STEP-BY-STEP
ASIAN COOKBOOK

STEP-BY-STEP

ASIAN COOKBOOK

RECIPES COMPILED BY ANNE McDOWALL

SALAMANDER

A SALAMANDER BOOK

Published by Salamander Books Ltd
8 Blenheim Court
Brewery Road
London N7 9NY
United Kingdom

A member of Chrysalis Books plc

ISBN: 1 84065 336 1

1 2 3 4 5 6 7 8 9 10

All correspondence concerning the content of this volume should be addressed to Salamander Books Ltd.

CREDITS
Project managed by Stella Caldwell
Editor: Anne McDowall
Typeset by SX Composing DTP

Printed in Spain

CONTENTS

THE FOOD OF ASIA

The various cuisines of Asia have much in common, particularly where geography and religion – the two main influences on diet – are similar, but there are also unique traits, between and within each country. Here we give a brief introduction to the food of each of the six countries whose recipes are featured in this book. In addition, each chapter opener indicates from which country the recipe comes (though some are obviously common to several). The order of recipes within each chapter follows the order given below, from west to east and south to north.

INDIA

Indian food encompasses the cooking of many different regions and the foods are quite different from state to state. In the north, where the climate is temperate, sheep are reared and the lamb dishes are generally cooked slowly in the oven. Travelling south through Delhi and the Punjab, the diet becomes much richer; here they cook mainly with ghee and eat both goat and chicken. In these northern regions, instead of rice, the preference is for breads. To the east, around the Bay of Bengal, there is an abundance of fish from the many rivers and from the bay itself. Coconut palms grow in the hot and humid climate, so coconut features strongly in many recipes. On the west coast, in Gujarat, the people are mainly vegetarian, eating pulses and vegetables; likewise in Tamil Nadu in the far south east. The humid tropical conditions of the south west, in Goa and Malabar, encourage date and coconut palms and banana plants to flourish and there is also an abundance of fish and shellfish. Southern Indians eat more rice than the northerners and they prefer to steam foods. The dishes are traditionally very hot, much more so than in the north.

But religion influences diet at least as much as geography. There are hundreds of different religions, each with their own customs and taboos: Moslems and Jews don't eat pork, while Hindus and Sikhs are prohibited from eating beef. Although many Hindus are strict vegetarians, others eat fish and shellfish.

The imaginative use of spices sets Indian cooking apart from other cuisines; it is by far the most aromatic of all types of cooking. The most commonly used spices are cumin, coriander, mustard, black pepper, turmeric, cinnamon, cardamom and cloves.

CHINA

China is a vast country, extending from the sub-tropical regions of Hunan and Kwantung in the south, right up to the dry plains of Mongolia in the north, while the western borders go right into central Asia, reaching almost to the frontier of Afghanistan. Because it is such a vast country, there are dramatic contrasts in geography and climate across China. The great diversity of regional history, customs, life and culture have caused a distinct cuisine to evolve in each of the four major provinces.

The cooking of Beijing and northern China is a fusion of three distinct influences, high-class court and mandarin dishes, rustic Mongolian and Manchurian fare, and the indigenous cooking of the cold, northerly climate. Here rice is less important than wheat and a variety of pancakes, noodles and dumplings are found. Barbecuing, lacquer roasting, spit-roasting, slow-simmering and deep-frying are the most common cooking techniques in the north. Sauces are richly flavoured with dark soy sauce, garlic, spring onions, spices and sesame oil. Lamb, generally disliked elsewhere in China, is common here.

The Szechuan cuisine of the West tends to be hearty rather than delicate and is renowned for highly spiced foods, especially dishes containing chillies. Szechuan cooks have perfected a fascinating range of hot-sour, savoury-spiced and sweet-hot-piquant dishes, many of which are characterised by the crunch and bite of pickles. Many dishes are relatively dry and more reminiscent of southern stir-fries than of the sauce-rich dishes of the east.

Above: This bustling food market on the streets of Hong Kong is typical of many throughout Asia. As well as buying meat, fish and vegetables, locals will buy snacks such as dim sum and spring rolls (see pages 34 and 41) to eat on the street.

The cooking of the east is more starchy, and richer, not only in the amount of oil used in cooking, but also in the range of ingredients, the amount of soy sauce, and the number and combinations of spices. Rice is used a lot, not only plain as an accompaniment, but also combined with vegetables, and as a stuffing. With a long coastline, and well-watered lands, there is a fine selection of seafood and plenty of freshwater fish and a great range of vegetables is also available. The people of Shanghai are sweet-toothed and make savoury dishes that are generally sweeter than elsewhere.

Southern cooking is probably the most inventive, rich and colourful in China. It has been influenced by a steady stream of foreign traders and travellers, and is richly endowed with year-round produce from land and sea. Fruits flourish and are combined in meat and savoury dishes more here than elsewhere. Vegetables are used in quantity, but meat sparsely. Stir-frying is the most popular cooking method, but steaming and roasting are also common and the use of oil in cooking is kept to a minimum. Every meal includes rice and dishes often contain thick but delicate sauces. The area produces some of the best soy sauce in the country and, because of this, specializes in 'red cooking' – slowing baking or braising in soy sauce.

MALAYSIA

Malaysian cuisine is a fusion of the different cooking styles and dishes of three nationalities – Indian, Chinese and indigenous Malay. These have merged to make a unique, harmonious blend that is an identifying characteristic of the cuisine of this tropical peninsula.

The Indians contributed spices such as cumin, turmeric and chillies, and their art of blending spices is reflected in the many Malaysian curries. Indian-style flat-breads, chutneys and relishes frequently accompany meals. The Chinese influence is evident in the use of soy sauce, hoisin sauce, spring rolls and stir-fries and is particularly strong in the Nonya cooking of Singapore, which combines the Chinese emphasis on texture and balance of tastes with the Malaysian predilection for curries and chilli dishes. A definite Thai flavour can be detected in the use of lemon grass, coriander and galangal. The many years of Portuguese, Dutch and British occupation have also left their mark on Malaysian cooking.

Malaysian cuisine is a very healthy one. Chicken is the most widely eaten meat. With a large Muslim population and significant number of Hindus, pork and beef are not used to any great extent. Besides, the climate is not conducive to rearing livestock for eating. Fish and seafood are plentiful and widely eaten. Rice is the staple food, while noodles are also used to bulk out meat dishes, to thicken soups and generally add substance to the diet. Both rice and noodles are also popular as snacks.

Desserts are light and refreshing. A Malaysian meal does not usually include a dessert beyond, perhaps, some of the tropical fruits, such as mangoes, lychees, pineapples, rambutans and star-fruit, that grow in profusion. Coconut palms thrive, so coconut is a predominant ingredient. Coconut milk provides the liquid in many of the country's curries, and the national soup, Laksa Lemak (see page 22). It is also the basis of desserts such as coconut custard.

THAILAND

Thai food is an original and rich amalgam of evocative aromas, subtle blends of herbs and spices and contrasting textures and tastes and contains flavours and techniques that are familiar from Chinese, Indian and Japanese cooking. The dishes are light and fresh and characterized by flavours such as the citrus-limes, spiked with clean pine notes, fresh coriander, coconut milk, garlic and chillies. A fresh sweet-sour taste is also typically Thai, derived from tangy lime or tamarind and palm sugar. Mild fish sauce provides the main savoury flavouring.

Rice is a very important part of the diet. As well as being the foundation of many one-course dishes, rice plays a vital supporting role for other dishes, and balances highly spiced ones. Thai dishes are created to be mixed and eaten with rice – Thai curries can be searingly hot, though they are cooked quickly and do not have the rich heaviness that results from long, slow simmering. Coconut milk is used to soften the pungency of the spices and combines flavours to give a sophisticated subtlety to the finished dish.

Thailand has a long coastline and many inland rivers, which provide fish and shellfish, which are both ubiquitous and varied. Meat is considered more of a luxury and is often 'stretched' by combining with vegetables, rice, noodles, fish or shellfish or plenty of coconut-based sauce. Chicken is more abundant, but the birds are smaller than Western ones. Duck is popular, particularly for special occasions. Dairy products are not used. Vegetables are important, but they are not often cooked on their own or served as a specific dish. Instead they are combined with meat, poultry or fish, eaten as a salad, either hot or cold, or simply served with 'Nam Prik' (see page 232).

VIETNAM

At first sight, there seems to be little difference between Vietnamese and Thai cooking, but on closer examination, you will discover that, partly because of their geographical proximity, the influence of Chinese cuisine is more strongly felt in Vietnam than in Thailand, while the latter seems to have absorbed more influences from the Indian subcontinent.

There is an amazing variety of regional cuisine in Vietnam. Apart from the extensive external influence of China, Vietnam has also a long-established vegetarian tradition derived from Mahayana Buddhism, which originated in India and was introduced into Vietnam by way of China and Thailand. In addition, there is still evidence of the more recent French colonial influence, not to mention the American influence of the 1960s.

Ho Chi Minh City in the south is the most cosmopolitan of all Vietnamese cities and the home of incredible tropical seafood and specialities from the Mekong River delta. With its hot, humid climate and fertile lands, this region also produces a great variety of vegetables, fruits and meats. The French influence is particularly strong here. The small island of Phu Quoc off the Vietnam/Cambodia border, is reputed to produce the best fish sauce (nuoc mam) in Vietnam.

Hue, the former Imperial capital in the centre of the country, has the most sophisticated cuisine and, as the temperate climate is ideal for the cultivation of exotic vegetables, it specializes in vegetarian food. Ho An of the central coast was home of the most important ports in Southwest Asia between the seventeenth and nineteenth centuries, and the Dutch, Portuguese, American, Japanese and Chinese merchants all came here.

In Hanoi, the capital of Vietnam, which is in the north close to the Chinese border, the food is less spicy, and the Chinese influence particularly strong, with stir-fried dishes and clay-pot cooking. The climate is milder here than in the south, and the Red River delta with the Gulf of Tongking produces a wealth of fish and shellfish, as well as vegetables and other foods.

JAPAN

Japan was an agricultural nation for thousands of years until after the war. Houses were traditionally constructed mostly of wood, so wood was, and still is, a very valuable resource. With few other fuel resources, the Japanese had to find various ways of appreciating both their agricultural produce and the plentiful supply of fish caught in the surrounding seas without burning lots of wood and charcoal. Consequently, the Japanese developed ways of eating raw or near raw food.

In Japan, eating raw fish is considered the best, if not the only, way to appreciate the real flavour of fish, and sashimi (prepared raw fish) has pride of place in a Japanese meal. Fish for sashimi must be really fresh, refrigerated until ready to use and handled as little as possible. Another Japanese speciality is sushi, based on boiled rice, flavoured with a rice vinegar mixture while warm, then fanned to cool it quickly and give it a glossy sheen. There is wide variety of sushi, such as sushi rolls made with vegetables or fish enclosed in sushi rice, wrapped in nori seaweed, then rolled up and sliced.

Due to Shintoism, the ancient mythological religion, and later Buddhism, which was introduced from China, the Japanese remained a non-carnivorous nation until the opening up of the country to western influences towards the end of the nineteenth century. Today, despite Japan's economic growth and the pressure from overseas governments to open up the domestic market, Japan is still largely a nation of fish and vegetable eaters. When meat is used, it is sliced thickly and normally cooked with vegetables. As a result, Japanese cooking is naturally healthy without even trying to be so.

GLOSSARY OF INGREDIENTS

Asafoetida A pale brown resin made from the sap of a giant fennel-like plant native to India and Iran. It has a garlicky flavour and is used sparingly as a flavouring in Indian dishes. It is available in powdered or lump form.

Bamboo shoots The young shoots of certain varieties of bamboo, these are pale yellow in colour with a crunchy texture and fairly bland flavour. They are available in cans, whole or sliced; rinse in fresh water before use. Will keep a week if stored in fresh water in a covered container in the refrigerator.

Banana leaves Used to make containers for steamed foods. Aluminium foil can be used instead, but the food will not have the same delicate flavour.

Basil Thai (or 'holy') basil leaves are darker and their flavour slightly deeper, more spicy and less 'fresh' than ordinary sweet basil, with a touch of lemony flavour. Bundles of leaves can be frozen whole in a polythene bag for up to about 2 weeks; remove leaves as required and add straight to dishes. Substitute Thai sweet basil or ordinary sweet basil, if necessary.

Bean sprouts These are the sprouting shoots of the mung bean. They have a mild, watery taste and crisp texture and can be steamed or stir-fried, or eaten raw. Always use fresh sprouts in preference to canned ones. They will keep fresh in the refrigerator for 3-4 days.

Black beans Small black soy beans, fermented in salt and spices, are available in cans or plastic packets, and also as a paste or a sauce.

Bok choy Also known as *pak choi*, *Chinese cabbage* and, in Japan, '*hakusai*', this leafy vegetable has a slightly bulbous base and long leaves that have white stalks and ribs topped by dark green leaves. The stalks have a mild, refreshing flavour and the leaves taste pleasantly tangy and bitter. It is best cooked quickly to retain both the flavour and texture, but can also be served raw and is particularly good for making pickles. It keeps fresh for quite a long time stored in the refrigerator. Bok choy is available in many supermarkets, but if you are unable to find it use Chinese leaves or spinach.

Candlenuts Creamy coloured waxy nuts used to add thickness and texture to curries and casseroles. Raw macadamia or cashew nuts can be substituted.

Cardamom A member of the ginger family common in Indian dishes. Its long light-green or brown pods contain seeds with a strong, lemony flavour and heady aroma. Ground cardamom is available, but it is better to grind the seeds as needed. Whole pods should be removed from the dish before eating.

Chilli sauce A bright red, hot sauce made from red chillies, vinegar, garlic, sugar and salt. It can be used in cooking but is more often served as a dip. Vietnamese chilli sauce is much more fiery than standard Chinese chilli sauce or western Tabasco sauce.

Chillies A very important feature of Asian cooking, and used in large amounts. Some supermarkets now sell specific varieties of chillies, and label them to show the degree of hotness, but as a rule, smaller varieties are hotter than large ones. *Dried chillies*, which are always red, have a more earthy fruity flavour, and fresh *green chillies* have a '*greener*', less rounded flavour than red ones, which are riper. Thais favour small and very fiery '*bird's eye*' *chillies*. The seeds and white veins inside a chilli are not only hotter than the flesh, but have less flavour, and are generally removed before cooking. Chillies contain an oil that can irritate the eyes and skin, so avoid touching your eyes and mouth when preparing chillies and wash your hands well.

Chinese leaves A member of the cabbage family, similar to bok choy, but with paler leaves. It has a stout, elongated head of relatively tightly packed, firm, crinkly, pale yellow-green leaves with a thick white centre vein and a mild, delicate flavour. It can be lightly stir-fried or steamed or eaten raw.

Cinnamon Whole cinnamon sticks are highly aromatic and pungent and should be broken into 2-3 pieces before use to release their flavour. Remove from the dish before serving. Ground cinnamon has a much milder flavour and should only be used as a substitute if very fresh.

Cloves A common spice in Indian cooking. Whole cloves keep their flavour better than the powder and can be ground as needed.

Coconut cream The layer that forms on the top of coconut milk when it is left to stand. It is usually added almost at the end of cooking.

Coconut milk This is not the liquid that comes from a coconut, but is made by soaking coconut flesh in hot water (see page 224). Once cool, coconut milk should be kept in the refrigerator. It may separate on standing; either spoon off the thick layer and use as coconut cream or stir it back into the milk. Ready prepared coconut milk, sold in cans and plastic pouches, sometimes has a thicker consistency than home-made coconut milk.

Coriander Ideally, buy whole bunches and stand them in cold water in a cool place. Large coriander bunches often include the roots, which have a more muted taste than the leaves. Fresh roots will last for several days if kept wrapped in a cool place, or can be frozen. If unavailable, use coriander stalks.

Creamed coconut Sold in hard white blocks, which should be kept in a cool place or the refrigerator. Creamed coconut can be used to make coconut milk – grate or chop 85 g (3 oz) and dissolve in 300 ml (10 fl oz/1¼ cups) hot water – or it can be added, after grating or chopping, straight to the hot cooking liquid in a pan towards the end of cooking.

Cumin Commonly used in Indian cooking, these small seeds have a nutty flavour and aroma. Whole seeds will keep fresh longer than ground cumin.

Curry leaves A small, dark green leaf used in some southern Indian dishes.

Daikon Also known as *mooli*, or *Chinese radish*, the daikon resembles a large parsnip. The white, crisp and slightly pungent flesh is a staple of Japanese cooking, but also used in Chinese dishes. It is eaten raw in salads (usually grated), cooked in vegetable dishes, pickled and used in sauces.

Dried shrimp Used throughout South-east Asia, these are sold in clear plastic packets (check the shrimp are a good pinkish colour). They need to be soaked in hot water for 10-15 minutes and are usually ground before use. Keep them in an airtight container in a cool place. (See also *shrimp paste*.)

Fish sauce Used in South-east Asia much as soy sauce is used in China, fish sauce is a thick salty brown liquid made from salted shrimp or fish.

Five-spice powder A mix of ground star anise, Szechuan peppercorns, fennel, cloves and cinnamon, which gives a fragrant, spicy, sweet flavour to Chinese dishes. Some brands include other spices, such as ginger and coriander seeds.

Galangal Resembles fresh root ginger (to which it is related), but the skin is thinner, paler, more translucent and tinged with pink and it is less hot, with citrus, pine notes. To use, peel and thinly slice or chop. The whole root will keep for up to 2 weeks if wrapped in paper and kept in the cool drawer of the refrigerator, or it can be frozen: allow to thaw just sufficiently to enable the amount required to be sliced off, then return the root to the freezer. Galangal is also sold dried or in slices, but fresh root ginger is the best substitute if fresh galangal is unavailable.

Ghee A form of clarified butter (after the moisture has evaporated, the milk solids are allowed to brown), this is a common cooking medium in India. It has a long shelf life, high smoke point and a nutty, caramel-like flavour.

Ginger When buying fresh root ginger, choose firm, heavy pieces that have a slight sheen. Keep it in a cool place for up to a week or, for longer storage, wrap it in absorbent kitchen paper, place in a polythene bag and store in the salad drawer of the refrigerator. Once peeled and chopped or sliced, it adds a sweet, spicy flavour to all kinds of sweet and savoury dishes. *Vinegared ginger* is widely used in Japanese cooking and is available in packets.

Hoisin sauce A thick, dark reddish brown sauce made from soy beans, vinegar, spices, garlic and sugar, with a sweet flavour. Also known as *Chinese barbecue sauce*, it is most versatile – it can be used for dipping and marinating, as well as for cooking. Refrigerate after opening and it will keep for many months.

Kaffir lime leaves Dark green, highly aromatic leaves with a clean citrus-pine smell and flavour. Kaffir lime leaves freeze well, laid flat in a heavy-duty plastic bag. Use the grated peel of ordinary limes if kaffir leaves are not available, substituting 1½ teaspoons for 1 kaffir lime leaf.

Konbu (kelp) A giant seaweed sold in dried form in Japanese supermarkets. Full of vitamins and minerals, it is a health food best eaten simmered with other vegetables. It is also used for dashi (Japanese fish stock).

Konnyaku A jelly-like cake made from yam flour, it has no taste or nutritional value but is eaten for its texture. It is available fresh in packets at Japanese supermarkets.

Lemon grass A deliciously fragrant, lemony herb that is indispensable to Far Eastern cooking. To use, cut off the root tip and top end to leave the lower 1-15 cm (4-6 in) or so, peel away the tough outer layers, then thinly slice the inner part. To prevent drying out, store with the end in a little cold water. Lemon grass also freezes well; to defrost, hold briefly under running hot water. The grated rind of ½ lemon can be substituted for 1 lemon grass stalk.

Lily buds Also known as *golden needles* or yellow flowers in Chinese, these are the dried buds of the 'tiger' lily flower. Soak in warm water for 30 minutes or so, then rinse in fresh water and discard the hard tip before use.

Long beans Although these can grow to over 1 metre (3 feet) it is best to use younger ones. Green beans or French beans can replace them.

Lychees Available in cans, but fresh lychees are now becoming more readily available. The nobbly, brittle coating is easily cracked to reveal the delicious crisply fruity white flesh surrounding a smooth central stone.

Mango Select fruit that feels heavy for its size and is free of bruises or damage; a ripe mango yields to gentle pressure and should have an enticing, scented aroma. The fresh inside should have a wonderful, luxurious and slightly exotic texture and flavour. If a mango is a little firm when bought, leave it in a warm sunny place to finish ripening. The central stone is large and flat and usually difficult to separate from the flesh without using a knife.

Mint There are many varieties of mint in the Far East and it may be used at almost every meal. Thai mint has a spearmint flavour. If Thai mint leaves are not available, spearmint or garden mint are the best substitutes.

Mirin This is thick sweet rice wine, which gives a very subtle sweet flavour to dishes. If not available, sweet sherry can be substituted but reduce the amount of sugar in the dish by half.

Miso A very salty paste made from fermented soy beans, miso is used in Japanese soup and salad dressing and is also good in marinades for fish and meat. The orangey-brown variety is slightly sweeter than the more salty reddish-brown one.

Mushrooms Asian cooks generally use dried mushrooms, which have a much more intense fragrance and flavour than fresh ones. Dried mushrooms must be soaked before cooking: put them in a bowl, cover with boiling water, cover the bowl, leave for about 30 minutes until swollen and pliable, then drain well and squeeze dry. Discard the hard stalks before use.
Chinese (dried) mushrooms – Also known as *shiitake* or *black mushrooms*, they have a pronounced flavour. Dried mushrooms vary in quality and thickness; choose the thickest (usually the most expensive) ones.
Straw mushrooms – These have a pleasant, delicate flavour with an interesting texture. They are available in cans, and should be drained and rinsed before use, as well as dried.
Black fungus – Also known as *tree* or *wood ears*, and always sold in dried form, these dried mushrooms have a crunchy texture with a subtle flavour.

From top to bottom: coconut milk, galangal, lemon grass, green chillies, fresh noodles, curry leaves, kaffir lime leaves, garlic, candlenuts, fresh noodles, red chillies, bok choy.

Mustard seeds White and yellow seeds have the mildest flavour, black the strongest. Brown seeds are moderately hot and generally have husks attached.

Noodles Most types are interchangeable, but two – rice vermicelli and bean thread noodles – can be crisp-fried. Egg noodles are rarely seen in Vietnam, where only rice flour noodles are used. Dried noodles are usually soaked in cold water for 10-20 minutes until softened before cooking; in general, the weight doubles after soaking. After draining, cooking is usually brief.
Egg noodles – In Asia both fresh and dried egg noodles, which are wheat flour-based, are used in a variety of different widths, but in the West fresh noodles can be quite difficult to come by. They may be found packed in plastic bags in the refrigerated section of Chinese grocery stores. Fresh 'nests' should be shaken loose before using. Some dried egg noodles are soaked before use; others are cooked like dried pasta, by dropping into a saucepan of boiling water. Some varieties cook quickly so test frequently.
Rice noodles – Also known as *rice sticks*, these semi-transparent noodles come in 3 different widths and are sold in bundles. There are also very fine strands, known as *rice vermicelli*. The noodles are usually soaked for about 5 minutes in boiling water then rinsed in cold water before cooking, but vermicelli rice noodles are also sometimes served crisp and are then used dry. Fresh rice noodles are packaged cooked and wet in wide, pliable 'hanks'. To use, cut into ribbons, without unwinding, and stir into a dish just to warm through.
Bean thread noodles – Also called *glass*, *shining*, *mung bean* or *cellophane* noodles, these are fine noodles made from mung beans. Tough and semi-transparent when raw, they need to be soaked before cooking.
Soba noodles – Japanese thin, flat noodles made from buckwheat and wheat flour. They are greyish-brown in colour.
Somen – Japanese wheat flour noodles, fine, glossy and white in appearance and usually sold dried. Various colours and flavours are available.
Udon – These wide, flat ribbonlike Japanese wheat-flour noodles are available dried, fresh or precooked in a variety of widths.

Nori Dried seaweed available in wafer-thin sheets, it has a sweet, salty flavour and is used in Japanese cooking to wrap sushi or as a garnish or flavouring.

Oils Vegetable oil is used when the taste is not a part of a recipe. Groundnut (peanut) oil is used for its characteristic flavour. Other oils, with a lower burning point, are used for flavourings.
Groundnut (peanut) oil – A slightly sweet, mild oil that withstands heat very well. Use it in moderation as it has a high saturated fat content.
Sesame oil – Asian sesame oil is made from roasted sesame seeds so is dark in colour and has a delicious, rich nutty flavour. Because the flavour is quite pronounced, the oil is used only in small amounts, rather like a seasoning. Sesame oil is sold in small bottles that should be stored in the dark in a cool place, but not the refrigerator as the oil will become cloudy.
Chilli oil – Hot, pungent oil that should be heated gently as it burns easily. It is best used as a flavouring rather than a cooking agent.

Oyster sauce A thick brown sauce made from concentrated oysters cooked in soy sauce, then mixed with seasonings. It is often added to Chinese stir-fried dishes, particularly beef. Its taste is not fishy, but richly meaty.

Palm sugar A delicious honey-coloured, raw sugar, with a slight caramelized flavour, much used in Malaysia and Thailand. It is sold in lump and free-flowing forms in cans and plastic packets in Malaysian and Thai food shops. Light brown sugar is an adequate substitute.

Papaya Also known as *paw-paw*. Use the unripe green papaya for salads or in cooking. When it turns yellow or red, it is eaten as a fruit.

Pea aubergine Very small aubergines about the size of a pea, and usually the same colour, although they can be white, purple or yellow. The fresh, slightly bitter taste is used raw in hot sauces and cooked in curries.

Plum sauce This thick, sweet condiment, made from plums, apricots, garlic, vinegar and seasonings, is used in Chinese cooking or as a dip.

Preserved vegetables Various types of vegetables, preserved, or pickled, in salt, are available in cans and plastic pouches, but if a label simply specifies 'preserved vegetable' it will invariably mean mustard greens. They have a crunchy texture and hot, spicy flavour, but are salty so rinse before use. Once opened, jars should be covered and stored in the refrigerator and canned vegetables should be transferred to a glass or pottery container.

Rambutans A Malaysian variety of *lychee*, but with a more acidic flavour.

Rice The staple food of Asia. A number of different types are used.
Fragrant long-grain rice – Also known as *Thai fragrant rice* and *jasmine rice*, this is the rice most used in South-east Asian cooking. Ordinary long-grain rice can be substituted if necessary.
Basmati rice – This rice, with its long, slim grains and nutty flavour, is the rice most often used in Indian recipes. Long-grain rice can be substituted.
'Sticky' (or glutinous) rice – An aptly named short, round grain variety. It can be formed into balls and eaten with fingers, or used for desserts.
Ground, browned rice – This is sometimes added to dishes to give texture. Dry-fry raw long-grain white rice until well browned, then grind finely.
Japanese rice – Authentic Japanese rice – short grained and slightly sticky – is kept for the home market. Californian medium-grain rice is a good substitute.

Rice paper Made from rice flour, salt and water, then dried in the sun on bamboo mats, rice paper is available in round or large square sheets and is used for wrapping spring rolls and other foods. The sheets must be dipped in warm water for a few seconds before use.

Rice wine Made from glutinous rice, yeast and spring water, this wine is used extensively in Asian cooking. Similar to sherry in colour, bouquet and alcohol content (18 percent), it has its own distinctive (rich and sweetish) flavour. Pale, dry sherry may be substituted or, if a sweet, spicy flavour is required, sweet sherry may be used. (See also *mirin* and *sake*.)

Saffron The dried yellow-orange stigma of a crocus's purple flower, saffron is used as a flavouring (it has a slightly bitter, honeylike flavour) and colouring agent in Indian cooking. Although expensive, only a few threads are needed.

Sake A strong rice wine made from fermented rice and water. Along with tea, it is Japan's most famous drink and the one most frequently served with meals, usually lukewarm.

Sansho pepper A delicately pungent Japanese green pepper, which is not used for cooking but as a condiment at the table. It is available in bottles.

Sesame paste A flavouring often used in South-east Asian cooking made from toasted white sesame seeds.

Shallots The red variety commonly found in Asia is smaller than the Western type. It has quite a pronounced flavour that is fruity rather than pungent. Shallots are used in large amounts instead of onions, and are included as part of a spice paste. Ordinary shallots, or the white parts of spring onions,.can be substituted

Shrimp paste Known as *belaccan* in Malaysia but more often found elsewhere as *trasi* or *blachan* – the Indonesian and Burmese names. Shrimp paste is made from fermented shrimps, dried and pounded to a paste, and is used in small amounts. It is always cooked before use. It may be ground to a paste with other flavourings, or it may be toasted, grilled or fried. Break off the amount you need and either hold it in tongs over a naked flame, turning it so it roasts evenly, or spread it onto a piece of foil and grill it. Alternatively, wrap it in foil and cook it in a dry frying pan until it is crumbly and smells fragrant. Raw shrimp paste has a strong smell so keep it in a tightly covered jar; the smell disappears on cooking.

Soy sauce The essential ingredient in Chinese and Japanese cooking, soy sauce (*shoyu* in Japan) is made from soy beans, flour and water, which are fermented and aged for several months. *Light soy sauce* (sometimes known as thin soy sauce) is thinner, paler in colour and saltier than *dark (thick) soy sauce*, which is heavier, sweeter and has a more rounded flavour. Light soy is used with vegetables, seafood and soups; dark soy with dark meats and for dipping sauces. When soy sauce is used, additional salt is often not necessary.

Star anise These attractive pods, in the shape of an eight-pointed star, have a mild liquorice flavour. They should be removed from a dish before serving.

Star fruit Long almost translucent yellow, ridged fruit, also known as *carambola*. The whole fruit is edible, and when cut across the width, the slices resemble five-pointed stars. Raw star-fruit have a pleasant, citrus-like juicy sharpness, but when poached the flavour is more distinctive.

Szechuan peppercorns These reddish coloured, mildly spicy, aromatic dried berries should be toasted and crushed or ground before use. To toast, dry-fry in a wok for a few minutes. Crush in a mortar and pestle.

Tamarind This has a distinctive fruity/lemony sharpness. The sticky brown-black 'pulp' can be found in Asian stores, peeled, seeded and wrapped as a block in a square packet. To make *tamarind water*, break off a 25 g (1 oz) piece, pour over 300 ml (10 fl oz/1¼ cups) boiling water, break up the lump with a spoon, then leave for about 30 minutes, stirring occasionally. Strain off the tamarind water, pressing on the pulp; discard the remaining debris. Keep the water in a jar in the refrigerator. Ready-to-use tamarind syrup can sometimes be bought; it is usually more concentrated, so less is used. To make *tamarind paste*, soak 115 g (4 oz) tamarind in 225 ml (8 fl oz/1 cup) hot water for about 3 hours, then strain it through a fine sieve to extract as much liquid as possible. Ready-prepared tamarind paste is also available.

Tofu Also known as *bean curd*, tofu is made from puréed yellow soy beans and has a distinctive soft texture and neutral flavour. It is low in fat and high in protein and so is widely used as a health food. In Japan tofu shops still make it every day and traditionally there are two kinds, silk or cotton, made from soya milk sieved through silk or cotton cloth. You can buy fresh as well as prepacked tofu at Asian food shops. The fresh one available outside Japan is normally a cotton tofu and the prepacked one is a silk tofu. Firm tofu – the type recommended for cooking – is sold in solid cakes, which are kept in water and drained and chopped before use. Handle and cook with care to prevent tofu breaking up.

Turmeric A rhizome similar to ginger, though smaller and more delicate in appearance. It is usually used fresh in Asia, but in the West is more usually used ground; ½ teaspoon ground turmeric is equivalent to 2.5 cm (1 in) fresh. Fresh turmeric needs to be peeled before use.

Vinegars *Rice vinegar* is the mildest of all vinegars, with a sweet, delicate flavour and comes in several varieties. *White rice vinegar* is clear, with a mild, delicate flavour. *Red rice vinegar* is sweet and spicy. If possible use a pale rice vinegar for light-coloured sweet-and-sour dishes, and try a dark variety for dipping sauces. If unable to find either, use cider vinegar. *Chinese black vinegar* is thicker than most vinegars, made from grains other than rice and aged to impart complex, smoky flavours with a light, pleasant bitterness. It is used sparingly as a seasoning. Substitute balsamic vinegar, sherry or a good red wine vinegar if Chinese black vinegar is not available.

Wasabi This is hot, green horseradish used in Japanese raw fish dishes. It is sold as a paste in tubes or in powdered form. The latter needs to be mixed with an equal quantity of warm water before use.

Water chestnuts Round, white root vegetables about the size of a walnut, water chestnuts are crunchy in texture with a mild, slightly sweet flavour. They are available fresh from Chinese supermarkets but are more commonly sold in cans. Rinse well before using. Once opened, store in fresh water in the refrigerator for up to a week.

Won won skins Thin, pastry-like sheets made from egg and flour. They can be bought fresh or frozen and are available in squares or rounds. They can be kept in the refrigerator, wrapped, for about 5 days.

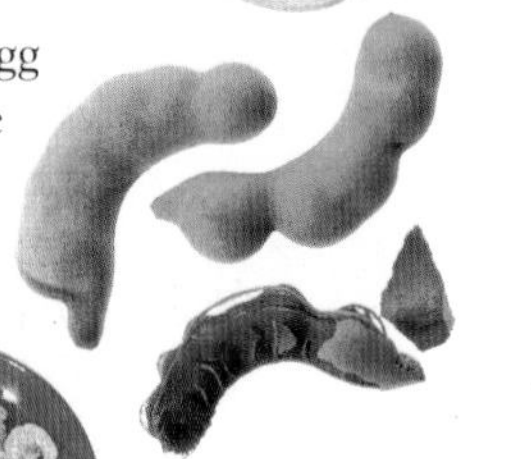

Yellow bean sauce This thick, spicy, aromatic sauce is made from fermented yellow beans and is quite salty. It is often used in sauces for fish and poultry. It may be chunky or smooth.

From top to bottom: galangal powder, tamarind, dried shrimp, turmeric, basmati rice, fragrant long-grain rice, shallots, palm sugar, soy sauce, pestle and mortar.

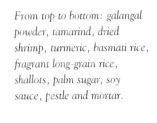

PREPARING, COOKING AND SERVING FOOD

Cutting ingredients, particularly vegetables, is a very important part of Asian cooking; indeed more time is often spent in preparing ingredients than in cooking them, particularly for stir-frying, where it is important that ingredients are cut in equal-size pieces so that they cook evenly.

Roll cutting – cut a diagonal slice from the vegetable. Make a one-quarter turn of the vegetable towards you and make a diagonal slice slightly above and partly across the face of the first slice. Continue cutting in this way.

Diagonal cutting – hold a heavy chef's knife or Chinese cleaver at a 45° angle and move it along the length of the width of slice desired.

Shredding – cut the sides and ends of the vegetables so that they are flat. Work the knife across the vegetables, just in front of the fingers. Cut the vegetable lengthways across the slices to the width of a matchstick.

COOKING UTENSILS

Asian cooks use few, practical and versatile utensils, designed to make the most efficient and economical use of heat. Many of these items will be found in a well-equipped Western kitchen and for those specifically Asian utensils, a Western alternative will usually suffice.

Pestle and mortar Used during the preparation of the majority of savoury dishes. A small blender or coffee grinder kept specifically for the purpose will take away the effort but will not produce quite the same results. When used for fibrous ingredients, such as galangal and lemon grass, the pestle and mortar crushes the fibres rather than cuts them and so releases the flavouring juices and oils more successfully.

Clockwise from top left: wok, Chinese hot pot, bamboo steamer, Chinese cleavers, chopsticks, wire ladle, clay pot, pestle and mortar.

Knives and cleavers Asian cooks generally use cleavers for all tasks that require a knife, but a selection of good-quality sharp knives will suffice.

Chopping board A large, heavy wooden board is ideal.

Wok Used for frying, stir-frying, deep-frying and steaming. A useful size to buy is about 30-35 cm (12-14 in) in diameter across the top. Choose one that has good deep sides and some weight. Carbon steel is preferable to light stainless steel or aluminium as these tend to develop hot spots which cause sticking, and do not withstand intense heat so well. Non-stick woks and electric ones do not reach sufficiently high temperatures. A frying pan could be used for frying and stir-frying, a deep-fat frying pan for deep frying and a saucepan for steaming.

The wok may also have a lid, which is used when braising and red-cooking, and a metal ring or stand to hold the wok steady over the heat.

A wok rack may be used in the wok when steaming to support the steaming basket above the level of the water.

Steamer Bamboo steamers are used throughout the Far East. These are designed to sit over a wok and often two or more are stacked on top of each other so that a number of dishes can be cooked at the same time. The steam is absorbed by the bamboo lid, preventing water dripping onto the food. So that all the nourishing juices and flavour are retained, the food is often placed on a plate in the steamer and served directly from it.

Rice cooker Because of the amount of rice eaten and the number of people cooked for, many households now use an electric rice cooker. A heavy saucepan with a tight-fitting lid will be adequate for Western needs.

Karahi or balti pan A traditional Indian deep-round-bottomed vessel with two circular carrying handles. Food is cooked in this and, if used with a stand, it is brought to the table, where food is served directly from it.

Long-handled spatula Metal or wooden and curved and shaped like a shovel, these long spatulas are used for scooping and tossing food in the wok.

Sieves and strainers The best ones are wire baskets with bamboo handles, which are used to scoop noodles and other ingredients out of boiling water, stock or oil, while cooking, or during a 'pot-style' meal.

Fondue (hot pot) Traditionally, a charcoal- or spirit-burning Chinese hot pot (also known as a Mongolian fire kettle) is used for table-top cooking. A fondue set is quite adequate.

Chopsticks Used for cooking (stirring and mixing) as well as eating; the chopsticks used for stir-frying are longer.

When using chopsticks to eat, an equal amount of chopstick should protrude on each side of the hand and the tapered ends should point downwards. The lower chopstick, which remains stationary, is held with the tips of the fourth and little finger, the upper part of the chopstick resting comfortably in the base of the thumb and the index finger. The upper one is held firmly with the thumb, index and middle fingers as you would a pencil. Use the thumb to brace the stationary chopstick securely against the top of the fourth finger. There should be about 2.5 cm (1 in) space between the sticks. Press the upper chopstick down with the index and third finger so that it meets the stationary chopstick to pick up the food. Tap the ends of the chopsticks gently on the table to align them.

Clay pots Small earthenware pots are used as casseroles in Vietnamese cooking, in particular. The Western versions are usually too large for Asian dishes, so try a set of small Asian clay pots.

Daikon grater Commonly used in Japanese cooking, which uses a lot of grated daikon and ginger, this differs from an ordinary cheese grater in having a curved base, which catches the juices from the ingredients.

Makisu A piece of bamboo blind the size of a table mat, which is used mainly for rolling sushi. Use any flexible place mat of a similar texture.

Moulds A rectangular mould is used to make pressed sushis and flower-shaped ones for pretty pieces of sushis and hors d'oeuvres.

Whisk About 25 cm (10 in) long and consisting of thin strips of bamboo tied together at the top, this is used for cleaning the wok.

COOKING METHODS

Whether food is being cooked for a family meal or formal banquet, it is generally lightly done. Stir-frying is the most common cooking method throughout most of the Far East, but the following are also popular ways of cooking food. Because of the importance of contrasts in texture as well as taste, several methods may be used to prepare food for a single meal.

Stir-frying For successful stir-frying, food should be finely sliced or shredded with every piece cut to the same size. Heat the wok over a high heat before pouring in a little oil. Once the oil is almost at smoking point, add the ingredients. Toss them, keeping them moving from the centre to the sides.

Steaming A healthy cooking method, as few of the food's nutrients are lost, steaming also preserves the colour and texture of ingredients. Steaming is far more popular in the East than in the West and is a common way to cook meat, poultry, fish, dim sum and other pastries and desserts. It was developed as a fuel-saving measure, as several foods can be cooked at once in baskets stacked above each other. Foods that require the most cooking are put to cook first, and those needing less time are placed on top as cooking proceeds.

Grilling Foods to be grilled benefit from being marinated before cooking. This adds flavour and helps to keep the foods moist when exposed to direct heat, which is particularly important when using little or no fat.

Braising Rich, slow-cooked dishes make a pleasant change to stir-fries. Foods are initially seared in a little oil then further cooked in a liquid, such as stock, thickened with cornflour to form a sauce, or coconut milk. Cooking in this way ensures nutrients and flavour are retained in the sauce.

Deep-frying Done in a wok, this needs less oil. Foods are often marinated first, then sometimes coated in batter. Often the food if fried until almost cooked, then removed from the oil, the oil reheated and the food added again to finish cooking and become really crisp.

Oven-cooking Few Asian cooks have ovens, but it is a method often used in restaurants. The most renowned oven-cooked method is Cantonese red-roasting, in which meat, fish or root vegetables are cooked slowly in dark soy sauce, sometimes with other flavourings added. During the lengthy cooking, which may be as long as four hours, the soy imparts a fairly dark, reddish brown colour and a rich flavour to the food. Because soy sauce is very salty, sugar may be added to counteract this.

SERVING AND EATING

Throughout Asia, meals tend to be sociable times, particularly the main meal of the day, which is normally eaten in the evening. A traditional meal will usually comprise several dishes, served simultaneously, which everyone shares. Diners will often have their own bowl of soup and rice and will help themselves to other dishes. Importance is given to selecting dishes to provide a contrast of textures as well as flavours, so a soft, steamed dish may be served with a crisp fried one; a strongly spiced one with a bland one, and so on. Desserts do not usually feature, except at formal banquets, but there is usually fresh fruit. Many of the sweets and starters featured in this book will be eaten as snacks during the day, often bought from street-vendors. Food presentation is also important and garnishes are common. A couple of simple ones are shown on the following page.

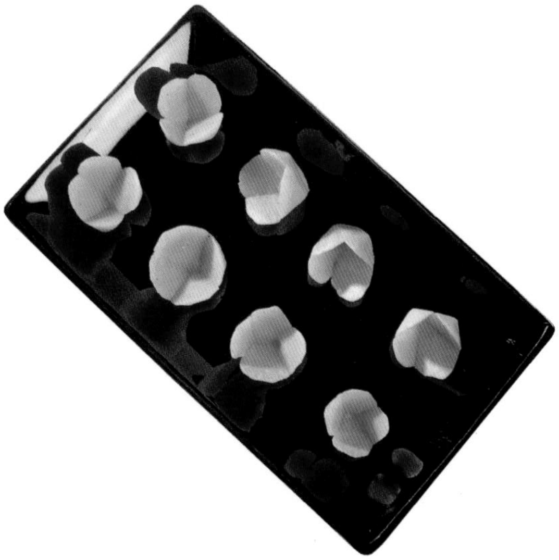

CARROT FLOWERS

1 long carrot, about 2.5 cm (1 in) in diameter

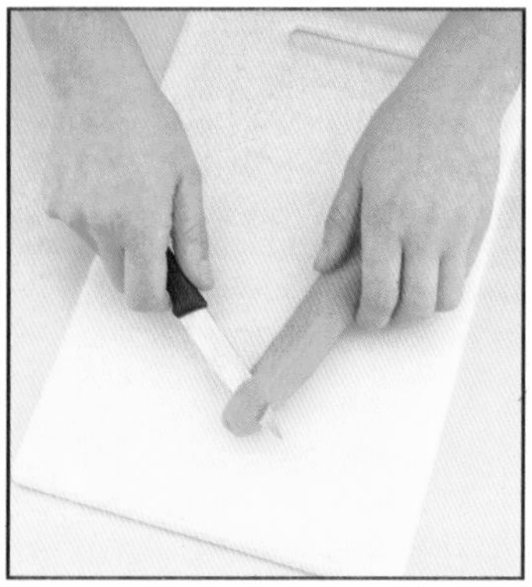

Use a small sharp knife to make a cut towards the pointed end of the carrot, to form a petal shape about 0.5 cm (¼ in) wide. Repeat cuts around the carrot to form a flower with 4 petals.

Angle the knife in such a way that with a slight twist, the flower comes away from the carrot. Repeat this process along the length of the carrot.

Drop the flowers into a pan of boiling salted water for about 1 minute, to improve the colour. Drain and rinse in cold water. Dry well. Use as a garnish, singly or in clusters.

GARNISHES

2 small firm tomatoes
6-8 radishes
4 spring onions
4 small red or green chillies, seeded

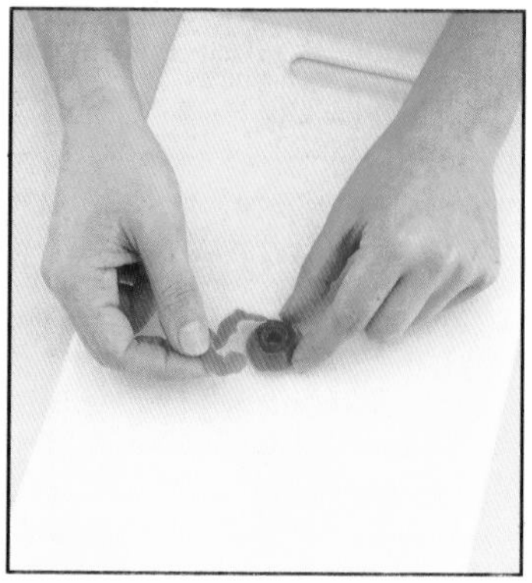

To make tomato roses, use a small sharp knife to peel off the skin, like an apple, in one piece. Curl the skin into a circle, then invert it to form a rose.

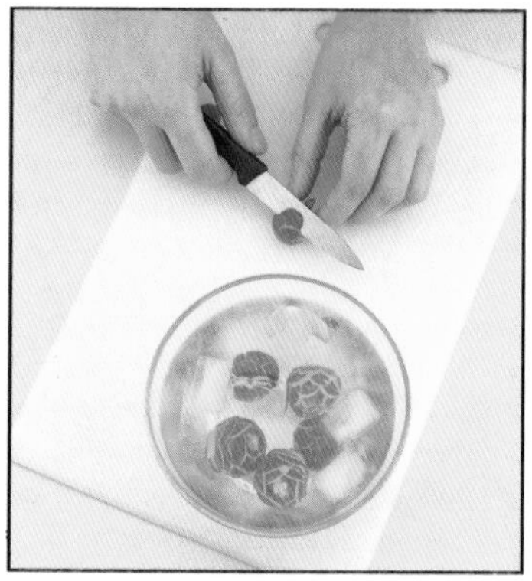

To make radish flowers, cut thin petals all the way round each radish, starting at the root and finishing at the top. Plunge them into iced water and leave for 1 hour or so; the petals will open up to form a flower. Drain and pat dry before use.

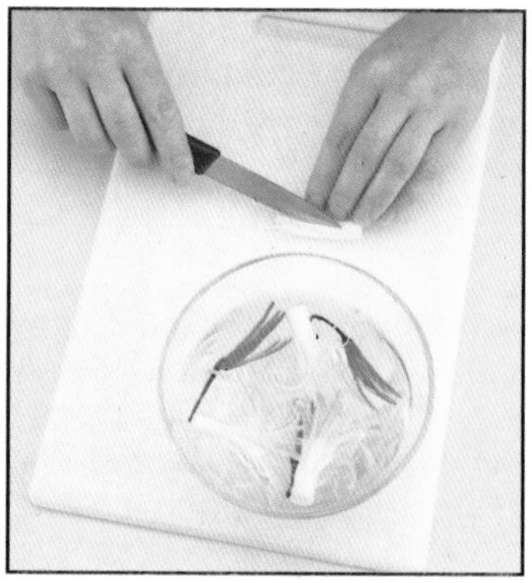

To make spring onion and chilli flowers, make fine cuts about halfway along the length of the vegetables to form fine petals. Place in a bowl of iced water and leave for 5-10 minutes; they will open up to form curly flowers. Dry well before using them as garnishes.

SOUPS

CHINESE CHICKEN STOCK

1 (1.25 kg/2½ lb) chicken, giblets removed
2 slices fresh root ginger
1 clove garlic
2 spring onions
large pinch salt
large pinch ground white pepper

Skin chicken and trim away any visible fat. Wash and place in a large saucepan with ginger, garlic, spring onions, salt and pepper. Add 2 litres (3½ pints/9 cups) cold water.

Bring to the boil, skimming away surface scum using a large flat ladle. Reduce heat, cover and simmer for 2 hours. Leave to cool slightly.

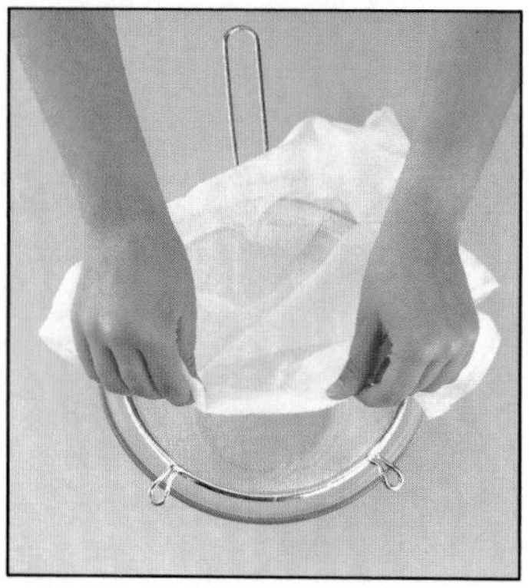

Line a sieve with clean muslin and place over a large bowl. Ladle stock through sieve and discard chicken and vegetables. Cover and chill. Skim away any fat that forms on surface before using. Store in the refrigerator for up to 3 days or freeze for up to 3 months.

Makes 1.75 litres (3 pints/7½ cups).

CHINESE BEEF STOCK

900 g (2 lb) lean stewing beef
2.5 cm (1 in) piece fresh root ginger, peeled
1 clove garlic
2 shallots
1 stick celery
2 carrots
2 tablespoons dark soy sauce
large pinch salt
large pinch freshly ground black pepper

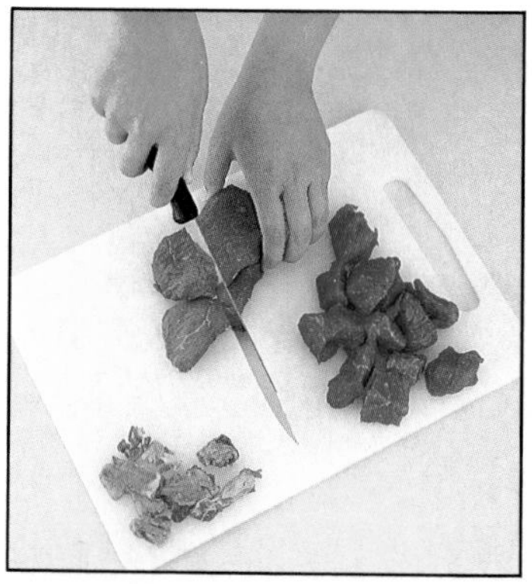

Trim any visible fat and silver skin from beef. Cut into 5 cm (2 in) pieces. Wash and pat dry with absorbent kitchen paper.

Place beef in a large saucepan with ginger, garlic, shallots, celery, carrots, soy sauce, salt and pepper and add 2 litres (3½ pints/9 cups) cold water. Bring to the boil, skimming away surface scum using a large, flat ladle. Reduce heat, cover and simmer for 2 hours. Leave to cool slightly.

Line a sieve with clean muslin and place over a large bowl. Ladle stock through sieve and discard beef and vegetables. Cover and chill. Skim away any fat that forms on surface before using. Store in the refrigerator for up to 3 days or freeze for up to 3 months.

Makes 1.75 litres (3 pints/7½ cups).

CHINESE VEGETABLE STOCK

1 stalk lemon grass
2 slices fresh root ginger
1 clove garlic
2 spring onions
1 large carrot, sliced
2 sticks celery
115 g (4 oz) bean sprouts
large pinch salt
large pinch ground white pepper

Break lemon grass to release its flavour and place in a large saucepan with 2 litres (3½ pints/9 cups) cold water and all remaining ingredients.

Bring to the boil, skimming away surface scum using a large, flat ladle. Reduce heat, cover and simmer 45 minutes. Leave to cool slightly.

Line a sieve with clean muslin and place over a large bowl. Ladle stock through sieve and discard vegetables. Cover and store in the refrigerator for up to 3 days or freeze for up to 3 months.

Makes 1.5 litres (2½ pints/6 cups).

CHICKEN & ASPARAGUS SOUP

225 g (8 oz) fresh asparagus
1 litre (1¾ pints/4 cups) Chinese Chicken Stock (see page 16)
2 tablespoons light soy sauce
2 tablespoons dry sherry
2 teaspoons brown sugar
55 g (2 oz) rice vermicelli
1 cm (½ in) piece fresh root ginger, peeled and chopped
350 g (12 oz) lean cooked chicken, finely shredded
salt and ground white pepper
2 spring onions, finely chopped, to garnish

Trim ends from asparagus spears and slice spears into 2.5 cm (1 in) pieces. Pour stock into a large saucepan along with soy sauce and sherry. Stir in brown sugar. Bring to the boil and add asparagus and noodles. Simmer, covered, for 5-6 minutes.

Stir in chopped ginger and shredded chicken and season with salt and pepper. Simmer for 3-4 minutes to heat through. Garnish with chopped spring onions and serve.

Serves 4.

CHICKEN DUMPLING SOUP

225 g (8 oz) lean minced chicken
1 tablespoons light soy sauce
3 tablespoons chopped fresh chives
1 clove garlic, finely chopped
2 egg whites
1 teaspoon sugar
salt and freshly ground pepper
16 won ton skins
1 litre (1¾ pints/4 cups) Chinese Chicken Stock (see page 16)
2 tablespoons rice wine

In a bowl, mix chicken, soy sauce, 1 tablespoon of the chives and the garlic. Bind together with 1 egg white and stir in sugar, salt and pepper.

Place a little chicken mixture in centre of each won ton skin, brush edges with egg white and bring corners together, pinching edges to seal. Cook dumplings in a large pan of boiling water for 1 minute. Drain. Bring stock to the boil and stir in rice wine, dumplings and remaining chives. Simmer for 2 minutes. Serve immediately.

Serves 4.

HOT & SOUR TURKEY SOUP

115 g (4 oz) lean minced turkey
25 g (1 oz) dried Chinese mushrooms, soaked in hot water for 20 minutes
115 g (4 oz) preserved vegetables, shredded
1 litre (1¾ pints/4 cups) Chinese Chicken Stock (see page 16)
2 teaspoons brown sugar
2 tablespoons red rice vinegar
large pinch ground white pepper
1 tablespoon dark soy sauce
2 teaspoons cornflour mixed with 4 teaspoons cold water
2 spring onions, finely chopped
2 tablespoons chopped coriander leaves

Cook turkey in a saucepan of boiling water for 3 minutes. Drain and set aside. Drain mushrooms and squeeze out excess water. Discard stems and slice caps.

Place minced turkey, mushrooms, preserved vegetables, stock, brown sugar, red rice vinegar, pepper and soy sauce in a saucepan. Stir to combine. Bring to the boil and simmer for 3 minutes. Add cornflour mixture and cook, stirring, until thickened. Add chopped spring onions and coriander and serve.

Serves 4.

BEEF & EGG DROP SOUP

1 tablespoon dark soy sauce
225 g (8 oz) extra-lean minced beef
1 clove garlic, crushed
1 whole cinnamon stick, broken
2 tablespoons tomato purée
ground white pepper
1 litre (1¾ pints/4 cups) Chinese Beef Stock (see page 16)
2 teaspoons cornflour mixed with 4 teaspoons cold water
1 egg white, lightly beaten
2 tablespoons chopped coriander leaves, to garnish

In a wok, heat soy sauce, add beef, garlic and cinnamon stick and stir-fry for 3-4 minutes or until beef is browned all over. Drain well on absorbent kitchen paper. Transfer beef mixture to a large saucepan and stir in tomato purée and white pepper. Pour in stock and bring to the boil, skimming away surface scum with a flat ladle. Cover and simmer for 20 minutes.

Discard cinnamon stick. Add cornflour mixture and cook, stirring, until thickened. With soup still simmering, pour in egg white in a thin stream, stirring until thin strands of egg form in the soup. Garnish with coriander and serve.

Serves 4.

CRAB & SWEETCORN SOUP

225 g (8 oz) baby sweetcorn
1 cm (½ in) piece fresh root ginger, peeled and finely chopped
1 clove garlic, finely chopped
175 g (6 oz) crab meat
2 tablespoons rice wine
1 tablespoon light soy sauce
1 litre (1¾ pints/4 cups) Chinese Vegetable Stock (see page 17)
salt and ground white pepper
2 teaspoons cornflour mixed with 4 teaspoons cold water
2 spring onions, shredded, to garnish

Bring a small saucepan of water to the boil, add baby sweetcorn and cook for 3-4 minutes or until just softened. Drain. In a bowl, mix together ginger, garlic, crab meat, rice wine and soy sauce.

Pour stock into a saucepan, bring to the boil and add sweetcorn and crab mixture. Simmer for 5 minutes. Season with salt and pepper, add cornflour mixture and cook, stirring, until thickened. Garnish with spring onions and serve.

Serves 4.

THREE MUSHROOM SOUP

- 4 dried Chinese mushrooms, soaked in hot water for 20 minutes
- 25 g (1 oz) oyster mushrooms
- 55 g (2 oz) button mushrooms
- 1 litre (1¾ pints/4 cups) Chinese Vegetable Stock (see page 17)
- 1 cm (½ in) piece fresh root ginger, peeled and finely chopped
- 1 clove garlic, finely chopped
- 2 tablespoons dry sherry
- 2 tablespoons dark soy sauce
- 115 g (4 oz) fresh tofu, drained and diced
- 2 teaspoons cornflour mixed with 4 teaspoons cold water
- 2 tablespoons shredded basil leaves

Drain soaked mushrooms and squeeze out excess water. Discard stems and slice caps. Slice oyster mushrooms and cut button mushrooms in half.

Pour stock into a saucepan and add ginger, garlic, sherry and soy sauce. Bring to the boil, reduce heat and carefully stir in mushrooms and tofu. Simmer for 5 minutes then add cornflour mixture and cook, stirring, for another 2 minutes or until thickened. Stir in basil and serve.

Serves 4.

BLACK-EYED PEA SOUP

- 175 g (6 oz) black-eyed peas
- 1 large carrot
- 115 g (4 oz) daikon, peeled
- 1 bunch spring onions
- 1 litre (1¾ pints/4 cups) Chinese Vegetable Stock (see page 17)
- 2 tablespoons light soy sauce
- 2 cloves garlic, finely chopped
- 1 fresh red chilli, seeded and finely chopped
- salt and freshly ground pepper
- carrot and daikon flowers (see page 14), to garnish

Place peas in a saucepan, add enough water to cover and bring to the boil. Cover and simmer for 45 minutes or until tender. Drain and rinse. Cut carrots and daikon into thin strips. Cut spring onions into fine shreds.

Pour stock into a saucepan and stir in soy sauce. Bring to the boil and add prepared vegetables, garlic and chilli. Simmer for 4 minutes, then add peas. Season with salt and pepper and cook for 3 minutes. Skim surface, garnish and serve.

Serves 4.

WON TON SOUP

85 g (3 oz) boneless, skinless chicken
85 g (3 oz) lean pork
85 g (3 oz) Chinese sausage
85 g (3 oz) peeled prawns
1 onion, chopped
1 carrot, chopped
1 stick celery, chopped
6 water chestnuts
2 tablespoons soy sauce
1 tablespoon sesame oil
30 won ton skins
1.75 ml (3 pints/7½ cups) chicken stock
55 g (2 oz) mangetout
1 carrot, cut into fine strips

Dice one-quarter of chicken, pork, sausage and prawns. Set aside. Put remaining chicken, pork, sausage and prawns in a food processor. Add onion, carrot, celery, water chestnuts, soy sauce and sesame oil. Process to a smooth paste.

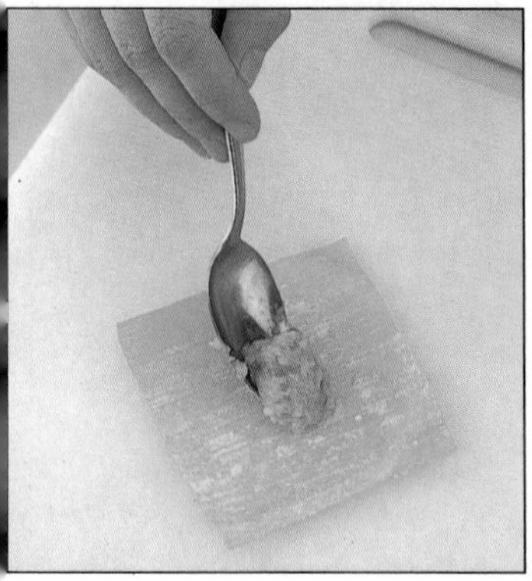

Spoon a little of meat paste onto centre of each won ton skin. Lightly moisten edges and draw them together to make small packets. In a large saucepan, bring stock to the boil. Add won tons in batches. Return to the boil and simmer for 4-5 minutes. Add mangetout, carrot strips and reserved meats and prawns. Return to the boil and simmer for a further 4-5 minutes.

Serves 6.

CHICKEN & NOODLE SOUP

175 g (6 oz) rice vermicelli
225 g (8 oz) boneless, skinless chicken breast
550 ml (20 fl oz/2½ cups) chicken stock
550 ml (20 fl oz/2½ cups) coconut milk
15 g (½ oz) tamarind paste (see page 11)
15 g (½ oz) fresh root ginger, grated
1 stalk lemon grass, very finely chopped
3 tablespoons shrimp paste, toasted (see page 11)
200 g (7 oz) raw, peeled medium prawns
85 g (3 oz) bean sprouts
85 g (3 oz) peeled, seeded and chopped cucumber
fried onion rings, sliced chillies and coriander leaves, to serve (optional)
Malaysian Spicy Sauce (see page 227), to serve (optional)

Cook noodles in boiling water for 3-4 minutes. Drain and refresh under running cold water. Drain very well and set aside. In a saucepan, put chicken and stock. Bring to a simmer and poach for 8 minutes. Lift chicken from stock (reserve stock). When cool enough to handle, shred and set aside. Add coconut milk to pan, with tamarind, ginger, lemon grass and shrimp paste. Bring to the boil then simmer for 5 minutes.

Add prawns. Simmer for 3-4 minutes, then add bean sprouts and cucumber. Heat through for 1-2 minutes. Serve with small dishes of fried onion rings, sliced chillies and coriander leaves. Serve accompanied by spicy sauce (see page 227).

Serves 4-6.

LAKSA LEMAK

3 dried red chillies, cored, seeded and chopped
3 cloves garlic, crushed
6 shallots, chopped
5 cm (2 in) piece fresh root ginger, chopped
1 tablespoon ground coriander
1½ teaspoons ground turmeric
115 g (4 oz) rice vermicelli
2 tablespoons vegetable oil
700 g (1½ lb) boneless, skinless chicken breast, cubed
675 ml (24 fl oz/3 cups) chicken stock
450 g (1 lb) raw, unpeeled medium prawns
225 g (8 oz) tofu, cut into 2.5 cm (½ in) cubes
225 g (8 oz) bean sprouts
450 ml (16 fl oz/2 cups) coconut milk
small bunch spring onions

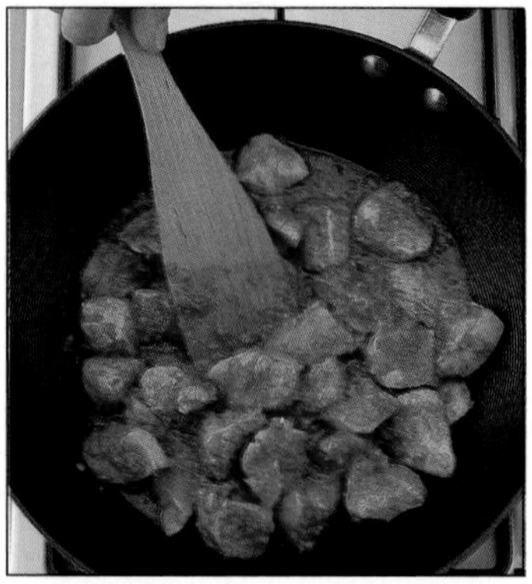

Soak chillies in 3 tablespoons hot water in a blender for 10 minutes. Add garlic, shallots, fresh root ginger, coriander and turmeric and grind to a paste. Soak noodles in hot water for 3-5 minutes, stirring occasionally. Drain. In a wok or saucepan over medium heat, heat oil. Stir in spice paste and cook for 3-4 minutes. Add chicken and cook, stirring, for 3-4 minutes. Add stock; simmer gently for 20-25 minutes.

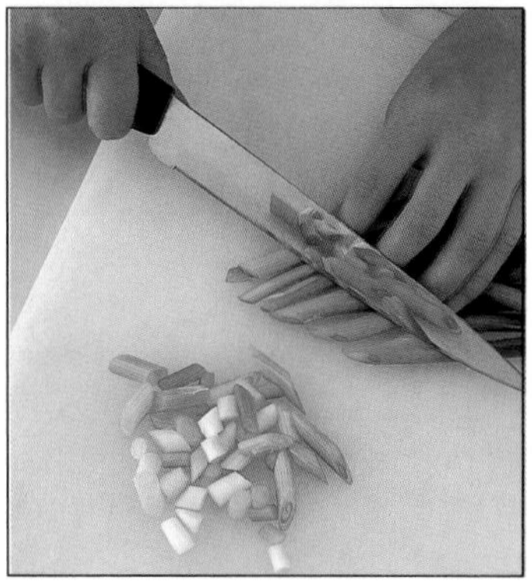

Add prawns and simmer for 3-4 minutes until they turn pink. Add tofu, bean sprouts, noodles and coconut milk. Stir and simmer for 5 minutes. Thickly slice spring onions on diagonal, including some green. Add half to pan and stir in. Serve garnished with remaining spring onions.

Serves 6.

PENANG HOT-SOUR SOUP

225 g (8 oz) whole fish, such as trout
1.2 litres (2 pints/5 cups) fish or chicken stock
4-5 dried chillies, cored, seeded and chopped
6 shallots, chopped
1 stalk lemon grass, chopped
3 slices galangal, chopped
1 teaspoon shrimp paste
1 tablespoon paprika
¼ teaspoon ground turmeric
15 fresh mint leaves
1 teaspoon brown sugar
1 teaspoon vegetable oil
3 tablespoons tamarind paste (see page 11)
225 g (8 oz) rice vermicelli
salt

In a saucepan, put fish and stock. Cover and simmer for 15 minutes. Lift fish from pan. When cool enough to handle, remove flesh from skin and bones. Return bones to pan and simmer gently, uncovered, for 15 minutes, then strain. Mash fish. Put chillies and 4 tablespoons hot water in a blender and soak for 10 minutes. Add shallots, lemon grass, galangal, shrimp paste, paprika and turmeric. Mix to a smooth paste. Add to pan with strained stock.

Add mint, sugar, oil, tamarind and 225 ml (8 fl oz/1 cup) water. Simmer, uncovered, for 15 minutes. Add fish and simmer for 30 minutes. Soak noodles in hot water for 15 minutes until soft; drain. Cook in boiling salted water for 1 minute; drain. Put in warmed soup bowls.

Serves 3-4.

SEAFOOD & COCONUT SOUP

3 stalks lemon grass, cut into 5 cm (2 in) lengths
5 cm (2 in) piece galangal, thinly sliced
2.5 cm (1 in) piece fresh root ginger, thinly sliced
2 teaspoons finely chopped red chilli
1 litre (1¾ pints/4 cups) coconut milk
10 kaffir lime leaves
200 g (7 oz) boneless, skinless chicken breast, cut into 2.5 cm (1 in) cubes
5 tablespoons fish sauce
juice ½ lime
200 g (7 oz) raw unpeeled large prawns, peeled and deveined
200 g (7 oz) firm white fish fillets, cut into 2.5 cm (1 in) cubes
small handful each coriander and Thai basil leaves
coriander sprigs, to garnish

In a saucepan, put lemon grass, galangal, ginger and chilli. Add 225 ml (8 fl oz/1 cup) water. Bring to the boil then simmer for 5 minutes. Add coconut milk and lime leaves. Simmer for 10 minutes. Add chicken, fish sauce and lime juice to pan. Poach for 5 minutes. Add prawns and fish. Poach for a further 2-3 minutes until prawns turn pink.

Add coriander and basil to pan. Stir, then ladle into warm soup bowls. Remove and discard lemon grass and lime leaves before eating. Garnish with coriander.

Serves 4.

TOFU SOUP

1 litre (1¾ pints/4 cups) well-flavoured vegetable stock
225 g (8 oz) tofu, cut into 1 cm (½ in) cubes
1 fresh red chilli, cored, seeded and finely chopped
6 shallots, finely chopped
1 small carrot, finely chopped
2 spring onions, sliced into rings
4 tablespoons light soy sauce
2 teaspoons light brown sugar
salt

Pour stock into a saucepan. Add tofu, chilli, shallots, carrot, spring onions, soy sauce and sugar.

Bring to the boil, uncovered. Stir briefly then simmer for 2-3 minutes.

Add salt to taste. Ladle soup into warmed soup bowls. Serve as part of a main meal to counterbalance hot dishes.

Serves 4.

VERMICELLI SOUP

1.2 litres (2 pints/5 cups) chicken stock
1 small onion, chopped
2 stalks lemon grass, chopped and crushed
2 kaffir lime leaves, shredded
1 tablespoon lime juice
3 cloves garlic, chopped
2 fresh red chillies, seeded and chopped
4 cm (1½ in) piece galangal, peeled and chopped
1½ tablespoons fish sauce
2 teaspoons crushed palm sugar
115 g (4 oz) clear vermicelli, soaked in cold water for 10 minutes, drained
2 tablespoons roughly chopped coriander leaves
Thai holy basil leaves, to garnish

Put stock, onion, lemon grass, lime leaves, lime juice, garlic, chillies and galangal into a saucepan and simmer for 20 minutes.

Stir in fish sauce and sugar. When sugar has dissolved, add noodles and cook for 1 minute. Stir in coriander. Spoon into warmed bowls and garnish with basil leaves.

Serves 4-6.

LEMON GRASS SOUP

175-225 g (6-8 oz) raw large prawns
2 teaspoons vegetable oil
625 ml (20 fl oz/2½ cups) light fish stock
2 thick stalks lemon grass, finely chopped
3 tablespoons lime juice
1 tablespoon fish sauce
3 kaffir lime leaves, chopped
½ fresh red chilli, seeded and thinly sliced
½ fresh green chilli, seeded and thinly sliced
½ teaspoon crushed palm sugar
coriander leaves, to garnish

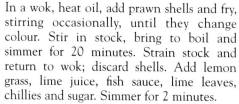

Peel prawns and remove dark veins running down their backs; reserve prawns.

In a wok, heat oil, add prawn shells and fry, stirring occasionally, until they change colour. Stir in stock, bring to boil and simmer for 20 minutes. Strain stock and return to wok; discard shells. Add lemon grass, lime juice, fish sauce, lime leaves, chillies and sugar. Simmer for 2 minutes.

Add prawns and cook just below simmering point for 2-3 minutes until prawns are cooked. Serve in warmed bowls garnished with coriander.

Serves 4.

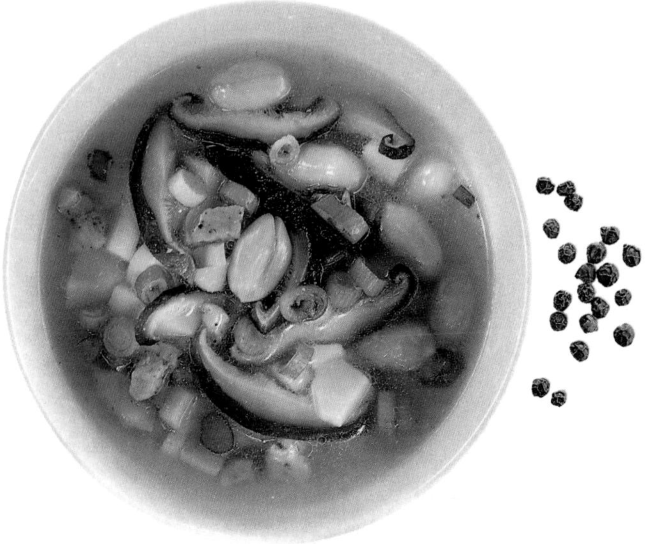

PORK & PEANUT SOUP

- 4 coriander roots, chopped
- 2 cloves garlic, chopped
- 1 teaspoons black peppercorns, cracked
- 1 tablespoon vegetable oil
- 225 g (8 oz) lean pork, finely chopped
- 4 spring onions, chopped
- 675 ml (24 fl oz/3 cups) veal stock
- 55 g (2 oz/⅓ cup) skinned peanuts
- 6 pieces dried Chinese black mushrooms, soaked for 20 minutes, drained and chopped
- 115 g (4 oz) bamboo shoots, roughly chopped
- 1 tablespoon fish sauce

Using a pestle and mortar, pound coriander, garlic and peppercorns to a paste.

In a wok, heat oil, add peppercorn paste and cook for 2-3 minutes, stirring occasionally. Add pork and spring onions and stir for 1½ minutes.

Stir stock, peanuts and mushrooms into wok, then cook at just below boiling point for 7 minutes. Add bamboo shoots and fish sauce and continue to cook gently for 3-4 minutes.

Serves 3-4.

CHICKEN & COCONUT SOUP

- 950 ml (30 fl oz/3¾ cups) coconut milk
- 115 g (4 oz) chicken breast fillet, cut into strips
- 2 stalks lemon grass, bruised and thickly sliced
- 2 spring onions, thinly sliced
- 3-4 fresh red chillies, seeded and sliced
- juice 1½ limes
- 1 tablespoon fish sauce
- 1 tablespoon coriander leaves, freshly torn into shreds
- coriander leaves, to garnish

Bring coconut milk to just below boiling point in a saucepan. Add chicken and lemon grass.

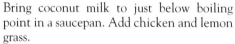

Adjust heat so liquid gives just an occasional bubble, then poach chicken, uncovered, for about 4 minutes until tender.

Add spring onions and chillies. Heat briefly, then remove from heat and stir in lime juice, fish sauce and shredded coriander. Serve garnished with coriander leaves.

Serves 4.

CHICKEN SOUP

1 tablespoon vegetable oil
½ teaspoon minced garlic
2 shallots or 1 small onion, thinly sliced
675 ml (24 fl oz/3 cups) chicken stock
225 g (8 oz) cooked chicken meat, boned and thinly shredded
25 g (1 oz) bean thread vermicelli, soaked then cut into short lengths
1 tablespoon black fungus, soaked and cut into small pieces
12-16 lily buds, soaked and trimmed
2 tablespoons fish sauce
salt and freshly ground black pepper
2-3 spring onions, sliced
coriander sprigs, to garnish

Heat oil in a wok or pan and stir-fry garlic and shallots or onion until aromatic; do not brown them. Add chicken stock and bring to boil. Add chicken, vermicelli, fungus, lily buds and fish sauce, bring back to boil and simmer for about 3 minutes.,

Taste and adjust seasoning, then add spring onions. Serve soup hot, garnished with coriander sprigs.

Serves 4-6.

Variation: If ready-cooked chicken is not available, raw chicken fillet can be used instead, but increase cooking time by at least 2 minutes, or until chicken is cooked.

VIETNAMESE FISH SOUP

1 tablespoon vegetable oil
2 cloves garlic, finely chopped
2 shallots or 1 small onion, chopped
1 tablespoon each chilli sauce and tomato purée
2 medium tomatoes, chopped
3 tablespoons fish sauce
2 tablespoons sugar
675 ml (24 fl oz/3 cups) chicken stock
2 tablespoons tamarind water or lime juice
225 g (8 oz) firm fish fillet, cut into small slices
115 g (4 oz) fresh scallops, sliced
115 g (4 oz) raw peeled prawns
12 clams or mussels, scrubbed clean
2-3 tablespoons dry white wine or sherry
salt and freshly ground black pepper
coriander sprigs, to garnish

Heat oil in a wok or pan and lightly brown garlic and shallots or onion. Add chilli sauce, tomato purée, chopped tomato, fish sauce and sugar. Blend well, then simmer for 2-3 minutes. Add stock with tamarind water or lime juice and bring to the boil.

Just before serving, add seafood and wine or sherry to stock, bring back to boil, cover and simmer for 3-4 minutes until clam or mussel shells have opened; discard any that remain closed after cooking. Taste soup and adjust seasoning. Serve hot, garnished with coriander sprigs.

Serves 4-6.

Note: Take care not to overcook seafood. If using ready-shelled clams or mussels, reduce cooking time by half.

VIETNAMESE BEEF SOUP

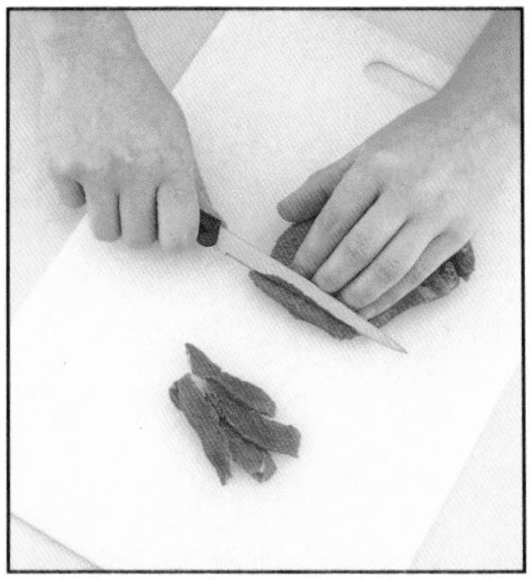

175-225 g (6-8 oz) beef steak, thinly sliced
¼ teaspoon freshly ground black pepper
½ teaspoon minced garlic
½ teaspoon sugar
2 teaspoons soy sauce
1 tablespoon vegetable oil
1 teaspoon finely chopped lemon grass
2 shallots, thinly sliced
675 ml (24 fl oz/3 cups) beef or chicken stock
1 tablespoon fish sauce
salt to taste
2 spring onions, chopped
chopped coriander leaves , to garnish

In a bowl, marinate beef slices with pepper, garlic, sugar and soy sauce for at least 2-3 hours. Heat oil in a wok or pan and stir-fry chopped lemon grass and shallots for about 1 minute. Add beef or chicken stock and bring to the boil.

Add beef and fish sauce and bring back to the boil. Adjust seasoning and serve at once, garnished with chopped spring onions and coriander.

Serves 4.

PAPAYA & PORK SOUP

1 litre (1¾ pints/4 cups) stock or water
4 pork chops, each weighing about 85 g (3 oz)
1 small unripe green papaya, peeled and cut into small cubes
2 tablespoons fish sauce
salt and freshly ground black pepper
1 tablespoon chopped spring onions
coriander sprigs, to garnish

Bring stock or water to the boil in a wok or pan and add pork. Bring back to the boil and skim off scum, then reduce heat, cover and simmer gently for 25-30 minutes.

Add papaya cubes and fish sauce, bring back to the boil and cook soup for a further 5 minutes.

To serve, place salt, pepper and chopped spring onions in a tureen. Pour boiling soup with its contents over it, garnish with coriander sprigs and serve at once. The meat should be so tender that one can easily tear it apart into small pieces for eating.

Serves 4.

VERMICELLI & MUSHROOM SOUP

1 tablespoon vegetable oil
½ teaspoon minced garlic
½ teaspoon finely chopped fresh root ginger
1 tablespoon chopped spring onion
1 litre (1¾ pints/4 cups) vegetarian stock or water
2 tablespoons soy sauce
1 tablespoon sugar
55 g (2 oz) dried bean curd skins, soaked then cut into small pieces
55 g (2 oz) bean thread vermicelli, soaked then cut into short lengths
8-10 Chinese dried mushrooms, soaked and sliced
salt and freshly ground black pepper
coriander sprigs, to garnish

Heat oil in a wok or pan and stir-fry garlic, ginger and spring onions for 20 seconds, or until fragrant. Add stock or water and bring to a rolling boil. Add soy sauce and sugar and simmer for about 30 seconds. (The soup can be made in advance up to this point, then brought back to the boil).

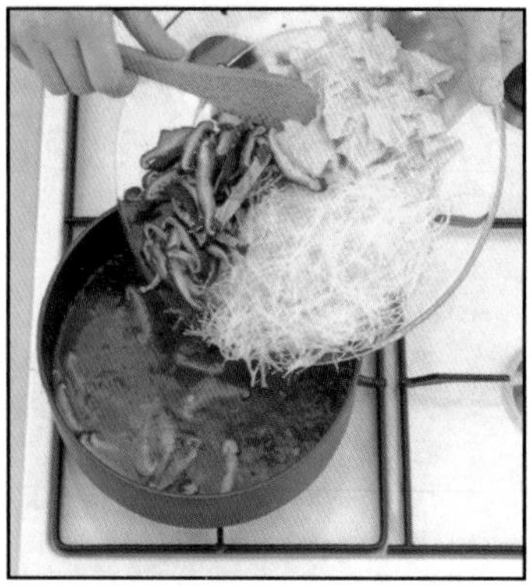

Add bean curd skins, vermicelli and mushrooms and cook for 2-3 minutes. Adjust seasoning and garnish with coriander sprigs.

Serves 4-6.

Variation: For non-vegetarians, add 1-2 tablespoons dried shrimp, soaked, if wished. Chicken or meat stock can be used instead of vegetable stock.

MIXED VEGETABLE SOUP

1 tablespoon vegetable oil
1 teaspoon minced garlic
1 small onion, chopped
1 teaspoon chilli sauce
1 tablespoon sugar
675 ml (24 fl oz/3 cups) vegetarian stock or water
2 tablespoons soy sauce
3 tablespoons tamarind water (see page 11) or 2 tablespoons lime juice
1 cake tofu, cut into small cubes
225 g (8 oz) bok choy or spinach, chopped
175 g (6 oz) bean sprouts
3-4 firm tomatoes, cut into thin wedges
salt and freshly ground black pepper
5-6 fresh basil leaves, coarsely chopped

Heat oil in a wok or pan and stir-fry garlic and onion for about 30 seconds. Add chilli sauce and sugar and stir to make a smooth paste. Add stock or water, bring to the boil, then add soy sauce and tamarind water or lime juice. Simmer for 1 minute. (The soup can be made in advance up to this point.)

Bring soup back to a rolling boil and add tofu, bok choy, bean sprouts and tomatoes. Cook for about 2 minutes. Adjust seasoning and serve soup piping hot, garnished with chopped basil leaves.

Serves 4-6.

DASHI

10 cm (4 in) square dried konbu (kelp)
40 g (1½ oz) hana-katsuo (dried bonito flakes)

Wipe konbu with a damp cloth, place in a saucepan with 675 ml (24 fl oz/3 cups) water and leave to soak for about 1 hour. Heat uncovered, over medium heat for about 10 minutes, removing konbu just before reaching boiling point so it retains its subtle flavour. If the thickest part of the konbu is still hard, return it to the pan for a few more minutes, adding a little water to prevent it boiling. Reserve konbu.

Add 25 g (1 oz) of the hana-katsuo to the pan. Bring back to the boil (do not stir) and immediately remove from the heat. Using a tablespoon or ladle, remove foam from the surface and leave to stand for a few minutes until the hana-katsuo settles down to the bottom of pan. Strain liquid through a sieve lined with muslin and reserve hana-katsuo. This dashi (known as first dashi) is good for clear soups; however, for strongly flavoured soups, noodle broths and simmering, second dashi is used.

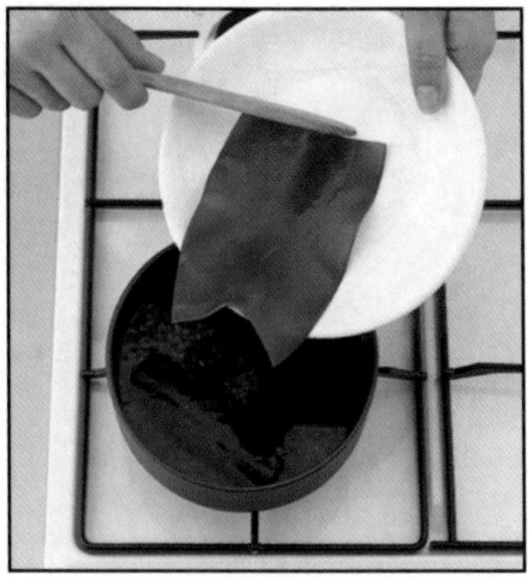

To make second dashi, put reserved konbu and hana-katsuo in a saucepan with 675 ml (24 fl oz/3 cups) water and bring to the boil. Lower the heat and simmer, uncovered, for 10-15 minutes until dashi is reduced by one third. Add the last 15 g (½ oz) hana-katsuo and remove from heat. Skim off foam, leave to stand and strain as for first dashi.

Serves 4.

Note: For instant dashi, mix dashi-no-moto (freeze-dried dashi powder) with water.

CLEAR SOUP WITH CHICKEN

100 g (3½ oz) chicken breast fillet
2 tablespoons cornflour
12 mangetout
DASHI SOUP:
1 quantity dashi, opposite
1 tablespoon soy sauce
½ teaspoon salt

Slice chicken breast crossways diagonally into 8 pieces and pat lightly with cornflour.

Bring a saucepan of water to the boil and drop in chicken pieces, one at a time so that they do not stick together. Cook for a few minutes (do not overcook), then drain in a mesh bowl or a colander. Keep them warm. Remove strings from mangetout, trim ends and slice diagonally. Cook in boiling water for 1-2 minutes until soft but still crunchy. Set aside.

Heat dashi and season with soy sauce and salt. Place 2 pieces of cooked chicken breast and 3 mangetout in each of 4 individual soup bowls. Pour hot soup over them and serve at once.

Serves 4.

CLEAR SOUP WITH PRAWNS

4 raw king prawns or 8 medium size prawns
3 tablespoons sake or 6 tablespoons white wine
45 g (1½ oz) dried somen (very fine) noodles
cress, to garnish
DASHI SOUP:
1 quantity dashi (see page 29)
1 tablespoon soy sauce
½ teaspoon salt

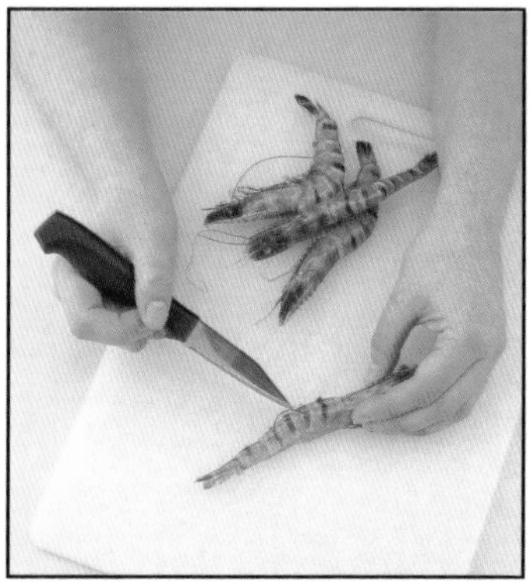

Make a slit lengthways along the back of each prawn and remove black vein-like intestine.

Place prawns in a saucepan with sake and 3 tablespoons water, or with white wine only, and steam for 2-3 minutes. Remove from heat and cool down in the saucepan. Peel prawns, leaving tail shell on. Cook noodles in boiling water for about 3 minutes then rinse in cold water, changing water several times. Divide noodles between 4 individual soup bowls. Place one large prawn or 2 medium size ones on each portion of noodles.

Heat dashi and season with soy sauce and salt. Pour hot soup gently over prawns and noodles and garnish with a few sprigs of cress.

Serves 4.

MISO SOUP WITH TOFU

2 tablespoons dried wakame (seaweed)
3 tablespoons miso
115 g (4 oz) firm tofu, cut into tiny dice
1 spring onion, finely chopped
ground sansho pepper (optional)
STOCK:
450 ml (16 fl oz/2 cups) second dashi (see page 29), or 550 ml (20 fl oz/2½ cups) water and 1-2 teaspoons dashi-no-moto (freeze-dried dashi powder)

First make second dashi, following method on page 29, or add dashi-no-moto to boiling water and stir to dissolve.

Meanwhile, soak wakame in plenty of water for 10-15 minutes until fully opened up. Drain and cut wakame into small pieces, if necessary.

Put miso in a teacup and mix with a few spoonfuls of stock. Return stock to a low heat (do not boil) and add diluted miso. Add wakame and tofu to the pan and turn up the heat. Just before it reaches boiling point, add finely chopped spring onion and remove from heat. Serve hot in individual soup bowls, sprinkled with a little ground sansho pepper, if wished.

Serves 4.

STARTERS

CHEESY STUFFED TOMATOES

8 tomatoes
2 tablespoons vegetable oil
1 small onion, finely chopped
1 clove garlic, crushed
2.5 cm (1 in) piece fresh root ginger, grated
1 teaspoon ground cumin
½ teaspoon turmeric
½ teaspoon cayenne pepper
2 teaspoons ground coriander
salt
115 g (4 oz/½ cup) fresh Indian cheese or natural fromage frais
25 g (1 oz/¼ cup) Cheddar cheese, grated
1 tablespoon chopped coriander leaves

Cut a slice from the top of each tomato. Scoop out centres and discard seeds, then chop pulp and reserve. Turn tomatoes upside down on absorbent kitchen paper and leave to drain. Heat oil in a small frying pan, add onion and fry for 5 minutes, stirring occasionally, until soft. Stir in garlic and ginger and fry for 1 minute. Stir in cumin, turmeric, cayenne pepper and ground coriander. Season with salt and fry for 1 minute more.

Stir in tomato pulp and cook, uncovered, for about 5 minutes, until thick. Preheat oven to 190C (375F/Gas 5). Stir fresh cheese or fromage frais and half the Cheddar into spice mixture and spoon into tomato shells. Sprinkle remaining Cheddar over the tops and place on a baking tray. Cook for 10-15 minutes, until tops are golden brown and tomatoes soft. Sprinkle with chopped coriander and serve hot.

Serves 4.

ONION BHAJIS

85 g (3 oz/¾ cup) chick-pea flour, sifted
1 tablespoon vegetable oil plus extra for deep-frying
1 teaspoon ground coriander
1 teaspoon ground cumin
2 fresh green chillies, seeded and finely chopped
115 ml (4 fl oz/½ cup) warm water
salt
2 onions, finely sliced
herb sprigs, to garnish

Put flour in blender or food processor fitted with a metal blade.

Add oil, coriander, cumin, chillies and water. Season with salt. Process until well blended and smooth, then pour batter into a bowl. Cover and leave in a warm place for 30 minutes. Stir in onions.

Half-fill a deep-fat fryer or deep pan with oil and heat to 190C (375F) or until a cube of day-old bread browns in 40 seconds. Drop about five two-tablespoon amounts into oil and fry for 5-6 minutes, until golden. Drain on absorbent kitchen paper. Serve hot, garnished with sprigs of herbs.

Serves 4.

Note: Make sure that oil doesn't become too hot: the bhajis must fry slowly so centres cook through.

PRAWNS & MUSTARD SEEDS

450 g (1 lb) raw king prawns
1 tablespoon mixed black and yellow mustard seeds
½ teaspoon turmeric
½ teaspoon cayenne pepper
salt
25 g (1 oz/2 tablespoons) butter or ghee, melted
strips orange and lime zest, to garnish

Peel prawns, leaving tail shells on, then make a small incision along spines and remove black vein. Push 2 or 3 prawns at a time onto short wooden skewers, then set aside.

Reserve 1 teaspoon mustard seeds, and grind remainder in a mortar and pestle or coffee grinder. Transfer to a small bowl and mix in turmeric and cayenne and season with salt. Add 85 ml (3 fl oz/⅓ cup) water and blend until smooth. Add prawns, turning to coat them in marinade and leave in a cool place for 30 minutes to marinate.

Heat grill. Drain skewered prawns and place on a grill rack, brush with butter and sprinkle with reserved mustard seeds. Cook for 3-5 minutes, turning over once and basting occasionally with any remaining marinade, until prawns are just tender. Serve hot, garnished with orange and lime zest.

Serves 4.

SPICY PRAWN PATTIES

350 g (12 oz) white fish fillets, such as sole, plaice, cod or whiting
175 g (6 oz) peeled cooked prawns, chopped
4 spring onions, chopped
2.5 cm (1 in) piece fresh root ginger, grated
2 tablespoons chopped coriander leaves
1 tablespoon chopped fresh mint
115 g (4 oz/2 cups) fresh white bread crumbs
salt and cayenne pepper
1 egg yolk, beaten
2 tablespoons lemon juice
85 g (3 oz/¾ cup) chick-pea flour
1 tablespoon ground coriander
55 ml (2 fl oz/¼ cup) vegetable oil for frying
mint sprigs and lemon slices, to garnish

Remove any skin and bones from fish, wash and pat dry with absorbent kitchen paper. Mince fish, then transfer to a bowl. Stir in prawns, spring onions, ginger, coriander, mint, 55 g (2 oz/1 cup) bread crumbs and salt and pepper. Add egg yolk and lemon juice and mix well. Divide mixture into 16 pieces and form each into a 1 cm (½ in) thick round. Roll patties in remaining bread crumbs to coat completely.

Put flour and ground coriander in a small bowl, season with salt and cayenne pepper, then add 115 ml (4 fl oz/½ cup) water and mix to a smooth batter. Heat oil in a frying pan. Dip prawn patties in batter, then fry for 2-3 minutes on each side until golden brown. Drain on absorbent kitchen paper and serve hot, garnished with mint and lemon slices.

Serves 4.

PORK DIM SUM

450 g (1 lb) minced pork
115 g (4 oz) raw shelled prawns, minced
1½ tablespoons soy sauce
½ tablespoon Chinese rice wine or dry sherry
½ tablespoon sesame oil
½ tablespoon sugar
pinch pepper
1 egg white
1½ tablespoons cornflour
30 won ton skins
fresh or frozen peas or chopped hard-boiled egg yolks, to garnish

To make filling, mix together minced pork, minced prawns, soy sauce, rice wine or sherry, sesame oil, sugar, pepper and egg white until mixture is well blended and smooth. Stir in cornflour. Divide into 30 portions. Cut off edges of won ton skins to form circles, if necessary. Place 1 portion of filling in the centre of a won ton skin. Gather edges of won ton skin around meat filling. Dip a teaspoon in water and use to smooth the surface of the meat.

Garnish by placing a green pea or piece of chopped egg yolk on top of meat. Gather edge to seal in filling. Repeat with remaining won ton skins and meat filling. Line a steamer with a damp cloth; steam over high heat for 5 minutes. Remove and serve.

Makes 30 dumplings.

PRAWN DIM SUM

450 g (1 lb) raw shelled prawns, ground
115 g (4 oz) can bamboo shoots, chopped
4 tablespoons water
1½ tablespoons soy sauce
½ tablespoon Chinese rice wine or dry sherry
½ teaspoon sugar
½ teaspoon sesame oil
pinch pepper
1½ tablespoons cornflour
DOUGH:
450 g (1 lb/4 cups) plain flour
115 ml (4 fl oz/½ cup) boiling water
70 ml (2½ fl oz/⅓ cup) cold water
1 tablespoon vegetable oil

To make filling, mix together ground prawns, bamboo shoots, water, soy sauce, rice wine or sherry, sugar, sesame oil and pepper until well blended and smooth. Stir in cornflour. Divide into 30 portions. To make dough, put 300 g (10 oz/2½ cups) of flour in a medium size bowl. Reserve remaining flour and use for hands if they become sticky. Stir in boiling water. Add cold water and oil. Mix to form dough and knead until smooth. Roll dough into a long, rope shape and cut into 30 pieces. Roll each portion into a thin 5 cm (2 in) circle.

Place 1 portion of filling in the centre of a dough circle. Bring opposite edges together and pinch them together to hold. Repeat with remaining circles and filling. Line a steamer with a damp cloth. Set dumplings about 2.5 cm (1 in) apart. Steam over high heat for 5 minutes. Remove and serve.

Makes 30 dumplings.

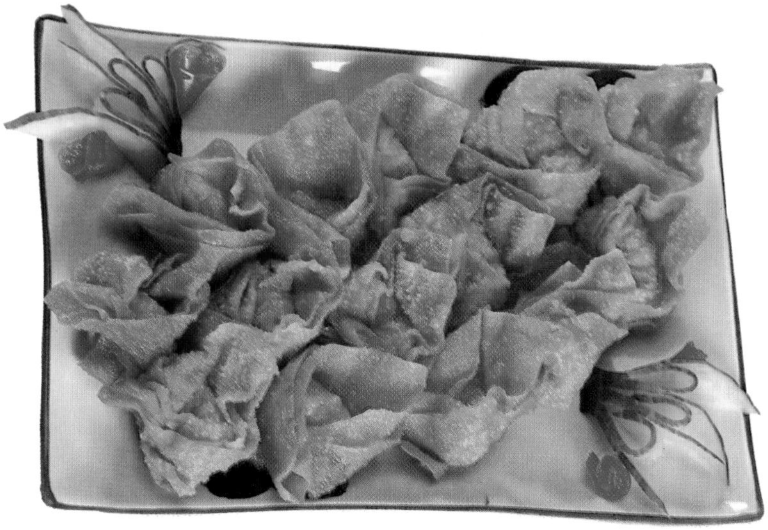

FRIED WON TONS

175 g (6 oz) minced pork
115 g (4 oz) can water chestnuts, finely chopped
1 tablespoon cornflour
½ teaspoon salt
½ teaspoon Chinese rice wine or dry sherry
dash sesame oil
pinch pepper
30 won ton skins
vegetable oil, for frying

Mix together minced pork, water chestnuts, 1 tablespoon water, cornflour, salt, rice wine or sherry, sesame oil and pepper until combined. Divide into 30 portions.

Put 1 tablespoon of filling in the centre of a won ton skin. Diagonally fold skin in half to form a triangle. Fold edge containing filling over about 1 cm (½ in).

Bring 2 points together, moisten one inner edge and pinch edges together to hold. Repeat with remaining won tons and filling. Heat a wok, then add vegetable oil. deep-fry won tons over a medium heat until golden. Drain on absorbent kitchen paper and serve.

Makes 30 won tons.

CRISPY SEAWEED

800 g (1¾ lb) young spring greens
550 ml (20 fl oz/2½ cups) vegetable oil
1 tablespoon brown sugar
½ teaspoon sea salt
½ teaspoon ground cinnamon
85 g (3 oz/¾ cup) flaked almonds, to garnish (optional)

Remove thick ribs from leaves and discard. Wash leaves and drain and dry thoroughly with absorbent kitchen paper. Using a very sharp knife or Chinese cleaver cut leaves into very fine shreds.

In a wok heat oil until smoking, then remove from heat and add greens. Return to a medium heat and stir for 2-3 minutes, or until shreds begin to float. Using a slotted spoon remove from oil and drain on absorbent kitchen paper.

In a small bowl, mix together sugar, salt and cinnamon. Place 'seaweed' on a dish and sprinkle with sugar mixture. Serve cold garnished with flaked almonds, if wished.

Serves 4.

PRAWNS WITH GINGER DIP

16 uncooked large prawns, peeled, with tails left on
coriander leaves and fresh root ginger strips, to garnish
MARINADE:
1 tablespoon light soy sauce
1 teaspoon rice wine
1 teaspoon sesame oil
1 clove garlic, crushed
DIP:
1 tablespoon white rice vinegar
1 teaspoon sugar
2 tablespoons chopped coriander leaves
1 cm (½ in) piece fresh root ginger, peeled and finely chopped

Using a small sharp knife, cut along back of each prawn and remove thin black cord. Rinse and dry prawns with absorbent kitchen paper and place on a plate. Mix together light soy sauce, rice wine, sesame oil and garlic and brush over prawns. Cover and chill for 1 hour.

To make dip, mix together white rice vinegar, sugar, chopped coriander and fresh root ginger, cover and chill. Preheat grill. Place prawns on the grill rack and cook for 1-2 minutes on each side, basting with marinade, until cooked through. Garnish with coriander leaves and ginger strips and serve with dip.

Serves 4.

CHILLI PRAWN BALLS

450 g (1 lb) cooked, peeled large prawns, thawed and dried, if frozen
1 fresh red chilli, seeded and chopped
3 spring onions, finely chopped
grated zest 1 small lemon
2 tablespoons cornflour
1 egg white, lightly beaten
salt and freshly ground black pepper
strips fresh red chilli, to garnish

Place prawns, chilli, spring onions, lemon zest, cornflour, egg white and black pepper in a blender or food processor and process to form a firm dough-like mixture.

Divide prawn mixture into 12 portions and form each portion into a smooth ball, flouring hands with extra cornflour if necessary, to prevent sticking.

Bring a wok or large saucepan of water to the boil, arrange prawn balls on a layer of greaseproof paper in a steamer and place over water. Cover and steam 5 minutes or until cooked through. Garnish with sliced chilli to serve.

Serves 4.

STEAMED FISH DUMPLINGS

175 g (6 oz) skinless cod fillet
1 slice lean bacon, trimmed of fat and finely chopped
1 teaspoon light soy sauce
1 teaspoon oyster sauce
1 tablespoon chopped fresh chives
1 teaspoon cornflour
12 round won ton skins
1 egg white, lightly beaten
chopped fresh chives, to garnish

Place cod fillet, bacon, soy sauce, oyster sauce, chives and cornflour in a blender or food processor and process to form a firm mixture. Divide into 12 portions.

Place a portion of filling in the centre of each won ton skin and lightly brush edges of won ton skin with egg white.

Fold over to form crescent shapes and crimp edges to seal. Bring a wok or large saucepan of water to the boil, arrange dumplings on a layer of greaseproof paper in a steamer and place over water. Cover and steam 10 minutes or until cooked through. Garnish with chives to serve.

Serves 4.

PEARL PATTIES & SHERRY DIP

150 g (5 oz/¾ cup) long-grain white rice
350 g (12 oz) extra-lean minced beef
2 spring onions, finely chopped
1 clove garlic, crushed
1 tablespoon dark soy sauce
1 tablespoon dry sherry
2 teaspoons cornflour
DIP:
2 tablespoons dry sherry
2 tablespoons dark soy sauce
1 teaspoon sugar
1 clove garlic, crushed

Place rice in a bowl, add enough water to cover and soak for 1 hour. Drain well and dry on absorbent kitchen paper. Mix together beef, spring onions, garlic, soy sauce, sherry and cornflour to form a firm mixture. Divide into 16 portions and shape into 4 cm (1½ in) diameter patties.

Press each patty into rice to coat on both sides. Bring a wok or large saucepan of water to the boil. Arrange patties on a layer of greaseproof paper in a steamer, making sure they don't overlap – you will probably need 2 steamers. Place over water, cover and steam for 20 minutes. To make dip, mix together dry sherry, soy sauce, sugar and garlic. Serve dip with patties.

Serves 4.

GRILLED FIVE-SPICE CHICKEN

2 boneless, skinless chicken breasts, each weighing about 175 g (6 oz), trimmed
2 small red peppers, halved
2 small yellow peppers, halved
chopped fresh chives, to garnish
MARINADE:
1 clove garlic, crushed
1 fresh red chilli, seeded and chopped
3 tablespoons light soy sauce
1 teaspoon five-spice powder
1 teaspoon brown sugar
2 teaspoons sesame oil

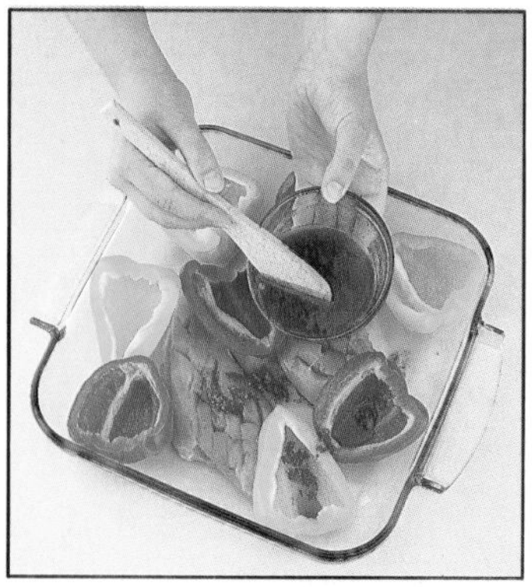

Using a small sharp knife, score chicken breasts on both sides in a criss-cross pattern, taking care not to slice all the way through. Place in a shallow dish with peppers. To make marinade, mix together garlic, chilli, soy sauce, five-spice powder, brown sugar and sesame oil and pour over chicken and peppers and turn to coat. Cover and chill for 1 hour.

Preheat grill. Remove chicken and peppers from marinade, place on grill rack and cook for 4-5 minutes on each side, or until chicken is cooked through, basting with marinade. Slice chicken breasts and serve with a piece of red and yellow pepper, garnished with chives.

Serves 4.

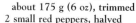

MARINATED MUSHROOMS

25 g (1 oz) dried Chinese mushrooms, soaked in hot water for 20 minutes
115 g (4 oz) oyster mushrooms
1115 g (4 oz) button mushrooms
1 tablespoon sunflower oil
2 tablespoons light soy sauce
2 sticks celery, chopped
2 cloves garlic, thinly sliced
1 whole cinnamon stick, broken
chopped celery leaves, to garnish
MARINADE:
3 tablespoons light soy sauce
3 tablespoons dry sherry
freshly ground black pepper

Drain Chinese mushrooms and squeeze out excess water. Discard stems and thinly slice caps. Slice oyster and button mushrooms. Heat oil in a wok and stir-fry mushrooms for 2 minutes.

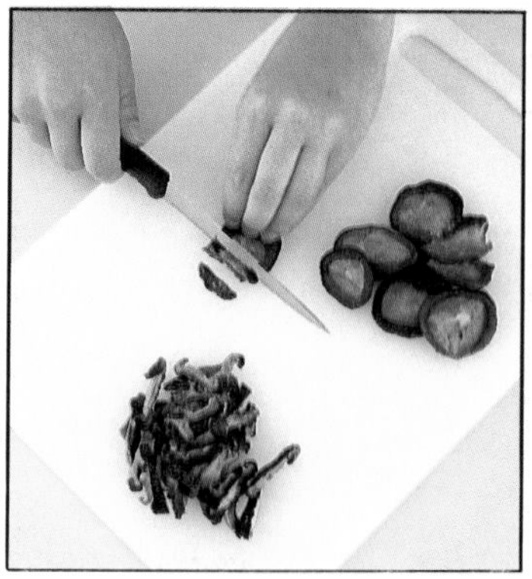

Add soy sauce, celery, garlic and cinnamon stick and stir-fry for 2-3 minutes or until just cooked. Transfer to a shallow dish and leave to cool. To make marinade, mix together soy sauce, dry sherry and black pepper and pour over cooled mushroom mixture. Cover and chill for 1 hour. Discard cinnamon stick, garnish and serve.

Serves 4.

POT-STICKER DUMPLINGS

115 g (4 oz/1 cup) plain flour
1 tablespoon sunflower oil
FILLING:
115 g (4 oz) lean minced pork
1 cm (½ in) piece fresh root ginger, peeled and finely chopped
1 tablespoon dark soy sauce
1 tablespoon dry sherry
large pinch ground white pepper

Place flour in a bowl and gradually add 115 ml (4 fl oz/½ cup) hot water, mixing well to form a dough. Turn out on to a floured surface and knead until smooth.

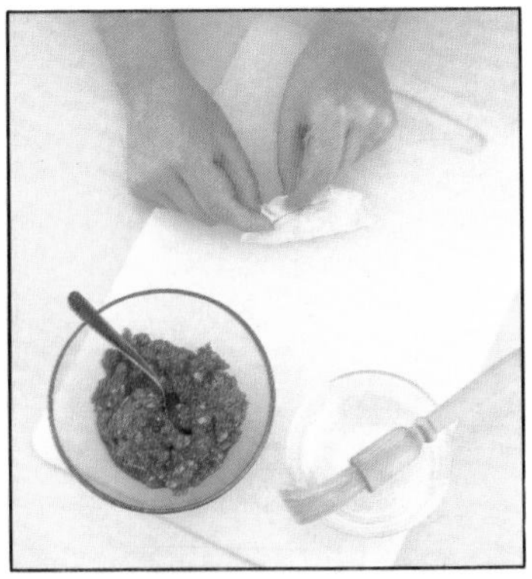

Return to the bowl, cover and set aside for 20 minutes. To make filling, mix together minced pork, ginger, soy sauce, sherry and pepper. Divide dough into 16 portions and, on a floured surface, flatten each portion into a 5 cm (2½ in) diameter round. Take one round at a time, keeping remaining rounds covered with a damp tea towel, and place a little filling in the centre. Brush edge of dough with water and bring together over filling, pinching edges together to seal. Cover with a damp tea towel while you make remainder.

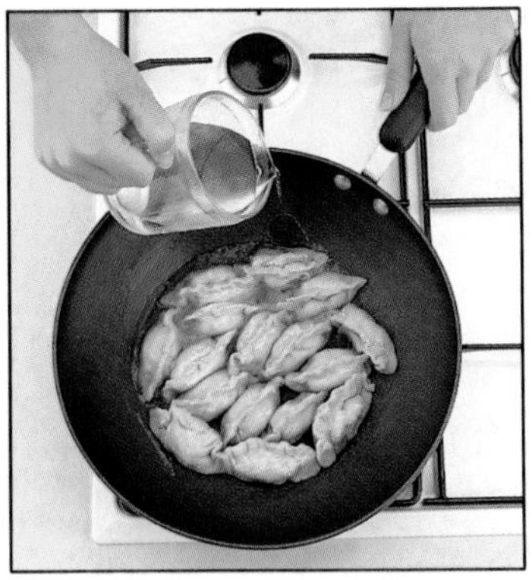

Heat oil in a wok and place dumplings, flat side down, in the wok. Cook for 2 minutes until lightly browned on bottom. Add 150 ml (5 fl oz/⅔ cup) water, cover and cook for 10 minutes. Uncover and cook for 2 minutes. Drain and serve with a crisp salad and hoisin sauce as a dip.

Serves 4.

GINGERED MELONS

½ honeydew melon
½ cantaloupe melon
115 g (4 oz) can water chestnuts, rinsed
2.5 cm (1 in) piece fresh root ginger, peeled and finely chopped
55 ml (2 fl oz/¼ cup) dry sherry
4 pieces stem ginger in syrup, sliced
2 tablespoons dried melon seeds

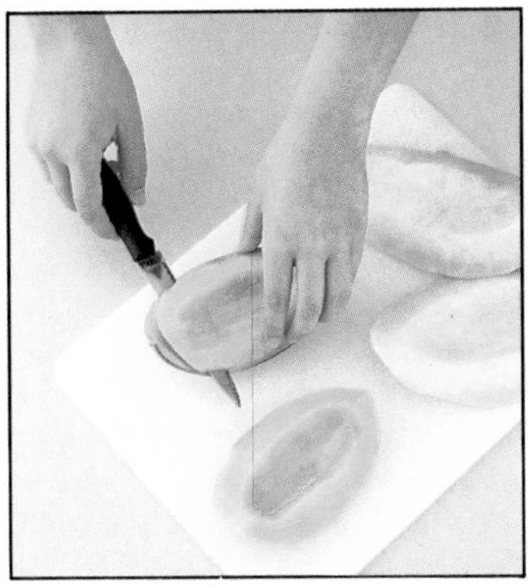

Using a spoon, scoop out seeds from both melons. Cut in half, peel away skin and thinly slice melon flesh. Slice water chestnuts.

Arrange melon slices on serving plates and top with sliced water chestnuts.

Mix together chopped ginger, dry sherry and stem ginger with its syrup and spoon over melon and water chestnuts. Cover and chill for 30 minutes. Sprinkle with melon seeds and serve.

Serves 4.

CURRY PUFFS

225 g (8 oz/1 cup) unsalted butter
575 g (1 lb 4 oz/5 cups) plain flour
3 tablespoons vegetable oil plus extra for deep-frying
4 shallots, thinly sliced
2 cloves garlic, finely crushed
1 teaspoon grated fresh root ginger
1 fresh green chilli, cored, seeded and finely chopped
4 teaspoons curry powder
450 g (1 lb) minced beef, lamb or chicken
1 potato, finely diced
1 tablespoon lime juice, or to taste
6 tablespoons chopped celery leaves
celery leaves, to garnish

Melt butter with 2 tablespoons water.

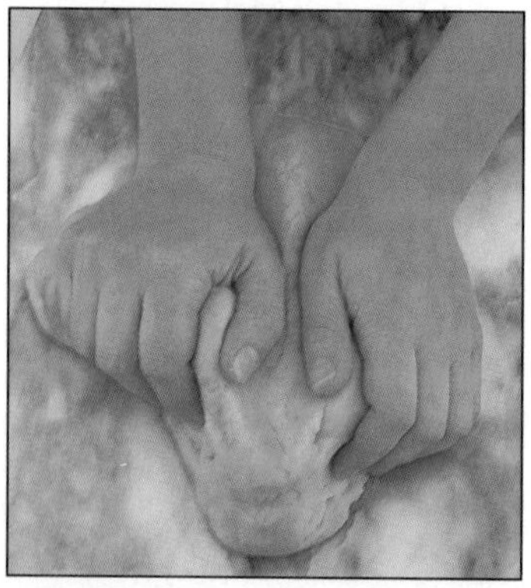

In a bowl, combine butter mixture with flour, a pinch of salt and about 6 tablespoons of water to give a medium-soft dough. Transfer to a work surface and knead for about 10 minutes. Form into a ball. Brush with oil and put in a plastic bag. Leave for at least 30 minutes.

Heat oil in a frying pan. Add shallots and fry for 4-5 minutes until browned. Stir in garlic, ginger, chilli and curry powder. Add meat and cook until pale, stirring to break up lumps. Stir in potato, lime juice, salt to taste and 2 tablespoons water. Simmer gently, covered, for 15-20 minutes until meat and potatoes are tender.

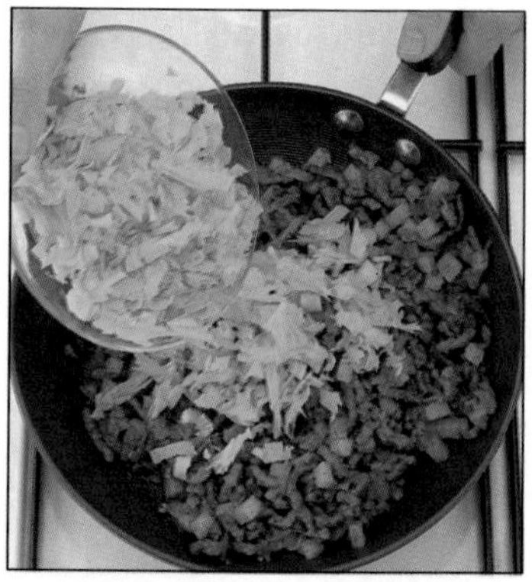

Add celery leaves and cook for 2 minutes. If necessary, increase heat and boil to drive off excess moisture, stirring. Knead dough. Break off a 2.5 cm (1 in) piece. Form into a smooth ball then roll to a 10 cm (4 in) disc.

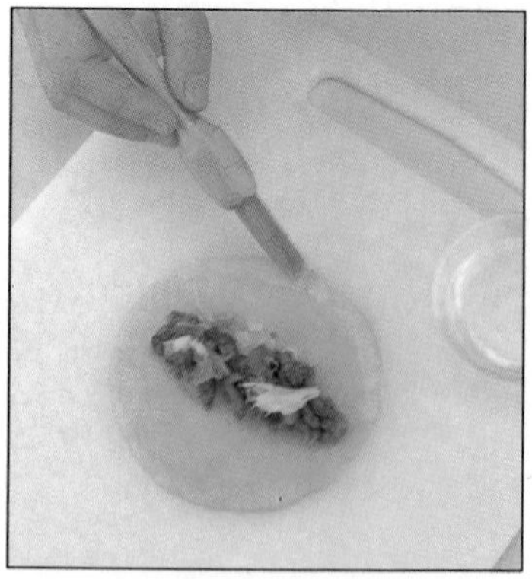

Put 2 teaspoons meat mixture along centre. Brush edge of dough circle with water and fold dough over filling.

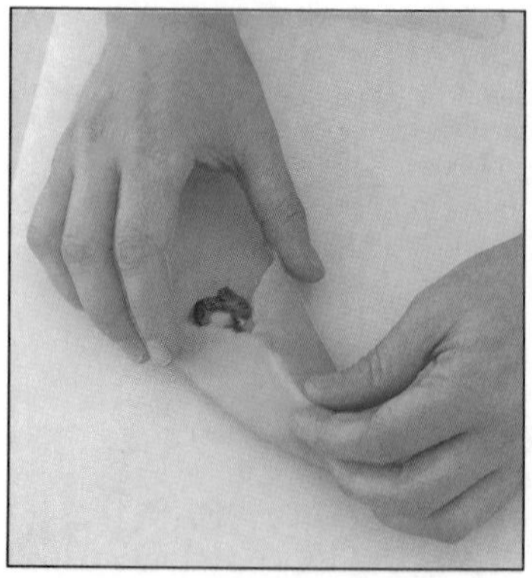

Pinch edges together to seal. Place, pinched end up, on a plate. Repeat with remaining filling and dough. Heat enough oil for deep-frying in a wok or deep-fryer over medium-low heat. Place a few curry puffs in the wok or fryer at one time, so they are not crowded, and fry slowly until golden. Turn them over so they cook evenly. Remove with a slotted spoon and drain on absorbent kitchen paper. Serve warm, garnished with celery leaves.

Makes about 30.

MALAYSIAN SPRING ROLLS

150 g (5 oz) boneless, skinless chicken breast
115 g (4 oz) raw prawns in shell
2 tablespoons groundnut (peanut) oil
1 cm (½ in) piece fresh root ginger, grated
1 clove garlic, finely crushed
3 shallots, very finely chopped
1 small carrot, grated
1 stick celery, very finely chopped
1 fresh red chilli, cored, seeded and finely chopped
2 spring onions, chopped
1 teaspoon sesame oil
2 teaspoons soy sauce
12 spring roll wrappers
1 egg, beaten
115 ml (4 fl oz/½ cup) vegetable oil
Malaysian Dipping Sauce (see page 227), to serve

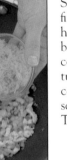

Skin and finely chop chicken. Peel and finely chop prawns. In a wok or sauté pan, heat oil. Add chicken and stir-fry until beginning to turn opaque. Stir in prawns and continue to stir-fry until prawns begin to turn pink. Add ginger, garlic, shallots, carrot, celery, chilli, spring onions, sesame oil and soy sauce and fry for a further 1 minute. Transfer to a bowl and leave until cold.

Spread 1 wrapper on the work surface; keep remaining wrappers between 2 damp tea towels. Put 1-2 tablespoons filling on lower half of wrapper.

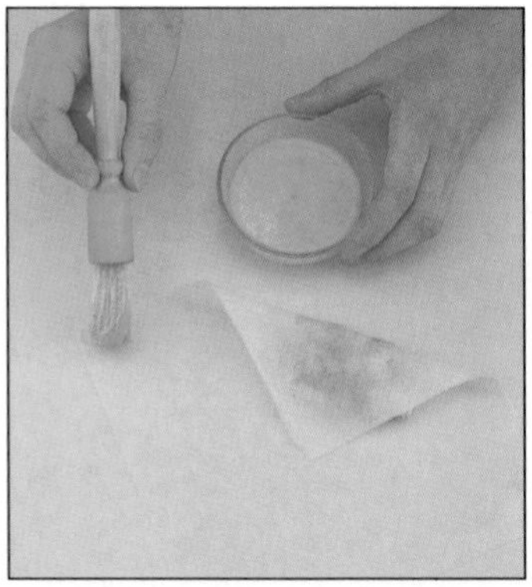

Fold bottom corner up and over filling. Moisten side corners with beaten egg. Fold sides over to cover bottom corner and filling. Press firmly to seal. Moisten top corner with beaten egg.

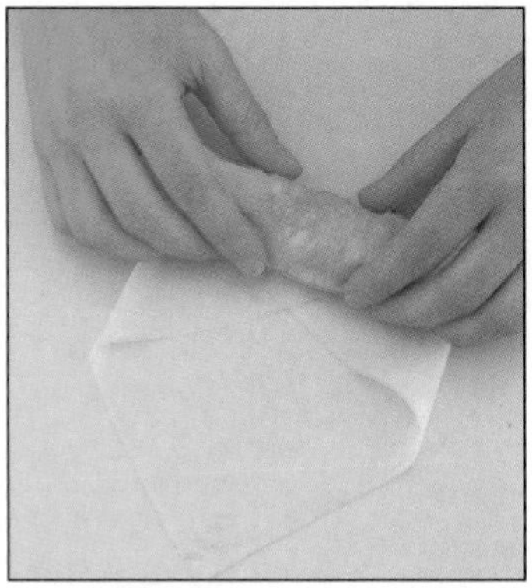

Roll wrapper over tightly to make a neat cylinder. Press top corner of roll to seal. Place seam side down and cover with a damp tea towel. Repeat with remaining wrappers and filling.

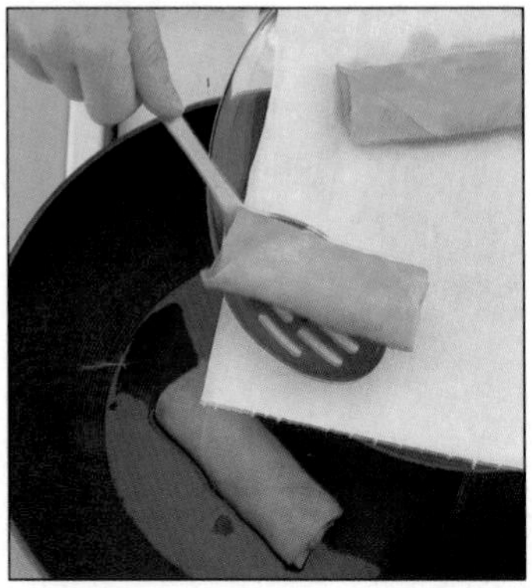

In a wok or sauté pan, heat vegetable oil. Fry rolls in batches for 3-5 minutes, turning occasionally, until golden and crisp. Remove with a slotted spoon and drain on absorbent kitchen paper. Keep warm while frying remaining rolls. Serve with dipping sauce.

Serves 6.

NONYA PACKETS

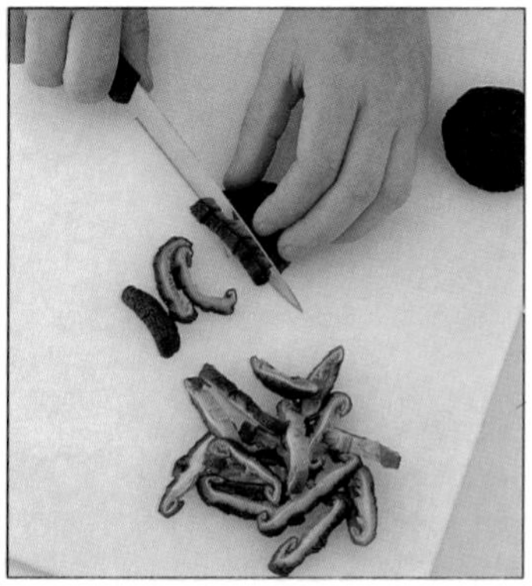

4 dried Chinese black mushrooms
225 g (8 oz) boneless, skinless chicken breast, thinly sliced into strips
1 tablespoon oyster sauce
1½ teaspoons rice wine
1½ teaspoons sesame oil
1 cm (½ in) piece fresh root ginger, grated
1½ teaspoons light soy sauce
1 clove garlic, finely crushed
½ fresh red chilli, cored, seeded and finely chopped
2 spring onions, including some green, chopped

Soak mushrooms in 3 tablespoons hot water for 30 minutes. Drain. Discard stems and finely slice caps.

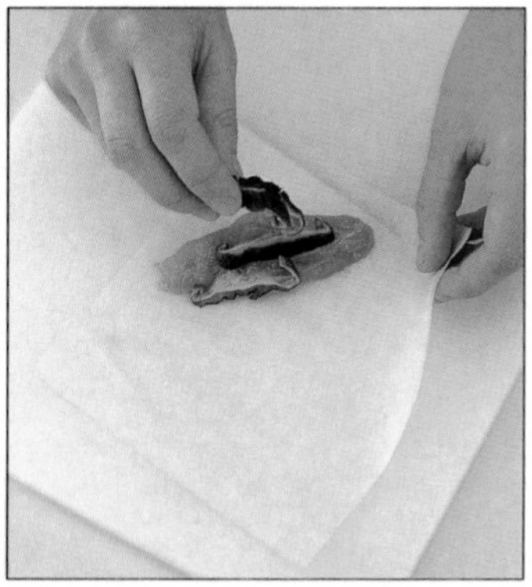

In a bowl, mix chicken, oyster sauce, rice wine, sesame oil, ginger, soy sauce, garlic and chilli. Cover and leave in a cool place for up to 1 hour, or in the refrigerator for up to 8 hours (return to room temperature 30 minutes before cooking). Cut ten 15 x 15 cm (6 x 6 in) squares of nonstick baking parchment. Lay 1 on the work surface with a point towards you. Put several pieces of chicken near the point. Add some mushroom strips and spring onions. Fold point over filling, make a firm crease. Fold left and right hand corners to centre.

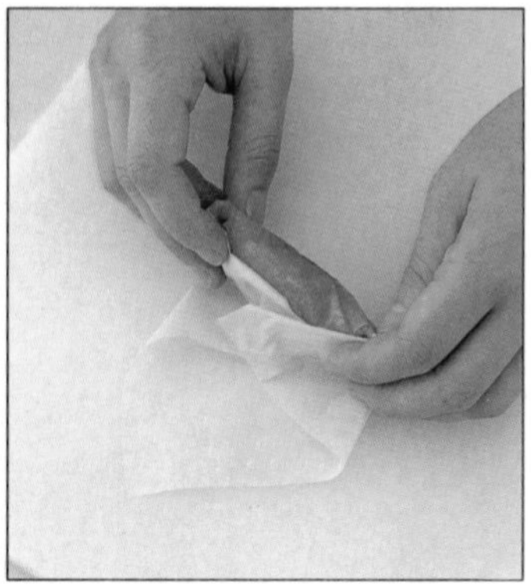

Continue to fold package over, away from you. Tuck in the last flap to make a package about 7.5 × 5 cm (3 × 2 in). Repeat with remaining chicken and nonstick baking parchment. Half fill a wok or deep-fat fryer with oil and heat to 185-190C (360-375F). Fry packets in batches for about 8 minutes, pushing them under occasionally and turning over once or twice. Remove with a slotted spoon. Keep warm while cooking remaining packages. Serve unopened.

Serves 5-6.

GRILLED CHICKEN SKEWERS

6 large chicken thighs, total weight about 1 kg (2¼ lb)
2 cloves garlic, finely chopped
150 ml (5 fl oz/⅔ cup) coconut milk
2 teaspoons ground coriander
1 teaspoon each ground cumin and ground turmeric
juice 1 lime
leaves 8 sprigs coriander, chopped
3 tablespoons light soy sauce
2 tablespoons fish sauce
3 tablespoons light brown sugar
½ teaspoon crushed dried chillies

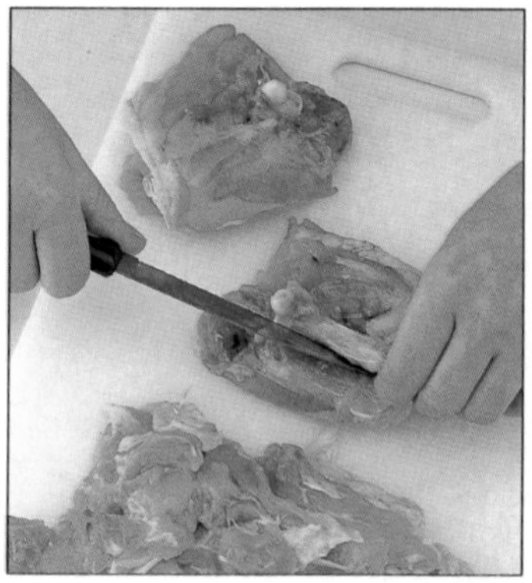

Using a sharp knife, slit along underside of each chicken thigh and remove bone, scraping flesh from bone.

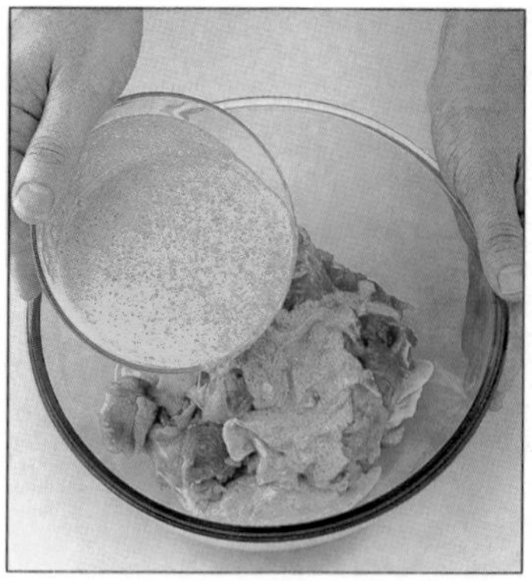

Cut each boned thigh into 6 pieces. Put in a bowl. In a small bowl, mix together garlic, coconut milk, coriander, cumin and turmeric. Pour over chicken. Stir to coat then cover and refrigerate for for 2-12 hours. To make sauce, in a small serving bowl, mix together lime juice, coriander, soy sauce, fish sauce, sugar and chillies. Set aside.

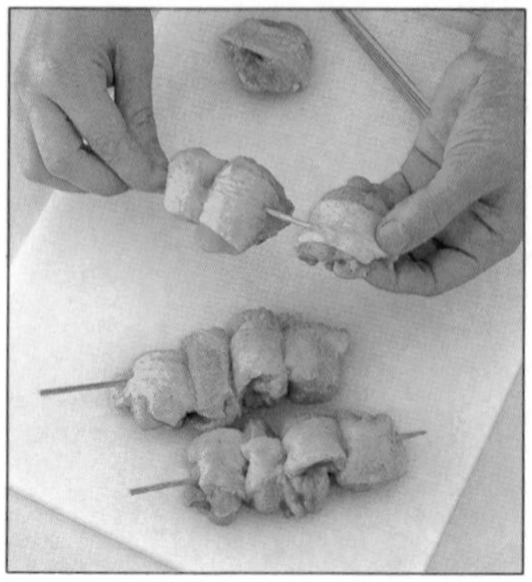

Soak 8 short wooden or bamboo skewers for 30 minutes. Preheat grill. Thread chicken, skin side up, on skewers. Place on oiled grill rack and cook for 4-5 minutes. Turn over and cook for a further 2-3 minutes until juices run clear. Serve with sauce.

Serves 4-6.

POH PIAH

2 tablespoons vegetable oil
4 shallots, finely chopped
2 cloves garlic, crushed
1 fresh red chilli, cored, seeded and finely chopped
115 g (4 oz) lean pork, minced
115 g (4 oz) crab meat
8 water chestnuts, finely chopped
115 g (4 oz) bamboo shoots, shredded
1 tablespoon light soy sauce
1½ tablespoons salted yellow beans
12 spring roll wrappers
Malaysian Spicy Sauce (see page 227), to serve

TO SERVE:
115 g (4 oz) small prawns
115 g (4 oz) Chinese sausage, steamed and sliced
115 g (4 oz) bean sprouts, blanched
1 bunch spring onions
115 g (4 oz) crisp lettuce leaves, shredded
½ medium cucumber, chopped and coarsely grated

For the filling, in a wok or frying pan, heat oil. Add shallots, garlic and chilli. Cook, stirring occasionally, until softened and transparent. Stir pork into pan and stir-fry until it changes colour. Add crab meat, water chestnuts, bamboo shoots, soy sauce and yellow beans.

Stir together ingredients for about 2 minutes until well mixed. Leave to cool. Put cooled meat mixture and remaining ingredients in individual bowls. Each person helps themselves to filling ingredients then rolls up the wrapper, tucking in ends, and eats it at once. Serve with spicy sauce and other accompaniments.

Makes 12.

SPICY SPARE RIBS

1.35 kg (3 lb) spare ribs, trimmed and divided into ribs
4 tablespoons vegetable oil
2 spring onions, thinly sliced
MARINADE:
2.5 cm (1 in) piece fresh root ginger, grated
4 cloves garlic, finely crushed
1 fresh red chilli, cored, seeded and finely chopped
3 tablespoons rice vinegar
85 ml (3 fl oz/⅓ cup) dark soy sauce
2 tablespoons groundnut (peanut) oil
1 tablespoon light brown sugar
1 teaspoon Chinese five-spice powder

Whisk marinade ingredients together. Put ribs in a dish and pour marinade over.

Turn ribs to coat in marinade, cover and refrigerate for 2-3 hours, turning occasionally. Lift ribs from marinade. Pat dry. Reserve marinade. In a wok or sauté pan, heat oil over high heat. Add 3-4 ribs and cook, stirring, for 2-3 minutes until evenly browned. Using tongs, transfer to absorbent kitchen paper. Repeat with remaining ribs.

Pour off all but 2 tablespoons oil from the pan. Return ribs to pan. Add reserved marinade and enough water to completely cover ribs. Bring to the boil. Lower heat, cover and simmer gently for about 1 hour, stirring occasionally, until meat is tender and shrinks slightly from the bone. Boil until cooking liquid is reduced to a thick sauce. Transfer ribs to warmed plates and spoon a little sauce over each serving. Sprinkle with sliced spring onions.

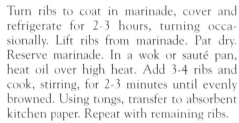

Serves 6.

SPLIT PEA FRITTERS

225 g (8 oz) yellow split peas, soaked overnight in cold water
3-4 fresh red chillies, cored, seeded and chopped
2 cloves garlic, chopped
2 spring onions, sliced
3 tablespoons chopped coriander leaves
1 teaspoon ground roasted cumin seeds
large pinch ground turmeric
1 egg, beaten
salt
vegetable oil for deep-frying (optional)
banana leaves (optional)
Malaysian Dipping Sauce or Spicy Sauce (see page 227), to serve

Drain split peas and put in a saucepan with 300 ml (10 fl oz/1½ cups) water. Bring to the boil. Boil, stirring, for 10 minutes. Drain. Put in a food processor with chillies, garlic and spring onions. Mix until coarsely chopped. Add coriander, cumin, turmeric, egg and salt to taste and mix together. Form into about 50 small balls, pressing mixture firmly together with your hands. Refrigerate for about 1 hour.

Preheat oven to 230C (450F/Gas 8). Roll patties in a little oil, put on baking sheets and bake for 15-17 minutes until golden brown. Turn over halfway through. Alternatively, heat oil in a deep-fat fryer to 180C (350F), or until a cube of bread browns in 30 seconds. Deep-fry fritters in batches for 2-3 minutes until golden. Drain on absorbent kitchen paper. Serve fritters hot on banana leaves, if wished, accompanied by the dipping sauce of your choice.

Makes about 50.

SWEET POTATO RINGS

500 g (1 lb 2 oz) sweet potatoes, peeled and cubed
2 tablespoons vegetable oil, plus oil for frying
1 onion, finely chopped
2 cloves garlic, finely crushed
1 fresh red chilli, cored, seeded and chopped
1 tablespoon curry powder
1 egg, beaten
salt and freshly ground black pepper
115 g (4 oz/1 cup) plain flour
dried bread crumbs for coating
coriander sprigs, to garnish

Steam sweet potato cubes for 6-8 minutes until tender. Pass through a vegetable mill into a bowl, or mash thoroughly.

Meanwhile, in a wok or frying pan, heat oil and fry onion, garlic and chilli until onion is lightly coloured. Stir in curry powder and cook for 1 minute. Add onion mixture to sweet potato with egg, and salt and pepper to taste. Beat together until evenly mixed then stir in flour to bind together; if mixture is too soft, add a little more flour. Leave to cool then refrigerate for at least 1 hour.

With oiled hands, form mixture into balls about 4 cm (1½ in) in diameter. Press lightly to flatten into cakes. With floured end of a wooden spoon press through centre of each cake to make a ring. Thoroughly coat rings in bread crumbs, pressing them in. Chill for at least 1 hour. Heat 1 cm (½ in) depth of oil in a frying pan and fry rings until crisp and golden. Using a fish slice, transfer to absorbent kitchen paper to drain. Serve warm, garnished with coriander sprigs.

Serves 4.

GOLD BAGS

115 g (4 oz) cooked peeled prawns, finely chopped
55 g (2 oz) canned water chestnuts, finely chopped
2 spring onions, white part only, finely chopped
1 teaspoon fish sauce
freshly ground black pepper
16 won ton skins
vegetable oil for deep-frying
Thai Dipping Sauce 1 (see page 231), to serve
coriander sprig, to garnish

In a bowl, mix together prawns, water chestnuts, spring onions, fish sauce and black pepper.

Place a small amount of prawn mixture in centre of each won ton skin. Dampen edges of skins with a little water, then bring up over filling to form a 'dolly bag'. Press edges together to seal.

In a wok, heat oil to 190C (375F). Add bags in batches and fry for about 2-3 minutes until crisp and golden. Using a slotted spoon, transfer to absorbent kitchen paper to drain. Serve hot with dipping sauce. Garnish with coriander sprig.

Makes 16.

SWEETCORN CAKES

350 g (12 oz) sweetcorn kernels
1 tablespoon Green Curry Paste (see page 230)
2 tablespoons plain flour
3 tablespoons rice flour
3 spring onions, finely chopped
1 egg, beaten
2 teaspoons fish sauce
vegetable oil for deep-frying
2.5 cm (1 in) piece cucumber
Thai Dipping Sauce 2 (see page 232), to serve
1 tablespoon ground roasted peanuts

Place sweetcorn in a blender and add curry paste, plain flour, rice flour, spring onions, egg and fish sauce and mix together until sweetcorn is slightly broken up. Form into about 16 cakes. Heat oil in a wok to 180C (350F), then deep-fry one batch of sweetcorn cakes for about 3 minutes until golden brown.

Using a slotted spoon, transfer to absorbent kitchen paper to drain. Keep warm while frying remaining cakes. Peel cucumber, quarter lengthways, remove seeds, then slice thinly. Place in a small bowl and mix in dipping sauce and ground peanuts. Serve with warm sweetcorn cakes.

Makes about 16.

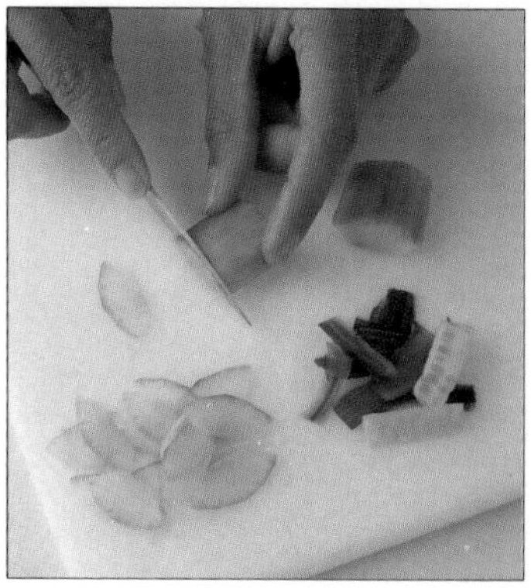

CRAB ROLLS

225 g (8 oz) cooked chicken, very finely chopped
115 g (4 oz) cooked crab meat, flaked
4 spring onions, finely chopped
25 g (1 oz) bean sprouts, finely chopped
1 small carrot, grated
2 teaspoons fish sauce
freshly ground black pepper
about 9 rice paper wrappers (spring roll wrappers), each about 18 cm (7 in) in diameter
vegetable oil for deep-frying
Thai holy basil leaves, Thai mint leaves and lettuce leaves, to serve
Thai Dipping Sauce 1 (see page 231), to serve

In a bowl, mix together chicken, crab meat, spring onions, bean sprouts, carrot, fish sauce and black pepper. Brush both sides of each wrapper liberally with water and set aside to soften. Cut each wrapper into 4 wedges. Place a small amount of filling near wide end of one wedge, fold end over filling, tuck in sides and roll up. Repeat with remaining wedges and filling.

In a wok, heat oil to 190C (375F). Fry rolls in batches for 2-3 minutes until crisp and golden. Drain on absorbent kitchen paper. Serve hot. To eat, sprinkle each roll with herbs, then wrap in a lettuce leaf and dip into dipping sauce.

Makes about 36.

FISH PARCELS WITH GALANGAL

2 fresh red chillies, seeded and finely chopped
2 cloves garlic, finely chopped
1 shallot, finely chopped
4 cm (1½ in) piece galangal, finely chopped
2 stalks lemon grass, finely chopped
1 tablespoon fish sauce
20 Thai holy basil leaves
450 g (1 lb) boneless firm white fish, such as halibut, cod, hake or monkfish, cut into about 2 cm (¾ in) pieces
banana leaves (optional)

Using a pestle and mortar or small blender, briefly mix together chillies, garlic, shallot, galangal, lemon grass and fish sauce. Turn into a bowl, stir in basil leaves and fish. Divide between 3 or 4 pieces banana leaf or aluminium foil. Fold leaves or foil over fish to make neat parcels. Secure leaves with a wooden cocktail stick (toothpick), or fold foil edges tightly together.

Put parcels in a steaming basket. Place over boiling water and steam for about 7 minutes until fish is lightly cooked.

Serves 3-4.

STEAMED CRAB

1 clove garlic, chopped
1 small shallot, chopped
6 coriander sprigs, stalks finely chopped
175 g (6 oz) cooked crab meat
115 g (4 oz) lean pork, very finely chopped and cooked
1 egg, beaten
1 tablespoon coconut cream (see page 8)
2 teaspoons fish sauce
freshly ground black pepper
1 fresh red chilli, seeded and cut into fine strips

Grease 4 individual heatproof dishes and place in a steaming basket.

Using a pestle and mortar, pound garlic, shallot and coriander stalks to a paste. In a bowl, stir together crab meat, pork, garlic paste, egg, coconut cream, fish sauce and plenty of black pepper until evenly mixed.

Divide between dishes, arrange coriander leaves and strip of chilli on top of each one. Place steaming basket over a saucepan of boiling water and steam for about 12 minutes until mixture is firm.

Serves 4.

Note: Crab shells may be used instead of dishes for cooking.

STUFFED COURGETTES

55 g (2 oz/1¼ cups) shredded fresh coconut
6 tablespoons chopped coriander leaves
1 fresh green chilli, seeded and finely chopped
4 courgettes, each weighing about 225 g (8 oz)
5 tablespoons vegetable oil
few drops fish sauce
2 tablespoons lime juice
1 teaspoon crushed palm sugar
freshly ground black pepper

In a small bowl, combine coconut, coriander and chilli; set aside.

Cut each courgette into 4 lengths, about 4 cm (1½ in) long. Stand each on one cut side and cut 2 deep slits like a cross, down 2.5 cm (1 in) of the length. Gently prize apart cut sections and fill with coconut mixture. Pour oil and 115 ml (4 fl oz/½ cup) water into a wide frying pan. Stand courgettes, filled side uppermost, in pan.

Sprinkle over a little fish sauce. If any coconut mixture remains, spoon over courgettes. Sprinkle over lime juice, sugar, black pepper and a few drops of fish sauce. Heat to simmering point, cover tightly and simmer gently for 5-6 minutes. Using 2 spoons, turn courgette pieces over, re-cover and cook for a further 7-10 minutes.

Serves 4-6.

STEAMED EGGS

4 eggs, beaten
2 spring onions, thinly sliced
85 g (3 oz) cooked peeled prawns, finely chopped
freshly ground black pepper
1 fresh red chilli, seeded and thinly sliced
1 tablespoon chopped coriander leaves
70 ml (2½ fl oz/⅓ cup) coconut milk (see page 224)
2 teaspoons fish sauce
coriander sprigs and red chilli rings, to garnish

In a small blender or food processor, mix eggs, spring onions, prawns, pepper, chilli, coriander, coconut milk and fish sauce until evenly combined.

Pour into greased individual heatproof dishes. Place in a steaming basket, then position over a saucepan of boiling water. Cover and steam for 10-12 minutes until just set in centre.

Remove from heat, leave to stand for a minute or two. Turn out on to a plate, then invert on to a warmed plate. Garnish with coriander sprigs and red chilli rings.

Serves 2-4.

STUFFED EGGS

4 large eggs, at room temperature
4 tablespoons minced cooked pork
4 tablespoons finely chopped peeled prawns
1 teaspoon fish sauce
1 clove garlic, chopped
1½ tablespoons chopped coriander leaves
finely ground black pepper
lettuce leaves, to serve
coriander sprigs, to garnish

Form 4 'nests' from aluminium foil to hold eggs upright. Place in a steaming basket. Cook eggs in pan of gently boiling water for 1½ minutes; remove.

Carefully peel a small part of pointed end of eggs. With the point of a slim, sharp knife, cut a small hole down through exposed white of each egg; reserve pieces of white that are removed. Pour liquid egg yolk and white from egg into a small bowl. Thoroughly mix in pork, prawns, fish sauce, garlic, coriander and pepper. Carefully spoon into eggs and replace removed pieces of white.

Set steaming basket over a saucepan of boiling water and place eggs, cut end uppermost, in foil 'nests'. Cover basket and steam eggs for about 12 minutes. When cool enough to handle, carefully peel off shells. Serve whole or halved on lettuce leaves, garnished with coriander sprigs.

Serves 4.

EGG NESTS

1 tablespoon chopped coriander roots
1 clove garlic, chopped
½ teaspoon black peppercorns, cracked
1 tablespoon groundnut (peanut) oil
½ small onion, finely chopped
115 g (4 oz) lean pork, very finely chopped
115 g (4 oz) raw peeled prawns, chopped
2 teaspoons fish sauce
3 tablespoons vegetable oil
2 eggs
3 fresh red chillies, seeded and cut into fine strips
20-30 coriander leaves
coriander sprigs, to garnish

Using a pestle and mortar, pound together coriander roots, garlic and peppercorns. In a wok, heat groundnut oil, add peppercorn mixture and onion and stir-fry for 1 minute.

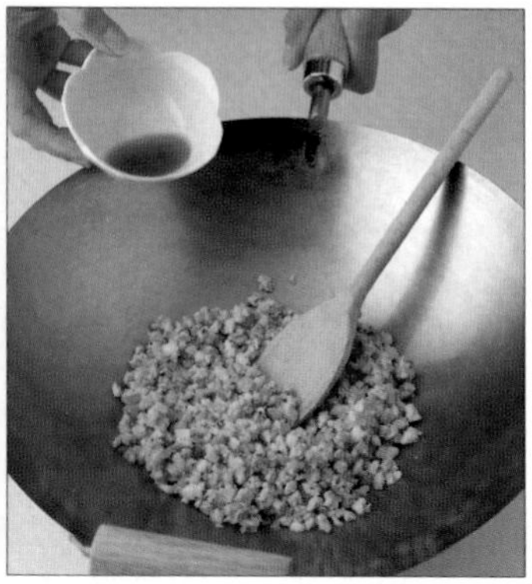

Add pork, stir-fry for 1 minute, then stir in prawns for 45 seconds. Quickly stir in fish sauce, then transfer mixture to a bowl. Using absorbent kitchen paper, wipe out wok.

Add vegetable oil to wok and place over medium heat. In a small bowl, beat eggs. Spoon egg into a cone of nonstick baking parchment with a very small hole in pointed end. Move cone above surface of pan, so trail of egg flows on to it and sets in threads. Quickly repeat, moving in another direction directly over threads. Repeat until there are 4 crisscrossing layers of egg.

Using a spatula, transfer nest to absorbent kitchen paper. Repeat with remaining egg to make more nests. Place nests with flat side facing downwards. Place 2 strips of chilli to form a cross on each nest.

Top with coriander leaves, then about 1 tablespoon of pork mixture. Fold nests over filling, turn over and arrange on serving plate. Garnish with coriander sprigs.

Serves 4.

STUFFED CHICKEN WINGS

4 large chicken wings
lean pork, finely minced, (see method)
55 g (2 oz) cooked peeled prawns, chopped
3 spring onions, finely chopped
2 large cloves garlic, chopped
3 coriander roots, chopped
2 tablespoons fish sauce
freshly ground black pepper
vegetable oil for deep-frying
rice flour for coating
Thai Dipping Sauce 2 (see page 232), to serve
lettuce leaves, to garnish

Bend chicken wing joints backwards against joint. Using a small sharp knife or kitchen scissors, cut around top of bone that attaches wing to chicken body. Using blade of knife, scrape meat and skin down length of first bone, turning skin back over unboned portion. Break bone free at joint.

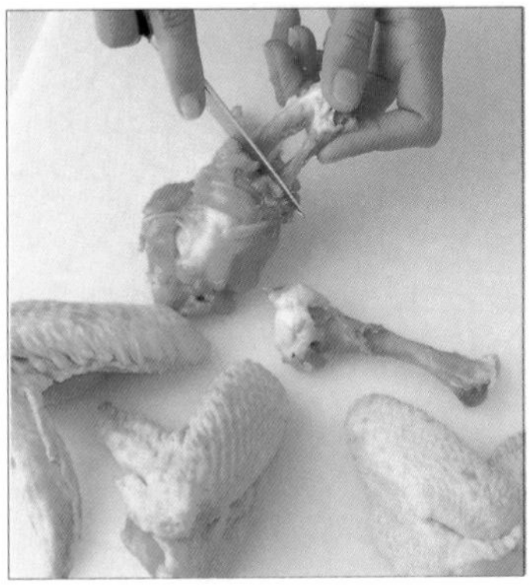

Ease skin over joint and detach from flesh and bone. Working down next adjacent bones, scrape off flesh and skin taking care not to puncture skin. Break bones free at joint, leaving end section.

Chop chicken flesh from wings. Make up to 175 g (6 oz) with pork, if necessary. Place chicken and pork, if used, in a bowl and thoroughly mix together with prawns and spring onions. Divide between chicken wings; set aside.

Using a pestle and mortar, pound together garlic and coriander roots. Stir in fish sauce and plenty of black pepper. Pour over chicken wings, stirring them to coat with mixture, then set aside for 30 minutes.

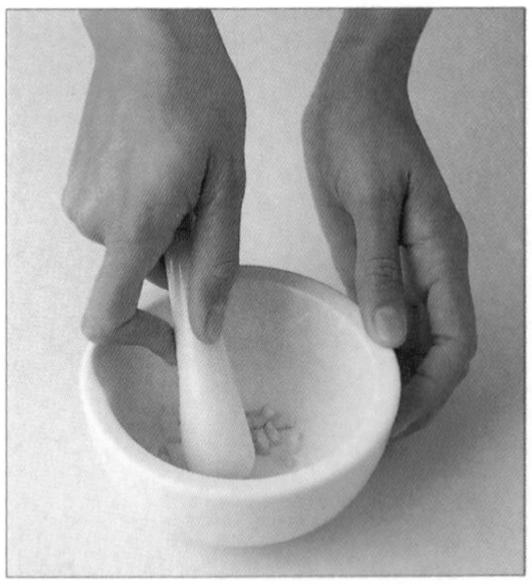

Heat oil in a wok to 180C (350F). Remove chicken wings from bowl, then toss in rice flour to coat completely. Add 2 at a time to oil and deep-fry for about 3-4 minutes until browned. Using a slotted spoon, transfer to absorbent kitchen paper to drain. Keep warm while frying remaining 2 chicken wings. Serve with sauce and garnish with lettuce leaves.

Serves 4.

PORK TOASTS

175 g (6 oz) lean pork, minced
55 g (2 oz) cooked peeled prawns, finely chopped
2 cloves garlic, finely chopped
1 tablespoon chopped coriander leaves
1½ spring onions, finely chopped
2 eggs, beaten
2 teaspoons fish sauce
freshly ground black pepper
4 day-old slices bread
1 tablespoon coconut milk
vegetable oil for deep-frying
coriander leaves, fine rings fresh red chilli and cucumber slices, to garnish

In a bowl, mix together pork and prawns using a fork, then thoroughly mix in garlic, coriander, spring onions, half of egg, fish sauce and black pepper. Divide between bread, spreading it firmly to edges. In a small bowl, stir together remaining egg and coconut milk and brush over pork mixture. Trim crusts from bread, then cut each slice into squares.

In a wok, heat oil to 190C (375F). Add several squares at a time, pork-side down, and fry for 3-4 minutes until crisp, turning over halfway through. Using a slotted spoon, transfer to absorbent kitchen paper to drain, then keep warm in oven. Check temperature of oil in between frying each batch. Serve warm, garnished with coriander and slices of chilli and cucumber.

Serves 4-6.

PORK & NOODLE PARCELS

3 cloves garlic, chopped
4 coriander roots, chopped
175 g (6 oz) lean pork, minced
1 small egg, beaten
2 teaspoons fish sauce
freshly ground black pepper
about 55 g (2 oz) egg thread noodles (1 'nest')
vegetable oil for deep-frying
Thai Dipping Sauce 1 (see page 231), to serve

Using a pestle and mortar or small blender, pound or mix together garlic and coriander roots. In a bowl, mix together pork, egg, fish sauce and pepper, then stir in garlic mixture.

Place noodles in a heatproof sieve and dip in boiling water for 5 seconds if fresh, about 2 minutes if dried, until separated. Remove and rinse immediately in cold running water. Form pork mixture into approximately 12 balls. Neatly and evenly wind 3 or 4 strands of noodles around each ball to cover completely.

In a wok, heat oil to 180C (350F). Using a slotted spoon, lower 4-6 balls into oil and cook for about 3 minutes until golden and pork is cooked through. Using a slotted or draining spoon, transfer to absorbent kitchen paper to drain. Keep warm while cooking remaining balls. Serve hot with dipping sauce. Garnish with coriander sprig.

Makes about 12 parcels.

PRAWN CRYSTAL ROLLS

225 g (8 oz) cooked peeled prawns
115 g (4 oz) cooked pork, coarsely chopped
115 g (4 oz) cooked chicken meat, coarsely chopped
2 tablespoons grated carrot
2 tablespoons chopped water chestnuts
1 tablespoon chopped preserved vegetables
1 teaspoon finely chopped garlic
2 spring onions, finely chopped
1 teaspoon sugar
2 tablespoons fish sauce
salt and freshly ground black pepper
10-12 sheets dried rice paper
flour and water paste
fresh mint and coriander leaves
iceberg or Webb's lettuce leaves
Spicy Fish Sauce (see page 233), to serve

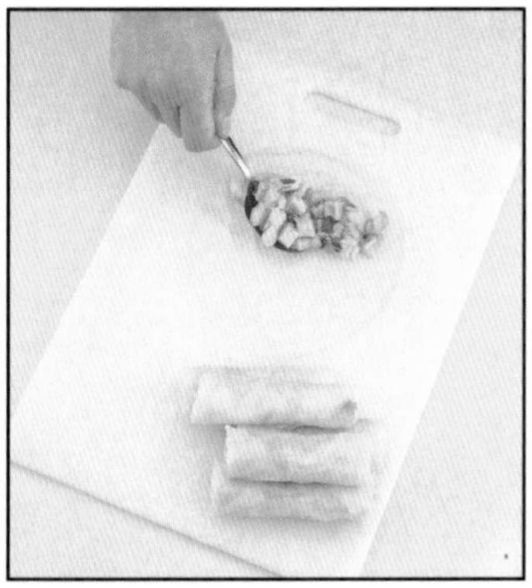

Cut any large prawns in half. In a bowl, mix prawns, pork, chicken, grated carrot, water chestnuts, preserved vegetables, garlic, spring onions, sugar, fish sauce and salt and pepper. Fill a bowl with warm water, then dip sheets of rice paper in water one at a time. If using large sheets of rice paper, fold in half then place about 2 tablespoons of filling on to long end of rice paper, fold sides over to enclose filling and roll up, then seal end with a little flour paste. (The roll will be transparent, hence the name 'crystal'.)

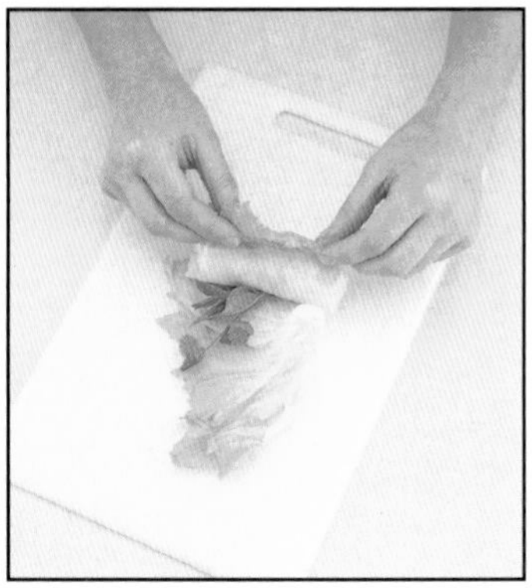

To serve, place some mint and coriander in a piece of lettuce leaf with a crystal roll and wrap into a neat parcel, then dip roll into Spicy Fish Sauce before eating.

Serves 4.

SESAME PRAWN TOASTS

225-300 g (8-10 oz) raw peeled prawns, chopped
½ teaspoon minced garlic
½ teaspoon finely chopped fresh root ginger
2 shallots or 1 small onion, finely chopped
1 egg, beaten
salt and freshly ground black pepper
1 tablespoon cornflour
1 French baguette
3-4 tablespoons white sesame seeds
oil for deep-frying
chopped coriander leaves, to garnish

In a bowl, mix prawns, garlic, ginger, shallots, egg, salt, pepper and cornflour. Chill in the refrigerator for at least 2 hours.

Cut bread into 1 cm (½ in) slices and spread thickly with prawn mixture on one side, then press that side down on to sesame seeds so that entire surface is covered by seeds, making sure seeds are firmly pressed into prawn mixture.

Heat oil in a wok or deep-fat fryer to 180C (350F) and deep-fry toasts, in batches, spread-side down, for 2-3 minutes until they start to turn golden brown around edges. Remove and drain on absorbent kitchen paper. Serve hot, garnished with chopped coriander leaves.

Serves 6-8.

PRAWN PASTE ON SUGAR CANE

400 g (14 oz) raw peeled prawns
55 g (2 oz) fresh fatty pork, chopped
½ teaspoon chopped garlic
salt and freshly ground black pepper
1 teaspoon sugar
1 tablespoon cornflour
1 egg white, beaten
30 cm (12 in) piece sugar cane
coriander sprigs, to garnish
Spicy Fish Sauce (see page 233), to serve

Using a pestle and mortar, pound prawns, pork and garlic to a smooth paste. Mix with salt, pepper, sugar, cornflour and egg white.

Preheat grill. Peel sugar cane, cut into 10 cm (4 in) lengths and split lengthways into quarters. Mould prawn paste on to sugar cane, leaving about 2.5 cm (1 in) of sugar cane at one end uncovered, to use as a handle.

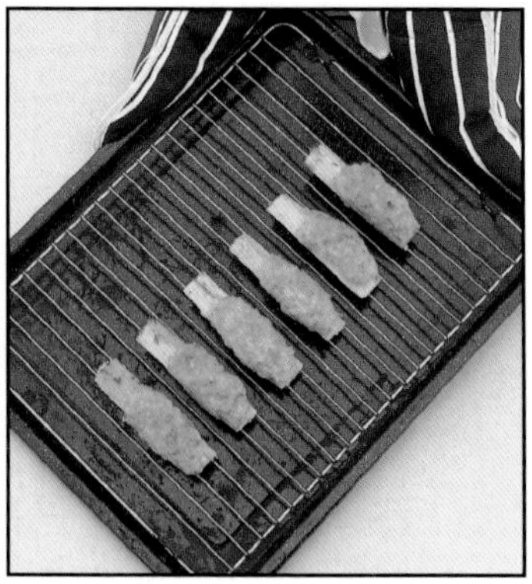

Grill sticks under a moderately hot grill for 5-6 minutes, turning to ensure even cooking. Garnish with coriander. To serve, dip each stick in Spicy Fish Sauce before eating. When prawn paste is eaten, sugar cane can be sucked and chewed.

Serves 4-6.

Variation: Instead of grilling, sugar cane can be deep-fried in hot oil for 4-5 minutes until golden brown.

SQUID WITH SPICY CHILLIES

450 g (1 lb) fresh squid, cleaned (see page 194)
½ teaspoon minced garlic
½ teaspoon chopped fresh root ginger
salt and freshly ground black pepper
1 tablespoon fish sauce
2 tablespoons vegetable oil
2 spring onions, finely shredded
3-4 small red chillies, seeded and sliced
coriander sprigs, to garnish

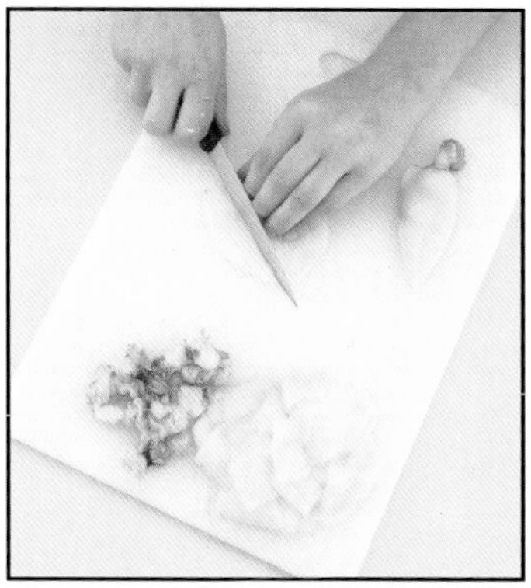

Pull head off each squid, discard head and transparent backbone, but reserve tentacles. Cut open body and score inside of flesh in a criss-cross pattern.

Cut squid into small pieces about 2.5 × 4 cm (1 × 1½ in). Blanch squid and tentacles in a saucepan of boiling water for 1 minute only – cooking for any longer will toughen squid. Remove and drain, then dry well on absorbent kitchen paper. Mix garlic, ginger, salt, pepper and fish sauce in a bowl, add blanched squid and leave to marinate for 25-30 minutes.

Meanwhile, heat oil in a small saucepan until hot but not smoking. Remove pan from heat, add spring onions and chillies and leave to infuse for 15-20 minutes. Arrange squid with marinade on a serving plate, pour oil with spring onions and chillies all over squid and garnish with coriander sprigs. Serve cold.

Serves 4-6.

SEAFOOD SKEWERS

12 scallops
12 large raw peeled prawns
225 g (8 oz) firm white fish fillet, such as halibut, cod or monkfish, cut into 12 cubes
1 medium onion, cut into 12 pieces
1 red or green pepper, cut into 12 cubes
115 ml (4 fl oz/½ cup) dry white wine or sherry
1 tablespoon chopped dill
1 tablespoon chopped Thai holy basil leaves
1 tablespoon lime juice or vinegar
salt and freshly ground black pepper
vegetable oil for brushing
Spicy Fish Sauce (see page 233), to serve

In a bowl, mix scallops, prawns, fish, onion and peppers with wine, dill, basil, lime juice or vinegar, salt and pepper. Leave to marinate in a cool place for at least 2-3 hours. Meanwhile, soak 6 bamboo skewers in hot water for 25-30 minutes and prepare barbecue or preheat grill. Thread seafood and vegetables alternately on to skewers so that each skewer has 2 pieces of each ingredient.

Brush each skewer with a little oil and cook on barbecue or under the hot grill for 5-6 minutes, turning frequently. Serve hot with fish sauce as a dip.

Serves 6.

CHICKEN SATAY

450 g (1 lb) boneless, skinless chicken breast, cut into 2.5 cm (1 in) cubes
1 teaspoon minced garlic
2 shallots or 1 small onion, finely chopped
1 tablespoon ground coriander
1 teaspoon sugar
1 tablespoon mild curry powder
2 tablespoons fish sauce
1 tablespoon lime juice or vinegar
salt and freshly ground black pepper
vegetable oil for brushing
chopped onion and cucumber, to garnish
roasted peanuts, crushed and mixed with Vietnamese Hot Sauce (see page 234), to serve

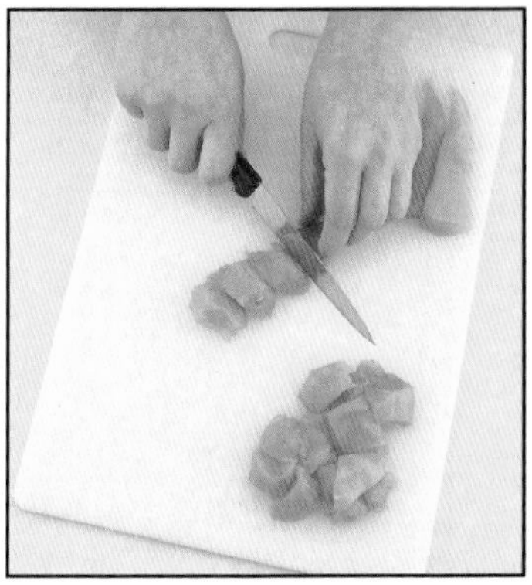

In a bowl, mix chicken with garlic, shallots or onion, coriander, sugar, curry powder, fish sauce, lime juice or vinegar, and salt and pepper, then leave to marinate for 2-3 hours. Meanwhile, soak 16 bamboo skewers in hot water for 25-30 minutes. Prepare barbecue or preheat grill.

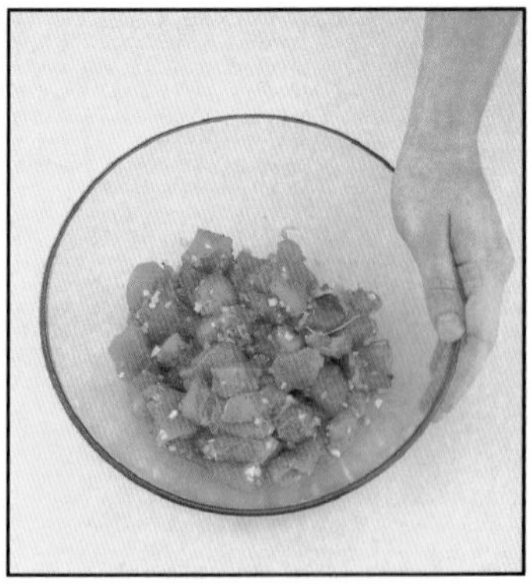

Thread 4 meat cubes on to one end of each skewer. Brush each skewer with a little oil and cook on barbecue or under the hot grill for 5-6 minutes, turning frequently. Garnish with chopped onion and cucumber and serve hot with sauce as a dip.

Serves 8.

Variation: Pork fillet, beef steak or lamb can be prepared and cooked in the same way.

MONGOLIAN-STYLE LAMB

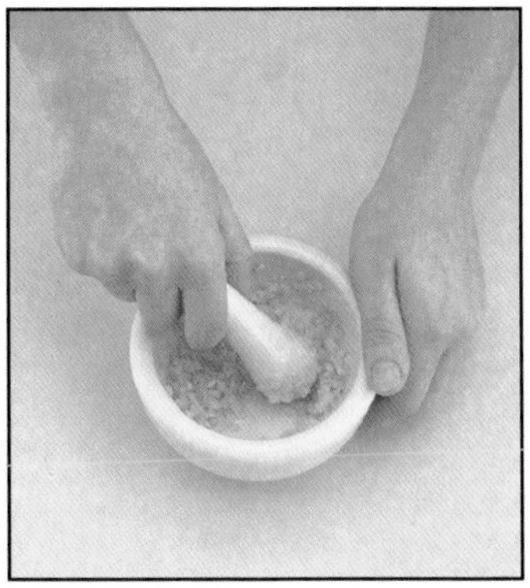

2 cloves garlic, chopped
1 tablespoon chopped fresh root ginger
2 shallots or white part 3 spring onions, chopped
1 tablespoon five-spice powder
salt and freshly ground black pepper
1 teaspoon chilli sauce
2 tablespoons fish sauce
700 g (1½ lb) leg of lamb fillet, boneless
12-16 crisp lettuce leaves (iceberg or Webb's)
fresh mint and coriander leaves
Spicy Fish Sauce (see page 233)

With pestle and mortar, pound garlic, ginger and shallots to a paste. Mix with five-spice powder, salt, pepper, chilli and fish sauces.

Cut lamb fillet into 6 long strips. Rub spice mixture all over lamb strips and leave to marinate for 3-4 hours. Pack meat, with marinade, in a heatproof dish or bowl. Place in a steamer and steam over high heat for 2-3 hours.

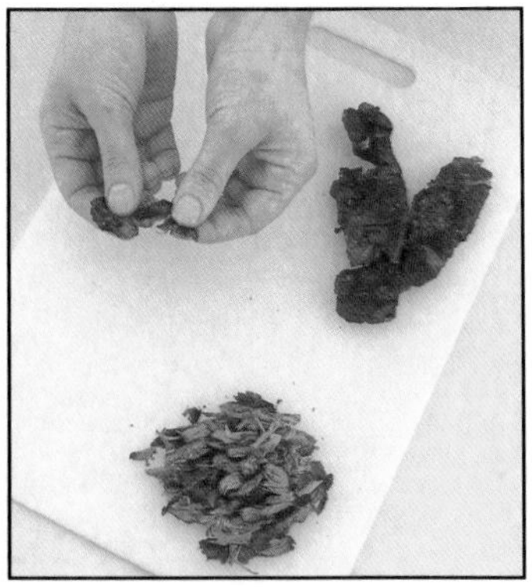

Prepare barbecue or preheat grill. Remove meat strips from steamer and grill them on barbecue or under the grill for 3-4 minutes, turning frequently so that they are slightly charred but not burnt. Pull meat into small shreds and wrap in lettuce leaves with some mint and coriander. Dip rolls in Spicy Fish Sauce before eating.

Serves 6-8.

QUAIL WRAPPED IN LETTUCE

225-330 g (8-10 oz) quail meat, boned and minced
salt and freshly ground black pepper
½ teaspoon sugar
2 teaspoons fish sauce
3 tablespoons vegetable oil
½ teaspoon minced garlic
½ teaspoon minced fresh root ginger
1 tablespoon chopped spring onion
2 tablespoons chopped Chinese mushrooms, soaked
2 tablespoons chopped water chestnuts
1 tablespoon chopped preserved vegetables
2 tablespoons oyster sauce
12 iceberg or Webb's lettuce leaves
fresh mint and coriander leaves
Spicy Fish Sauce (see page 233)

In a bowl, mix quail meat with salt, pepper, sugar and fish sauce and leave to marinate for 15-20 minutes. Heat oil in a wok or frying pan and lightly brown garlic and ginger. Add quail meat and stir-fry for about 1 minute. Add spring onion, mushrooms, water chestnuts and preserved vegetables and blend well. Stir-fry for 2 minutes, then stir in oyster sauce. Transfer to a serving dish.

To serve, place 2 tablespoons of mixture on a lettuce leaf with some mint and coriander and roll it up tightly, then dip roll into Spicy Fish Sauce before eating.

Serves 4-6.

Variation: Pigeon, duck or other game birds can be cooked and served in the same way.

MIXED SUSHI

3-4 dried shiitake mushrooms
1½ tablespoons sugar
3½ tablespoons soy sauce
½ carrot, peeled and shredded
250-350 ml (9-12 fl oz/1-1½ cups) dashi (see page 29)
3 tablespoons sake
100 g (3½ oz) crab sticks, shredded
25 g (1 oz) french beans, trimmed
vegetable oil for frying
1 egg, beaten with a pinch salt
VINEGARED RICE:
700 g (1½ lb/3⅔ cups) Japanese rice
2 tablespoons mirin
100 ml (3½ fl oz/½ cup) rice vinegar
2½ tablespoons sugar
¼ teaspoon salt

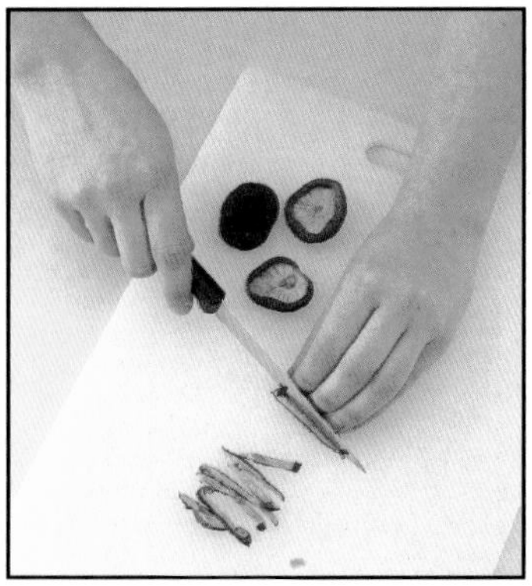

Soak rice following method on page 209. Meanwhile, soak mushrooms in warm water for 30 minutes, then drain, reserving 70 ml (2½ fl oz/⅓ cup) of water. Discard stems and cut caps into thin strips. Put reserved soaking water in a pan with sugar, 1½ tablespoons soy sauce and mushroom caps and cook for 20 minutes or until almost all liquid is absorbed. Parboil carrot and cook in dashi seasoned with 2 tablespoons each soy sauce and sake for 3-4 minutes. Sprinkle remaining sake over crab sticks. Lightly cook beans and slice diagonally.

Heat a frying pan, pour in some vegetable oil, then remove from heat and wipe off excess oil. Return to medium heat and pour in egg so that a paper-thin layer covers the entire surface. Break air bubbles and fry both sides for 30 seconds. Turn on to a board, leave to cool, then cut into shreds. Make sweet vinegared rice (see page 209). While warm, fold in mushrooms, carrots and crab sticks. Garnish with beans and egg shreds.

Serves 4-6.

HAND-ROLLED SUSHI

700 g (1½ lb/3⅔ cups) Japanese rice
4-5 dried shiitake mushrooms
2½ tablespoons sugar
1 tablespoon mirin
2 tablespoons soy sauce, plus extra for dipping
225 g (8 oz) fresh tuna
115 g (4 oz) smoked salmon
8 raw king prawns
1 avocado
⅓ cucumber, shredded
1 punnet cress
8 sheets nori (wafer-thin dried seaweed)

Soak Japanese rice following method on page 209.

Meanwhile, soak shiitake mushrooms in warm water for 30 minutes then drain, reserving 70 ml (2½ fl oz/⅓ cup) of soaking water. Trim off stems and discard; cut caps into thin strips. Place in a pan with sugar, mirin, 2 tablespoons soy sauce and reserved soaking water; cook for 10 minutes. Slice tuna into 5 × 1 cm (2 × ½ in) thin pieces. Cut smoked salmon into similar sized slices. Peel, de-vein and lightly boil prawns. Drain and slice horizontally in half. Peel, stone and thinly slice avocado.

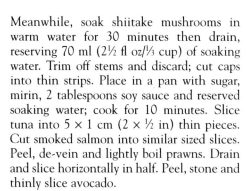

Boil rice (see page 209) and divide between 4.individual serving bowls with lids on to keep rice warm. On a large serving plate, arrange all prepared ingredients and place it in centre of table. Lightly grill both sides of nori sheets over low heat and cut each one into 4 squares so that each diner has 8 small sheets. At table, take one sheet in your palm, put in a little boiled rice spreading it with a spatula or fork. Wrap any ingredients in it, dip in soy sauce and eat.

Serves 4.

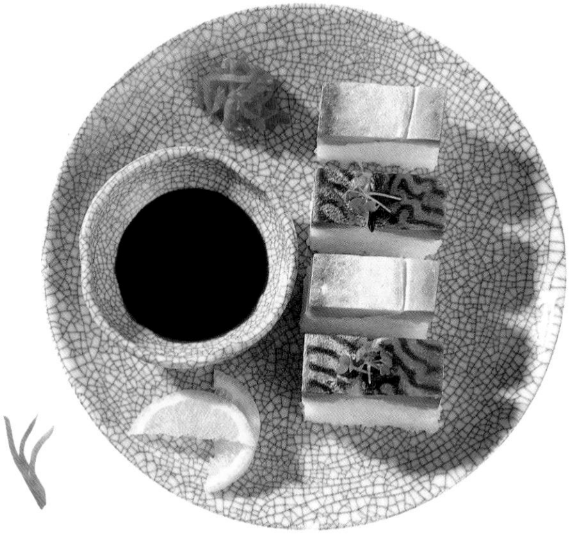

MACKEREL SUSHI

500 g (1 lb 2 oz) mackerel fillet
salt and rice vinegar
VINEGARED RICE:
200 g (7 oz/1 cup) Japanese rice
2½ tablespoons rice vinegar
½ tablespoon sugar
½ tablespoon salt
GARNISH:
lemon wedges and cress
vinegared ginger slices (optional)

Place mackerel fillets in a dish, cover completely with plenty of salt and leave overnight in the refrigerator.

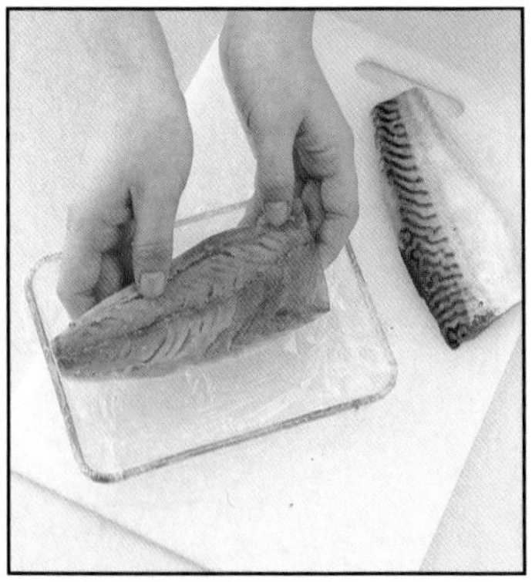

Make vinegared rice following method on page 209. Remove mackerel and rub off salt with absorbent kitchen paper. Carefully remove all bones with tweezers. Wash off any remaining salt with rice vinegar. Using your fingers, remove transparent skin from each fillet, leaving silver pattern on flesh intact. Place a fillet, skinned side down, in a wet wooden mould or rectangular container, about 25 x 7.5 x 5 cm (10 x 3 x 2 in), lined with a large piece of cling film. Fill gaps with small pieces taken from the other fillet so the mould is lined.

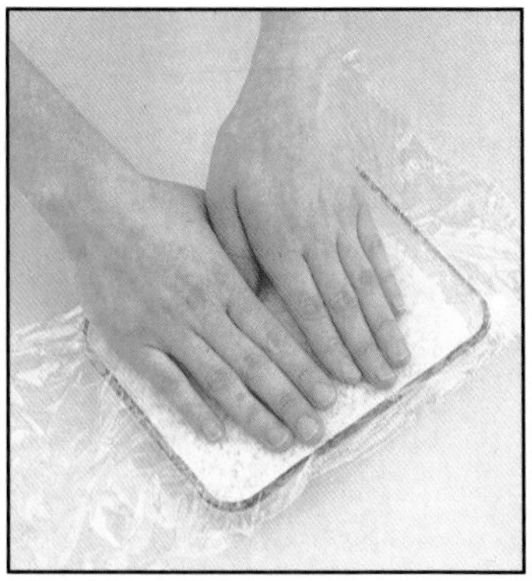

Press vinegared rice down firmly on top of fish with fingers. Put the wet wooden lid on, or fold in cling film, and place a weight on top. Leave in a cool place (but do not refrigerate) for several hours. Remove from container, unwrap, and cut into small pieces with a sharp knife, wiping the knife with a vinegar-soaked cloth or paper after each cut. Garnish with lemon, cress, and vinegared ginger slices, if wished. Serve with soy sauce handed separately in small individual dishes.

Serves 4-6.

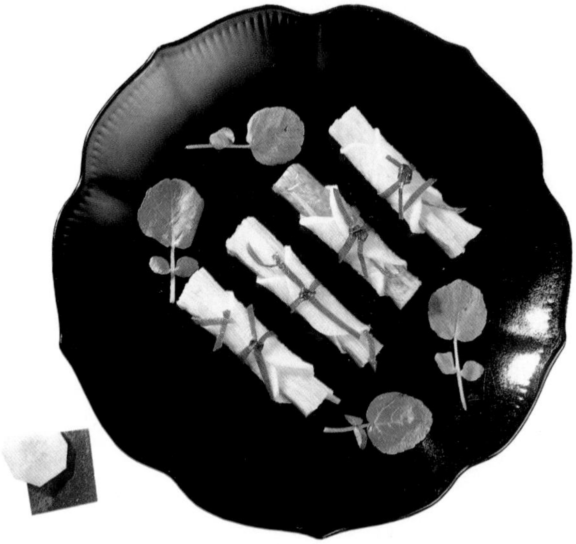

CRAB STICK DAIKON ROLL

10 cm (4 in) square dried konbu (kelp)
1 large daikon, peeled
200 g (7 oz) crab sticks
4 cm (1½ in) piece fresh root ginger, peeled and cut into matchsticks
watercress, to garnish
DRESSING:
2 dried or fresh red chillies
8 tablespoons dashi (see page 29)
4 tablespoons rice vinegar
3 tablespoons sugar
salt and 2-3 teaspoons vegetable oil

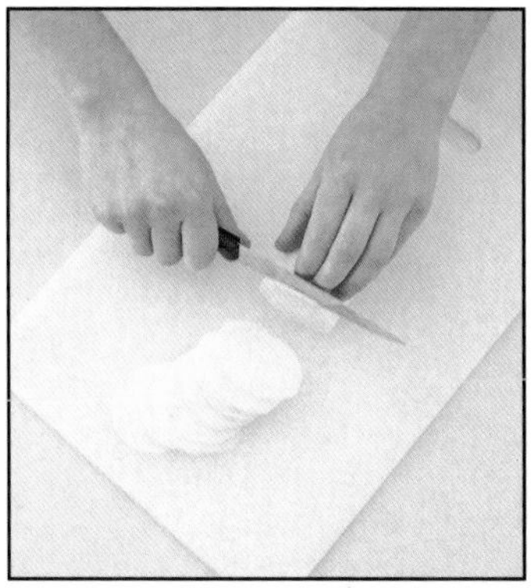

Slice daikon into very thin rounds and spread out on a wire rack. Dry for 24 hours.

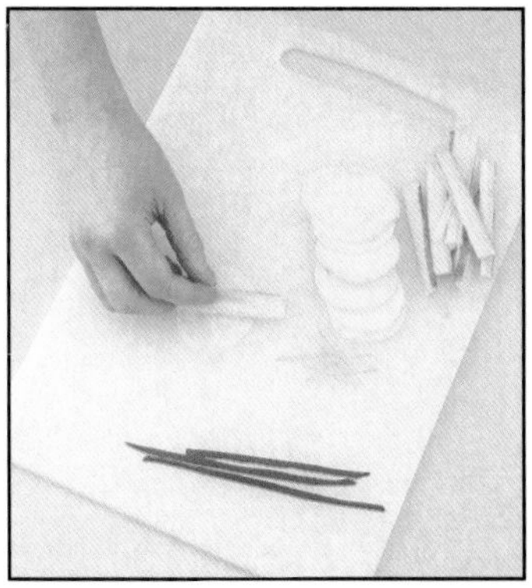

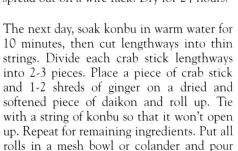

The next day, soak konbu in warm water for 10 minutes, then cut lengthways into thin strings. Divide each crab stick lengthways into 2-3 pieces. Place a piece of crab stick and 1-2 shreds of ginger on a dried and softened piece of daikon and roll up. Tie with a string of konbu so that it won't open up. Repeat for remaining ingredients. Put all rolls in a mesh bowl or colander and pour over boiling hot water. Drain and set aside.

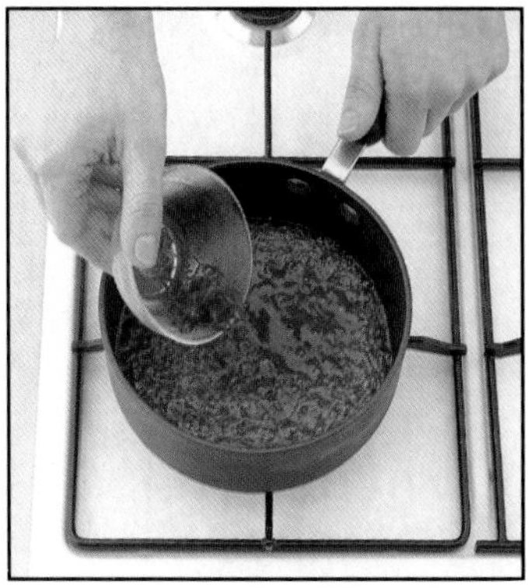

If using dried chillies, soak in warm water for 10 minutes. Whether using dried or fresh cut in half lengthways and remove seeds, then slice diagonally into thin strips. Put dashi, rice vinegar, sugar, a little salt and oil in a saucepan and bring to the boil. Stir to dissolve sugar and add chilli strips. Boil for a few seconds and remove from heat. Leave to cool. Place daikon rolls in a bowl, pour over dressing and marinate overnight. Transfer to a serving dish and garnish with watercress.

Serves 4-8.

VEGETABLE TEMPURA

1 carrot
1 turnip or parsnip
200 g (7 oz) French beans, trimmed
vegetable oil for deep-frying
½ daikon, peeled and grated
4-5 cm (1½-2 in) piece fresh root ginger, peeled and grated
lemon wedges, to garnish
BATTER:
1 egg yolk
200 ml (7 fl oz/1 cup) ice cold water
200 g (7 oz/1¾ cups) plain flour, sifted
SAUCE:
200 ml (7 fl oz/1 cup) dashi (see page 29)
70 ml (2½ oz/⅓ cup) soy sauce
70 ml (2½ oz/⅓ cup) mirin

Cut carrot and turnip into 5 cm (2 in) long shreds. Cut beans diagonally into fine strips. Heat plenty of oil in a wok or deep-frying pan to 170C (340F). Meanwhile, make batter. In a large mixing bowl, lightly beat egg and pour in ice cold water. Stir just 2-3 times, then add flour. Using 3 or 4 chopsticks or a fork, very lightly mix batter with just a few strokes. Do not whisk or overmix – the batter should be very lumpy. Put all the vegetable shreds into the bowl and gently fold in.

Carefully drop a tablespoon at a time of battered vegetables into oil. Fry a few at a time and remove from oil when both sides are light golden and drain on absorbent kitchen paper. Repeat until all battered vegetables are cooked. Arrange them on a large serving plate or individual plates with heaps of grated daikon and ginger. Garnish with lemon wedges. Quickly heat dashi, soy sauce and mirin in a pan and pour it into small individual bowls. Serve hot.

Serves 4.

GRILLED TOFU WITH MISO SAUCE

500 g (1 lb 2 oz/2 cakes) firm tofu
toasted sesame seeds for sprinkling
bamboo leaves, to garnish
MISO SAUCE:
100 g (3½ oz) miso
1 egg yolk
1 tablespoon each sake, mirin and sugar
4 tablespoons dashi (see page 29)
juice ½ lime

Wrap each tofu cake in a tea towel and place a light weight, such as a plate, on top to squeeze out water. Leave to stand for at least 1 hour.

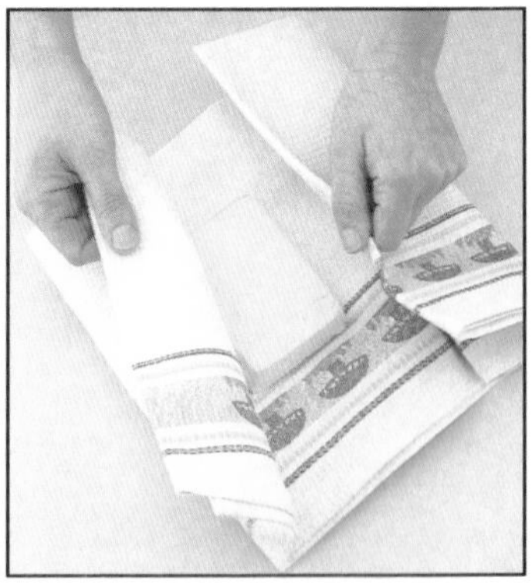

To make sauce, put miso in a bowl and blend in egg yolk, sake, mirin and sugar. Place bowl over a saucepan of simmering water. Gradually add dashi and stir until sauce becomes thick but not too hard, then add lime juice. Remove from heat immediately and cool to room temperature (it will keep well in the refrigerator, if wished.)

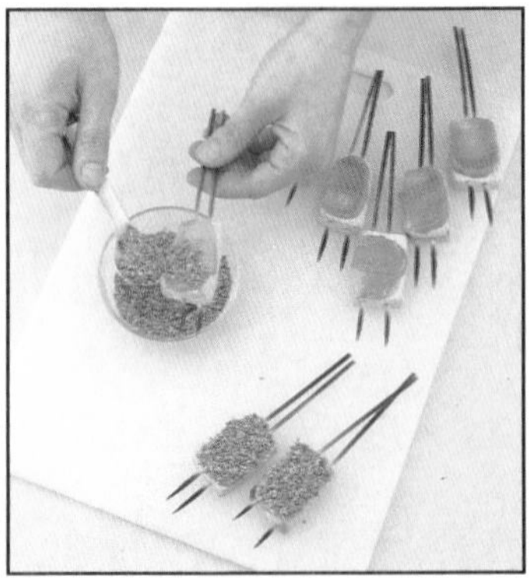

Preheat grill. Unwrap tofu cakes and cut into 5 × 2 × 1 cm (2 × ¾ × ½ in) slices. Skewer each slice lengthways with 2 bamboo skewers. Grill them under high heat for a few minutes on each side until lightly browned and heated through. Remove from heat and, using a butter knife, thickly spread one side with miso sauce. Sprinkle with toasted sesame seeds. Grill miso-covered side for 1-2 minutes. Serve hot on skewers on a bed of bamboo leaves.

Serves 4 as a starter.

SEAFOOD

PRAWN & FISH BALL CURRY

450 g (1 lb) white fish fillets, such as sole, plaice, cod, whiting or monkfish, skinned
115 g (4 oz) peeled cooked prawns
85 g (3 oz/1½ cups) fresh white bread crumbs
2 eggs, beaten separately
2 tablespoons chopped coriander leaves
2 teaspoons lemon juice
salt and pepper
2 tablespoons vegetable oil plus extra for frying
1 large onion, finely chopped
2 fresh green chillies, seeded and chopped
4 cloves garlic, crushed
½ teaspoon turmeric
150 ml (5 fl oz/⅔ cup) coconut milk (see page 224)
440 g (14 oz) can chopped tomatoes

Wash fish and remove any bones. Mince fish and prawns, then transfer to a large bowl. Stir in 55 g (2 oz/1 cup) bread crumbs, 1 egg, coriander and lemon juice and season with salt and pepper. Mix well and form into 24 balls. Roll balls in remaining egg, then in remaining bread crumbs to coat completely. Chill for 30 minutes. Meanwhile, heat 2 tablespoons oil in a heavy-based pan, add onion and cook, stirring, for 5 minutes until soft.

Add chillies, garlic and turmeric and fry for 2 minutes more. Stir in coconut milk and tomatoes and cook, uncovered, for 20 minutes, stirring occasionally, until thickened. Half-fill a deep-fat pan or fryer with oil and heat to 190C (375F) or until a cube of day-old bread browns in 40 seconds. Fry fish balls for 3-5 minutes, until golden. Drain well and serve with sauce.

Serves 4.

HOT MUSSELS WITH CUMIN

1.5 kg (3½ lb) mussels
2 tablespoons vegetable oil
1 large onion, finely chopped
2.5 cm (1 in) piece fresh root ginger, grated
6 cloves garlic, crushed
2 fresh green chillies, seeded and finely chopped
½ teaspoon turmeric
2 teaspoons ground cumin
85 g (3 oz/1¾ cups) shredded fresh coconut
2 tablespoons chopped coriander leaves
coriander sprigs, to garnish

Scrub mussels clean in several changes of fresh cold water and pull off beards.

Discard any mussels that are cracked or do not close tightly when tapped. Set aside. Heat oil in a large saucepan and add onion. Fry, stirring, for 5 minutes, until soft, then add ginger, garlic, chillies, turmeric and cumin. Fry 2 minutes, stirring constantly.

Add mussels, coconut and 225 ml (8 fl oz/1 cup) water and bring to the boil. Cover and cook over a high heat, shaking pan frequently, for about 5 minutes or until almost all the shells have opened. Discard any that do not open. Spoon mussels into a serving dish, pour over cooking liquid and sprinkle with chopped coriander. Garnish with coriander sprigs and serve at once.

Serves 4.

CORIANDER & CHILLI FISH

800 g (1¾ lb) white fish fillets, such as monkfish, sole or plaice
4 teaspoons lemon juice
salt and pepper
85 g (3 oz) coriander leaves
4 fresh green chillies, seeded and chopped
3 cloves garlic, crushed
225 ml (8 fl oz/1 cup) natural yogurt
vegetable oil for deep-frying
lemon wedges and coriander leaves, to garnish

Trim any skin and bones from fish, then cut flesh into 2.5 × 7.5 cm (1 × 3 in) strips.

Spread fish strips in a shallow non-metallic dish and sprinkle with lemon juice and salt and pepper. Set aside in a cool place. Put coriander, chillies, garlic and 1-2 tablespoons water in a blender or food processor fitted with a metal blade and process until smooth, frequently scraping mixture down from sides. Squeeze out excess liquid from paste, place in a shallow dish and stir in yogurt.

Heat oil in a deep-frying pan to 180C (350F) or until a cube of day-old bread browns in 35 seconds. Drain fish and pat dry with absorbent kitchen paper. Dip strips in yogurt mixture, coating them all over, and fry a few at a time for 2-3 minutes, until golden brown. Drain on absorbent kitchen paper, then serve at once, garnished with lemon wedges and coriander leaves.

Serves 4.

SOLE WITH DILL STUFFING

4 sole fillets, each weighing about 175 g (6 oz), skinned
3 tablespoons lemon juice
salt and pepper
2 tablespoons vegetable oil
1 clove garlic, crushed
2.5 cm (1 in) piece fresh root ginger, grated
¼ teaspoon cayenne pepper
¼ teaspoon turmeric
4 spring onions, finely chopped
8 tablespoons finely chopped fresh dill
dill sprigs, to garnish

Wash fish fillets and pat dry with absorbent kitchen paper.

Lay fillets skinned-side up on a work surface and sprinkle with lemon juice and salt and pepper, then set aside. Preheat oven to 180C (350F/Gas 4). Heat 1½ tablespoons oil in a frying pan. Add garlic, ginger, cayenne, turmeric and spring onions and cook over a low heat for 3 minutes or until onions are soft and golden, stirring occasionally. Remove from heat and set aside to cool, then stir in dill.

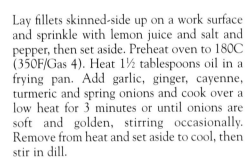

Divide stuffing between fillets and spread evenly over skinned side of fish. Roll fillets up from thickest end. Grease a shallow ovenproof dish with remaining oil and arrange sole rolls, seam-side down, in the dish with 55 ml (2 fl oz/¼ cup) water. Cover with aluminium foil and cook for 15-20 minutes or until fish flakes easily. Serve hot, with cooking juices spooned over and garnished with sprigs of dill.

Serves 4.

FISH IN HOT SAUCE

4 whole fish, such as mackerel, trout, grey mullet or blue fish, each weighing about 225 g (8 oz), cleaned
4 dill sprigs
4 lime slices
55 ml (2 fl oz/¼ cup) vegetable oil
4 spring onions, sliced
1 cm (½ in) piece fresh root ginger, grated
1 clove garlic, crushed
1 teaspoon mustard seeds
¼ teaspoon cayenne pepper
1 tablespoon tamarind paste (see page 11)
2 tablespoons tomato purée
dill sprigs and lime slices, to garnish

Wash fish and pat dry with absorbent kitchen paper. Slash 2 or 3 times on each side, tuck a sprig of dill and a lime slice inside each fish, then set aside. Heat 2 tablespoons of oil in a small pan. Add onions and cook, stirring, for 2-3 minutes, until softened. Add ginger, garlic and mustard seeds and fry for 1 minute more, until mustard seeds start to pop.

Stir in cayenne pepper, tamarind paste, tomato purée and 85 ml (3 fl oz/⅓ cup) water. Bring to the boil and simmer, uncovered, for about 5 minutes, until thickened slightly. Meanwhile, heat grill. Place fish on grill rack, brush with remaining oil and cook for about 5 minutes on each side, basting occasionally with oil, until flesh flakes easily. Serve hot with sauce, garnished with dill and lime slices.

Serves 4.

STEAMED FISH & VEGETABLES

4 whole red mullet, red snapper or sea bream, each weighing about 225 g (8 oz), cleaned
4 teaspoons Garam Masala (see page 224)
½ teaspoon turmeric
2 tablespoons chopped coriander leaves
1 tablespoon chopped fresh parsley
2.5 cm (1 in) piece fresh root ginger, grated
4 lemon slices
2 tablespoons vegetable oil
8 new potatoes, sliced
3 carrots, sliced
4 courgettes, sliced
salt and pepper
coriander leaves, to garnish

Wash fish and pat dry with absorbent kitchen paper, then slash 3 times on each side. Mix garam masala, turmeric, coriander, parsley and ginger together and rub into flesh and skin of fish. Tuck a slice of lemon inside each fish and set aside. Heat oil in a frying pan, add potatoes and carrots and fry, stirring frequently, for 5-6 minutes, until slightly softened and beginning to brown.

Add courgettes to pan and fry for 1 minute more. Season with salt and pepper. Using a slotted spoon, transfer vegetables to a steamer. Lay fish on top, cover and steam for 20-25 minutes or until fish flakes easily and vegetables are tender. Serve at once, garnished with coriander.

Serves 4.

COCONUT SPICED COD

4 cod steaks, each weighing 175-225 g (6-8 oz)
salt and pepper
2 tablespoons vegetable oil
1 onion, chopped
115 g (4 oz/1⅓ cups) desiccated coconut
5 cm (2 in) piece fresh root ginger, grated
2 cloves garlic, crushed
2 green chillies, seeded and chopped
½ teaspoon chilli powder
grated zest and juice 1 lemon
2 tablespoons chopped coriander leaves
2 tomatoes, skinned, seeded and diced
oregano leaves, to garnish

Wash cod steaks and pat dry with absorbent kitchen paper. Place in a greased ovenproof dish and sprinkle with salt and pepper. Heat oil in a frying pan, add onion and fry, stirring, for about 5 minutes or until soft. Stir in coconut, ginger, garlic, chillies and chilli powder and fry, stirring, for 3-5 minutes, until golden brown.

Stir in lemon zest and juice and simmer, covered, for 10 minutes to soften coconut. Preheat oven to 160C (325F/Gas 3). Stir coriander and tomatoes into coconut mixture and spoon over cod steaks. Cook for 20-25 minutes, until fish flakes easily. Serve hot, garnished with oregano leaves.

Serves 4.

Note: Cover with foil during cooking if coconut begins to brown too much.

GRILLED SPICED FISH

4 whole plaice or flounder, each weighing about 225 g (8 oz), skinned
salt and pepper
150 ml (5 fl oz/⅔ cup) natural yogurt
2 cloves garlic, crushed
2 teaspoons Garam Masala (see page 224)
1 teaspoon ground coriander
½ teaspoon chilli powder
1 tablespoon lemon juice
lemon wedges and parsley sprigs, to garnish

Wash fish, pat dry with absorbent kitchen paper and place in a shallow non-metallic dish. Sprinkle with salt and pepper.

Mix together yogurt, garlic, garam masala, coriander, chilli powder and lemon juice. Pour over fish and cover. Leave in a cool place for 2-3 hours to allow fish to absorb flavours.

Heat grill. Transfer fish to a grill rack and cook for about 8 minutes, basting with cooking juices and turning over halfway through cooking, until fish flakes easily. Serve hot, garnished with lemon wedges and parsley sprigs.

Serves 4.

Note: Use fillets instead of whole fish, if preferred, and grill for about 2 minutes less.

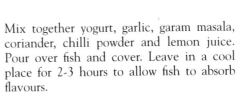

FISH IN A PACKET

4 fish steaks, such as sea bass, cod or salmon, each weighing 175-225 g (6-8 oz)
1-2 fresh or frozen banana leaves (optional)
salt and pepper
55 g (2 oz/1¼ cups) finely grated fresh coconut
55 g (2 oz) fresh mint, chopped
4 cloves garlic, crushed
1 teaspoon ground cumin
4 fresh green chillies, seeded and chopped
2 tablespoons lemon juice
55 ml (2 fl oz/¼ cup) cider vinegar
1 tablespoon vegetable oil
8 dried curry leaves (optional)
mint leaves and lemon slices, to garnish

Wipe fish steaks and place each in the centre of a 30 cm (12 in) square of banana leaf or piece of aluminium foil. Sprinkle fish with salt and pepper. Mix together coçonut, mint, garlic, cumin, chillies and lemon juice. Spoon a quarter of mixture over each fish steak. Fold sides of banana leaf or foil over to seal completely. Tie banana leaf parcels with fine string, if necessary.

Pour vinegar, oil and 175 ml (6 fl oz/¾ cup) water into base of a large steamer, add curry leaves (if using) and bring to the boil. Steam parcels for 12-15 minutes or until fish flakes easily. Open parcels and serve, garnished with mint and lemon slices.

Serves 4.

CREAMY SAFFRON FISH CURRY

700 g (1½ lb) white fish fillets, such as sole, plaice, whiting or cod
pinch saffron threads
3 tablespoons vegetable oil
2 onions, chopped
3 cloves garlic, crushed
2.5 cm (1 in) piece fresh root ginger, grated
1 teaspoon turmeric
1 tablespoon ground coriander
2 teaspoons Garam Masala (see page 224)
salt and cayenne pepper
2 teaspoons chick-pea flour
225 ml (8 fl oz/1 cup) natural yogurt
55 ml (2 fl oz/¼ cup) double (thick) cream
lemon zest and red pepper strips, to garnish

Wash fish, remove any skin and bones and pat dry with absorbent paper. Cut into large chunks and set aside. Put saffron in a small bowl with 2 tablespoons boiling water and leave to soak for about 5 minutes. Heat oil in a large shallow pan, add onions and cook, stirring, for about 5 minutes, until soft but not coloured.

Add garlic, ginger, turmeric, coriander, garam masala and salt and pepper and fry for 1 minute more. Stir in flour and cook for 1 minute, then remove from heat. Stir in yogurt and cream, then return to heat and slowly bring to the boil. Add fish, saffron and soaking water and simmer gently, covered, for 10-15 minutes, until fish is tender and flakes easily. Serve fish hot, garnished with shreds of lemon zest and strips of red pepper.

Serves 4.

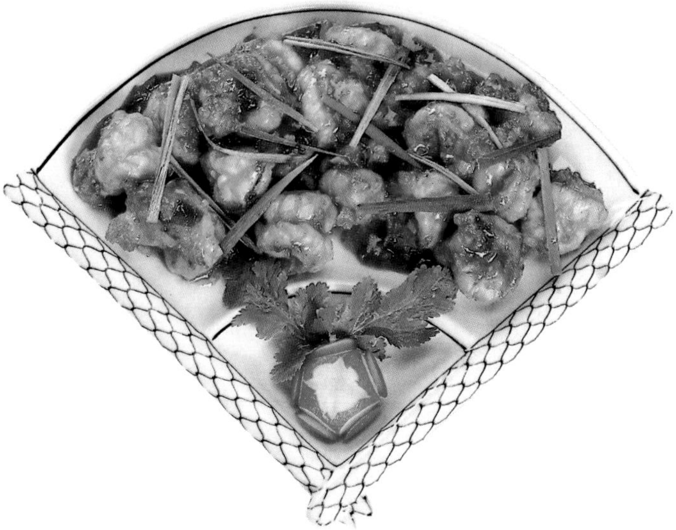

KUNG PO PRAWNS

450 g (1 lb) prepared raw prawns
4 tablespoons cornflour mixed with 5-6 tablespoons water
550 ml (20 fl oz/2½ cups) groundnut (peanut) oil
2 spring onions, finely chopped
1 cm (½ in) piece fresh root ginger, peeled and finely chopped
1 tablespoon rice wine or dry sherry
1 tablespoon light soy sauce
1 teaspoon brown sugar
2 teaspoons sherry vinegar
sea salt and black pepper

Dip prawns in cornflour mixture to coat evenly; allow excess batter to drain off.

In a wok, heat oil until smoking, add prawns and deep-fry for about 3 minutes until golden brown. Using a slotted spoon, remove and then drain on absorbent kitchen paper. Pour oil from wok, leaving just 2 tablespoonsful.

Add spring onion and ginger to wok and stir-fry for 1 minute. Stir in rice wine, soy sauce, brown sugar, sherry vinegar, salt and pepper and bring to the boil. Add prawns to sauce and heat gently until sauce has thickened.

Serves 4.

PHOENIX PRAWNS

8 large prepared prawns
2.5 cm (1 in) piece fresh root ginger, peeled and grated
3 spring onions, chopped
2 tablespoons rice wine or dry sherry
1 teaspoon sesame oil
1 tablespoon light soy sauce
½ teaspoon sea salt
550 ml (20 fl oz/2½ cups) vegetable oil
BATTER:
4 egg whites
2 tablespoons cornflour
2 tablespoons plain flour
175 g (6 oz/1½ cups) dry bread crumbs, for coating

Using a cleaver or large knife slightly flatten prawns along their length; place in a dish. In a bowl, mix together ginger, spring onions, rice wine or dry sherry, sesame oil, soy sauce and salt. Pour over prawns and leave for 30 minutes. Make batter in a bowl by beating together egg whites until thick, then beat in cornflour and flour. Dip prawns in batter to coat thickly and evenly, then coat well with dry bread crumbs.

In a wok heat vegetable oil until very hot, add prawns and deep-fry for 5 minutes until golden. Drain on absorbent kitchen paper.

Serves 4.

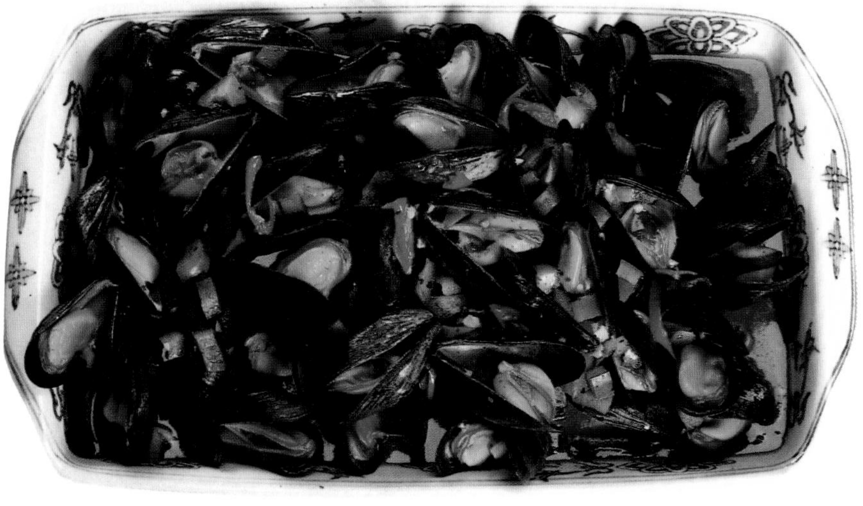

MUSSELS WITH BEANS & CHILLI

3.25 kg (8 lb) mussels, scrubbed and rinsed
125 ml (4 fl oz/½ cup) vegetable oil
4 cloves garlic, finely chopped
2 red hot chillies, seeded if desired, finely chopped
½ green pepper, seeded and chopped
3 spring onions, sliced
1 teaspoon cornflour dissolved in 2 teaspoons cold water
4 tablespoons rice wine or dry sherry
3 tablespoons black bean paste
2 teaspoons ground ginger
1 tablespoon brown sugar
2 tablespoons hot chilli paste
3 tablespoons oyster sauce
750 ml (24 fl oz/3 cups) Chinese Chicken Stock (see page 16)

Place mussels in a large saucepan, add 450 ml (16 fl oz/2 cups) water, cover and place over a high flame for about 5 minutes, shaking pan occasionally, or until mussels have opened; this may have to be done in batches. Remove from heat, drain and discard any mussels which have not opened.

In a wok, heat oil, add garlic, chilli, green pepper and spring onions and stir-fry for 1 minute. In a bowl mix together cornflour mixture, rice wine or dry sherry, black bean paste, ground ginger, brown sugar, hot chilli paste, oyster sauce and stock. Stir into wok and bring to the boil, stirring. Simmer until lightly thickened. Add mussels to wok and heat through for 5 minutes, occasionally shaking wok.

Serves 4-6.

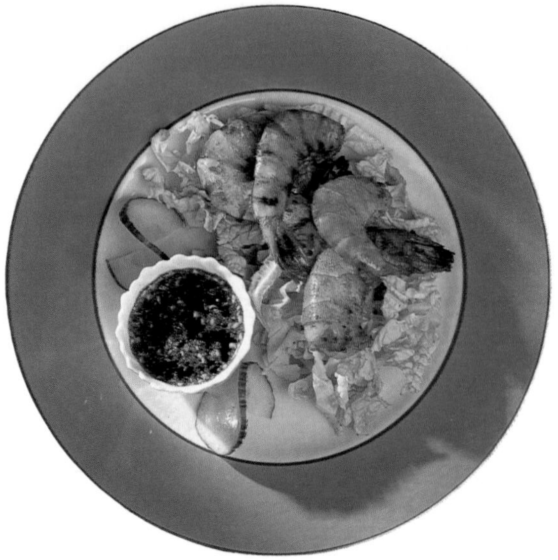

SALT & PEPPER PRAWNS

16 uncooked large prawns
1 teaspoon chilli powder
1 teaspoon coarse sea salt
1 teaspoon Szechuan peppercorns, crushed
2 cloves garlic, finely chopped
1 tablespoon groundnut (peanut) oil
DIP:
½ teaspoon Szechuan peppercorns, toasted and ground
2 tablespoons light soy sauce
2 tablespoons dry sherry
1 teaspoon brown sugar

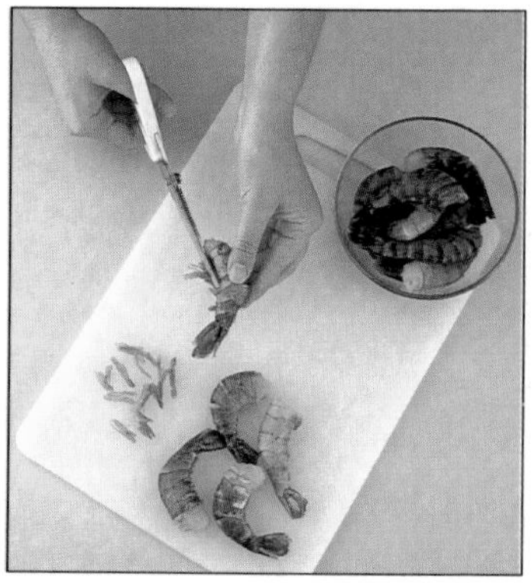

Cut heads off prawns. Use scissors to remove legs, leaving shells.

Rinse prawns and pat dry with absorbent kitchen paper. In a bowl, mix together prawns, chilli powder, salt, peppercorns and garlic. Heat oil in a wok until very hot and stir-fry prawns for 2-3 minutes or until prawns are pink and cooked through. Drain on absorbent kitchen paper.

Mix together ingredients for dip. Serve prawns immediately with dip and a salad.

Serves 4.

Note: Serve with a finger bowl of water and lemon slices, to freshen hands.

STIR-FRIED SCALLOPS

450 g (1 lb) fresh bay scallops, cleaned and trimmed
225 g (8 oz) baby sweetcorn
225 g (8 oz) mangetout
1 tablespoon sunflower oil
2 shallots, chopped
1 clove garlic, finely chopped
1 cm (½ in) piece fresh root ginger, peeled and finely chopped
2 tablespoons yellow bean sauce
1 tablespoon light soy sauce
1 teaspoon sugar
1 tablespoon dry sherry

Rinse scallops and dry with absorbent kitchen paper.

Slice baby sweetcorn in half lengthways and remove ends from mangetout. Heat oil in a wok and stir-fry shallots, garlic and ginger for 1 minute.

Add scallops, baby sweetcorn and mangetout and stir-fry for 1 minute. Stir in yellow bean sauce, soy sauce, sugar and sherry and simmer for 4 minutes or until scallops and vegetables are cooked through. Serve on a bed of rice.

Serves 4.

Note: Scallops are sometimes sold with edible orange roe still attached.

SCALLOPS WITH BLACK BEANS

12 scallops on their half-shells
2 tablespoons groundnut (peanut) oil
2 cloves garlic, finely chopped
3 spring onions, finely chopped
1 fresh hot green chilli, seeded and chopped
3 tablespoons fermented salted black beans, soaked for 20 minutes, drained
2 tablespoons dark soy sauce
2 teaspoons brown sugar
3 tablespoons Chinese Chicken Stock (see page 16)
2 teaspoons cornflour

Place scallops on their shells in a steaming basket, place over a wok or saucepan of boiling water, cover and cook for 6 minutes.

Meanwhile, in a wok, heat oil, add garlic, spring onions, chilli and black beans and stir-fry for 2 minutes, mashing the beans. Stir in soy sauce and sugar for 1-2 minutes.

Blend stock with cornflour until smooth. Stir into wok, bring to the boil, stirring and simmer until thickened. Keep warm. Transfer scallops to a warmed serving plate and spoon a little sauce over each.

Serves 4.

CURRIED CRAB

700 g (1½ lb) cooked large crab claws, thawed and dried, if frozen
1 tablespoon sunflower oil
2 cloves garlic, thinly sliced
5 tablespoons Chinese Vegetable Stock (see page 17)
1 tablespoon Madras curry paste
1 tablespoon light soy sauce
1 teaspoon brown sugar
1 large green pepper, thinly sliced
225 g (8 oz) small broccoli florets

Wrap the end of a rolling pin in cling film and tap the main part of the crab claws until shell cracks, leaving pincers intact. Peel away hard shell to expose crab flesh, leaving shell on pincers. Heat oil in a wok and stir-fry crab and garlic for 1-2 minutes or until crab is lightly browned. Drain on absorbent kitchen paper and set aside.

Mix together stock, curry paste, soy sauce and brown sugar and add to wok with green pepper and broccoli. Simmer for 5 minutes, stirring occasionally. Return crab and garlic to wok and simmer for 2-3 minutes, stirring to coat crab with sauce. Serve immediately with rice, vegetables and lemon wedges.

Serves 4.

SQUID FLOWERS WITH PEPPERS

550 ml (20 fl oz/2½ cups) groundnut (peanut) oil
450 g (1 lb) squid, cleaned (see page 194)
2 slices fresh root ginger, peeled and finely chopped
1 large green pepper, seeded and cut into 2.5 cm (1 in) squares
1 teaspoon sea salt
1 tablespoon dark soy sauce
1 teaspoon rice vinegar
½ teaspoon brown sugar
ground black pepper
1 teaspoon sesame oil

In a wok, heat oil until smoking, add squid and fry for 1 minute. Remove and drain on absorbent kitchen paper.

Pour oil from wok, leaving just 1 tablespoon. Add ginger and green pepper and stir-fry for 5 minutes until pepper begins to soften. Stir in sea salt, soy sauce, rice vinegar, brown sugar and black pepper.

Bring to the boil, stirring, then reduce heat so sauce is simmering, then add squid and gently heat through. Transfer to a warmed serving plate and sprinkle with sesame oil.

Serves 4.

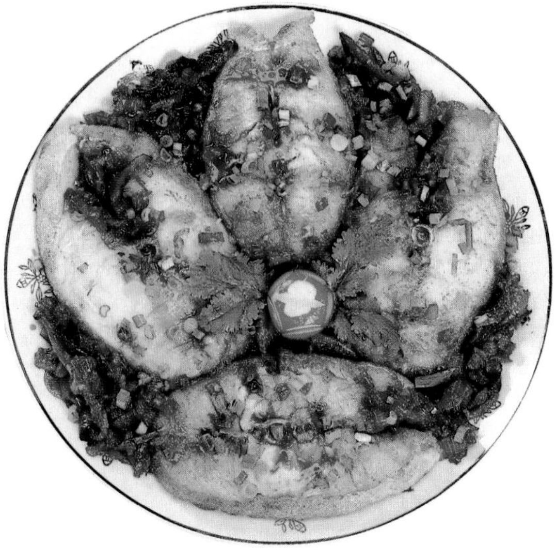

HUNAN FISH STEAKS

550 ml (20 fl oz/2½ cups) vegetable oil
4 cod steaks, each weighing about 175 g (6 oz)
SAUCE:
4 dried black winter mushrooms, soaked in hot water for 25 minutes
2 medium onions, finely chopped
3 slices fresh root ginger, peeled and finely chopped
2 cloves garlic, finely chopped
2 tablespoons Chinese radish pickle, chopped
3 dried red chillies
175 ml (6 fl oz/¾ cup) Chinese Chicken Stock (see page 16)
3 tablespoons dark soy sauce
2 tablespoons brown sugar
2 teaspoons sea salt
4 tablespoons rice wine or dry sherry

TO SERVE:
4 spring onions, chopped
2 teaspoons sesame oil

In a wok, heat oil until just smoking. Add fish steaks 2 at a time and deep-fry for 1½ minutes each side. Remove, drain on absorbent kitchen paper and keep warm. Reheat oil before adding remaining steaks. Pour oil from wok, leaving just 3 tablespoonsful. Stir in sauce ingredients and boil, stirring, until reduced by half.

Reduce heat so sauce is just simmering, add fish steaks and heat through gently, turning occasionally, for 5 minutes. Transfer fish to a warmed serving plate, pour over sauce, sprinkle with finely chopped spring onions and sesame oil.

Serves 4.

CANTONESE LOBSTER

1 (1.35 kg/3 lb) lobster
2 tablespoons groundnut (peanut) oil
1 cm (½ in) piece fresh root ginger, peeled and grated
4 spring onions, coarsely chopped
1 teaspoon sea salt
175 ml (6 fl oz/¾ cup) Chinese Chicken Stock (see page 16)
2 tablespoons dark soy sauce
2 tablespoons rice wine or dry sherry

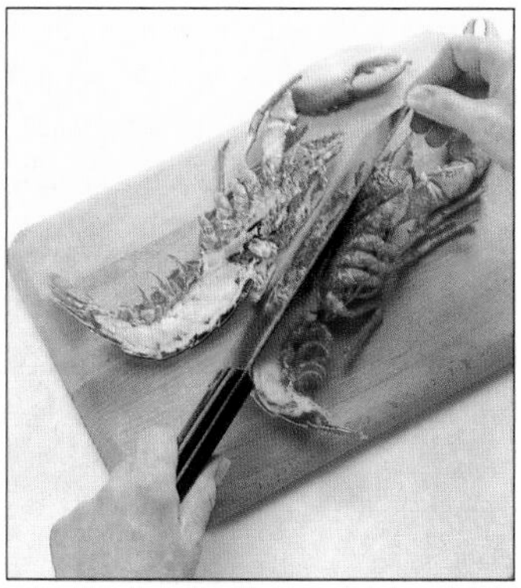

Insert the point of a large, heavy knife in the back of the lobster's head, then move the knife towards the tail in a series of cutting movements to split the lobster in half.

Remove and discard head sac and black intestinal thread. Crack the claws. In a wok, over a moderate heat, heat oil, add lobster pieces, cover and cook for 4 minutes. Remove and drain on absorbent kitchen paper. Pour oil from wok leaving just 1 tablespoonful. Stir ginger, spring onions, salt, stock, soy sauce and rice wine into the wok and bring to the boil.

Return lobster pieces to wok, cover and simmer for 5 minutes. Transfer lobster to a warmed serving plate and pour sauce over.

Serves 4.

COD WITH OYSTER SAUCE

700 g (1½ lb) piece cod fillet, skinned
2 shallots, shredded
115 g (4 oz) oyster mushrooms, sliced
2 cloves garlic, finely sliced
115 g (4 oz) cooked, peeled large prawns, thawed and dried, if frozen
55 ml (2 fl oz/¼ cup) oyster sauce
2 tablespoons dry sherry
salt and freshly ground black pepper
grated zest 1 lime and 1 lemon
2 tablespoons chopped coriander leaves

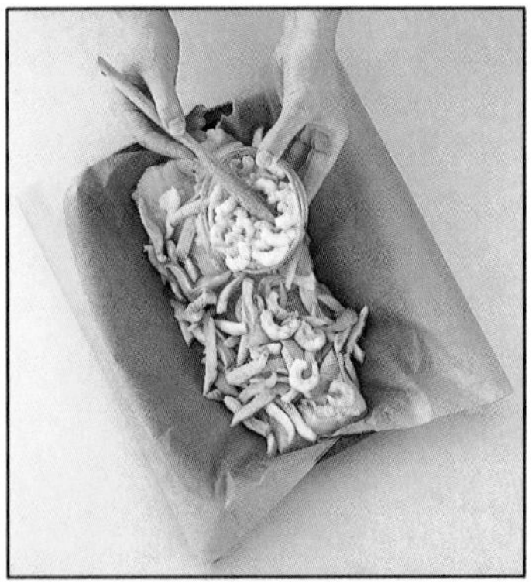

Preheat oven to 180C/350F/Gas 4. Rinse cod fillet and pat dry with absorbent kitchen paper. Place on a large piece of nonstick baking parchment and put in a roasting pan. Top cod with shallots, mushrooms, garlic and prawns then drizzle with oyster sauce and sherry. Season with salt and freshly ground pepper.

Bring ends of the nonstick baking parchment over fish and pleat together to seal. Bake for 25 minutes or until cod is cooked through. Carefully lift from paper, sprinkle with lime and lemon zest and coriander and serve with rice and salad.

Serves 4.

COD WITH VINEGAR SAUCE

1 tablespoon sunflower oil
6 shallots, sliced
2 tablespoons white rice vinegar
2 teaspoons sugar
1 tablespoon light soy sauce
300 ml (10 fl oz/1¼ cups) Chinese Vegetable Stock (see page 17)
1 teaspoon cornflour mixed with 2 teaspoons cold water
4 cod steaks, each weighing about 175 g (6 oz)
salt and freshly ground black pepper
2 tablespoons chopped fresh chives

Heat half oil in a wok and stir-fry shallots for 2-3 minutes.

Add vinegar, sugar and soy sauce and stir-fry for 1 minute. Pour in stock and bring to the boil. Simmer for 8-9 minutes or until thickened and slightly reduced. Stir in cornflour mixture and cook, stirring, until thickened. Keep warm.

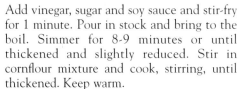

Preheat grill. Season cod steaks on both sides and place on grill rack. Brush with remaining oil and cook for 4 minutes on each side or until cooked through. Drain on absorbent kitchen paper. Remove skin. Stir chives into vinegar sauce, spoon over cod steaks and serve with noodles and grilled tomatoes.

Serves 4.

SMOKY GARLIC FISH STEW

700 g (1½ lb) firm white fish fillets, such as cod or monkfish, skinned and cut into 2.5 cm (1 in) cubes
4 large cloves garlic, roughly chopped
2 teaspoons light soy sauce
3 tablespoons sweet sherry
1 tablespoon cornflour
1 tablespoon sunflower oil
225 g (8 oz) shallots, sliced
2 tablespoons fermented black beans
4 spring onions, cut into 2.5 cm (1 in) pieces
2 tablespoons dark soy sauce

In a bowl, mix together cubed fish, garlic, light soy sauce, sherry and cornflour. Cover and chill for 30 minutes. Heat oil in a wok and stir-fry fish mixture and shallots for 3 minutes or until fish is lightly coloured. Remove with a slotted, spoon, drain on absorbent kitchen paper and set aside.

Add black beans, spring onions and dark soy sauce to wok and stir-fry for 2-3 minutes over high heat or until thick and syrupy. Replace fish mixture and cook for 2 minutes, stirring gently. Serve immediately with noodles and salad.

Serves 4.

LIME-GRILLED FISH KEBABS

350 g (12 oz) monkfish tails, skinned and cut into ¾ in cubes
12 oz trout fillets, skinned and cut into 2 cm (¾ in) pieces
2 limes
1 teaspoon sesame oil
large pinch five-spice powder
freshly ground pepper
strips lime zest, to garnish

Place monkfish and trout in a shallow dish. Juice 1 lime and grate zest. Mix juice and zest with sesame oil and five-spice powder, pour over fish, cover and chill for 30 minutes.

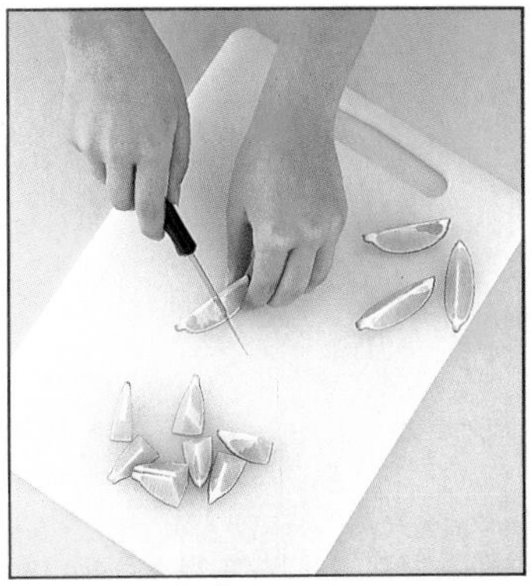

Soak 4 bamboo skewers in cold water. Halve and quarter remaining lime lengthways, then halve each quarter to make 8 wedges. Slice each piece of lime in half crossways to make 16 small pieces.

Preheat grill. Thread monkfish, trout and lime pieces on to skewers and place on grill rack. Brush with marinade and season with pepper. Grill for 2 minutes on each side, brushing occasionally with marinade to prevent drying out. Drain on absorbent kitchen paper, garnish with lime zest and serve with rice, vegetables and lime wedges.

Serves 4.

STUFFED RED MULLET

55 g (2 oz) oyster mushrooms
55 g (2 oz) cooked, peeled large prawns, thawed and dried, if frozen
grated zest 1 small lemon
2 tablespoons oyster sauce
4 red mullet or red snapper, each weighing about 225 g (8 oz), cleaned and scaled
55 ml (2 fl oz/¼ cup) dry sherry
1 large carrot, cut into thin strips
1 daikon, peeled and cut into thin strips
225 g (8 oz) small broccoli florets
lemon zest and chopped spring onions, to garnish

Finely chop mushrooms and prawns. Place in a small bowl and mix in lemon zest. Stir in oyster sauce and set aside. Rinse fish and pat dry with absorbent kitchen paper. Divide mushroom mixture into 4 portions and press into cavity of each fish. Place stuffed fish in a shallow dish and spoon over sherry. Cover and chill for 30 minutes.

Bring a wok or large saucepan of water to the boil. Arrange carrot and daikon strips and broccoli florets on nonstick baking parchment in 2 steamers, lay fish on top and spoon over sherry marinade. Place over boiling water, cover and steam for 10 minutes. Carefully turn fish over and steam for a further 8-10 minutes or until cooked through. Garnish with lemon zest and chopped spring onions to serve.

Serves 4.

STEAMED FISH CAKES

2.5 cm (1 in) piece fresh root ginger, peeled
700 g (1½ lb) cod fillets, skinned and chopped
1 egg white, lightly beaten
2 teaspoons cornflour
2 tablespoons chopped fresh chives
salt and ground white pepper
115 g (4 oz) oyster mushrooms
2 shallots
2 courgettes
1 red pepper, halved
1 yellow pepper, halved
1 clove garlic
fresh chives, to garnish
oyster sauce, to serve (optional)

Chop half the ginger and place in a food processor or blender with cod, egg white, cornflour, chives, salt and pepper. Process until finely chopped. Divide into 12 portions and shape into 7.5 cm (3 in) diameter patties. Line a large plate with nonstick baking parchment, arrange fish cakes on plate, cover and chill for 30 minutes. Using a sharp knife, thinly slice mushrooms, shallots, courgettes, peppers, remaining ginger and garlic.

Bring a wok or large saucepan of water to the boil. Arrange vegetables on nonstick baking parchment in a steamer, place fish cakes on top and place over boiling water. Cover and steam for 10 minutes or until cooked, turning fish cakes halfway through cooking time. Garnish with chives and serve with a salad and oyster sauce.

Serves 4.

SALMON WITH GINGER DIP

4 salmon fillets, each weighing 175 g (6 oz), skinned
2 tablespoons light soy sauce
1 tablespoon dry sherry
2.5 cm (1 in) piece fresh root ginger, peeled and cut into thin strips
1 teaspoon sunflower oil
freshly ground pepper
4 spring onions, shredded, to garnish
DIP:
2 tablespoons sweet sherry
1 tablespoon light soy sauce

Using a sharp knife, lightly score top of salmon fillets in diagonal lines, taking care not to slice all way through.

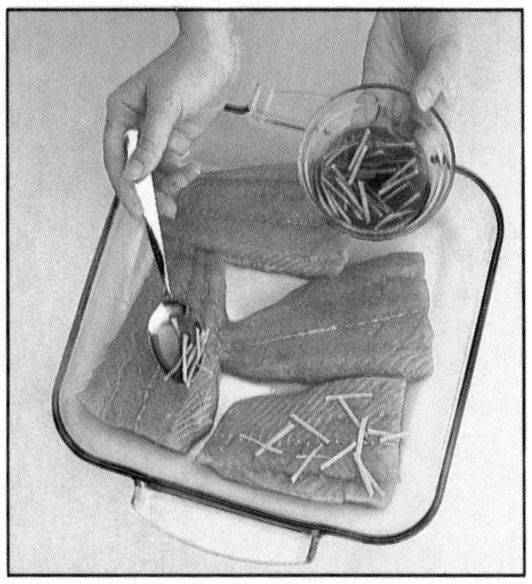

Place salmon in a shallow dish. Mix together soy sauce, sherry and ginger strips and spoon over salmon. Cover and chill for 1 hour.

Preheat grill and brush grill rack lightly with oil. Remove salmon from marinade and place on rack. Season with pepper and grill for 2-3 minutes on each side. Meanwhile, mix together sweet sherry and light soy sauce for dip and set aside. Drain salmon on absorbent kitchen paper. Garnish with spring onions and serve with dip.

Serves 4.

FIVE-SPICE SALMON STEAKS

4 salmon steaks, each weighing about 175 g (6 oz)
2 teaspoons five-spice powder
freshly ground black pepper
1 tablespoon groundnut (peanut) oil
1 clove garlic, finely chopped
2 tablespoons rice wine
1 tablespoon light soy sauce
1 teaspoon sesame oil
zest 1 lemon, cut into fine strips

Rinse salmon steaks and pat dry with absorbent kitchen paper. Rub both sides with five-spice powder and freshly ground black pepper.

Heat oil in a wok, add garlic and salmon and cook for 1-2 minutes on each side until salmon is lightly browned.

Add rice wine, soy sauce and sesame oil and simmer for 3-4 minutes or until salmon is just cooked through. Stir in lemon zest. Remove salmon with a slotted spoon and remove skin.

Serves 4.

FRAGRANT PRAWNS

2 dried shrimp
2 tablespoons vegetable oil
5 whole small fresh red chillies
1 small onion, finely chopped
3 cloves garlic, finely chopped
2.5 cm (1 in) piece fresh root ginger, grated
1 teaspoon curry powder
leaves from 2 stalks fresh curry leaves
450 g (1 lb) raw unpeeled medium prawns, peeled and deveined
1 tablespoon yellow bean sauce
1 teaspoon oyster sauce
1 teaspoon dark soy sauce
2 teaspoons rice wine
pinch sugar

Soak dried shrimp in hot water for 10 minutes. Drain and pound in a mortar or mix in a small blender. In a wok or sauté pan, heat oil over medium heat. Add chillies, onion, garlic and ginger. Fry for 1 minute. Add curry powder and curry leaves. Stir for 30 seconds.

Stir in prawns and dried shrimp then add yellow bean sauce, oyster sauce and soy sauce. Bring to a simmer, cover pan then cook gently for 2-3 minutes until prawns are beginning to turn pink. Add rice wine, and sugar to taste. Increase heat and stir for a few seconds. Serve immediately.

Serves 4.

PRAWNS ROBED IN SPICES

8 candlenuts or cashew nuts
2 teaspoons lime juice
2 large shallots, chopped
4 cloves garlic, crushed
2.5 cm (1 in) piece galangal, chopped
2.5 cm (1 in) piece fresh root ginger, chopped
1 stalk lemon grass, chopped
½ teaspoon ground turmeric
4 tablespoons vegetable oil
575 g (1¼ lb) raw unpeeled medium prawns, peeled and deveined

Put nuts in a blender and grind to a powder. Transfer to a small bowl. Stir in lime juice and 1 tablespoon water. Set aside.

Put shallots, garlic, galangal, ginger, lemon grass and turmeric in blender. Add 2-3 tablespoons water and mix to a paste. Heat oil in a wok or large non-stick frying pan over medium heat. Add spice paste and cook, stirring, for about 5 minutes until reduced and reddish-brown in colour.

Add prawns and nut mixture. Increase heat to high and fry, stirring, for 2-3 minutes until prawns are cooked and spice mixture clings to them. Using a slotted spoon transfer to a warm plate, leaving all oil behind.

Serves 3-4.

PRAWN KEBABS

115 ml (4 fl oz/½ cup) vegetable oil
6 tablespoons lime juice
1 cm (½ in) piece fresh root ginger, grated
2 large cloves garlic, finely crushed
1 fresh red chilli, cored, seeded and finely chopped
leaves from small bunch coriander, chopped
1 tablespoon light soy sauce
½ teaspoon light brown sugar
700 g (1½ lb) raw, unpeeled large prawns
Malaysian Dipping Sauce (see page 227), to serve

Whisk together oil, lime juice, ginger, garlic and chilli. Stir in coriander, soy sauce and sugar.

Soak 8 long wooden or bamboo skewers in water for 20-30 minutes, drain, then thread with prawns. Place skewers in a shallow non-reactive dish. Pour ginger mixture evenly over prawns. Turn skewers, cover and refrigerate for 1-2 hours, turning occasionally. Return to room temperature for 30 minutes.

Preheat grill. Transfer kebabs to oiled grill rack; reserve marinade. Cook prawns 5-7.5 cm (2-3 in) from heat, for 4-6 minutes, turning halfway through cooking time, until they turn pink. Brush with reserved marinade occasionally. Serve accompanied by Malaysian Dipping Sauce (see page 227).

Serves 4.

MUSSELS IN HOT SPICY SAUCE

4 dried red chillies, seeded
2 teaspoons shrimp paste, roasted (see page 11)
1 small onion, chopped
2.5 cm (1 in) piece fresh galangal
4 cloves garlic, 3 coarsely chopped and 1 finely chopped
1 stalk lemon grass, sliced
6-8 candlenuts or cashew nuts
1 teaspoon paprika
4 tablespoons vegetable oil
900 g-1.35 kg (2-3 lb) live mussels, cleaned

Put chillies in a small bowl. Add 4 tablespoons hot water and soak until slightly softened. Pour into a blender.

Add shrimp paste, onion, galangal, coarsely chopped garlic, lemon grass, nuts and paprika. Mix to a paste, adding a little extra water if necessary. In a wok or large sauté pan, heat oil over medium-high heat. Add finely chopped garlic and stir until just beginning to brown. Add spice paste and stir for 3 minutes.

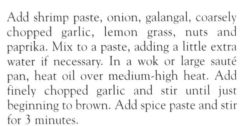

Pour in 350 ml (12 fl oz/1½ cups) water and bring to the boil. Add mussels. Return quickly to boil then cover pan and cook over medium-high heat for 3-5 minutes, shaking the pan halfway through, until all mussels have opened; discard any mussels that remain closed. Serve mussels in deep bowls with cooking juices spooned over.

Serves 4.

MILD FISH CURRY

55 g (2 oz/1¼ cups) desiccated coconut
3 small onions, chopped
2 cloves garlic, crushed
1 fresh red chilli, cored, seeded and chopped
2.5 cm (1 in) piece fresh root ginger, chopped
2 stalks lemon grass, chopped
2 teaspoons ground turmeric
3 tablespoons groundnut (peanut) oil
500 ml (18 fl oz/2¼ cups) coconut milk
450 g (1 lb) firm white fish fillet, such as cod, haddock or monkfish, skinned and cubed
3 tablespoons thick coconut milk
fresh red chilli, shredded, to garnish

Heat desiccated coconut in a small frying pan over medium-high heat until lightly darkened with a roasted aroma. Cool slightly, then pound in a mortar and pestle, or in small bowl using the end of a rolling pin. Set aside until required. Put onions, garlic, chilli, ginger, lemon grass and turmeric in a blender and mix to a paste. Heat oil in a wok or frying pan over medium-high heat. Add spice paste and fry for 3-4 minutes until fragrant but not coloured.

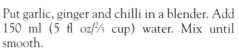

Stir coconut milk into spice paste. Bring to the boil, stirring, then lower heat and simmer for 3 minutes. Add fish to pan and cook gently for 3-4 minutes until just cooked through. Stir in thick coconut milk and pounded coconut. Serve garnished with shredded chilli.

Serves 3-4.

COCONUT CURRIED FISH

6 cloves garlic, chopped
2.5 cm (1 in) piece fresh root ginger, chopped
1 large fresh red chilli, cored, seeded and chopped
4 tablespoons vegetable oil
1 large onion, quartered and sliced
2 teaspoons ground cumin
½ teaspoon ground turmeric
400 ml (14 fl oz/1¾ cups) coconut milk
450 g (1 lb) firm white fish fillet, such as cod or halibut, cut into 5 cm (2 in) pieces
coriander sprigs and lime wedges, to garnish

Put garlic, ginger and chilli in a blender. Add 150 ml (5 fl oz/⅔ cup) water. Mix until smooth.

In a wok or sauté pan over medium heat, heat oil. Add onion and fry 5-7 minutes until beginning to colour. Add cumin and turmeric and stir for 30 seconds. Stir in garlic mixture. Cook, stirring, for about 2 minutes until liquid has evaporated.

Stir coconut milk into pan. Bring to the boil and bubble until sauce is reduced by half. Add salt to taste. Add fish and spoon sauce over it so it is covered. Heat to a simmer and cook gently for 4-6 minutes until fish just flakes when tested with the point of a sharp knife. Garnish with coriander sprigs and lime wedges. Serve with rice.

Serves 3-4.

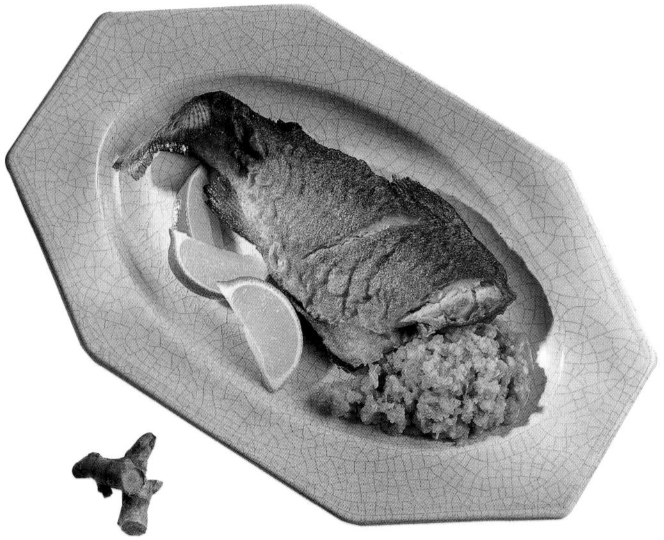

CRISP FISH WITH TURMERIC

2 whole fish, such as trout or bream, each weighing about 350 g (12 oz)
1 teaspoon ground turmeric
1½ teaspoons salt
115 ml (4 fl oz/½ cup) vegetable oil
SAUCE:
1 tablespoon tamarind
4 dried red chillies
1 stalk lemon grass, chopped
1 clove garlic, chopped
4 shallots, chopped
0.5 cm (¼ in) piece galangal, chopped
3 tablespoons vegetable oil
150 g (5 oz/1 cup) peanuts, toasted and ground
about 2 teaspoons light brown sugar
salt

To make sauce, soak tamarind in 2 tablespoons hot water for 4 hours. Press firmly through a sieve. In blender, soak chillies in 2 tablespoons hot water for 10 minutes. Add lemon grass, garlic, shallots and galangal. Grind to a paste. Heat oil in a wok or small frying pan over medium-high heat. Add chilli mixture and fry, stirring, for 3 minutes. Add tamarind liquid, peanuts, and sugar and salt to taste. Simmer for 2-3 minutes. Set aside.

With point of a sharp knife, score 3 diagonal lines on both sides of each fish. Score each lengthways down backbone. Mix together turmeric and salt. Rub into fish, working mixture into cuts. Leave for 1 hour. In a wok or sauté pan over medium heat, heat oil to 180C (350F). Cook fish for 5-6 minutes each side until golden and crisp. Remove with fish slice and drain on absorbent kitchen paper. Serve hot, accompanied by lime wedges and sauce.

Serves 4.

SPICED FISH IN BANANA LEAVES

575 g (1¼ lb) white fish fillets
banana leaves (optional)
oil for brushing
SPICE PASTE:
6 shallots, chopped
2 cloves garlic, crushed
2 fresh red chillies, seeded and chopped
2.5 cm (1 in) piece fresh root ginger, chopped
4 candlenuts or cashew nuts
½ teaspoon tamarind paste (see page 11)
2 teaspoons each ground coriander and ground cumin
¼ teaspoon ground turmeric

To make spice paste, put all ingredients in a blender with a pinch salt and mix to a paste.

Cut fish into 10 x 5 cm (4 x 2 in) pieces 1 cm (½ in) thick. Coat top of each piece thickly with spice paste. If using banana leaves, hold them over a flame to soften. Oil leaves thoroughly and cut into pieces to wrap around pieces of fish (or do this with aluminium foil). Secure with wooden cocktail sticks or toothpicks.

Preheat barbecue or grill. Cook fish parcels for 8-10 minutes, turning halfway through. Serve with banana leaf or foil partially torn away to reveal fish, and with lime wedges.

Serves 4.

MARINATED GRILLED FISH

4 flat fish, such as plaice or dabs, each weighing about 350 g (12 oz)
4 large cloves garlic, cut into fine slivers
2.5 cm (1 in) piece fresh root ginger, cut into fine slivers
4 tablespoons groundnut (peanut) oil
4 tablespoons light soy sauce
1 tablespoon sesame oil
1 tablespoon rice wine
4 spring onions, thinly sliced

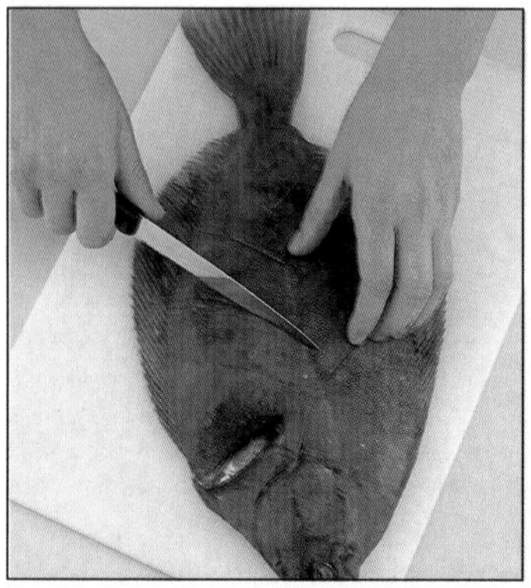

With the point of a sharp knife, cut 5 diagonal slashes, herringbone style, in both sides of each fish. Place in a shallow dish.

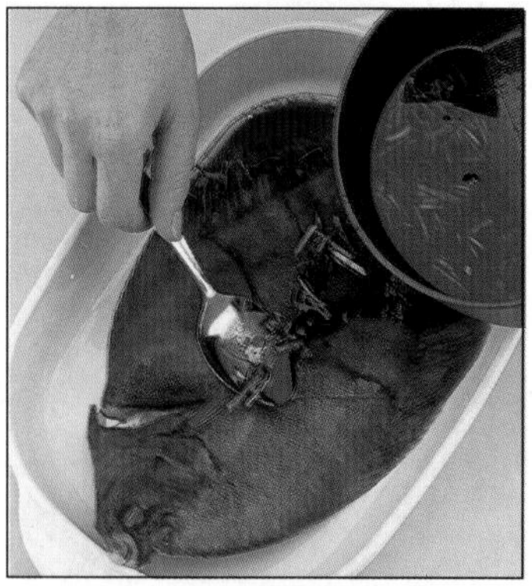

Put garlic, ginger, oil, soy sauce, sesame oil and rice wine in a small saucepan. Heat to simmering point and pour over fish, spooning marinade into slashes. Refrigerate for at least 1 hour, turning fish every 30 minutes.

Preheat grill. Lift fish from marinade and grill, pale skin side down, for 3 minutes. Turn carefully and grill for a further 1-2 minutes depending on thickness of fish. Grill in batches if necessary, keeping grilled fish warm. Reheat any remaining marinade and pour over fish. Scatter spring onions over and serve.

Serves 4.

SPICED SWEET & SOUR FISH

1 tablespoon cumin seeds
1 teaspoon coriander seeds
3 tablespoons vegetable oil
½ fresh red chilli, cored, seeded and chopped
3 cloves garlic, crushed
2 onions, chopped
2.5 cm (1 in) shrimp paste, roasted (see page 11)
3½ tablespoons lime juice
3 tablespoons dark soy sauce
brown sugar, to taste
2 whole fish, each weighing about 700 g (1½ lb)

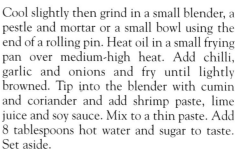

Heat cumin and coriander seeds in frying pan over medium-high heat until toasted, with a fragrant roasted aroma.

Cool slightly then grind in a small blender, a pestle and mortar or a small bowl using the end of a rolling pin. Heat oil in a small frying pan over medium-high heat. Add chilli, garlic and onions and fry until lightly browned. Tip into the blender with cumin and coriander and add shrimp paste, lime juice and soy sauce. Mix to a thin paste. Add 8 tablespoons hot water and sugar to taste. Set aside.

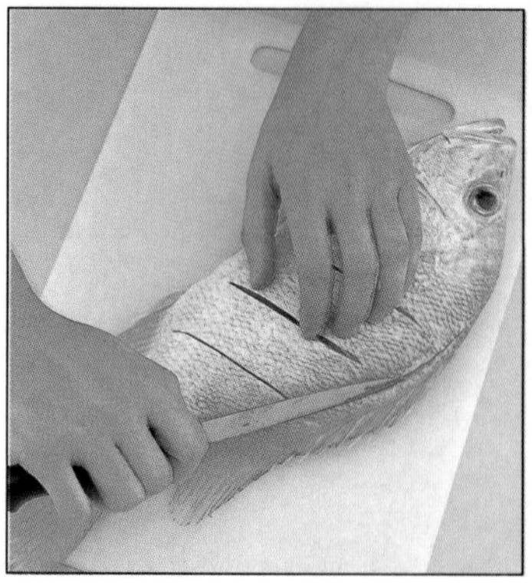

Preheat grill. Cut 3 deep slashes on both sides of each fish and score along backbone. Cook fish for 5-6 minutes on each side, depending on thickness. The flesh should just flake, when tested with point of a sharp knife, and the skin should be brown. Reheat sauce and pour some over each fish. Serve remaining sauce separately.

Serves 4-5.

SARAWAK MARINATED FISH

450 g (1 lb) very fresh white fish fillets, skinned and thinly sliced
85 ml (3 fl oz/⅓ cup) lime juice
2 fresh red chillies, cored, seeded and chopped
pinch salt
5 cm (2 in) piece fresh root ginger, grated
6 shallots, finely chopped
2 coriander sprigs, chopped
2 sprigs Chinese celery, or inner sticks celery, chopped

Put fish in a non-reactive dish. Pour over 3 tablespoons lime juice and leave for at least 30 minutes, stirring gently occasionally, until fish turns opaque.

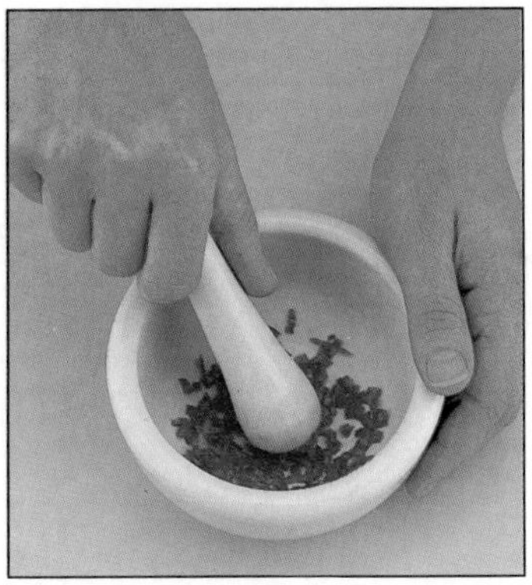

Meanwhile, in a mortar and using a pestle, pound chillies with a pinch of salt. Mix with remaining lime juice.

Drain lime juice from fish. Sprinkle ginger, shallots, coriander and celery over fish. Trickle chilli mixture evenly over fish and stir gently to mix ingredients together. Serve immediately.

Serves 4.

FISH STEAKS WITH CHILLI

5 dried red chillies, cored and seeded
½ small red pepper, chopped
5 shallots, chopped
4 cloves garlic, chopped
4 tablespoons vegetable oil
450 g (1 lb) fish steaks, such as cod, monkfish, salmon, snapper
coriander sprigs, to garnish
rice and lime juice, to serve

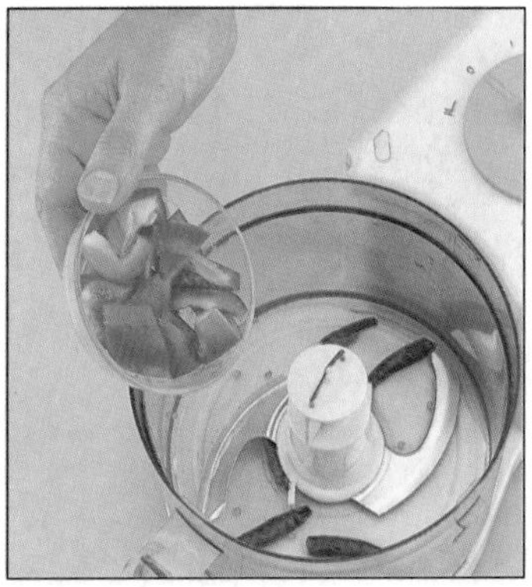

Put chillies in a blender. Pour 4 tablespoons hot water over and leave until softened. Add red pepper, shallots and garlic. Mix to a coarse paste.

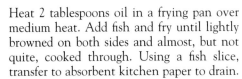

Heat 2 tablespoons oil in a frying pan over medium heat. Add fish and fry until lightly browned on both sides and almost, but not quite, cooked through. Using a fish slice, transfer to absorbent kitchen paper to drain.

Add remaining oil to pan. Add chilli paste and cook over medium-high heat for about 3 minutes until paste looks dryish. Stir in 2 tablespoons water. Lower heat, return fish to pan and baste with chilli paste. Cook gently for 1-2 minutes, basting with paste. Garnish with coriander, and serve with rice and with plenty of lime juice squeezed over.

Serves 3-4.

STIR-FRIED PRAWNS & GINGER

3 cloves garlic, crushed
4 cm (1½ in) piece fresh root ginger, thinly sliced
2 tablespoons vegetable oil
12-16 raw king prawns, peeled and deveined
2 red shallots, finely chopped
grated zest ½ kaffir lime
2 teaspoons fish sauce
3 spring onions, thinly sliced
lime juice, to serve
spring onion brushes (see page 14), to garnish

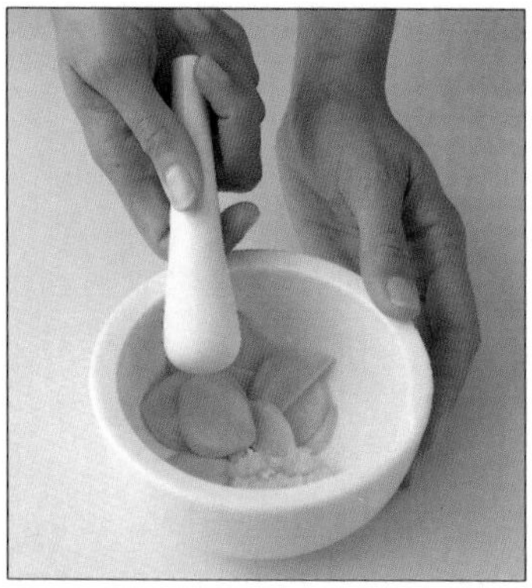

Using a pestle and mortar or small blender, pound or mix together garlic and ginger. In a wok, heat oil, add garlic paste and stir-fry for 2-3 minutes. Stir in prawns and shallots and stir-fry for 2 minutes.

Stir in lime zest, fish sauce and 3 tablespoons water. Allow to bubble for 1 minute until prawns become opaque and cooked through. Stir in spring onions, then remove from heat. Serve in a warmed dish, sprinkled with lime juice and garnished with spring onion brushes.

Serves 3-4.

PRAWNS IN COCONUT SAUCE

2 fresh red chillies, seeded and chopped
1 red onion, chopped
1 thick stalk lemon grass, chopped
2.5 cm (1 in) piece galangal, chopped
1 teaspoon ground turmeric
250 ml (8 fl oz/1 cup) coconut milk
14-16 raw king prawns, peeled and deveined
8 Thai holy basil leaves
2 teaspoons lime juice
1 teaspoon fish sauce
1 spring onion, including some green, cut into fine strips

Using a small blender, mix chillies, onion, lemon grass and galangal to a paste. Transfer to a wok and heat, stirring, for 2-3 minutes. Stir in turmeric and 115 ml (4 fl oz/½ cup) water, bring to the boil and simmer for 3-4 minutes until most of the water has evaporated.

Stir in coconut milk and prawns and cook gently, stirring occasionally, for about 4 minutes until prawns are just firm and pink. Stir in basil leaves, lime juice and fish sauce. Scatter over strips of spring onion to serve.

Serves 4.

PRAWNS WITH GARLIC

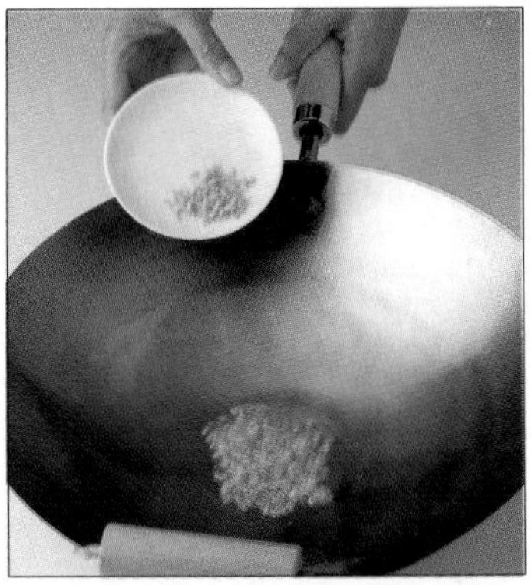

2 tablespoons vegetable oil
5 cloves garlic, chopped
0.5 cm (¼ in) slice fresh root ginger, very finely chopped
14-16 king prawns, peeled, tails left on
2 teaspoons fish sauce
2 tablespoons chopped coriander leaves
freshly ground black pepper
lettuce leaves, lime juice and diced cucumber, to serve

In a wok, heat oil, add garlic and fry until browned.

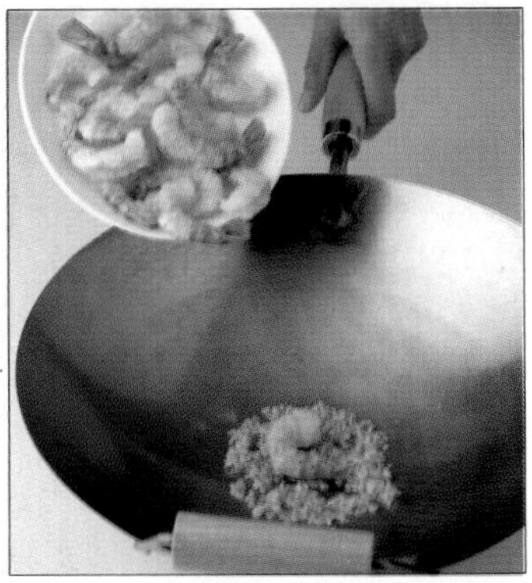

Stir in ginger, heat for 30 seconds, then add prawns and stir-fry for 2-3 minutes until beginning to turn opaque. Stir in fish sauce, coriander, 1-2 tablespoons water and plenty of black pepper. Simmer for 1-2 minutes.

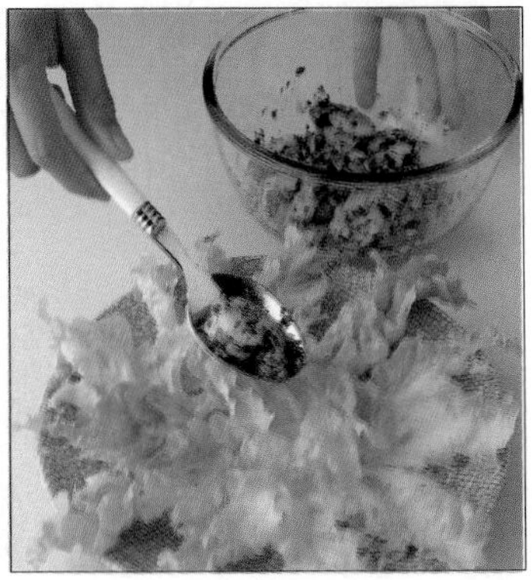

Serve prawns on a bed of lettuce leaves with lime juice squeezed over and scattered with cucumber.

Serves 4.

JACKETED PRAWNS

4 cm (1½ in) piece cucumber
Thai Dipping Sauce 1 (see page 231)
8 raw king prawns
vegetable oil for deep-frying
leaves from 1 coriander sprig, chopped
BATTER:
115 g (4 oz/⅔ cup) rice flour
3 tablespoons desiccated coconut
1 egg, separated
175 ml (6 fl oz/¾ cup) coconut milk
1 teaspoon fish sauce

Cut cucumber into quarters lengthways, remove and discard seeds, then thickly slice. Place in a small bowl and add dipping sauce. Set aside. Peel prawns, leaving tails on. Cut along back of each one and remove black spinal cord. Set prawns aside.

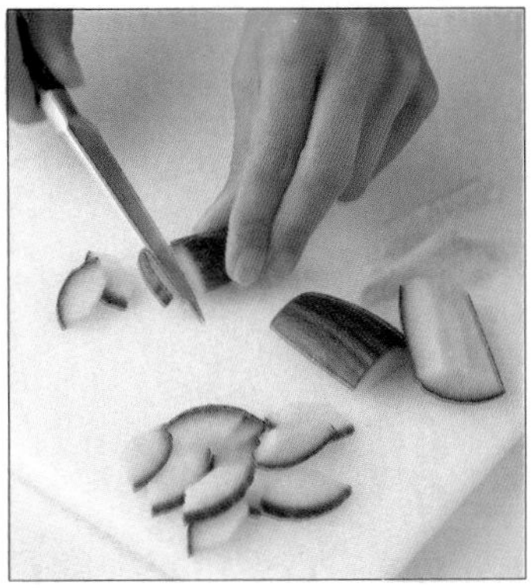

To make batter, in a bowl, stir together flour and coconut. Gradually stir in egg yolk, coconut milk and fish sauce. In a clean bowl, whisk egg white until stiff; fold into batter. In a wok, heat oil to 180C (350F). Dip prawns in batter to coat evenly. deep-fry in batches for 2-3 minutes until golden. Using a slotted spoon, transfer to absorbent kitchen paper. Keep warm while frying remainder. Add coriander to sauce and serve with prawns.

Serves 3-4.

PRAWN & CUCUMBER CURRY

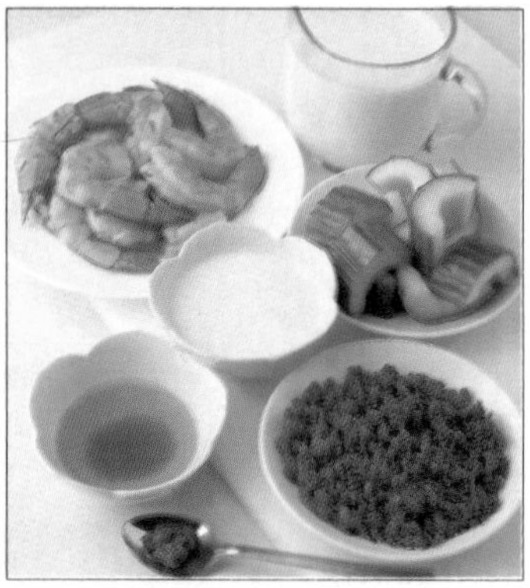

4 tablespoons coconut cream (see page 8)
3-4 tablespoons Red Curry Paste (see page 230)
225 g (8 oz) raw large peeled prawns
20 cm (8 in) length cucumber, halved lengthways, seeded and cut into 2 cm (¾ in) pieces
300 ml (10 fl oz/1¼ cups) coconut milk
2 tablespoons tamarind water (see page 11)
1 teaspoon crushed palm sugar
coriander leaves, to garnish

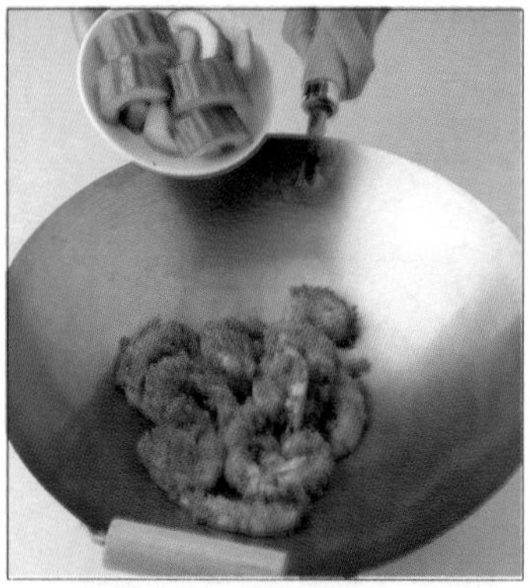

In a wok, heat coconut cream, stirring, until it boils, thickens and oil begins to form. Add curry paste. Stir in prawns to coat, then stir in cucumber. Add coconut milk, tamarind water and sugar.

Cook gently for about 3-4 minutes until prawns are just cooked through. Transfer to warmed serving dish and garnish with coriander.

Serves 3.

MUSSELS WITH BASIL

700 g (1½ lb) fresh mussels in shell, cleaned, bearded and rinsed
1 large clove garlic, chopped
7.5 cm (3 in) piece galangal, thickly sliced
2 stalks lemon grass, chopped
10 Thai holy basil sprigs
1 tablespoon fish sauce
Thai holy basil leaves, to garnish
Thai Dipping Sauce 2 (see page 232), to serve

Place mussels, garlic, galangal, lemon grass, basil sprigs and fish sauce in a large saucepan. Add water to a depth of 1 cm (½ in), cover pan and bring to the boil. Cook for about 5 minutes, shaking pan frequently, until mussels have opened; discard any that remain closed.

Transfer mussels to a large warmed bowl, or individual bowls, and strain over cooking liquid. Scatter over basil leaves. Serve with sauce to dip mussels into.

Serves 2-3.

FISH IN BANANA LEAF CUPS

85 g (3 oz) firm white fish, such as cod, hake, monkfish, very finely chopped
85 g (3 oz) cooked peeled prawns, very finely chopped
2-3 teaspoons Red Curry Paste (see page 230)
2 tablespoons ground peanuts
1 kaffir lime leaf, finely chopped
2 tablespoons coconut milk
1 egg
2 teaspoons fish sauce
leaf part ½ head Chinese leaves, finely shredded
2 banana leaf cups (see Note), if wished
2 teaspoons coconut cream (see page 8)
strips fresh red chilli, to garnish

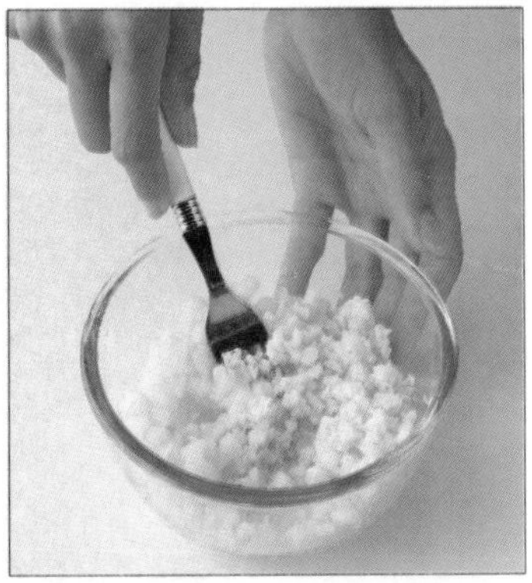

In a bowl, mix fish and prawns together using a fork. Mix in curry paste, peanuts and lime leaf. In a small bowl, mix together coconut milk, egg and fish sauce. Stir into fish mixture to evenly combine. Set aside for 30 minutes. Divide Chinese leaves between banana leaf cups, or heatproof individual dishes, to make a fine layer. Stir fish mixture and divide between cups or dishes.

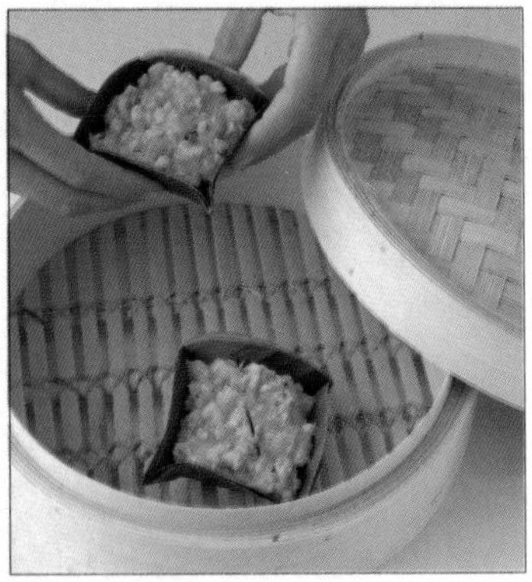

Place in a steaming basket over a saucepan of boiling water. Cover and steam for about 15 minutes until just set in centre. Place on a warmed serving plate, trickle coconut cream over top and garnish with strips of red chilli.

Serves 2.

Note: To make a banana leaf cup, cut two 10 cm (4 in) circles from banana leaf and place dull sides together. Form a 1 cm (½ in) pleat about 4 cm (1½ in) deep in the edge of circle and staple together. Repeat to make 4 corners.

FISH WITH CHILLI SAUCE

1 flat fish, such as pomfret, plump plaice or lemon sole, gutted and cleaned
vegetable oil for brushing
2 teaspoons vegetable oil
3 small dried red chillies, halved lengthways
2 cloves garlic, finely chopped
1 teaspoon fish sauce
85 ml (3 fl oz/⅓ cup) tamarind water (see page 11)
1 teaspoon crushed palm sugar

Preheat grill. Brush fish lightly with oil, then grill for about 4 minutes on each side until lightly coloured and flesh flakes when tested with the point of a knife. Using a fish slice, transfer to a warmed plate and keep warm.

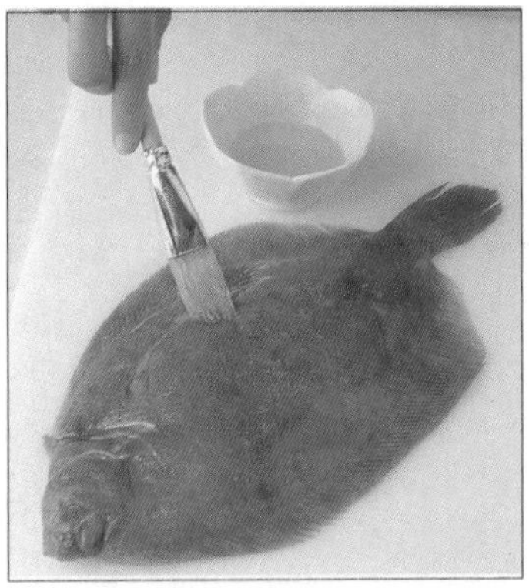

In a small saucepan, heat vegetable oil, add chillies and garlic and cook for 1 minute. Stir in fish sauce, tamarind water and palm sugar and simmer for 2-3 minutes until lightly thickened. Spoon over fish.

Serves 2.

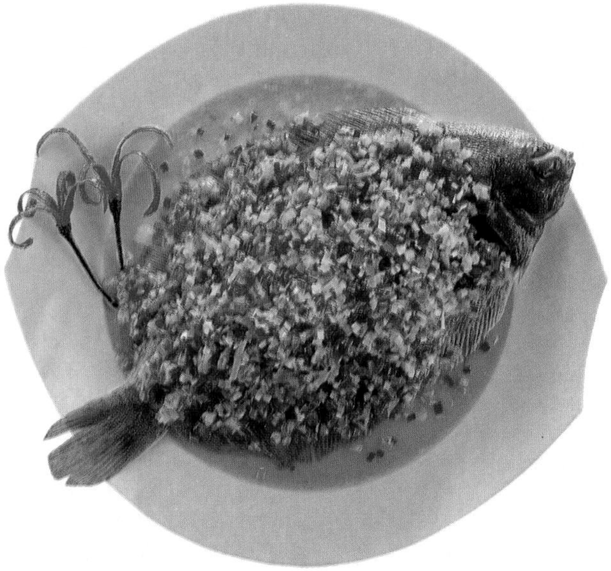

FISH WITH LEMON GRASS

2 tablespoons vegetable oil
1 flat fish, such as pomfret, plump lemon sole or plaice, gutted and cleaned
4 cloves garlic, finely chopped
2 fresh red chillies, seeded and finely chopped
1 red shallot, chopped
4½ tablespoons lime juice
½ teaspoon crushed palm sugar
1½ tablespoons finely chopped lemon grass
2 teaspoons fish sauce
chilli flowers (see page 14), to garnish

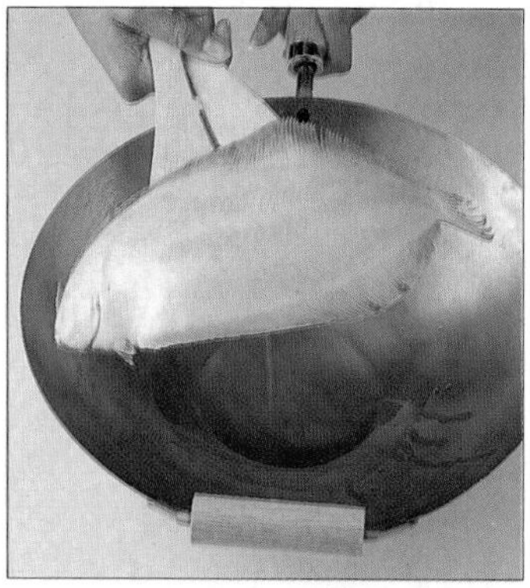

In a wok, heat oil, add fish, skin-side down first, and cook for 3-5 minutes on each side until lightly browned and cooked. Using a fish slice, transfer to a warmed serving plate, cover and keep warm. Add garlic to wok and fry, stirring occasionally, until browned.

Stir in chillies, shallot, lime juice, palm sugar, lemon grass and fish sauce. Allow to simmer gently for 1-2 minutes. Pour over fish and garnish with chilli flowers.

Serves 2.

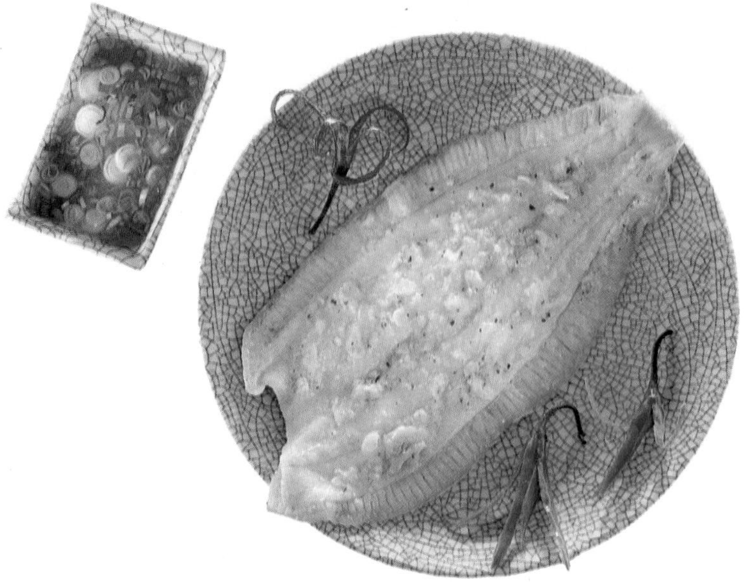

CORIANDER FISH & GARLIC

6 coriander roots, chopped
3 large cloves garlic, chopped
5 black peppercorns, crushed
2 fish fillets, such as trout or plaice
2 pieces banana leaf (optional)
3 tablespoons lime juice
½ teaspoon crushed palm sugar
1 spring onion, finely chopped
½ small fresh green chilli, seeded and thinly sliced
½ small fresh red chilli, seeded and thinly sliced
chilli flowers (see page 14), to garnish

Using a pestle and mortar or small blender, briefly mix together coriander roots, garlic and peppercorns. Spread evenly over inside of fish fillets; set aside for 30 minutes.

Wrap fish in banana leaves or pieces of aluminium foil, securing leaf with wooden cocktail stick (toothpick), or folding edges of foil tightly together. Grill for about 8 minutes. Meanwhile, in a bowl, stir together lime juice and sugar, then stir in spring onion and chillies. Serve with fish. Garnish with chilli flowers.

Serves 2.

FISH WITH MUSHROOM SAUCE

plain flour for coating
salt and freshly ground black pepper
1 whole flat fish, such as pomfret, plump lemon sole or plaice, weighing about 700 g (1½ lb), gutted and cleaned
2 tablespoons vegetable oil plus extra for deep-frying
3 cloves garlic, thinly sliced
1 small onion, halved and thinly sliced
4.5 cm (1¾ in) piece fresh root ginger, finely chopped
115 g (4 oz) shiitake mushrooms, sliced
2 teaspoons fish sauce
3 spring onions, sliced
spring onion brushes (see page 14), to garnish

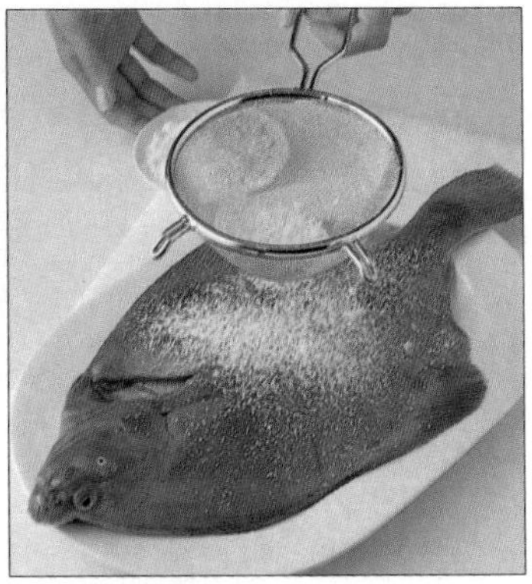

Season flour with salt and pepper, then use to lightly dust fish. Heat oil in a large deep-fat fryer to 180C (350F), add fish and cook for 4-5 minutes, turning halfway through, until crisp and browned.

Meanwhile, heat 2 tablespoons oil in a wok, add garlic, onion and ginger and cook, stirring occasionally, for 2 minutes. Add mushrooms and stir-fry for 2 minutes. Stir in fish sauce, 3-4 tablespoons water and spring onions. Simmer briefly. Using a fish slice, transfer fish to absorbent kitchen paper to drain. Transfer fish to a warmed serving plate and spoon over sauce. Garnish with spring onion brushes.

Serves 2.

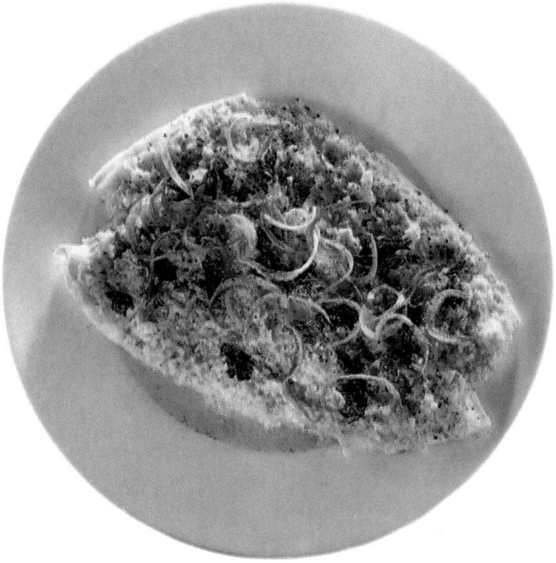

COCONUT FISH WITH GALANGAL

4 tablespoons vegetable oil
1 shallot, chopped
4 cm (1½ in) piece galangal, finely chopped
2 stalks lemon grass, finely chopped
1 small fresh red chilli, seeded and chopped
115 ml (4 fl oz/½ cup) coconut milk
2 teaspoons fish sauce
5 coriander sprigs
about 350 g (12 oz) white fish fillets, such as halibut or red snapper
1 small onion, sliced
freshly ground black pepper

In a wok, heat 1 tablespoon oil, add shallot, galangal, lemon grass and chilli. Stir for 3 minutes until lightly coloured. Transfer to a small blender, add coconut milk, fish sauce and stalks from coriander sprigs and process until well mixed. Place fish in a heatproof, shallow round dish that fits over a saucepan, and pour over spice sauce. Cover dish, place over pan of boiling water and steam for 8-10 minutes until flesh flakes.

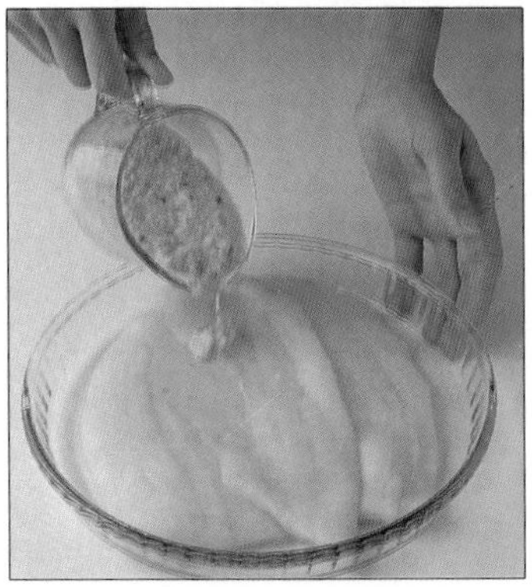

Meanwhile, heat remaining oil in a wok over moderate heat, add onion and cook, stirring occasionally, until browned. Using a slotted spoon, transfer to absorbent kitchen paper. Add coriander leaves to oil and fry for a few seconds. Using a slotted spoon, transfer to absorbent kitchen paper to drain. Scatter fried onions and coriander over fish and grind over plenty of black pepper.

Serves 3-4.

CURRIED PRAWNS

2 tablespoons vegetable oil
1 teaspoon chopped garlic
2 shallots, or 1 small onion, chopped
2-3 tablespoons mild curry powder
250 ml (9 fl oz/1 cup) Vietnamese Hot Sauce (see page 234)
250 ml (9 fl oz/1 cup) chicken stock or water
250 ml (9 fl oz/1 cup) coconut milk
300 g (10 oz) red potatoes, cut into chunks
2-3 carrots, sliced
3-4 lime or bay leaves
2 tablespoons fish sauce
300 g (10 oz) raw peeled prawns
½ teaspoon salt
1 teaspoon sugar
coriander sprigs, to garnish

Heat oil in a pan or pot and stir-fry garlic and shallots or onion for about 30 seconds. Blend in curry powder and cook for 30 seconds or until fragrant. Add Vietnamese Hot Sauce, stock or water and coconut milk then bring to the boil, stirring constantly. Add potatoes, carrots, lime or bay leaves and fish sauce, cover and simmer gently for 25-30 minutes.

Add prawns, salt and sugar, then increase the heat and cook for 5-6 minutes, stirring continuously. Serve at once, garnished with coriander sprigs.

Serves 4.

STIR-FRIED PRAWNS

3 tablespoons vegetable oil
1 teaspoon chopped garlic
½ teaspoon chopped fresh root ginger
1 tablespoon chopped spring onion
300 g (10 oz) raw peeled prawns, halved lengthways
115 g (4 oz) straw mushrooms, halved lengthways
55 g (2 oz) water chestnuts, sliced
3 tablespoons fish sauce
1 tablespoon sugar
about 2-3 tablespoons chicken stock or water
1 teaspoon chilli sauce (optional)
salt and freshly ground black pepper
coriander sprigs, to garnish

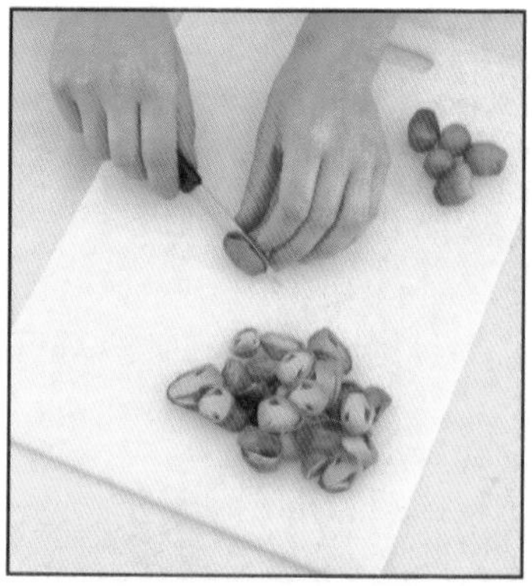

Heat oil in a wok or pan and stir-fry garlic, ginger and spring onion for about 20 seconds. Add prawns, mushrooms and water chestnuts and stir-fry for about 2 minutes.

Add fish sauce and sugar, stir for a few times, then add stock or water. Bring to the boil and stir for another minute or so. Finally, add chilli sauce, if using, and season with salt and pepper. Garnish with coriander sprigs and serve at once.

Serves 4.

SCALLOPS WITH VEGETABLES

3 tablespoons vegetable oil
1 teaspoon chopped garlic
1-2 small red chillies, seeded and chopped
2 shallots or 1 small onion, chopped
55 g (2 oz) mangetout
1 small carrot, thinly sliced
225 g (8 oz) fresh scallops, sliced
55 g (2 oz) sliced bamboo shoots
2 tablespoons black fungus, soaked and sliced
2-3 spring onions, cut into short sections
2 tablespoons fish sauce
1 teaspoon sugar
about 2-3 tablespoons chicken stock or water
1 tablespoon oyster sauce
salt and freshly ground black pepper
coriander sprigs, to garnish

Heat oil in a wok or pan and stir-fry garlic, chillies and shallots or onion for about 20 seconds. Add mangetout and carrot and stir-fry for about 20 minutes. Add scallops, bamboo shoots, black fungus and spring onions and stir-fry for 1 minute.

Add fish sauce and sugar, blend well and stir for 1 more minute, then add stock or water. Bring to the boil and stir for a few more seconds. Add oyster sauce and season with salt and pepper. Garnish with coriander sprigs and serve at once.

Serves 4.

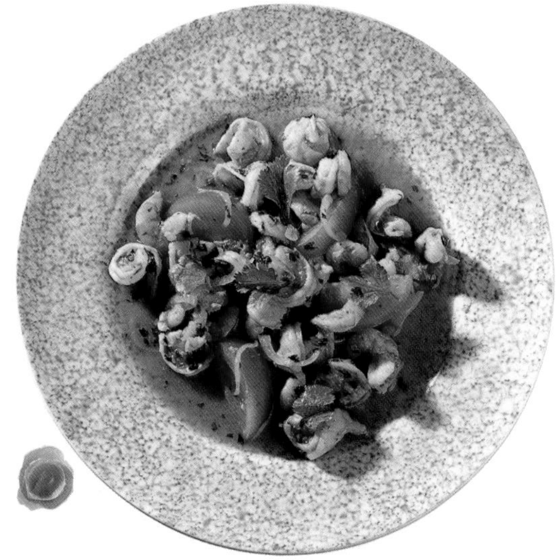

PRAWNS WITH LEMON GRASS

2 cloves garlic, chopped
1 tablespoon chopped coriander
2 tablespoons chopped lemon grass
½ teaspoon black or white peppercorns
3 tablespoons vegetable oil
350-400 g (12-14 oz) raw peeled prawns, cut in half lengthways if large
2 shallots or 1 small onion, sliced
2-3 small fresh chillies, seeded and chopped
2-3 tomatoes, cut into wedges
1 tablespoon fish sauce
1 tablespoon oyster sauce
2-3 tablespoons chicken stock or water
coriander sprigs, to garnish

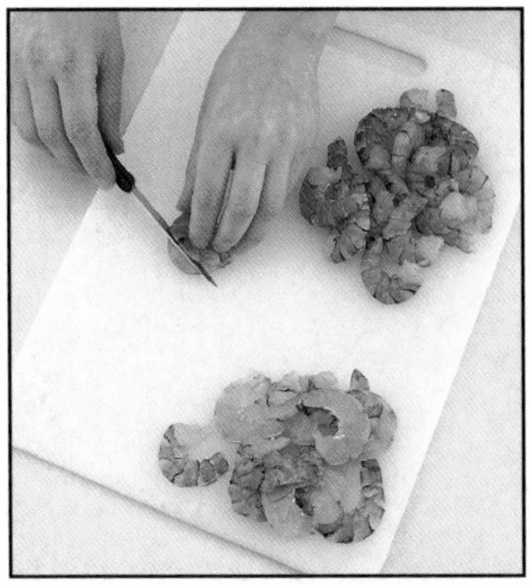

Using a pestle and mortar, pound garlic, coriander, lemon grass and peppercorns to a paste. Heat oil in a wok, or frying pan and stir-fry spicy paste for 15-20 seconds until fragrant. Add prawns, shallots or onion, chillies and tomatoes and stir-fry for 2-3 minutes.

Add fish sauce, oyster sauce and stock or water, bring to the boil and simmer for 2-3 minutes. Serve garnished with coriander sprigs.

Serves 4.

SPICY CRAB

1 clove garlic, chopped
2 shallots or white parts 3-4 spring onions, chopped
1 teaspoon chopped fresh root ginger
1 tablespoon chopped lemon grass
2-3 tablespoons vegetable oil
1 teaspoon chilli sauce
1 tablespoon sugar
3-4 tablespoons coconut milk
about 450 ml (16 fl oz/2 cups) chicken stock
3 tablespoons fish sauce
2 tablespoons lime juice or vinegar
meat from 1 large or 2 medium cooked crabs, cut into small pieces
salt and freshly ground black pepper
coriander sprigs, to garnish

Using a pestle and mortar, pound garlic, shallots or spring onions, ginger, and lemon grass to a fine paste. Heat oil in clay pot or flameproof casserole, add garlic mixture, chilli sauce and sugar and stir-fry for about 1 minute. Add coconut milk, stock, fish sauce and lime juice or vinegar and bring to the boil.

Add crab pieces and season with salt and pepper. Blend well and cook for 3-4 minutes, stirring constantly, then serve hot, garnished with coriander sprigs.

Serves 4.

Note: Uncooked crabs can be used for this dish, but increase cooking time by about 8-10 minutes.

STUFFED SQUID

25 g (1 oz) bean thread vermicelli, soaked then cut into short strands
15 g (½ oz) black fungus, soaked then shredded
225 g (8 oz) minced lean pork
salt and ground black pepper
2 spring onions, chopped
1 tablespoon fish sauce
1 egg, beaten
8-12 small squid, headless, cleaned (see page 194)
1-2 tablespoons vegetable oil
lettuce leaves
Spicy Fish Sauce (see page 233), as a dip

In a bowl, mix vermicelli, fungus, pork, salt, pepper, spring onions, fish sauce and egg.

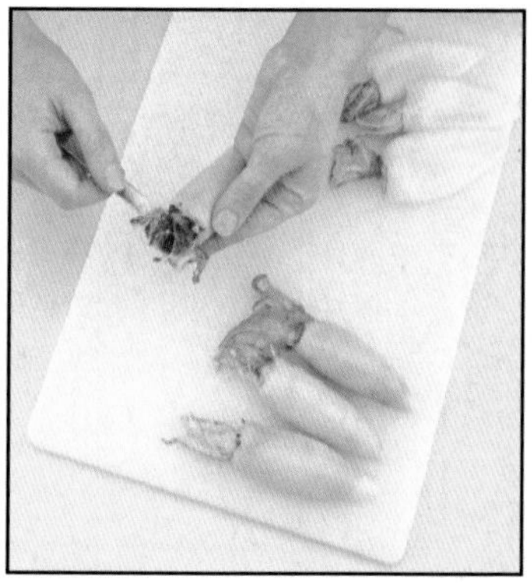

Fill squid with stuffing mixture, then steam them for 25-30 minutes.

Remove squid from the steamer. Heat oil in a frying pan and fry stuffed squid for 3-4 minutes, turning once. Serve hot on a bed of lettuce with Spicy Fish Sauce as a dip.

Serves 4-6.

Note: Squid are sometimes available ready cleaned, with tentacles still attached. If wished, the squid can be steamed in advance and then fried just before serving.

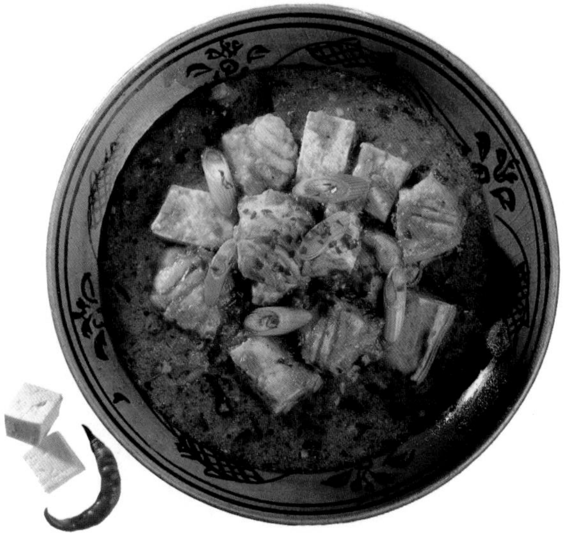

FISH IN CURRY SAUCE

450 g (1 lb) fish fillet or steak, such as halibut, cod or monkfish, cut into bite-sized pieces
freshly ground black pepper
2 tablespoons fish sauce
1 tablespoon sugar
1 tablespoon vegetable oil
1 clove garlic, finely chopped
2-3 shallots, finely chopped
2-3 tablespoons mild curry powder
250 ml (9 fl oz/1 cup) Vietnamese Hot Sauce (see page 234)
350 ml (12 fl oz/1½ cups) chicken stock or water
1 cake tofu, cut into small cubes
½ teaspoon salt
2-3 spring onions, cut into short lengths, to garnish
1-2 small red chillies, seeded and chopped (optional)

In a dish, marinate fish with pepper, fish sauce and sugar for 15-20 minutes. Heat oil in a saucepan and stir-fry garlic and shallots for about 1 minute. Add curry powder and hot sauce and cook for another minute, stirring constantly. Add stock or water, blend well and bring to the boil.

Add fish, tofu pieces and salt, stir very gently, then reduce heat, cover and simmer for 10 minutes. Serve hot, garnished with spring onions and chillies, if using.

Serves 4.

VIETNAMESE MIXED SEAFOOD

3 tablespoons vegetable oil
1 teaspoon minced garlic
2 shallots, chopped
115 g (4 oz) fish fillet, cut into bite-sized pieces
115 g (4 oz) prepared squid
115 g (4 oz) raw peeled prawns
115 g (4 oz) fresh scallops
115 g (4 oz) crab meat
4 tablespoons Sweet & Sour Sauce or Vietnamese Hot Sauce (see page 234)
3 tablespoons fish sauce
3-4 tablespoons chicken stock or water
2 spring onions, thinly sliced
freshly ground black pepper

Heat oil in a clay pot or flameproof casserole and stir-fry garlic and shallots for about 1 minute, or until fragrant. Add seafood and stir-fry very gently so that fish fillet does not break up. Cook for 2-3 minutes, then add Sweet and Sour Sauce or Vietnamese Hot Sauce and fish sauce with stock or water. Blend well and bring to the boil.

Cover and simmer gently for 3-4 minutes, then remove the lid and turn off the heat. Garnish with spring onions and pepper and serve hot straight from the pot.

Serves 4.

Variation: It is not essential to use as many as 5 different types of fish for this dish; if preferred, use any combination of 2 or 3 types.

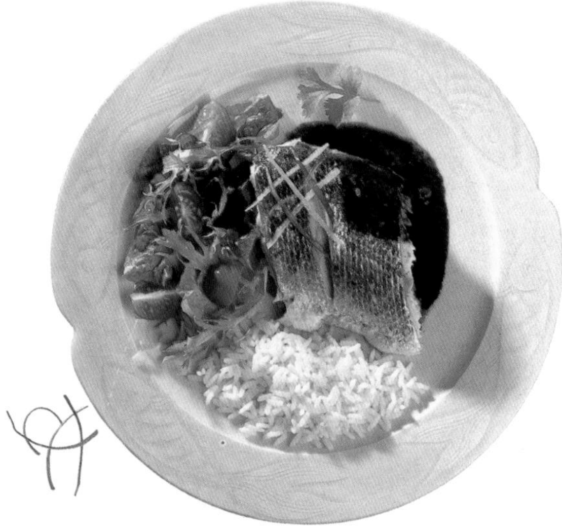

VIETNAMESE STEAMED FISH

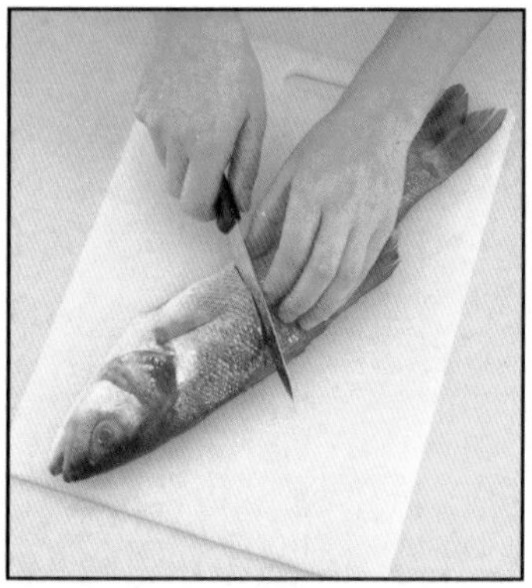

1 whole fish, such as sea bass, grey mullet or grouper, weighing about 900 g (2 lb), cleaned
salt and freshly ground black pepper
1 teaspoon sugar
1 teaspoon chopped fresh root ginger
1 tablespoon each chopped white and green parts spring onion
1 tablespoon fish sauce
2 teaspoons sesame oil
1 tablespoon shredded fresh root ginger
1 tablespoon vegetable oil
1 tablespoon black bean sauce
1 tablespoon soy sauce
2 small fresh red chillies, seeded and shredded
coriander sprigs, to garnish

Score fish on both sides at 2.5 cm (1 in) intervals. Rub inside and out with salt and pepper, then marinate in a shallow dish with sugar, ginger, white parts of spring onions, fish sauce and sesame oil for 30 minutes. Place fish with marinade in a hot steamer, or on a rack inside a wok, cover and steam for 15-20 minutes.

Remove dish from the steamer or wok, place ginger and green part of spring onions on top of fish. Heat vegetable oil in a small saucepan, add black bean sauce, soy sauce and chillies and stir-fry for 30 seconds, then drizzle it over fish. Garnish with coriander and serve with rice and a salad.

Serves 4.

Note: If fish is too big to fit into your steamer or wok, cut it in half crossways and re-assemble on a warmed plate to serve.

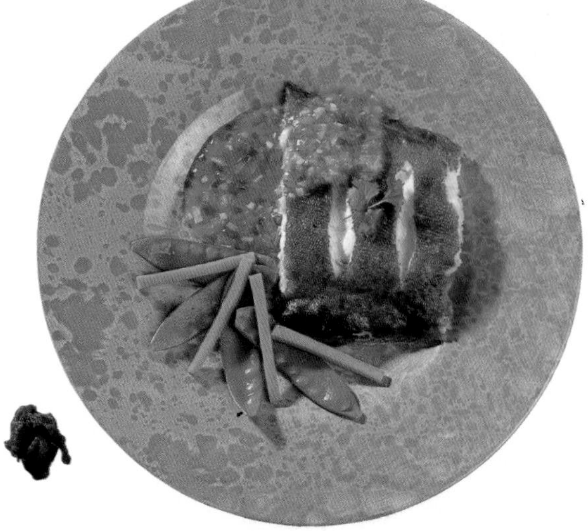

GRILLED FLAT FISH

575 g (1¼ lb) flat fish, such as plaice, cleaned
salt and freshly ground black pepper
1 tablespoon vegetable oil, plus extra for brushing
½ teaspoon minced garlic
½ teaspoon chopped fresh root ginger
2 shallots, finely chopped
2-3 small fresh red chillies, seeded and chopped
1 tablespoon chopped spring onion
2 tablespoons fish sauce
1 teaspoon sugar
1 tablespoon tamarind water or lime juice
2-3 tablespoons chicken stock or water
2 teaspoons cornflour

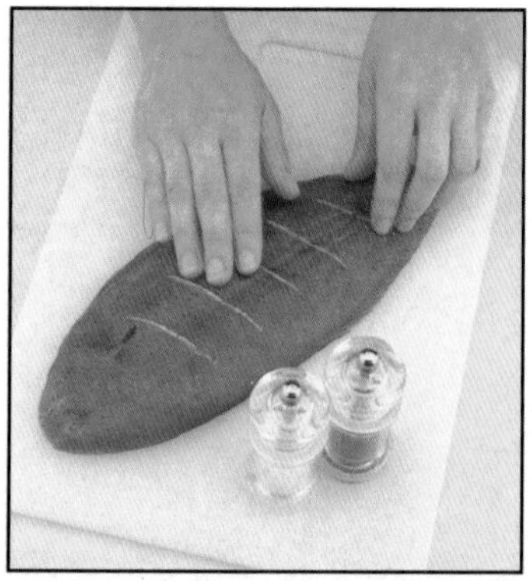

Score both sides of fish at 2.5 cm (1 in) intervals and rub with salt and pepper. Leave fish to stand for 25 minutes. Meanwhile, preheat grill. Brush both sides of fish with oil and grill under a hot grill for about 4 minutes each side until lightly brown but not burnt. Place on a warmed serving dish.

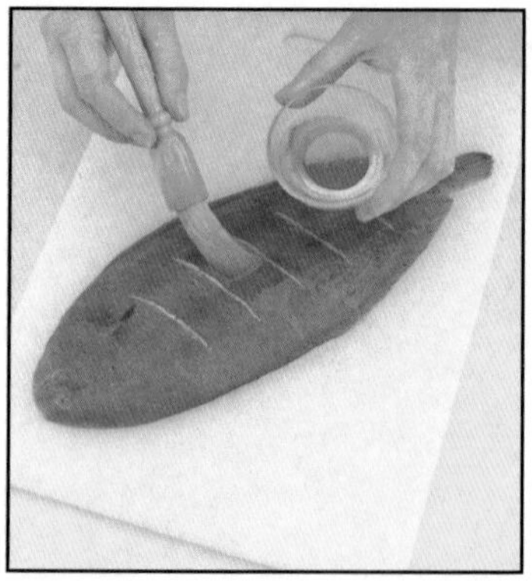

Heat oil in a small pan and stir-fry garlic, ginger, shallots, chillies and spring onion for 1 minute, then add fish sauce, sugar, tamarind water or lime juice and stock or water. Bring to the boil and simmer for 30 seconds. Mix cornflour with 1 tablespoon water and stir into sauce to thicken. Pour sauce over fish.

Serves 2.

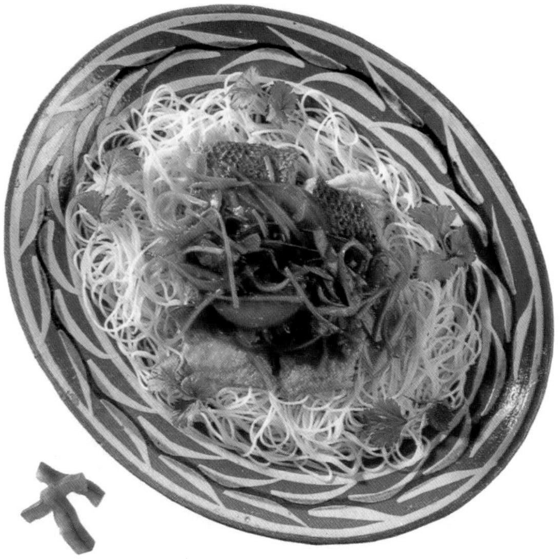

SWEET & SOUR FISH

1 (900 g/2 lb) whole fish, such as sea bass, grey mullet or carp, cleaned
salt and freshly ground black pepper
vegetable oil for deep-frying
about 2 tablespoons plain flour
1 small onion, shredded
1 small carrot, thinly shredded
1 small green pepper, seeded and thinly shredded
2 tomatoes, cut into small wedges
2 tablespoons fish sauce
250 ml (9 fl oz/1 cup) Sweet & Sour Sauce (see page 234)
about 115 ml (4 fl oz/½ cup) stock or water
1 teaspoon sesame oil (optional)
coriander sprigs, to garnish

Score both sides of fish at 2.5 cm (1 in) intervals. Rub fish inside and out with salt and pepper, then leave to stand for 15-20 minutes. Heat oil in a wok or deep-fat fryer to 180C (350F). Coat fish with flour and deep-fry for 3-4 minutes on each side until golden. Remove and drain on absorbent kitchen paper, then place fish on a warmed serving platter.

Pour off all but about 1 tablespoon oil from the wok, add onion, carrot, green pepper and tomatoes. Stir-fry for about 1 minute, then add fish sauce, Sweet and Sour Sauce and stock or water. Bring to the boil, then add sesame oil, if using. Pour sauce over fish, garnish with coriander and serve with rice vermicelli.

Serves 4.

Variation: Fish fillet or steak can be cooked in the same way.

FRIED FISH FILLET

450 g (1 lb) firm white fish fillet, such as halibut, cod, haddock or monkfish, cut into 2 cm (¾ in) pieces
salt and freshly ground black pepper
1 egg, beaten
3 tablespoons plain flour mixed with 2 tablespoons water
vegetable oil for deep-frying
fresh Thai holy basil and coriander sprigs, to garnish
Spicy Fish Sauce (see page 233), to serve

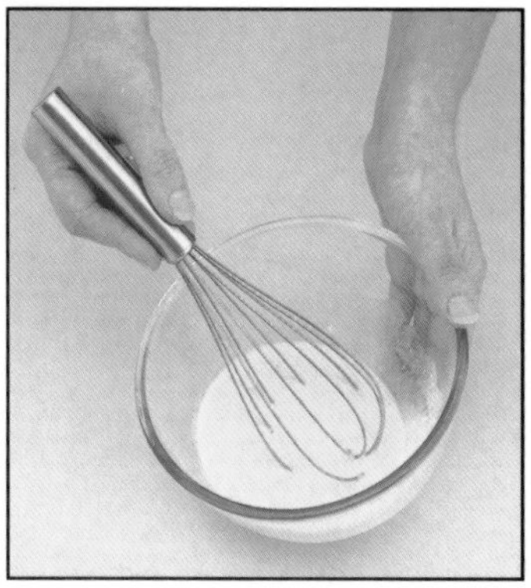

In a dish, season fish with salt and pepper and leave for 25-30 minutes. Make a batter by blending egg with flour and water paste.

Heat oil in a wok or deep-fat fryer to 180C (350F). Coat fish pieces with batter and deep-fry, in batches, for 3-4 minutes until golden. Remove and drain on absorbent kitchen paper.

Place fish pieces on a warmed serving dish with garnishes. Serve at once with Spicy Fish Sauce as a dip.

Serves 4.

Variation: A whole fish, boned, skinned and coated in batter, can be deep-fried first then cut into bite-sized pieces for serving.

TEMPURA

4 raw king prawns or 8 medium prawns
350-400 g (12-14 oz) whiting fillets
plain flour for coating
4-8 fresh shiitake or button mushrooms
8 asparagus tips or okra
vegetable oil for deep-frying
grated daikon, to garnish
fresh root ginger, to garnish

BATTER:
1 egg yolk, beaten
200 ml (7 fl oz/scant 1 cup) ice cold water
200 g (7 oz/scant 1 cup) plain flour, sifted

DIPPING SAUCE:
200 ml (7 fl oz/scant 1 cup) dashi (see page 29)
55 ml (2 fl oz/¼ cup) mirin
85 ml (3 fl oz/⅓ cup) soy sauce

Peel prawns, retaining tail shell, and devein. Make a few slits along the belly to prevent curling during cooking. Cut whiting fillets into pieces about 5 cm (2 in) long and roll in plain flour. If mushrooms are large, cut them in half. Heat oil for deep-frying to 170C (340F). Meanwhile, prepare batter: lightly mix egg yolk with ice cold water and add plain flour at once. Using chopsticks or a fork, very lightly fold in flour with just 4-5 strokes. The batter should be loosely mixed but still very lumpy.

Deep-fry asparagus tips or okra without any batter for 2-3 minutes, then drain on a wire rack. Dip mushrooms, prawns (one at a time, holding by tail) and whiting fillets in batter. Deep-fry one at a time in this order for 1-3 minutes until light golden. Drain them on the rack, then arrange one quarter of each on absorbent kitchen paper on individual plates. Boil dashi, mirin and soy sauce in a pan and pour into small individual bowls. Serve garnished with daikon and ginger.

Serves 4.

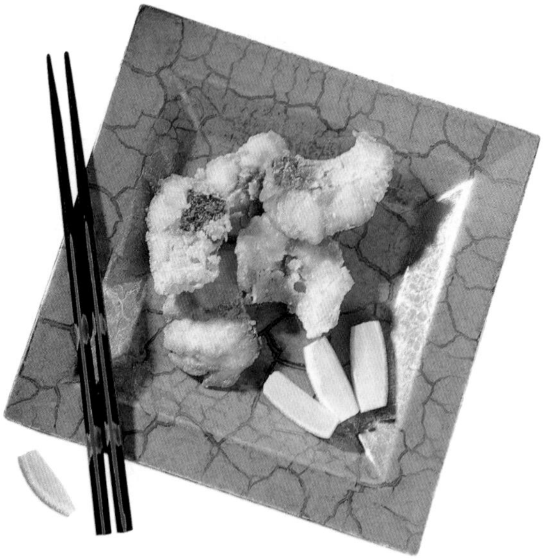

MACKEREL TATSUTA FRY

700 g (1½ lb) mackerel, filleted
115 g (4 oz/1 cup) cornflour
vegetable oil for deep-frying
lemon wedges, to garnish

MARINADE:
4 tablespoons sake
2 tablespoons soy sauce
2.5 cm (1 in) piece fresh root ginger, peeled and grated

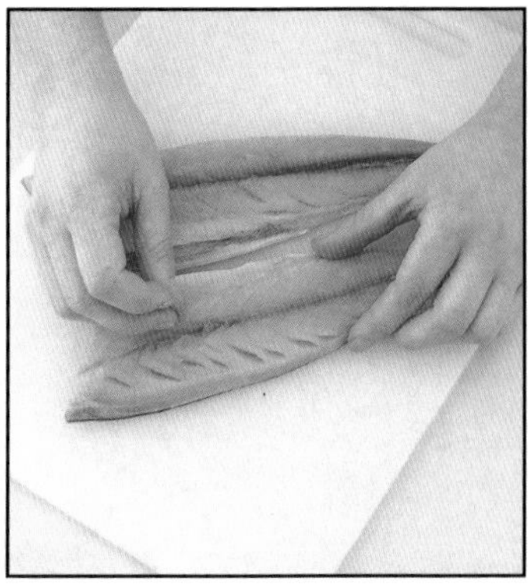

Remove large bones from mackerel fillets. Slice fillets crossways into bite-sized pieces, inserting the blade diagonally.

To make marinade, combine sake, soy sauce and ginger in a mixing bowl. Add mackerel pieces, turning to coat with marinade, then leave to marinate for 30 minutes. Drain and toss mackerel in cornflour to dust thoroughly.

Heat oil in a wok or a deep-frying pan to 160C (325F). Slide mackerel pieces into hot oil, a few pieces at a time, and fry for 2-3 minutes until golden brown, turning 2-3 times. Remove from oil and drain on a wire rack. Arrange a quarter of the fried mackerel pieces on each of 4 individual plates, on folded absorbent kitchen paper if wished. Alternatively, heap all the fish in the centre of a bamboo basket tray. Garnish with lemon wedges and serve at once.

Serves 4.

SALMON & NANBAN SAUCE

450 g (1 lb) salmon fillet, descaled
pinch salt
plain flour for coating
vegetable oil for deep-frying
3 spring onions, shredded, to garnish
NANBAN SAUCE:
4 tablespoons soy sauce
3 tablespoons rice vinegar
1½ tablespoons sake
2 teaspoons sugar
4½ tablespoons dashi (see page 29)
1-2 dried or fresh red chillies, seeded and chopped

Cut salmon fillet, with skin on, into 12 pieces and sprinkle with salt.

To make sauce, combine soy sauce, rice vinegar, sake, sugar, dashi and chillies in a saucepan and bring to the boil. Leave to cool. Pat dry salmon pieces with absorbent kitchen paper and dredge in plain flour. Heat oil in a wok or a deep-frying pan to 170C (340F). Shake off any excess flour from salmon pieces and deep-fry for 3-4 minutes until golden brown. Drain on a wire rack.

Transfer fried salmon pieces to a large serving plate and spread shredded spring onion on top. Pour over sauce and serve immediately.

Serves 4.

SWORDFISH TERIYAKI

2-3 swordfish steaks, each weighing about 225 g (8 oz)
6 tablespoons soy sauce
2 tablespoons sake
3 tablespoons mirin
4-5 fresh mint leaves, chopped
vegetable oil for frying
watercress sprigs, to garnish

Slice swordfish steaks in half horizontally to make a thickness of 1 cm (½ in), then cut into 6 x 4 cm (2½ x 1½ in) pieces. In a bowl, mix soy sauce, sake, mirin and mint. Add fish, mix well and leave to marinate for 30-40 minutes, turning over occasionally.

Heat a frying pan and spread a little oil evenly over the base. Drain fish pieces, reserving marinade, and fry a few pieces at a time over high heat until both sides become dark brown.

When all swordfish pieces are cooked, return them to the frying pan. Pour over marinade, gently mix in and remove from heat. Divide fish between 4 individual plates or heap it in the centre of a serving plate. Garnish with sprigs of watercress and serve at once.

Serves 4.

TOFU & FISH HOT POT

500 g (1 lb 2 oz) (2 cakes) tofu
250 g (9 oz) white fish or fillets, such as cod
4 Chinese leaves
55 g (2 oz) coriander leaves and/or 200 g (7 oz) spinach, trimmed
2-3 spring onions, finely chopped, to serve
SOUP:
15 cm (6 in) piece dried konbu (kelp) (optional)
500 ml (18 fl oz/2¼ cups) dashi (see page 29)
3 tablespoons soy sauce
½ tablespoon sugar

Cut tofu into bite-sized cubes and fish steaks or fillets into chunks with bone and skin still on.

Cut Chinese leaves in half lengthways and then crossways into 2.5 cm (1 in) long pieces. Chop coriander leaves and/or spinach roughly into 5 cm (2 in) lengths.

To make soup, put konbu in a pot (ideally a clay pot or enamelled casserole) and add dashi, soy sauce and sugar. Bring to the boil and then add some of each of the prepared ingredients. When it begins to boil again, transfer pot to a portable gas ring or electric hotplate on the dining table. Diners may then serve themselves to some soup and ingredients in individual bowls, sprinkled with chopped spring onion.

Serves 4.

ISHIKARI HOT POT

4 salmon steaks, scaled, skin left on
1 onion
2 potatoes
1-2 carrots
4-8 fresh shiitake or button mushrooms
55 g (2 oz) coriander leaves or watercress
250 g (9 oz) (1 cake) firm tofu
300 g (10 oz) (1 cake) konnyaku (optional)
25 g (1 oz/2 tablespoons) butter
10 cm (4 in) piece dried konbu (kelp) (optional)
3-5 tablespoons miso
2 spring onions, finely chopped, to serve

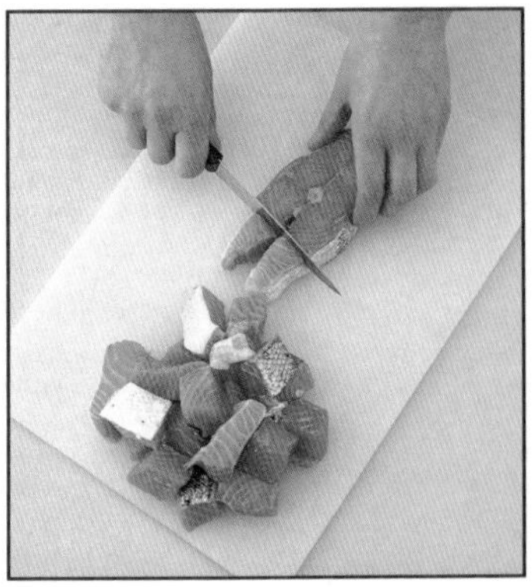

Cut salmon steaks into chunks. Halve onion and cut into 0.5 cm (¼ in) thick slices.

Slice potatoes and carrots into 1 cm (½ in) thick discs (if large, cut into half-moons) and parboil separately. Drain and set aside. Slice shiitake mushrooms diagonally into 4 slices. Chop coriander leaves or watercress into 6 cm (2¼ in) lengths. Cut tofu and konnyaku, if using, in half lengthways, then cut tofu into 1 cm (½ in) squares and konnyaku into 0.5 cm (¼ in) slices. Melt butter in a large cast-iron pot and stir-fry onion slices for 1-2 minutes. Add konbu and enough water to half fill pot.

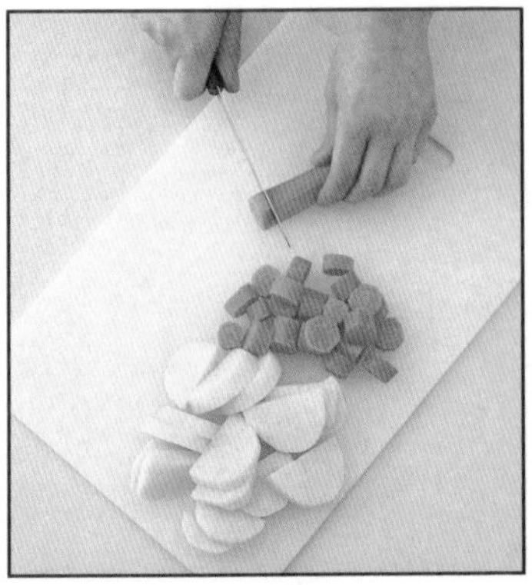

Bring to the boil over medium heat, discard konbu and lower heat. Dissolve miso in a bowl with some of soup, then stir back into pan. Add potatoes, carrots, salmon, mushrooms and konnyaku, cover and cook over low heat for 5 minutes. Add coriander or watercress and tofu; simmer for 3-4 minutes. Serve sprinkled with spring onion.

Serves 4-6.

Note: Ishikari is a river on the northern island of Japan which is famous for salmon.

POULTRY

LEMON & CORIANDER CHICKEN

4 chicken thighs, skinned
4 chicken drumsticks, skinned
55 ml (2 fl oz/¼ cup) vegetable oil
5 cm (2 in) piece fresh root ginger, grated
4 cloves garlic, crushed
1 fresh green chilli, seeded and finely chopped
½ teaspoon turmeric
1 teaspoon ground cumin
1 teaspoon ground coriander
salt and cayenne pepper
grated zest and juice 1 lemon
115 g (4 oz/3 cups) chopped coriander leaves
coriander leaves and lemon slices, to garnish

Wash chicken joints and pat dry with absorbent kitchen paper. Heat oil in a large frying pan, add chicken, and fry, stirring frequently, until browned all over. Remove from pan with a slotted spoon and set aside. Add ginger and garlic to pan and fry for 1 minute. Stir in chilli, turmeric, cumin and ground coriander and season with salt and cayenne pepper, then cook for 1 minute more.

Return chicken to pan, add 115 ml (4 fl oz/½ cup) water and lemon zest and juice. Bring to the boil, then cover and cook over a medium heat for 25-30 minutes or until chicken is tender. Stir in chopped coriander, then serve hot, garnished with coriander leaves and lemon slices.

Serves 4.

Variation: Use fresh parsley, or parsley and mint, instead of coriander, if preferred.

APRICOT & CHICKEN CURRY

1.25 kg (2½ lb) chicken joints, skinned
½ teaspoon chilli powder
1 tablespoon Garam Masala (see page 224)
2.5 cm (1 in) piece fresh root ginger, grated
2 cloves garlic, crushed
115 g (4 oz) ready-to-eat dried apricots
2 tablespoons vegetable oil
2 onions, finely sliced
400 g (14 oz) can chopped tomatoes
1 tablespoon sugar
2 tablespoons white wine vinegar
salt

Wash chicken and pat dry with absorbent kitchen paper. Cut each joint into 4 pieces and put in a large bowl. Add chilli powder, garam masala, ginger and garlic and toss well to coat chicken pieces. Cover and leave in a cool place for 2-3 hours to allow chicken to absorb flavours. In a separate bowl, put apricots and 150 ml (5 fl oz/⅔ cup) water and leave to soak for 2-3 hours.

Heat oil in a large heavy-based pan and add chicken. Fry over a high heat for 5 minutes or until browned all over. Remove from pan and set aside. Add onions to pan and cook, stirring, for about 5 minutes, until soft. Return chicken to pan with tomatoes and cook, covered, over low heat for 20 minutes. Drain apricots, add to pan with sugar and vinegar. Season with salt. Simmer, covered, for 10-15 minutes. Serve hot.

Serves 4.

TANDOORI CHICKEN

1.25 kg (2½ lb) chicken joints, skinned
1 tablespoon lime juice
salt
1 small onion
1 tablespoon Tandoori Masala(see Note)
2 teaspoons Garam Masala (see page 224)
2.5 cm (1 in) piece fresh root ginger, grated
300 ml (10 fl oz/1¼ cups) natural yogurt
lime wedges and coriander leaves, to garnish

Wash chicken joints and pat dry with absorbent kitchen paper, then make 2-3 cuts in meaty parts.

Place chicken in a shallow non-metallic dish. Sprinkle with lime juice and salt and set aside. Put onion, tandoori masala, garam masala, ginger, salt and yogurt into a blender or food processor fitted with a metal blade and process until smooth and frothy. Pour over chicken and cover loosely. Leave to marinate in a cool place for 6 hours or overnight.

Preheat oven to 200C (400F/Gas 6). Drain excess marinade from chicken joints and place them in a roasting tin. Cook for 25-30 minutes, until tender and well browned. Serve hot, garnished with lime wedges and coriander leaves.

Serves 4.

Note: To make Tandoori Masala, grind 1 tablespoon each of cumin and coriander seeds, stir in 1 tablespoon cayenne pepper and a few drops of red food colouring and mix well.

CHICKEN BIRYANI

575 g (1¼ lb) boneless chicken breasts, skinned
450 g (1 lb/2½ cups) basmati rice, washed
6 tablespoons vegetable oil
6 green cardamom pods, bruised
½ teaspoon cumin seeds
2 onions, finely sliced
4 cloves garlic, crushed
5 cm (2 in) piece fresh root ginger, grated
155 ml (5 fl oz/⅔ cup) natural yogurt
salt and pepper
large pinch saffron threads
2 tablespoons boiling water
few drops red food colouring
3 tablespoons flaked almonds, toasted, to garnish
2 tablespoons sultanas, to garnish

Cut chicken into 2 cm (¾ in) cubes. Set aside. Soak rice in cold water for 30 minutes, then drain. Heat 55 ml (2 fl oz/¼ cup) oil in a large heavy-based pan, add cardamom pods and cumin seeds and fry for 1 minute. Stir in onions, garlic, ginger and chicken and cook for about 5 minutes, stirring, over a high heat until chicken is browned all over. Stir in yogurt 1 tablespoon at a time, then add 115 ml (4 fl oz/½ cup) water. Cover and simmer for 15 minutes.

Heat remaining oil in separate pan, stir in rice and fry for 2-3 minutes, until golden, stirring all the time. Stir into chicken mixture and season with salt and pepper. Cover and simmer for 12-15 minutes, until rice and chicken are tender. Soak saffron in boiling water for 5 minutes. Stir food colouring into 2 tablespoons water. Pour liquids into separate parts of rice and fork in to colour it yellow, red and white. Serve hot, garnished with almonds and sultanas.

Serves 4.

GOLDEN STEAMED CHICKEN

115 g (4 oz/⅔ cup) basmati rice
1 (1.5 kg/3½ lb) chicken
3 tablespoons vegetable oil
½ teaspoon chilli powder
55 g (2 oz/⅓ cup) raisins
55 g (2 oz/⅓ cup) flaked almonds
1 tablespoon chopped fresh thyme
salt
½ teaspoon ground cumin
½ teaspoon turmeric
1 teaspoon ground coriander
2 teaspoons Garam Masala (see page 224)
cayenne pepper
115 ml (4 fl oz/½ cup) hot water
thyme sprigs, to garnish

Wash rice thoroughly and soak in cold water for 30 minutes, then drain. Wash chicken, pat dry with absorbent kitchen paper and set aside. Heat 1 tablespoon oil in a saucepan, add rice and fry, stirring, for 2-3 minutes, until golden brown. Stir in chilli powder, raisins, almonds, thyme, 175 ml (6 fl oz/¾ cup) water and salt. Bring to the boil, then cover and simmer for 10-12 minutes, until rice has absorbed all the liquid. Leave to cool, then use to stuff chicken.

Truss chicken, then place in a steamer and steam for 1 hour. Heat remaining oil in a large pan, add cumin, turmeric, coriander and garam masala. Season with salt and cayenne pepper and fry for 1 minute. Transfer chicken to this pan and fry for 5 minutes, turning chicken until well coated. Pour hot water down side of pan, cover and cook over a low heat for 15-20 minutes, until tender. Serve hot, garnished with thyme sprigs.

Serves 4.

CHICKEN WITH LENTILS

225 g (8 oz) boneless, skinless chicken breasts
225 g (8 oz/1¼ cups) red split lentils
½ teaspoon turmeric
55 ml (2 fl oz/¼ cup) vegetable oil
6 green cardamom pods, bruised
1 onion, finely sliced
1 cm (½ in) piece fresh root ginger, grated
salt and cayenne pepper
2 tablespoons lemon juice
1 teaspoon cumin seeds
2 cloves garlic, finely sliced

Wash chicken, pat dry and cut into cubes. Set aside.

Wash lentils, put in a large saucepan and add 950 ml (30 fl oz/3¾ cups) water and turmeric. Bring to the boil, then cover and simmer for 20-30 minutes or until tender. Drain thoroughly. Meanwhile, heat half the oil in a large saucepan, add cardamom pods and fry for 1 minute. Add onion and fry, stirring frequently, for about 8 minutes, until golden brown. Add chicken and fry for 5 minutes, until browned all over. Add ginger and fry for 1 minute more. Season with salt and cayenne pepper.

Stir in lemon juice and 115 ml (5 fl oz/⅔ cup) water and cover. Simmer for 25-30 minutes or until chicken is tender. Stir in lentil mixture and cook, stirring, for 5 minutes. Meanwhile, heat remaining oil, add cumin and garlic and fry, stirring, until garlic is golden. Transfer chicken and lentils to serving dish and pour garlic mixture over. Serve hot.

Serves 4.

CHICKEN IN SPICY SAUCE

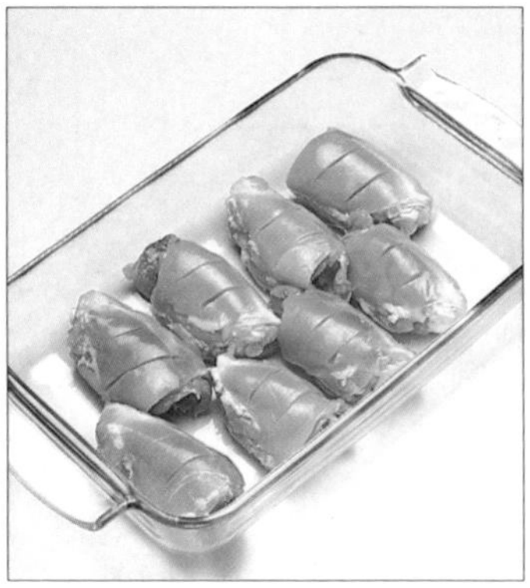

8 chicken thighs, skinned
225 g (8 oz) can tomatoes, drained
2 tablespoons tomato purée
2 tablespoons chilli sauce
2 teaspoons sugar
1 tablespoon Garam Masala (see page 224)
2 tablespoons light soy sauce
5 cm (2 in) piece fresh root ginger, grated
2 cloves garlic, crushed
juice 1 lime and 1 lemon
twists lime and lemon, to garnish

Wash chicken and pat dry with absorbent kitchen paper. Make 2-3 cuts in meaty parts and place in a shallow non-metallic dish.

Put tomatoes, tomato purée, chilli sauce, sugar, garam masala, soy sauce, ginger, garlic and lime and lemon juice in a blender or food processor fitted with a metal blade and process until smooth. Pour over chicken, cover and leave in a cool place for 2-3 hours to allow chicken to absorb flavours.

Preheat oven to 190C (375F/Gas 5). Put chicken and sauce in a roasting tin and cook, uncovered, for 45-50 minutes, basting with sauce 2-3 times, until tender and cooked. Serve hot, garnished with lime and lemon twists.

Serves 4.

CURRIED CHICKEN LIVERS

225 g (8 oz) chicken livers
2 tablespoons vegetable oil
2 onions, finely sliced
3 cloves garlic, crushed
2 teaspoons Garam Masala (see page 224)
½ teaspoon turmeric
salt and pepper
2 tablespoons lemon juice
2 tablespoons chopped fresh parsley
parsley sprigs, to garnish

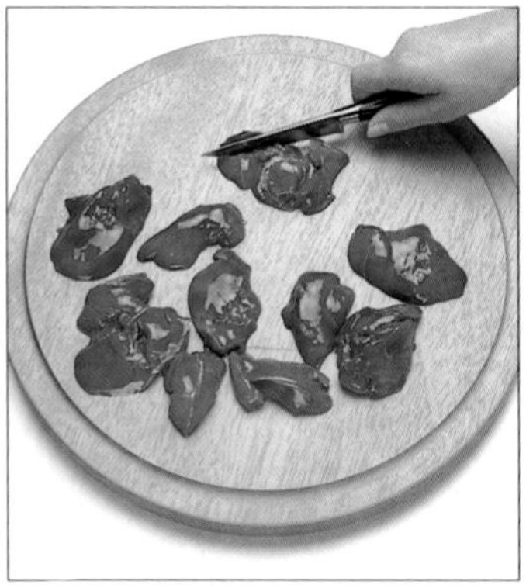

Wash chicken livers and remove any green tinged parts. Set aside.

Heat oil in a frying pan, add onions and cook over a medium heat, stirring, for about 8 minutes, until soft and golden brown. Stir in garlic, garam masala and turmeric and season with salt and pepper.

Fry for 1 minute, then stir in chicken livers and fry for about 5 minutes, stirring frequently, until livers are browned on outsides but still slightly pink in the centre. Sprinkle with lemon juice and parsley. Serve hot, garnished with sprigs of parsley.

Serves 4 as a starter.

Note: Frozen chicken livers can be used: thaw at room temperature for 3-4 hours before using.

DUCK & COCONUT CURRY

4 duck portions, skinned
2 tablespoons vegetable oil
1 teaspoon mustard seeds
1 onion, finely chopped
3 cloves garlic, crushed
5 cm (2 in) piece fresh root ginger, grated
2 fresh green chillies, seeded and chopped
1 teaspoon ground cumin
1 tablespoon ground coriander
1 teaspoon turmeric
1 tablespoon white wine vinegar
salt and cayenne pepper
300 ml (10 fl oz/1¼ cups) coconut milk (see page 224)
2 tablespoons shredded coconut, toasted, and lemon wedges, to garnish

Wash duck and pat dry with absorbent kitchen paper. Heat oil in a large frying pan, add duck and fry, stirring, over a high heat for 8-10 minutes, until browned all over, then remove from pan. Pour off all but 2 tablespoons of fat from pan, add mustard seeds and fry for 1 minute or until they begin to pop.

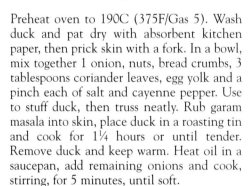

Add onion to pan and cook, stirring, over a medium heat for 8 minutes or until soft and golden. Stir in garlic, ginger, chillies, cumin, coriander and turmeric and fry for 2 minutes. Stir in vinegar and season with salt and cayenne pepper. Return duck to pan and turn pieces to coat them in spice mixture. Stir in coconut milk and bring to the boil. Cover and cook over a low heat for about 40 minutes or until duck is tender. Garnish and serve hot.

Serves 4.

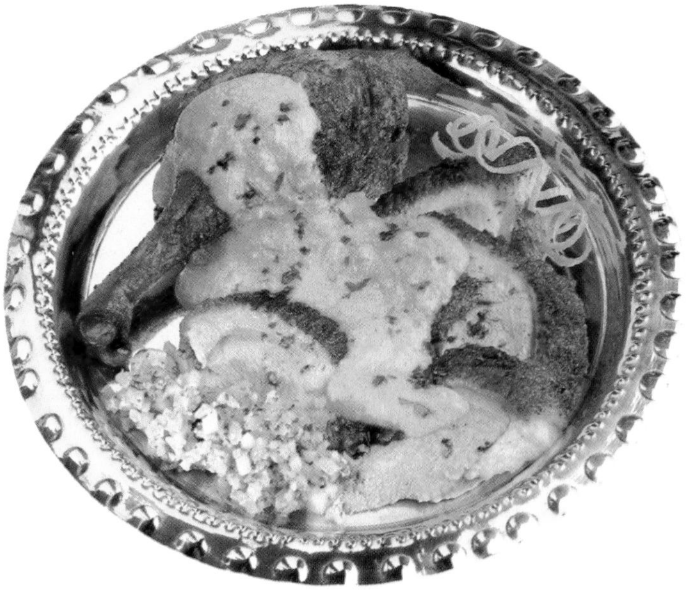

ROAST DUCK IN FRUIT SAUCE

1 (2 kg/4½ lb) duck
3 onions, chopped
115 g (4 oz/1 cup) chopped mixed nuts
55 g (2 oz/1 cup) fresh bread crumbs
4 tablespoons chopped coriander leaves
1 egg yolk
salt and cayenne pepper
1 tablespoon Garam Masala (see page 224)
2 tablespoons vegetable oil
2 cloves garlic, crushed
2.5 cm (1 in) piece fresh root ginger, grated
1 teaspoon turmeric
2 tablespoons ground coriander
1 teaspoon chick-pea flour
300 ml (10 fl oz/1¼ cups) natural yogurt
juice 2 lemons and 2 oranges

Preheat oven to 190C (375F/Gas 5). Wash duck and pat dry with absorbent kitchen paper, then prick skin with a fork. In a bowl, mix together 1 onion, nuts, bread crumbs, 3 tablespoons coriander leaves, egg yolk and a pinch each of salt and cayenne pepper. Use to stuff duck, then truss neatly. Rub garam masala into skin, place duck in a roasting tin and cook for 1¼ hours or until tender. Remove duck and keep warm. Heat oil in a saucepan, add remaining onions and cook, stirring, for 5 minutes, until soft.

Stir in garlic, ginger, turmeric, ground coriander, chick-pea flour and salt and cayenne pepper to taste. Cook for 1 minute, then stir in yogurt. Simmer for 10 minutes, then stir in lemon and orange juice and heat gently, without boiling. Carve duck, pour over sauce and sprinkle with remaining coriander. Serve hot.

Serves 4.

Note: This looks very attractive garnished with spirals of lemon and orange zest.

MURGHAL SHREDDED DUCK

450 g (1 lb) boneless duck breasts, skinned
55 ml (2 fl oz/¼ cup) vegetable oil
1 onion, finely chopped
1 quantity Cashew Nut Masala made with 115 g (4 oz/¾ cup) cashew nuts (see page 224)
1 teaspoon turmeric
55 g (2 oz/⅔ cup) desiccated coconut
85 g (3 oz/½ cup) sultanas
150 ml (5 fl oz/⅔ cup) natural yogurt
6 tablespoons double cream
55 g (2 oz/⅓ cup) unsalted cashew nuts
1 green chilli, seeded and chopped

Wash duck breasts and pat dry with absorbent kitchen paper.

Slice duck into 0.5 cm (¼ in) thick strips. Heat 3 tablespoons oil in a large frying pan, add duck and cook over a high heat for about 5 minutes, until browned all over. Remove duck from pan with a slotted spoon and set aside. Add onion to pan and cook, stirring, for 5 minutes or until soft. Stir in cashew nut masala and turmeric and fry for 2 minutes. Stir in coconut, sultanas, yogurt, cream and duck.

Cover and cook over a low heat for 15-20 minutes, stirring occasionally, until duck is tender. Just before serving, heat remaining oil in a small pan, add cashew nuts and fry for 2-3 minutes, until golden. Add chilli and fry for 1 minute more. Transfer duck to a warm serving dish, spoon over cashew nut and chilli mixture. Serve hot.

Serves 4-6.

DUCK WITH HONEY & LIME

4 duck portions, each weighing about 225 g (8 oz), skinned
2 tablespoons vegetable oil
1 onion, finely chopped
2 cloves garlic, crushed
2.5 cm (1 in) piece fresh root ginger, finely sliced
8 green cardamom pods, bruised
7.5 cm (3 in) cinnamon stick
3 tablespoons clear honey
juice 2 limes
twists lime, to garnish

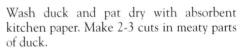

Wash duck and pat dry with absorbent kitchen paper. Make 2-3 cuts in meaty parts of duck.

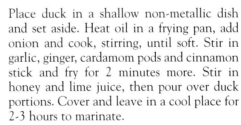

Place duck in a shallow non-metallic dish and set aside. Heat oil in a frying pan, add onion and cook, stirring, until soft. Stir in garlic, ginger, cardamom pods and cinnamon stick and fry for 2 minutes more. Stir in honey and lime juice, then pour over duck portions. Cover and leave in a cool place for 2-3 hours to marinate.

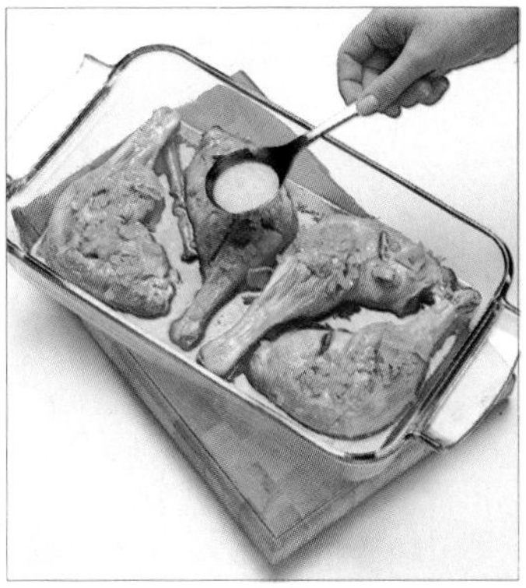

Preheat oven to 200C (400F/Gas 6). Transfer duck to a roasting tin if shallow dish is not ovenproof, then cook for 45-60 minutes, basting occasionally with marinade, until browned and tender. Serve hot, garnished with lime twists.

Serves 4.

CHICKEN WITH MUSHROOMS

450 g (1 lb) skinless, boneless chicken thighs
1 tablespoon sunflower oil
225 g (8 oz) button mushrooms, sliced
225 g (8 oz) spring onions, chopped
1 clove garlic, finely chopped
2.5 cm (1 in) piece fresh root ginger, peeled and finely chopped
150 ml (5 fl oz/⅔ cup) Chinese Chicken Stock (see page 16)
2 tablespoons rice wine
2 tablespoons dark soy sauce
2 tablespoons oyster sauce
425 g (15 oz) can straw mushrooms, drained
1 teaspoon cornflour mixed with 2 teaspoons cold water

Trim fat from chicken thighs. Cut meat into 2.5 cm (1 in) strips. Heat oil in a wok and stir-fry chicken strips for 3-4 minutes or until chicken is lightly browned all over.

Add sliced mushrooms, spring onions, garlic and ginger and stir-fry for 2 minutes. Stir in stock, rice wine, soy sauce, oyster sauce, straw mushrooms and cornflour mixture and simmer, stirring, for 5 minutes. Serve with noodles.

Serves 4.

GINGER CHICKEN PATTIES

450 g (1 lb) lean minced chicken
1 clove garlic, finely chopped
2.5 cm (1 in) piece fresh root ginger, peeled and finely chopped
3 tablespoons chopped coriander
1 tablespoon cornflour
115 g (4 oz/2 cups) cooked long-grain white rice
salt and freshly ground pepper
1 egg white, lightly beaten
2 teaspoons sunflower oil
coriander leaves, to garnish
DIP:
2 tablespoons light soy sauce
2 tablespoons dry sherry
1 cm (½ in) piece fresh root ginger, peeled and grated

In a bowl, mix together chicken, garlic, ginger and coriander. Stir in cornflour, rice, salt and pepper. Stir in egg white. Divide mixture into 8 portions and shape into 7.5 cm (3 in) diameter patties, dusting hands with extra cornflour if needed. Place on a plate, cover and chill for 30 minutes.

Preheat grill. Brush grill rack lightly with oil and place patties on rack. Brush tops lightly with oil and cook for 4 minutes. Turn patties over, brush again with oil and cook another for 3-4 minutes or until cooked through. Drain on absorbent kitchen paper. To make dip, mix together soy sauce, sherry and ginger in a small bowl. Garnish patties with coriander and serve with dip.

Serves 4.

CHICKEN & BASIL STIR-FRY

450 g (1 lb) boneless chicken thighs
1 tablespoon dark soy sauce
1 tablespoon cornflour
1 tablespoon groundnut (peanut) oil
2 cloves garlic, thinly sliced
1 fresh red chilli, seeded and thinly sliced
1 teaspoon chilli powder
1 tablespoon hoisin sauce
small bunch basil leaves, shredded
basil leaves and blanched red chilli strips, to garnish

Remove skin and fat from chicken. Cut meat into 2.5 cm (1 in) strips and place in a bowl. Stir in soy sauce and cornflour.

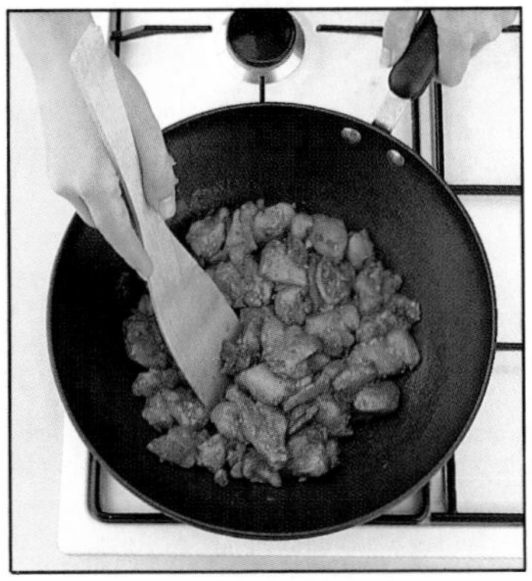

Heat oil in a wok and stir-fry chicken with garlic and chilli for 7-8 minutes.

Add chilli powder and hoisin sauce and cook for another 2 minutes. Remove from heat and stir in shredded basil. Garnish with basil leaves and chilli strips and serve on a bed of rice.

Serves 4.

LEMON & HONEY CHICKEN

4 boneless chicken breasts, each weighing 115 g (4 oz)
3 tablespoons honey
4 teaspoons light soy sauce
grated zest and juice 2 lemons
1 clove garlic, finely chopped
freshly ground pepper
1 tablespoon sunflower oil
2 tablespoons chopped fresh chives
thin strips lemon zest, to garnish

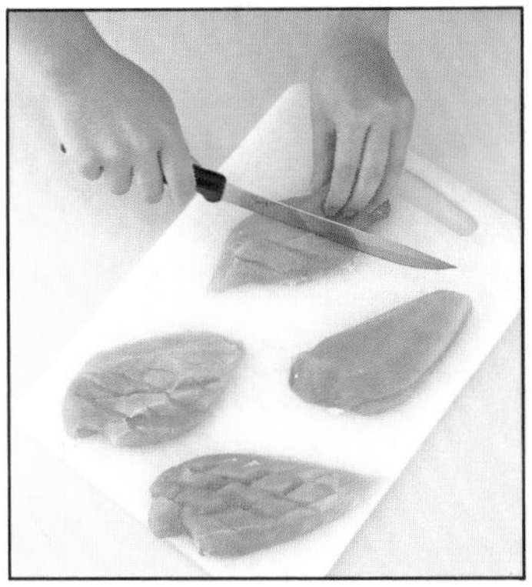

Remove skin and fat from chicken breasts. Using a sharp knife, score chicken breasts in a cross on both sides, taking care not to slice all the way through. Place in a shallow dish.

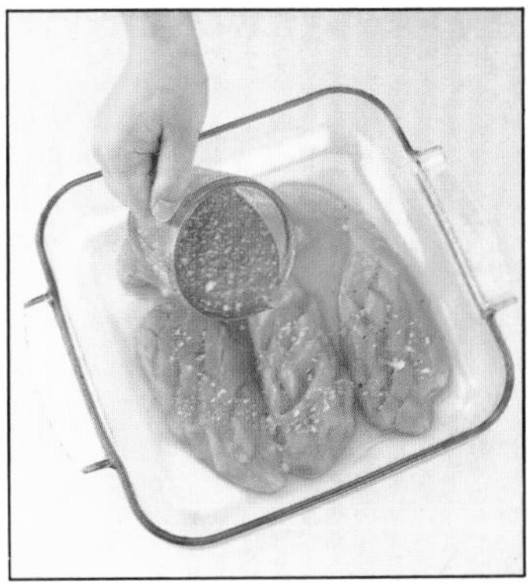

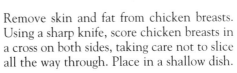

Mix together honey, soy sauce, lemon zest and juice, garlic and pepper. Pour over chicken, cover and chill 1 hour.

Heat oil in a wok. Drain chicken, reserving marinade, and cook for 2-3 minutes on each side, until lightly golden. Add marinade and simmer for 5 minutes, turning frequently, until chicken is cooked through and sauce syrupy. Stir in chives, garnish with lemon zest and serve on a bed of noodles.

Serves 4.

CHICKEN CHOW MEIN

- 225 g (8 oz) dried egg noodles
- 225 g (8 oz) boneless, skinless chicken breasts
- 1 tablespoon light soy sauce
- 1 tablespoon dry sherry
- 1 tablespoon sunflower oil
- 4 shallots, finely chopped
- 115 g (4 oz) mangetout, sliced diagonally
- 25 g (1 oz) prosciutto, trimmed and finely diced
- 1 teaspoon sesame oil
- 1 teaspoon sugar
- 2 spring onions, finely shredded, to garnish

Bring a large saucepan of water to the boil and cook noodles for 3-4 minutes. Drain well, rinse, put in cold water and set aside. Trim chicken breasts. Using a sharp knife, shred into 0.5 cm (¼ in) strips. In a bowl, mix chicken strips with soy sauce and sherry.

Heat sunflower oil in a wok and stir-fry chicken and shallots for 2 minutes. Add mangetout and prosciutto and stir-fry for 1 minute. Drain noodles well and add to pan along with sesame oil and sugar. Cook, stirring, for 2 minutes to warm through. Garnish with spring onions and serve.

Serves 4.

CHICKEN & PLUM CASSEROLE

- 25 g (1 oz) dried Chinese mushrooms, soaked in hot water for 20 minutes
- 450 g (1 lb) skinless, boneless chicken thighs
- 1 tablespoon sunflower oil
- 2 cloves garlic, thinly sliced
- 25 g (1 oz) prosciutto, trimmed and diced
- 225 g (8 oz) plums, halved and pitted
- 1 tablespoon brown sugar
- 3 tablespoons light soy sauce
- 2 tablespoons rice wine
- 3 tablespoons plum sauce
- 1 tablespoon chilli sauce
- 550 ml (20 fl oz/2½ cups) Chinese Chicken Stock (see page 16)
- 2 teaspoons cornflour mixed with 4 teaspoons cold water

Drain mushrooms and squeeze out excess water. Discard mushroom stems and thinly slice caps. Trim fat from chicken thighs and cut meat into 2.5 cm (1 in) strips. Heat oil in a wok and stir-fry chicken, garlic and prosciutto for 3-4 minutes. Add mushrooms and stir-fry for 1 minute.

Add plums, brown sugar, soy sauce, rice wine, plum sauce, chilli sauce and stock and simmer for 20 minutes or until plums have softened. Add cornflour mixture, and cook, stirring, until thickened. Serve on a bed of rice.

Serves 4.

CHICKEN WITH PEANUTS

450 g (1 lb) boneless chicken breasts
1 tablespoon chilli oil
2.5 cm (1 in) piece fresh root ginger, peeled and finely chopped
55 g (2 oz/⅓ cup) skinned peanuts
1 tablespoon Chinese Chicken Stock (see page 16)
1 tablespoon dry sherry
1 tablespoon dark soy sauce
1 teaspoon brown sugar
1 teaspoon five-spice powder
1 teaspoon white rice vinegar
4 spring onions, finely chopped

Remove skin and fat from chicken breasts. Cut into 2.5 cm (1 in) pieces.

Heat oil in a wok and gently stir-fry chicken, ginger and peanuts for 2 minutes or until chicken is just coloured.

Add stock, sherry, soy sauce, sugar, five-spice powder and rice vinegar and simmer for 5 minutes, stirring occasionally. Remove from heat and stir in spring onions.

Serves 4.

CHICKEN WITH CUCUMBER

225 g (8 oz) cucumber
2 teaspoons salt
450 g (1 lb) boneless chicken breasts
1 tablespoon groundnut (peanut) oil
2 cloves garlic, finely chopped
1 tablespoon light soy sauce
1 tablespoon dry sherry
2 tablespoons chopped fresh chives
cucumber twists, to garnish

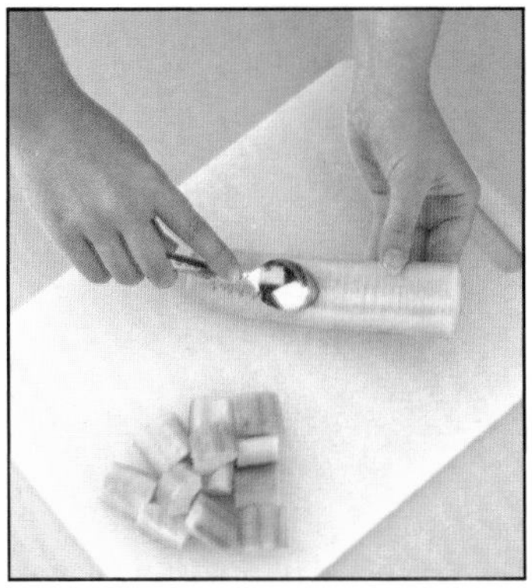

Peel cucumber, halve lengthways and scoop out seeds with a teaspoon. Cut into 2.5 cm (1 in) cubes, place in a bowl and sprinkle with salt. Set aside for 20 minutes.

Remove skin and fat from chicken. Cut into 1 cm (½ in) strips. Drain cucumber and rinse well. Pat dry with absorbent kitchen paper.

Heat oil in a wok and stir-fry chicken and garlic for 5 minutes. Add soy sauce, sherry, chives and cucumber and cook for 3 minutes. Garnish with cucumber twists and serve with noodles.

Serves 4.

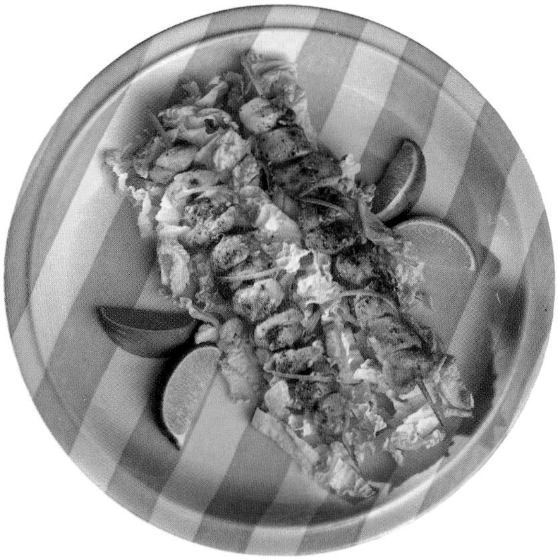

PEPPERED CHICKEN KEBABS

450 g (1 lb) boneless, skinless chicken breasts, cubed
1 tablespoon rice wine
1 tablespoon dark soy sauce
grated zest and juice 1 lime
2 teaspoons brown sugar
1 teaspoon ground cinnamon
1 teaspoon sunflower oil
1 teaspoon Szechuan peppercorns, toasted and crushed
strips lime zest and lime wedges, to serve

Place chicken in a shallow dish. Mix together rice wine, soy sauce, lime zest and juice, sugar and cinnamon. Pour over chicken.

Cover chicken and chill for 1 hour. Meanwhile, soak 8 bamboo skewers in cold water for 30 minutes. Remove chicken pieces from marinade, reserving marinade, and thread chicken on to skewers.

Preheat grill. Brush grill rack lightly with oil and place skewers on rack. Brush with marinade and sprinkle with peppercorns. Grill for 3 minutes, turn, brush again and grill for another 2-3 minutes or until cooked through. Drain on absorbent kitchen paper. Garnish with lime zest and serve with lime wedges.

Serves 4.

CHINESE BARBECUE CHICKEN

4 chicken quarters, each weighing 225 g (8 oz), skin and fat removed
2 cloves garlic, finely chopped
2.5 cm (1 in) piece fresh root ginger, peeled and finely chopped
55 ml (2 fl oz/¼ cup) hoisin sauce
2 tablespoons dry sherry
1 teaspoon chilli sauce
1 tablespoon dark soy sauce
1 tablespoon brown sugar
1 tablespoon chopped fresh chives, to garnish

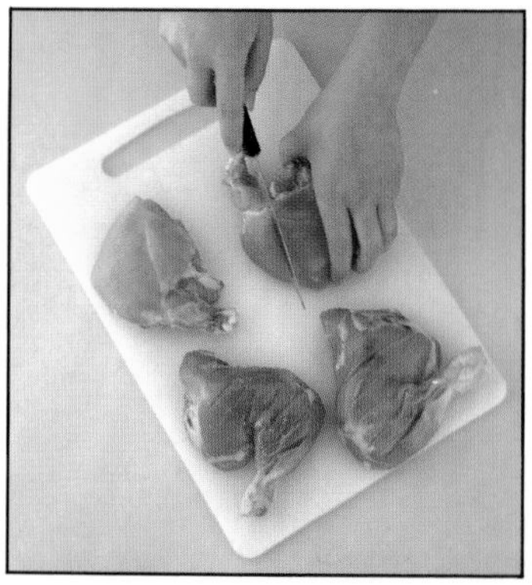

Rinse chicken quarters and pat dry with absorbent kitchen paper. Using a sharp knife, score top of quarters in diagonal lines.

Place chicken in a shallow dish. Mix together garlic, ginger, hoisin sauce, sherry, chilli sauce, soy sauce and brown sugar and spoon over prepared chicken quarters. Cover and chill overnight.

Preheat grill. Place chicken on grill rack and cook for 20 minutes, turning once, until cooked through. Garnish with chives and serve with rice and salad.

Serves 4.

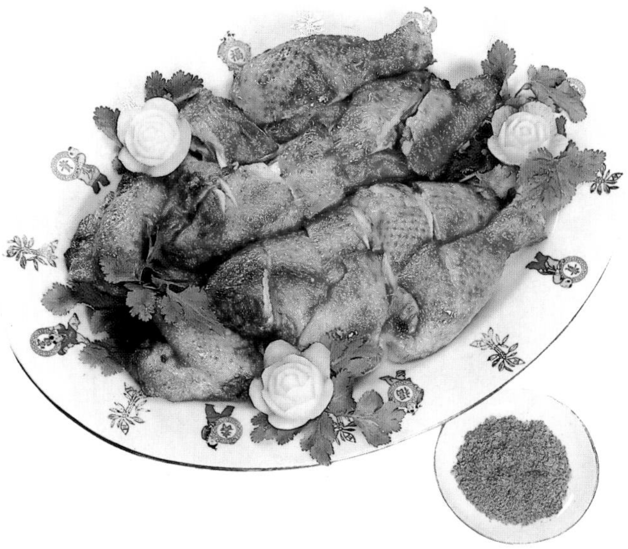

CRISPY SKIN CHICKEN

1 (1.5 kg/3½ lb) chicken
salt
1 tablespoon golden syrup
4 tablespoons plus 1 teaspoon sea salt
1 tablespoon Chinese five-spice powder
2 tablespoons rice vinegar
950 ml (30 fl oz/3¾ cups) vegetable oil

Bring a large saucepan of salted water to the boil. Lower in chicken, return to the boil, then remove pan from heat, cover tightly and leave chicken in the water for 30 minutes.

Drain chicken, dry with absorbent kitchen paper and leave in a cold dry place for at least 12 hours. In a small bowl, mix together golden syrup, 1 teaspoon salt,. ½ teaspoon five-spice powder and rice vinegar. Brush over chicken and leave in the refrigerator for 20 minutes. Repeat until all coating is used. Refrigerate chicken for at least 4 hours to allow coating to dry thoroughly on the skin.

Split chicken in half through the breast. In a wok, heat oil, add chicken halves and deep-fry for 5 minutes until golden brown. Lift chicken from oil and drain on absorbent kitchen paper. Cut into bite-sized pieces. In a small saucepan over a low heat, stir together remaining sea salt and remaining five spice powder for 2 minutes. Sprinkle over chicken.

Serves 4.

CHICKEN IN BLACK BEAN SAUCE

225 ml (8 fl oz/1 cup) groundnut (peanut) oil
450 g (1 lb) boneless, skinless chicken breast, cubed
10 button mushrooms, halved
½ red pepper, seeded and diced
½ green pepper, seeded and diced
4 spring onions, finely chopped
2 carrots, thinly sliced
2 tablespoons dried black beans, washed
1 cm (½ in) piece fresh root ginger, peeled and grated
1 clove garlic, finely chopped
2 tablespoons rice wine or dry sherry
225 ml (8 fl oz/1 cup) Chinese Vegetable Stock (see page 17)
1 tablespoon light soy sauce
2 teaspoons cornflour dissolved in 4 teaspoons cold water

In a wok, heat oil until smoking, add chicken cubes and deep-fry for 2 minutes. Using a slotted spoon, lift chicken from oil and drain on absorbent kitchen paper. Pour oil from wok, leaving just 2 tablespoons.

Add mushrooms to wok and stir-fry for 1 minute. Add red and green peppers, spring onions and carrots and stir-fry for 3 minutes. In a bowl, mash black beans with ginger, garlic and rice wine or dry sherry. Stir into wok then stir in stock and soy sauce. Cook for another 2 minutes. Stir in cornflour mixture and bring to the boil, stirring. Stir in chicken and heat through gently.

Serves 4.

DUCK WITH KIWI FRUIT

2 boneless duck breasts, each weighing 225 g (8 oz)
1 cm (½ in) piece fresh root ginger, peeled and finely chopped
1 clove garlic, finely chopped
2 tablespoons dry sherry
2 kiwi fruit
1 teaspoon sesame oil
SAUCE:
55 ml (2 fl oz/¼ cup) dry sherry
2 tablespoons light soy sauce
4 teaspoons honey

Remove skin and fat from duck. With a sharp knife, score flesh in diagonal lines. Beat with a meat tenderizer until 1 cm (½ in) thick.

Place duck breasts in a shallow dish and add ginger, garlic and sherry. Cover and chill for 1 hour. Peel and thinly slice kiwi fruit and halve crossways. Cover and chill until required. Preheat grill. Drain duck breasts and place on grill rack. Brush with sesame oil and cook for 8 minutes. Turn and brush again with oil. Cook for 8-10 minutes until tender and cooked through.

Meanwhile, make sauce. Put sherry, soy sauce and honey in a saucepan, bring to the boil and simmer for 5 minutes or until syrupy. Drain duck breasts on absorbent kitchen paper and slice thinly. Arrange duck slices and kiwi fruit on serving plates. Pour sauce over duck and serve with rice and vegetables.

Serves 4.

SOY-ROAST DUCKLING

1 (2.5 kg/5 lb) duckling, giblets removed
55 ml (2 fl oz/¼ cup) dark soy sauce
2 tablespoons brown sugar
2 cloves garlic, finely chopped
soft pancakes, spring onions and cucumber, to serve
DIP:
1 tablespoon sunflower oil
4 spring onions, finely chopped
1 clove garlic, finely chopped
3 tablespoons dark soy sauce
2 teaspoons brown sugar
2 tablespoons dry sherry

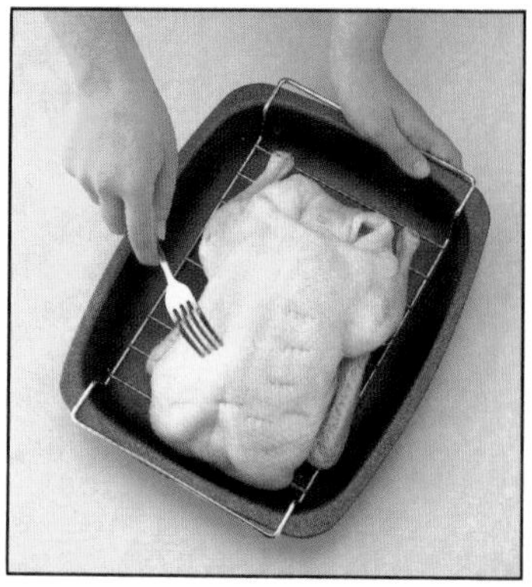

Rinse duckling and pat dry. Place on a wire rack in a roasting pan. Prick all over with a fork.

Sprinkle duckling with soy sauce, brown sugar and garlic. Bake for 2 hours 15 minutes or until juices run clear and skin is well browned. To make dip, heat oil in a wok and stir-fry spring onions and garlic for 1 minute. Combine with soy sauce, sugar and sherry in a bowl.

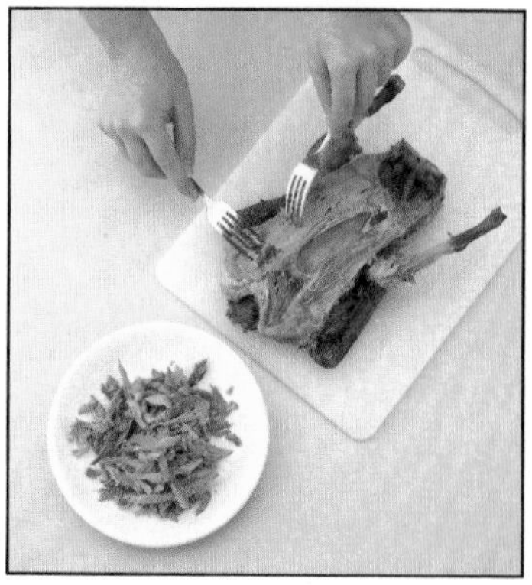

To serve, remove all skin and fat from duckling and shred flesh away from bone. Serve with dip, soft pancakes and shredded spring onions and cucumber.

Serves 4.

Note: Soft pancakes can be bought ready-made from Chinese stores and supermarkets.

DUCK WITH GREEN PEPPERS

1 egg white
3 tablespoons cornflour
sea salt
450 g (1 lb) boned duck breasts, cubed
550 ml (20 fl oz/2½ cups) groundnut (peanut) oil
2 green peppers, seeded and cut into 2.5 cm (1 in) squares
2 tablespoons light soy sauce
1 tablespoon rice wine or dry sherry
1 teaspoon brown sugar
115 ml (4 fl oz/½ cup) Chinese Chicken Stock (see page 16)
1 teaspoon sesame oil
white pepper

In a bowl, whisk together egg white, cornflour and 1 teaspoon salt. Stir in duck cubes to mix thoroughly. Leave for 20 minutes. In a wok, heat groundnut oil until very hot. Add duck and deep-fry for about 4 minutes, until crisp. Remove and drain on absorbent kitchen paper.

Add peppers to wok and deep-fry for 2 minutes, then drain on absorbent kitchen paper. Pour oil from wok, leaving about 2 tablespoonsful. Add soy sauce, rice wine or dry sherry, sugar, stock, sesame oil and salt and pepper to taste. Boil to the boil, then add cooked duck and peppers, reduce heat and gently heat through.

Serves 4.

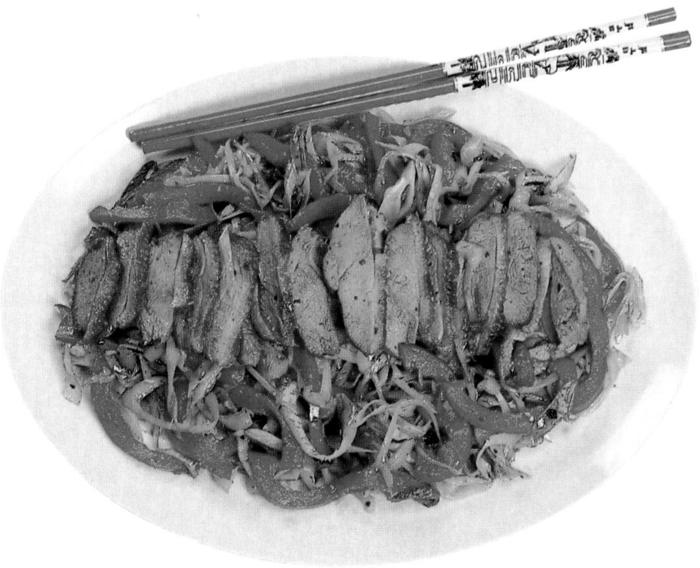

STIR-FRIED DUCK WITH LEEKS

4 tablespoons vegetable oil
2 leeks, thinly shredded
1 red pepper, seeded and sliced
1 cm (½ in) piece fresh root ginger, peeled and thinly sliced
3 cloves garlic, finely chopped
2 tablespoons black bean paste
450 g (1 lb) cooked boned duck, cut into strips
55 ml (2 fl oz/¼ cup) Chinese Chicken Stock (see page 16)
2 tablespoons light soy sauce
2 tablespoons rice vinegar
2 teaspoons brown sugar
2 teaspoons chilli sauce

In a wok, heat oil until just smoking. Add leeks, pepper, ginger and garlic. Stir-fry briefly to coat with oil, then stir in black bean paste and stir-fry for 5 minutes until vegetables begin to soften.

Add duck, stock, soy sauce, rice vinegar, brown sugar and chilli sauce and stir-fry for 2-3 minutes until duck is heated through.

Serves 4.

SZECHUAN TURKEY

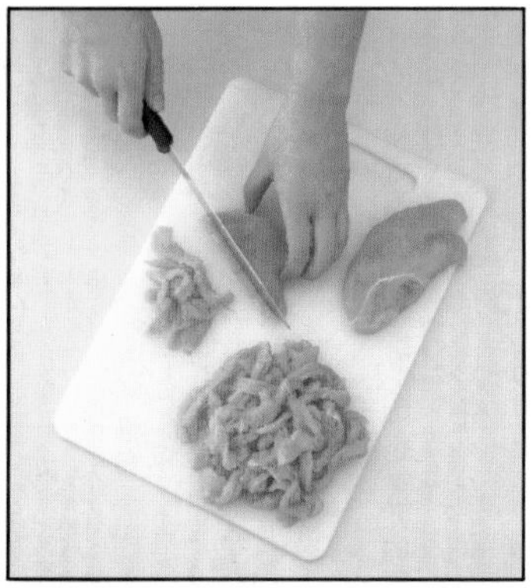

450 g (1 lb) lean boneless turkey
1 egg white, lightly beaten
large pinch salt
1 teaspoon cornflour
1 tablespoon sunflower oil
½ teaspoon Szechuan peppercorns, toasted and crushed
225 g (8 oz) preserved vegetables, shredded
225 g (8 oz) mangetout
115 g (4 oz) can water chestnuts, rinsed and sliced

Remove skin and fat from turkey. Cut into thin strips about 0.5cm (¼ in) thick.

Place turkey strips in a bowl and mix with egg white, salt and cornflour. Cover and chill for 30 minutes.

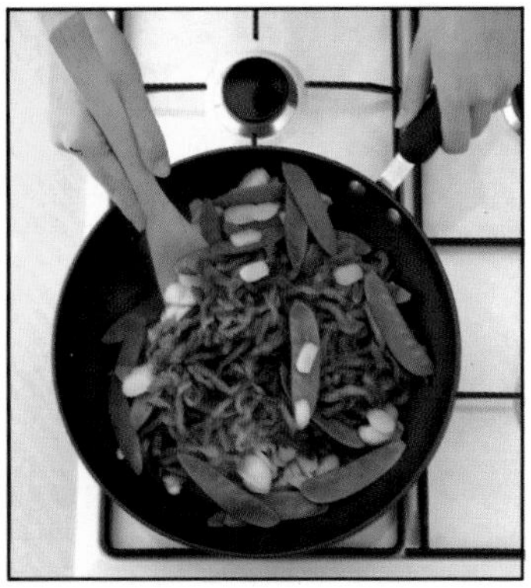

Heat oil in a wok and stir-fry turkey with crushed peppercorns for 2 minutes or until turkey is just coloured. Add preserved vegetables, mangetout and water chestnuts and stir-fry for 3 minutes or until just cooked through. Serve immediately.

Serves 4.

SWEET & SOUR TURKEY

450 g (1 lb) lean skinless boneless turkey
1 tablespoon sunflower oil
2 shallots, chopped
2 sticks celery, sliced
2 tablespoons light soy sauce
1 red pepper, sliced
1 yellow pepper, sliced
1 green pepper, sliced
115 g (4 oz) can bamboo shoots, drained
3 tablespoons plum sauce
2 tablespoons white rice vinegar
1 teaspoon sesame oil
2 tablespoons sesame seeds

Trim away any excess fat from turkey. Cut into 2.5 cm (1 in) cubes. Heat oil in a wok and stir-fry turkey, shallots and celery for 2-3 minutes or until lightly coloured.

Add soy sauce and peppers and stir-fry for 2 minutes. Stir in bamboo shoots, plum sauce and vinegar and simmer 2 minutes. Stir in sesame oil, sprinkle with sesame seeds and serve.

Serves 4.

BRAISED CHICKEN WITH SPICES

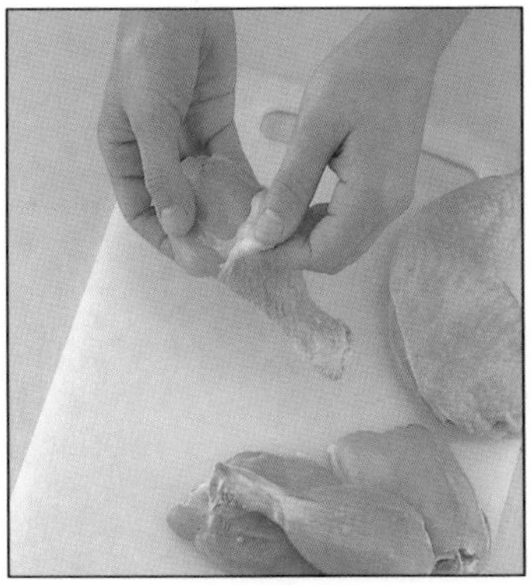

4 chicken thighs and 4 chicken drumsticks, total weight about 1 kg (2¼ lb)
4 cloves garlic, chopped
2 shallots, chopped
5 cm (2 in) piece fresh root ginger, chopped
400 ml (14 fl oz/1¾ cup) coconut milk
2 teaspoons ground coriander
2 teaspoons ground cumin
¼ teaspoon ground turmeric
2 tablespoons vegetable oil
6 green cardamom pods
6 star anise
6 dried red chillies
1 cinnamon stick
4 cloves
20 fresh curry leaves

Skin chicken pieces and set aside. Place garlic, shallots, ginger, coconut milk, coriander, cumin and turmeric into a small blender. Mix to a fine paste. In a heavy-based saucepan large enough to hold chicken in a single layer, heat oil over medium heat. Add cardamom pods, star anise, chillies, cinnamon, cloves and curry leaves. Fry, stirring, for 2-3 minutes. Add ⅓ of the coconut milk mixture. Bring to the boil then add chicken. Turn to coat then cook for 5 minutes.

Add remaining coconut milk mixture. Bring to a simmer then lower heat and cook gently, uncovered, for 50 minutes, stirring frequently. Cook for a further 10 minutes, stirring every minute. The chicken should be golden brown and most of the milk evaporated. Pour away oily residue. Increase heat to high. Add 3-4 tablespoons water and stir to deglaze pan. Serve chicken with Thai rice and sauce.

Serves 4.

CHICKEN & PINEAPPLE CURRY

5 shallots, chopped
3 large fresh red chillies, cored, seeded and chopped
3 cloves garlic, crushed
5 cm (2 in) piece galangal, chopped
1 stalk lemon grass, chopped
2 tablespoons vegetable oil
700 g (1½ lb) boneless, skinless chicken breast, cut into strips
2 tablespoons light brown sugar
2 x 400 ml (14 fl oz) cans (3½ cups) coconut milk
2 teaspoons tamarind paste (see page 11)
2 tablespoons fish sauce
4 kaffir lime leaves
1 small pineapple, about 450 g (1 lb), thinly sliced
grated zest and juice 1 lime, or to taste
small handful coriander leaves, chopped

Put shallots, chillies, garlic, galangal and lemon grass in a small blender. Mix to a paste; add 1 tablespoon of the oil, if necessary. In a wok or sauté pan, heat remaining oil. Add chicken and stir-fry until just turning pale golden brown. Remove and set aside.

Stir chilli paste into pan and stir-fry for 3-4 minutes until fragrant. Stir in sugar, coconut milk, tamarind, fish sauce and kaffir lime leaves. Bring to the boil, and boil for 4-5 minutes until reduced by half and lightly thickened. Return chicken to pan. Add pineapple and simmer for 3-4 minutes until chicken juices run clear. Add lime zest, and lime juice to taste. Stir in coriander.

Serves 6.

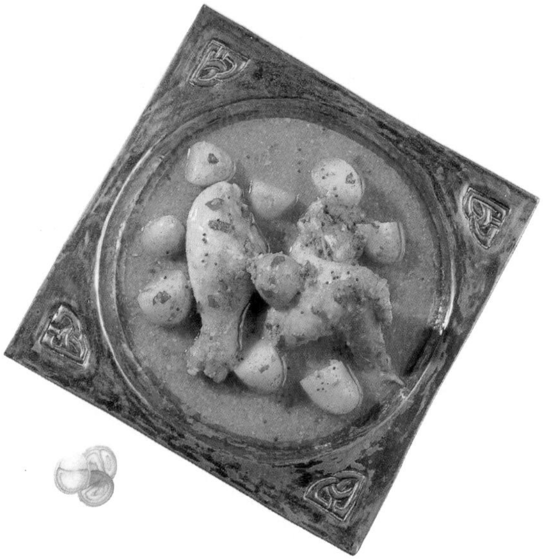

DEVIL'S CURRY

- 10 fresh red chillies, cored, seeded and chopped
- 5 cm (2 in) piece fresh root ginger, chopped
- 6 shallots, chopped
- 3 cloves garlic, chopped
- 1 tablespoon ground coriander
- ½ teaspoon ground turmeric
- 8 candlenuts or cashew nuts
- 6 tablespoons vegetable oil
- 6 shallots, thinly sliced
- 3 cloves garlic, thinly sliced
- 1 teaspoon black mustard seeds, lightly crushed
- 1.5 kg (3½ lb) chicken, jointed, or small chicken portions
- 300 g (10 oz) small potatoes, halved
- 2 teaspoons mustard powder
- 2 tablespoons rice vinegar
- 1 tablespoon dark soy sauce

Place chillies, ginger, chopped shallots and garlic, coriander, turmeric and nuts in a blender and mix to a paste. In a large wok or sauté pan, heat oil over medium-high heat. Add sliced shallots and garlic and fry until lightly browned. Stir in spice paste and cook for about 5 minutes, stirring. Add mustard seeds, stir once or twice then add chicken. Cook, stirring frequently, until chicken pieces turn white.

Add potatoes and 550 ml (20 fl oz/2½ cups) water. Bring to the boil, cover, then simmer for 15 minutes. Stir together mustard, vinegar and soy sauce. Stir into pan, re-cover and cook for another 15-20 minutes, stirring occasionally, until chicken is tender.

Serves 4-6.

AROMATIC CHICKEN

- 2 teaspoons tamarind paste (see page 11)
- salt
- 1 (1.5 kg/3½ lb) chicken, cut into pieces, or chicken portions, chopped
- 12 fresh green chillies, cored, seeded and chopped
- 2 small onions, chopped
- 5 cloves garlic, crushed
- 1 ripe tomato, chopped
- 5 tablespoons vegetable oil
- 4 kaffir lime leaves
- 1 stalk lemon grass, crushed

Blend tamarind paste with 1 teaspoon salt and 2 tablespoons hot water. Pour mixture over chicken and rub in. Leave for 1 hour.

Put chillies, onions, garlic and tomato in a blender and mix to a paste. In a wok or large heavy sauté pan, heat oil. Add chicken and marinade. Turn to brown on both sides then remove with a slotted spoon.

Add spice paste, lime leaves and lemon grass to pan. Cook, stirring, for 6-7 minutes until paste is browned. Return chicken to pan, add 300 ml (10 fl oz/1¼ cups) water and bring to a simmer. Cover and simmer gently for 30 minutes until chicken juices run clear, turning chicken occasionally.

Serves 4.

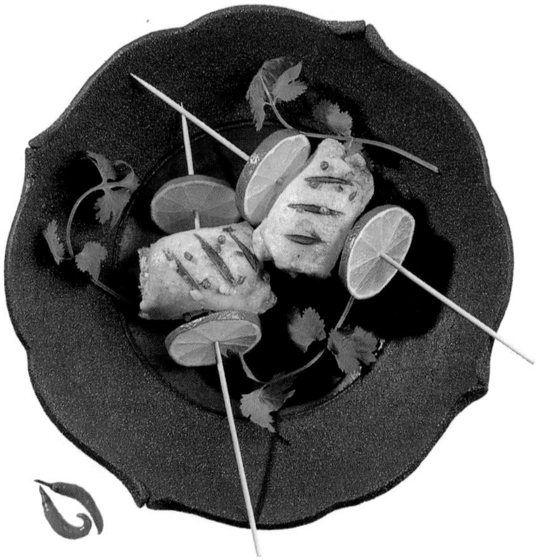

MALAY CHICKEN

2 teaspoons cumin seeds
2 teaspoons coriander seeds
8 boneless chicken thighs, total weight about 700 g (1½ lb)
1 bunch spring onions, white part only, finely chopped
2 tablespoons chopped coriander leaves
55 g (2 oz) creamed coconut, chopped
1 clove garlic, crushed and finely chopped
½ fresh red chilli, cored, seeded and chopped
2 teaspoons sunflower oil
1 teaspoon sesame oil
2 tablespoons lime juice
salt
lime slices
coriander sprigs, to garnish

Place cumin and coriander seeds in a small pan and heat until aroma is released. Grind in a blender or using a pestle and mortar and set aside. Open out chicken thighs. Mix together spring onions and coriander and spoon an equal quantity on each opened chicken thigh. Reform thighs. Place in a single layer in a non-reactive dish. Put coconut in a bowl and stir in 200 ml (7 fl oz/scant 1 cup) boiling water until dissolved. Stir in garlic, chilli, oils, lime juice, spices and salt. Pour over chicken, turn to coat in marinade then cover and refrigerate overnight.

Preheat grill or barbecue. Transfer chicken to room temperature. Soak bamboo skewers in water for 20-30 minutes. Remove chicken from marinade (reserve marinade) and thread 1 or 2 chicken thighs on to each skewer with a lime slice. Grill or barbecue for about 20 minutes, basting with remaining marinade, until chicken juices run clear when tested with the point of a sharp knife. Garnish with coriander sprigs.

Serves 4.

NONYA CHICKEN

2 tablespoons vegetable oil
800 g (1¾ lb) chicken portions, cut into large bite-sized pieces
2 fresh red chillies, sliced into rings
1 tablespoon dark soy sauce
1 tablespoon light soy sauce
1½ teaspoons light brown sugar
1 onion, sliced into 0.5 cm (¼ in) rings
sesame oil for sprinkling
toasted sesame seeds, to garnish

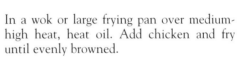

In a wok or large frying pan over medium-high heat, heat oil. Add chicken and fry until evenly browned.

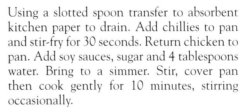

Using a slotted spoon transfer to absorbent kitchen paper to drain. Add chillies to pan and stir-fry for 30 seconds. Return chicken to pan. Add soy sauces, sugar and 4 tablespoons water. Bring to a simmer. Stir, cover pan then cook gently for 10 minutes, stirring occasionally.

Stir in onion, re-cover pan and continue to cook gently, stirring occasionally, for 5 minutes or until onion is soft and chicken juices run clear when chicken is pierced with a sharp knife. Sprinkle in a few drops of sesame oil. Serve scattered with toasted sesame seeds to garnish.

Serves 3-4.

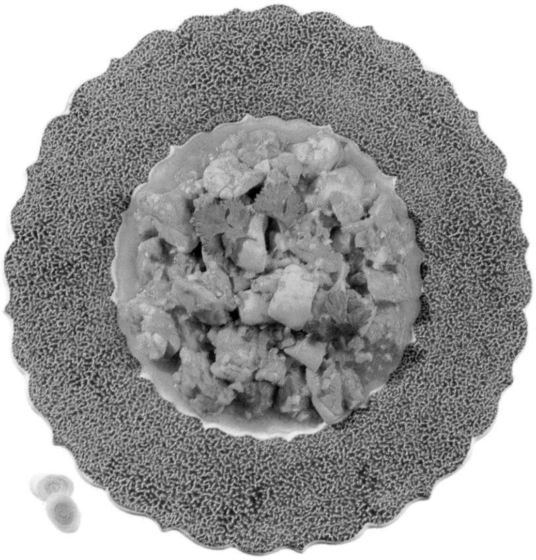

MALAYSIAN SPICED CHICKEN

8 chicken thighs, boned (see page 42) and chopped
3 tablespoons vegetable oil
1 clove garlic, finely chopped
2 tablespoons fish sauce
6 shallots, finely chopped
coriander leaves, to garnish
MARINADE:
2 small fresh red chillies, cored, seeded and chopped
1 stalk lemon grass, chopped
1 clove garlic, crushed
4 cm (1½ in) piece fresh root ginger, chopped
1 tablespoon ground turmeric
225 g (8 oz) canned tomatoes
1 tablespoon light brown sugar
salt

To make marinade, put chillies, lemon grass, garlic, ginger, turmeric, tomatoes, brown sugar and salt in a blender and mix together well. Put chicken in a non-reactive bowl. Pour marinade over chicken. Stir together, cover and refrigerate overnight. Return bowl of chicken to room temperature for 1 hour. In a wok or heavy sauté pan over high heat, heat oil. Add garlic and fry for 30 seconds. Add chicken and marinade. Stir and toss together, then stir in fish sauce and 4 tablespoons hot water. Cover, lower heat and simmer for 5 minutes.

Add shallots and continue to cook, uncovered, stirring occasionally, for about 10 minutes, until chicken juices run clear. Serve garnished with coriander.

Serves 4.

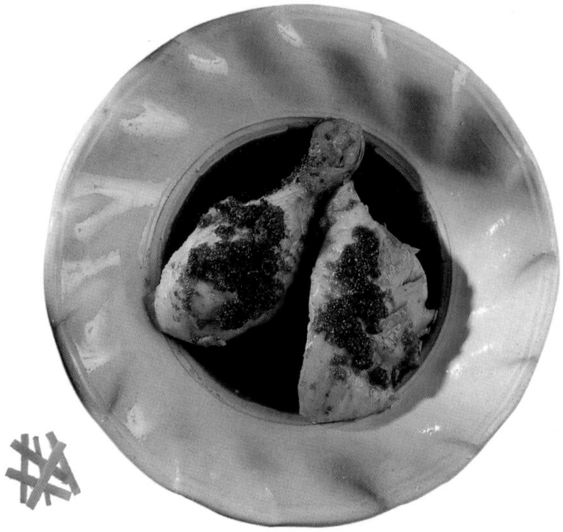

GINGER & SOY ROAST CHICKEN

4 cm (1½ in) piece fresh root ginger, coarsely chopped
1 onion, coarsely chopped
3 cloves garlic, coarsely chopped
1 (1.5 kg/3½ lb) chicken
5 tablespoons vegetable oil
3 tablespoons dark soy sauce
3 tablespoons rice vinegar
2½ tablespoons light brown sugar

Put ginger, onion and garlic in a blender. Mix to a paste, adding a little water if necessary.

Put chicken in a roasting tin. Rub inside and outside of chicken with half of ginger mixture. Cover and leave for 1 hour. Put remaining ginger paste in a bowl and stir in oil, soy sauce, rice vinegar, sugar and 6 tablespoons water.

Preheat oven to 180C (350F/Gas 4). Prop up tail end of chicken. Pour as much soy sauce mixture as possible into cavity of chicken. Roast chicken for 25 minutes, basting occasionally with remaining soy mixture. Pour remaining soy mixture around chicken and cook for a further 50 minutes, basting occasionally, until chicken juices run clear. Stir a little water into the tin if sauce begins to dry out too much.

Serves 4.

CHICKEN WITH RICE

2.5 cm (1 in) piece fresh root ginger, grated
4 spring onions, including some green, finely chopped
2 teaspoons rice wine
1 (1.25 kg/2½ lb) chicken
4 cloves garlic, lightly crushed
225 g (8 oz/1¼ cups) long-grain white rice
TO SERVE:
5 cm (2 in) piece fresh root ginger, grated
¼ teaspoon salt
2 teaspoons soy sauce
2 teaspoons rice vinegar
1 teaspoon sesame oil
2 spring onions, including some green, sliced

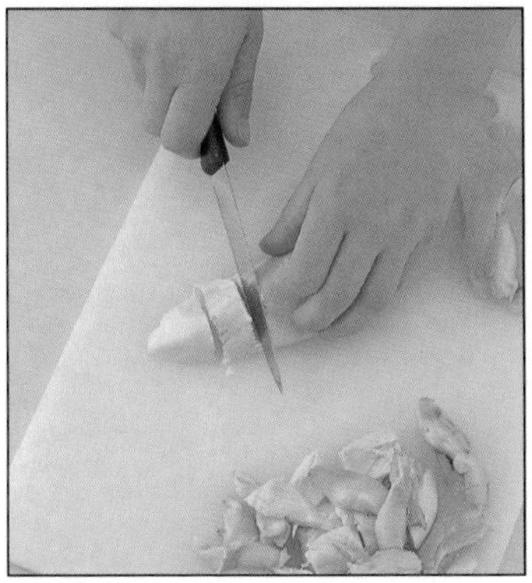

In a small bowl, mix together ginger, spring onions and rice wine. Rub over chicken and put some in cavity. Set aside to cool for 1 hour. Put chicken in a large saucepan and cover with water. Add garlic and bring to the boil over medium heat. Skim off any impurities. Cover pan and poach for 25 minutes. Remove from heat and leave to cool for 1½ hours. Remove chicken and plunge into a bowl of water and ice cubes for 10 minutes. Strain stock and measure 450 ml (16 fl oz/2 cups). Remove chicken skin and cut meat into chunks. Keep warm.

In another serving bowl, mix ginger and salt. In another bowl, mix soy sauce, rice vinegar and sesame oil. In a third bowl, put spring onions. Bring measured stock to the boil; add rice. Return to the boil, stir, cover and simmer for 12 minutes. Remove from heat and leave for 5 minutes until tender. Divide rice between 4 warm serving bowls and put chicken on top. Bring remaining stock to the boil. Spoon over chicken or serve separately. Serve with accompaniments.

Serves 4.

CHICKEN IN SPICED SAUCE

2 tablespoons vegetable oil
6 chicken thighs and 6 chicken drumsticks
2 stalks lemon grass, chopped
4 shallots, chopped
4 cloves garlic, chopped
7 cm (2½ in) piece fresh root ginger, chopped
3 tablespoons ground coriander
2 teaspoons ground turmeric
4 fresh bay leaves
350 ml (12 fl oz/1½ cups) coconut milk
4 tablespoons Chinese chilli sauce
about 2 tablespoons brown sugar, or to taste
55 g (2 oz/⅓ cup) chopped roasted candlenuts or cashew nuts
salt

In a large frying pan over medium heat, heat oil. Add chicken and brown evenly. Transfer to absorbent kitchen paper to drain. Pour all but 1½ tablespoons fat from pan. Put lemon grass, shallots, garlic and ginger in a blender. Mix to a paste. Gently heat pan of fat, add spice paste and stir for 2 minutes. Stir in coriander, turmeric and bay leaves and stir-fry for 1 minute. Stir in coconut milk, chilli sauce, sugar, nuts and salt and stir-fry for a further minute.

Return chicken to pan and turn in sauce. Cover and cook gently for 20 minutes, stirring and turning chicken frequently, until chicken juices run clear. Discard bay leaves before serving.

Serves 6.

CHICKEN IN COCONUT MILK

8 black peppercorns, cracked
6 coriander roots, finely chopped
4.5 cm (1¾ in) piece galangal, thinly sliced
2 fresh green chillies, seeded and thinly sliced
550 ml (20 fl oz/2½ cups) coconut milk
grated zest 1 kaffir lime
4 kaffir lime leaves, shredded
1 (1.35 kg/3 lb) chicken, cut into 8 pieces
1 tablespoon fish sauce
3 tablespoons lime juice
3 tablespoons chopped coriander leaves

Using a pestle and mortar or small blender, pound or mix together peppercorns, coriander roots and galangal.

In a wok, briefly heat peppercorn mixture, stirring, then stir in chillies, coconut milk, lime zest and leaves. Heat to just simmering point and add chicken portions. Adjust heat so liquid is barely moving, then cook gently for about 40-45 minutes until chicken is very tender and liquid reduced.

Stir in fish sauce and lime juice. Scatter coriander leaves over chicken and serve.

Serves 6-8.

CHICKEN WITH CORIANDER

6 coriander sprigs
1 tablespoon black peppercorns, crushed
2 cloves garlic, chopped
juice 1 lime
2 teaspoons fish sauce
4 large or 6 medium chicken drumsticks or thighs
lime wedges, to serve
spring onion brushes (see page 14), to garnish

Using a pestle and mortar or small blender, pound or mix together coriander, peppercorns, garlic, lime juice and fish sauce; set aside.

Using the point of a sharp knife, cut slashes in chicken. Spread spice mixture over chicken. Cover and set aside in a cool place for 2-3 hours, turning occasionally.

Preheat grill. Grill chicken, basting and turning occasionally, for about 10 minutes until cooked through and golden. Serve with wedges of lime and garnish with spring onion brushes.

Serves 2-4.

LEMON GRASS CHICKEN CURRY

350 g (12 oz) boneless chicken, chopped into small pieces
1 tablespoon Red Curry Paste (see page 230)
3 tablespoons vegetable oil
2 cloves garlic, finely chopped
1 tablespoon fish sauce
2 stalks lemon grass, finely chopped
5 kaffir lime leaves, shredded
½ teaspoon crushed palm sugar

Place chicken in a bowl, add curry paste and stir to coat chicken; set aside for 30 minutes.

In a wok, heat oil, add garlic and fry until golden. Stir in chicken, then fish sauce, lemon grass, lime leaves, sugar and 115 ml (4 fl oz/½ cup) water.

Adjust heat so liquid is barely moving and cook for 15-20 minutes until chicken is cooked through. If chicken becomes too dry, add a little more water, but the final dish should be quite dry.

Serves 3-4.

BARBECUED THAI CHICKEN

4 fresh red chillies, seeded and sliced
2 cloves garlic, chopped
5 shallots, finely sliced
2 teaspoons crushed palm sugar
115 ml (4 fl oz/½ cup) coconut cream (see page 8)
2 teaspoons fish sauce
1 tablespoon tamarind water (see page 11)
4 boneless chicken breasts
Thai holy basil leaves or coriander leaves, to garnish

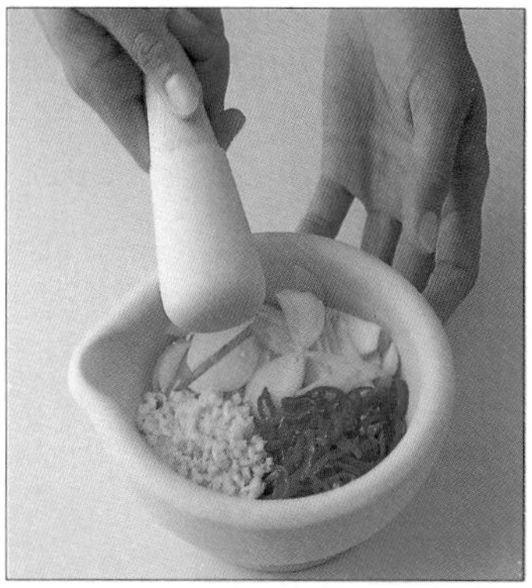

Using a pestle and mortar or small blender, pound or blend chillies, garlic and shallots to a paste. Work in sugar, then stir in coconut cream, fish sauce and tamarind water.

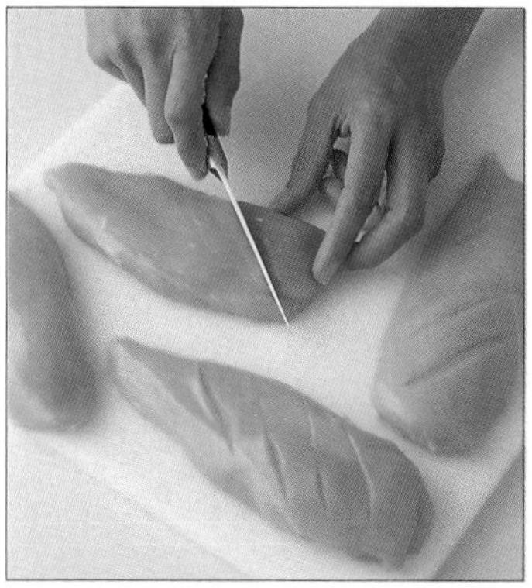

Using the point of a sharp knife, cut 4 slashes in chicken breast. Place chicken in a shallow dish and pour over spice mixture. Turn to coat, cover dish and set aside for 1 hour.

Preheat grill. Place chicken on a piece of aluminium foil and grill for about 4 minutes a side, basting occasionally, until cooked through. Garnish with basil or coriander leaves.

Serves 4.

THAI SPICED CHICKEN

5 shallots, chopped
3 cloves garlic, chopped
5 coriander roots, chopped
2 stalks lemon grass, chopped
2 fresh red chillies, seeded and chopped
4 cm (1½ in) piece fresh root ginger, finely chopped
1 teaspoon shrimp paste
1½ tablespoons vegetable oil
2 chicken legs, divided into thighs and drumsticks
1½ tablespoons tamarind water (see page 11)

Using a pestle and mortar or blender, pound or mix shallots, garlic, coriander, lemon grass, chillies, ginger and shrimp paste until smooth.

In a wok, heat oil, stir in spicy paste and cook, stirring, for 3-4 minutes. Stir in chicken pieces to coat evenly.

Add tamarind water and 85 ml (3 fl oz/⅓ cup) water. Cover and cook gently for about 25 minutes until chicken is tender.

Serves 3-4.

CHICKEN WITH BASIL LEAVES

2 tablespoons vegetable oil
2 cloves garlic, chopped
350 g (12 oz) boneless, skinless chicken breast, chopped
1 small onion, finely chopped
3 fresh chillies, seeded and thinly sliced
20 Thai holy basil leaves
1 tablespoon fish sauce
4 tablespoons coconut milk
squeeze lime juice
Thai holy basil leaves and chilli flower (see page 14), to garnish

In a wok, heat 1 tablespoon oil, add garlic, chicken, onion and chillies and cook, stirring occasionally, for 3-5 minutes until cooked through.

Stir in basil leaves, fish sauce and coconut milk. Stir briefly over heat. Squeeze over lime juice. Serve garnished with basil leaves and chilli flower.

Serves 2-3.

CHICKEN WITH GALANGAL

450 g (1 lb) boneless, skinless chicken breast
3 tablespoons vegetable oil
2 cloves garlic, finely chopped
1 onion, quartered and sliced
2.5 cm (1 in) piece galangal, finely chopped
8 pieces dried Chinese black mushrooms, soaked for 30 minutes, drained and chopped
1 fresh red chilli, seeded and cut into fine strips
1 tablespoon fish sauce
1½ teaspoons crushed palm sugar
1 tablespoon lime juice
12 Thai mint leaves
4 spring onions, including some green, chopped
Thai mint leaves, to garnish

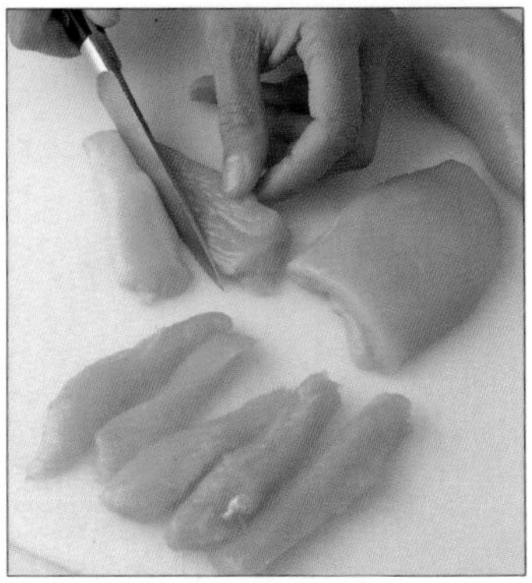

Using a sharp knife, cut chicken into 5 x 2.5 cm (2 x 1 in) pieces; set aside. In a wok, heat oil, add garlic and onion and cook, stirring occasionally, until golden. Stir in chicken and stir-fry for about 2 minutes.

Add galangal, mushrooms and chilli and stir-fry for 1 minute. Stir in fish sauce, sugar, lime juice, mint leaves, spring onions and 3-4 tablespoons water. Cook, stirring, for about 1 minute. Transfer to a warmed serving dish and scatter over mint leaves.

Serves 4.

CHICKEN WITH PEANUT SAUCE

2.5 cm (1 in) piece galangal, chopped
2 cloves garlic, chopped
1½ tablespoons Fragrant Curry Paste (see page 231)
4 tablespoons coconut cream (see page 8)
450 g (1 lb) boneless, skinless chicken breast, cut into large pieces
3 shallots, chopped
4 tablespoons dry-roasted peanuts, chopped
225 ml (8 fl oz/1 cup) coconut milk
½ teaspoon finely chopped dried red chilli
2 teaspoons fish sauce
freshly cooked broccoli, to serve

Using a pestle and mortar or small blender, pound or mix together galangal, garlic and curry paste. Mix in coconut cream. Place chicken in a bowl and stir in spice mixture; set aside for 1 hour.

Heat a wok, add shallots and coated chicken and stir-fry for 3-4 minutes. In a blender, mix peanuts with coconut milk, then stir into chicken with chilli and fish sauce. Cook gently for about 30 minutes until chicken is tender and thick sauce formed. Transfer to centre of a warmed serving plate and arrange cooked broccoli around.

Serves 4.

CHICKEN WITH MANGETOUT

3 tablespoons vegetable oil
3 cloves garlic, chopped
1 dried red chilli, seeded and chopped
3 red shallots, chopped
2 tablespoons lime juice
2 teaspoons fish sauce
350 g (12 oz) chicken, finely chopped
1½ stalks lemon grass, chopped
1 kaffir lime leaf, sliced
175 g (6 oz) mangetout
1½ tablespoons coarsely ground brown rice (see page 10)
3 spring onions, chopped
chopped coriander leaves, to garnish

In a wok, heat 2 tablespoons oil, add garlic and cook, stirring occasionally, until lightly browned. Stir in chilli, shallots, lime juice, fish sauce and 4 tablespoons water. Simmer for 1-2 minutes, then stir in chicken, lemon grass and lime leaf. Cook, stirring, for 2-3 minutes until chicken is just cooked through. Transfer to a warmed plate and keep warm.

Heat remaining oil in wok, add mangetout and stir-fry for 2-3 minutes until just tender. Transfer to a warmed serving plate. Return chicken to wok. Add rice and spring onions. Heat for about 1 minute, then transfer to serving plate. Garnish with chopped coriander.

Serves 3-4.

STEAMED CHICKEN CURRY

1 quantity Fragrant Curry Paste (see page 231)
375 ml (13 fl oz/1⅔ cups) coconut milk
450 g (1 lb) boneless, skinless chicken breast, sliced
4 kaffir lime leaves, shredded
8 Thai holy basil leaves
Thai holy basil sprig, to garnish

Using a small blender, mix together curry paste, 85 ml (3 fl oz/⅓ cup) coconut milk and an equal quantity of water; set aside. Place chicken in a heatproof bowl or dish, stir in remaining coconut milk and set aside for 30 minutes.

Stir curry-flavoured coconut milk, lime leaves and basil leaves into chicken in bowl or dish. Cover top tightly with aluminium foil and place in a steaming basket.

Cover with a lid. Position over a saucepan of boiling water. Steam for about 40 minutes until chicken is tender. Garnish with basil.

Serves 4-5.

Note: In Thailand the curry is steamed on a bed of lettuce and basil leaves, wrapped in a banana leaf.

THAI LEMON GRASS CHICKEN

1 (1.35 kg/3 lb) chicken, cut into 8 pieces
4 thick stalks lemon grass
4 spring onions, chopped
4 black peppercorns, cracked
2 tablespoons vegetable oil
1 fresh green chilli, seeded and thinly sliced
2 teaspoons fish sauce
fresh red chilli, cut into think slivers, to garnish

With the point of a sharp knife, cut slashes in each chicken piece; place in a shallow dish.

Bruise top parts of each lemon grass stalk and reserve. Chop lower parts, then pound with spring onions and peppercorns using a pestle and mortar. Spread over chicken and into slashes. Cover and set aside for 2 hours.

In a wok, heat oil, add chicken and cook, turning occasionally, for about 5 minutes until lightly browned. Add green chilli, bruised lemon grass stalks and 4 tablespoons water. Cover wok and cook over low heat for 25-30 minutes until chicken is cooked through. Stir in fish sauce. Transfer chicken pieces to a warmed serving dish, spoon over cooking juices and sprinkle with red chilli.

Serves 4-6.

DUCK CURRY

5 tablespoons coconut cream (see page 8)
5 tablespoons Green Curry Paste (see page 230)
1 (1.35 kg/3 lb) duck, skinned if desired, trimmed of excess fat and divided into 8 portions
550 ml (20 fl oz/2½ cups) coconut milk
1 tablespoon fish sauce
8 kaffir lime leaves, shredded
2 fresh green chillies, seeded and thinly sliced
12 Thai holy basil leaves
leaves from 5 coriander sprigs
coriander sprigs, to garnish

Heat coconut cream in a wok over a medium heat, stirring, until it thickens and oil begins to separate and bubble.

Stir in curry paste and cook for about 5 minutes until mixture darkens. Stir in duck pieces to coat with curry mixture. Lower heat, cover and cook for 15 minutes, stirring occasionally. If necessary, using a bulb baster, remove excess fat from the surface, or carefully spoon it off. Stir in coconut milk, fish sauce and lime leaves. Heat to just simmering point, then cook gently without boiling, turning duck over occasionally, for 30-40 minutes until meat is very tender. Remove surplus fat from surface, then stir in chillies.

Cook for a further 5 minutes. Stir in basil and coriander leaves and cook for a further 2 minutes. Garnish with coriander sprigs.

Serves 4.

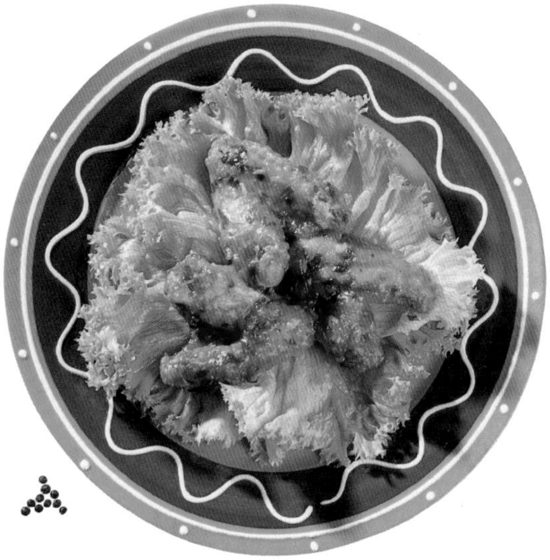

CHICKEN WINGS IN SPICY SAUCE

8-12 chicken wings
salt and freshly ground black pepper
1 tablespoon sugar
1 tablespoon fish sauce
oil for deep-frying
250 ml (9 fl oz/1 cup) Vietnamese Hot Sauce (see page 234)
about 85 ml (3 fl oz/⅓ cup) chicken stock or water
1 tablespoon clear honey
lettuce leaves

Trim off tip of each chicken wing (these are known as pinions), which can be used for making stock.

In a bowl, marinate chicken wings with salt, pepper, sugar and fish sauce for at least 30 minutes, longer if possible. Heat oil in a wok or deep-fat fryer to 160C (325F) and deep-fry chicken wings for 2-3 minutes until golden; remove and drain.

Heat Vietnamese Hot Sauce with chicken stock or water in a saucepan and add chicken wings. Bring to the boil and braise for 5-6 minutes, stirring constantly until sauce is sticky. Add honey and blend well. Serve hot or cold on a bed of lettuce leaves.

Serves 4-6.

CHICKEN & COCONUT CURRY

1 (1 kg/2¼ lb) chicken, cut into 10-12 pieces
salt and freshly ground black pepper
1 teaspoon sugar
1 tablespoon curry powder
3-4 tablespoons vegetable oil
3 red or white potatoes, peeled and cut into cubes
1 teaspoon chopped garlic
1 tablespoon chopped lemon grass
1 onion, cut into small pieces
250 ml (9 fl oz/1 cup) Vietnamese Hot Sauce (see page 234)
450 ml (16 fl oz/2 cups) stock or water
450 ml (16 fl oz/2 cups) coconut milk
3 bay leaves and 1 carrot, sliced
2 tablespoons fish sauce
coriander sprigs, to garnish

In a dish, marinate chicken pieces with salt, pepper, sugar and curry powder for at least 1 hour. Heat oil in a large pan and fry potatoes for 3-4 minutes until brown – it is not necessary to completely cook potatoes at this stage. Remove potatoes from pan and set aside.

In the same oil, stir-fry garlic, lemon grass and onion for about 30 seconds. Add chicken pieces and stir-fry for 2-3 minutes, then add Vietnamese Hot Sauce, stock or water, coconut milk and bay leaves. Bring to the boil, and add parboiled potatoes, carrot slices and fish sauce. Blend well, then cover and simmer for 15-20 minutes, stirring now and then to make sure nothing is stuck on the bottom of the pan. Garnish with coriander sprigs and serve.

Serves 4-6.

GRILLED CHICKEN DRUMSTICKS

1-2 cloves garlic, chopped
1-2 stalks lemon grass, chopped
2 shallots, chopped
1-2 small red or green chillies, chopped
1 tablespoon chopped coriander leaves
55 ml (2 fl oz/¼ cup) fish sauce
6-8 chicken drumsticks, skinned
lettuce leaves
Spicy Fish Sauce (see page 233), to serve

Using a pestle and mortar, pound garlic, lemon grass, shallots, chillies and coriander to a paste.

In a mixing bowl, thoroughly blend pounded mixture with fish sauce to a smooth paste. Add drumsticks and coat well with paste, then cover the bowl and leave to marinate for 2-3 hours, turning drumsticks every 30 minutes or so.

Prepare barbecue or preheat grill. Cook drumsticks over the barbecue or under the grill for 10-15 minutes, turning frequently and basting with marinade remaining in the bowl for the first 5 minutes only. Serve hot on a bed of lettuce leaves with Spicy Fish Sauce as a dip.

Serves 4-6.

VIETNAMESE CHICKEN STIR-FRY

225 g (8 oz) chicken fillet, boned and skinned
2 teaspoons cornflour
2 teaspoons fish sauce
salt and freshly ground pepper
2-3 tablespoons vegetable oil
½ teaspoon minced garlic
1 teaspoon finely chopped lemon grass
1 teaspoon chopped fresh root ginger
4-6 dried small red chillies
55 g (2 oz) mangetout, trimmed
½ red pepper, cored and cut into cubes
55 g (2 oz) sliced bamboo shoots, drained
1 teaspoon sugar
1 tablespoon rice vinegar
2 tablespoons oyster sauce
½ teaspoon sesame oil

Cut chicken into bite-sized slices or cubes. Mix cornflour with 1 tablespoon water. Place chicken in a bowl with cornflour paste and fish sauce. Season with salt and pepper and leave to marinate for 20-25 minutes. Heat oil in a wok or frying pan and stir-fry garlic, lemon grass, ginger and chillies for 30 seconds. Add chicken pieces and stir-fry for about 1 minute until colour of chicken changes.

Add mangetout, red pepper and bamboo shoots and cook for 2-3 minutes, stirring constantly, then add sugar, vinegar, oyster sauce and 3-4 tablespoons water. Blend well, bring to boil and add sesame oil. Serve at once with flat rice noodles.

Serves 4.

Variation: Use chicken stock instead of 3-4 tablespoons water.

CHICKEN HOT POT

450 g (1 lb) chicken thigh meat, boned and cut into small bite-sized pieces
salt and freshly ground pepper
2 teaspoons sugar
1 tablespoon each lime juice and fish sauce
1 tablespoon vegetable oil
2 cloves garlic, sliced, and 2 shallots, chopped
1 tablespoon dried small red chillies
2 tablespoons crushed yellow bean sauce
about 450 ml (16 fl oz/2 cups) chicken stock
2 spring onions, cut into short sections
coriander sprigs, to garnish

Marinate chicken with salt, pepper, sugar, lime juice and fish sauce for 1-2 hours.

Heat oil in a clay pot or flameproof casserole and stir-fry garlic, shallots and chillies for about 1 minute, then add yellow bean sauce and stir until smooth.

Add chicken pieces and stir-fry for 1-2 minutes. Add chicken stock, blend well and bring to the boil, then reduce heat, cover and simmer gently for 15-20 minutes. Uncover and stir in spring onions. Garnish with coriander sprigs and serve straight from the pot. Serve with rice.

Serves 4.

Note: The longer chicken is marinated, the better the flavour, so try to leave it for 2 hours.

CHICKEN WITH LEMON GRASS

450 g (1 lb) boned and skinned chicken fillet, cut into bite-sized slices or cubes
salt and freshly ground black pepper
1 teaspoon minced garlic
2 tablespoons finely chopped lemon grass
1 tablespoon sugar
1 teaspoon chilli sauce
3 tablespoons fish sauce
2-3 tablespoons vegetable oil
1 small onion, sliced
1-2 small red chillies, seeded and chopped

Mix chicken with salt, pepper, garlic, lemon grass, sugar, chilli sauce and 1 tablespoon fish sauce and marinate for 30 minutes.

Heat oil in a wok or frying pan and stir-fry onion slices for about 1 minute until opaque. Add chicken pieces, stir to separate them, then add remaining fish sauce and cook for 2-3 minutes until colour of chicken changes.

Add 55 ml (2 fl oz/¼ cup) water to marinade bowl to rinse out, then add to chicken. Bring to the boil and cook for 1 minute. Garnish with chopped chillies and serve with rice noodles.

Serves 4.

Variations: Firm white fish, pork or cubes of tofu can be cooked by the same method. Chicken stock can be used to rinse out the marinade bowl instead of water.

AROMATIC DUCK

2 half or 4 quarter portions duck (2 breasts and 2 legs)
salt and freshly ground black pepper
1 tablespoon five-spice powder
4-5 small pieces fresh root ginger
3-4 spring onions, cut into short sections
3-4 tablespoons Chinese rice wine or dry sherry
12 sheets dried rice paper, halved if large
fresh mint, basil and coriander leaves
Spicy Fish Sauce (see page 233), to serve

Rub salt, pepper and five-spice powder all over duck portions.

In a shallow dish, mix ginger, spring onions and rice wine or sherry, add duck portions and leave to marinate for at least 3-4 hours, turning duck pieces now and then. Steam duck portions with marinade in a hot steamer for 2-3 hours. Remove duck portions from liquid and leave to cool. (Duck can be cooked up to this stage in advance, if wished.)

Preheat oven to 230C (450F/Gas 8) and bake duck pieces, skin-side up, for 10-15 minutes, then pull meat off the bone. Meanwhile, soften dried rice paper in warm water. Place about 2 tablespoons of meat in each half sheet of rice paper, add a few mint, basil and coriander leaves, roll into a meat bundle, then dip roll in Spicy Fish Sauce before eating it.

Serves 4-6.

VIETNAMESE ROAST DUCK

1 teaspoon minced garlic
2-3 shallots, finely chopped
2 teaspoons five-spice powder
2 tablespoon sugar
55 ml (2 fl oz/¼ cup) red rice vinegar
1 tablespoon fish sauce
1 tablespoon soy sauce
4 quarter portions duck (2 breasts and 2 legs)
250 ml (9 fl oz/1 cup) coconut milk
salt and freshly ground black pepper
watercress, to serve
coriander sprigs, to garnish

In a bowl, mix garlic, shallots, five-spice powder, sugar, vinegar, fish and soy sauces.

Add duck pieces and leave to marinate for at least 2-3 hours, or overnight in the refrigerator, turning occasionally. Preheat oven to 220C (425F/Gas 7). Remove duck portions from marinade and place, skin-side up, on a rack in a baking tin and cook in the oven for 45 minutes, without turning or basting.

Remove duck and keep warm. Heat marinade with drippings in the baking tin, add coconut milk, bring to boil and simmer for 5 minutes. Season with salt and pepper, then pour sauce into a serving bowl. Serve duck portions on a bed of watercress, garnished with coriander sprigs.

Serve 4-6.

Note: The duck portions can be chopped through the bone into bite-sized pieces for serving, if wished.

DUCK BREASTS IN SPICY SAUCE

4 duck breasts, boned but not skinned
salt and freshly ground black pepper
1 teaspoon chopped garlic
2 shallots or 1 small onion, finely chopped
1 tablespoon chopped lemon grass
1 tablespoon chopped fresh root ginger
2-3 tablespoons vegetable oil
1 teaspoon sugar
2 tablespoons fish sauce
1 teaspoon chilli sauce
115 ml (4 fl oz/½ cup) chicken stock or water
2 teaspoons cornflour
½ teaspoon sesame oil
1-2 small red chillies, seeded and shredded
coriander sprigs, to garnish

Make a few shallow criss-cross cuts on skin side of duck breasts. Rub salt and pepper all over and leave for 15-20 minutes. Meanwhile, using a pestle and mortar, pound garlic, shallots or onion, lemon grass and ginger to a paste.

Heat oil in a wok or pan and fry duck pieces, skin-side down, for 2-3 minutes, then turn pieces over and cook for a further 2 minutes. Add garlic mixture and stir to coat well, then add sugar, fish and chilli sauces. Cook, stirring, for 1 minute. Add stock or water, bring to the boil and braise for 5-6 minutes, stirring. Mix cornflour with 1 tablespoon water and stir into sauce. Blend in sesame oil. Slice duck, garnish with chillies and coriander and serve with rice vermicelli.

Serves 4-6.

GRILLED QUAIL

4 cleaned quail, each split down backbone and pressed flat
salt and freshly ground black pepper
1 teaspoon minced garlic
1 tablespoon finely chopped lemon grass
1 teaspoon sugar
1 tablespoon fish sauce
1 tablespoon lime juice or vinegar
1-2 tablespoons vegetable oil
lettuce leaves
coriander sprigs, to garnish
Spicy Fish Sauce (see page 233), to serve

Rub 4 quail all over with plenty of salt and pepper.

In a mixing bowl, blend garlic, lemon grass, sugar, fish sauce and lime juice or vinegar. Add quail, turning to coat in mixture, then leave to marinate for 2-3 hours, turning over now and then.

Prepare a barbecue or preheat grill. Brush quail with oil and cook over barbecue or under grill for 6-8 minutes on each side, basting with remaining marinade during first 5 minutes of cooking. Serve quail on a bed of lettuce leaves, garnished with coriander sprigs, with Spicy Fish Sauce as a dip.

Serves 4.

CHICKEN-ROLLED ASPARAGUS

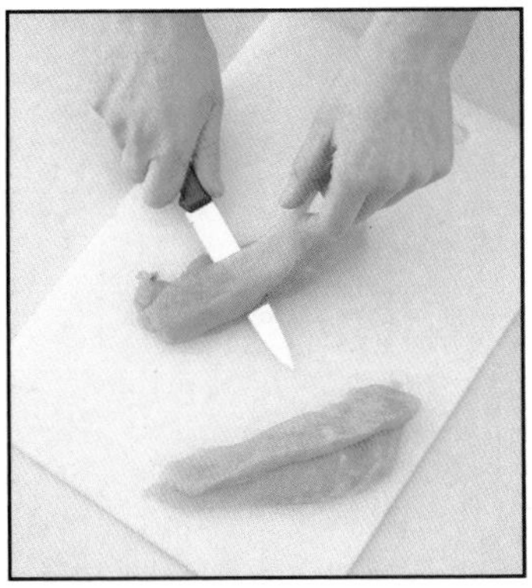

4 boneless, skinless chicken breasts
55 ml (2 fl oz/¼ cup) sake or white wine
salt and freshly ground black pepper
12 asparagus tips or 32-40 stalks French beans, trimmed
vegetable oil for frying
225 ml (8 fl oz/1 cup) dashi (see page 29), or chicken stock
250 g (9 oz) spinach, trimmed
MUSTARD SAUCE:
2 teaspoons mustard
3 tablespoons soy sauce

Cut chicken fillets in half along natural line and slice thickest half horizontally in two.

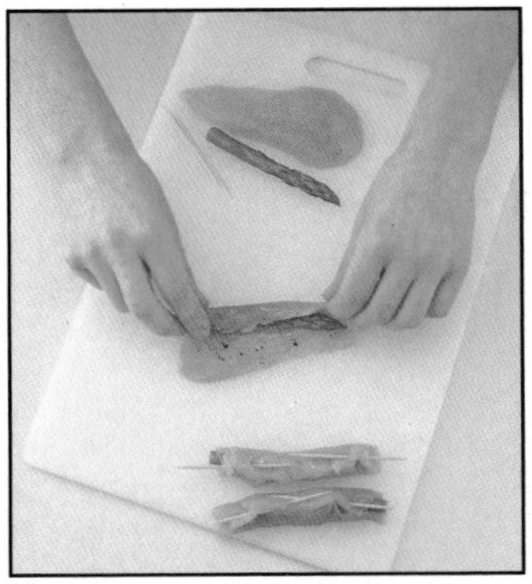

By making a few slits on thick parts, even out thickness to make 3 thin flat pieces, about 0.5 cm (¼ in) thick, from each chicken breast. Sprinkle with a little sake and salt and pepper. Parboil asparagus (or French beans) in lightly salted water and drain. Place an asparagus tip (or 4-5 French beans) on a chicken piece, roll up and secure with wooden cocktail sticks. If asparagus is too long, trim to length of chicken. Repeat with remaining chicken and asparagus or beans. Heat oil in a frying pan and pan-fry chicken rolls until light golden.

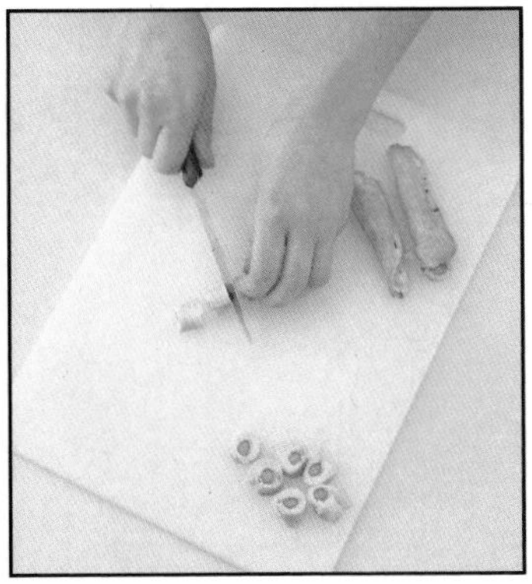

Add remaining sake and dashi or stock to the pan, bring to the boil, then simmer for 15 minutes. Cook spinach in boiling salted water for 1 minute, drain and chop into bite-sized lengths. Dissolve mustard with soy sauce and add 2-3 tablespoons of cooking juices to make a sauce. Cut chicken rolls into bite-sized pieces. Divide spinach between 4 individual serving plates, heaping it into a nest, pour sauce over the top, then arrange chicken pieces, cut-side up, on top.

Serves 4.

CHICKEN & CABBAGE ROLLS

450 g (1 lb) minced chicken
1 tablespoon miso
3 tablespoon soy sauce
1 tablespoon sugar
salt
4 large leaves Savoy cabbage
4 spring onions, shredded
sake
cooked and shredded carrot, to garnish
1-2 teaspoons mustard

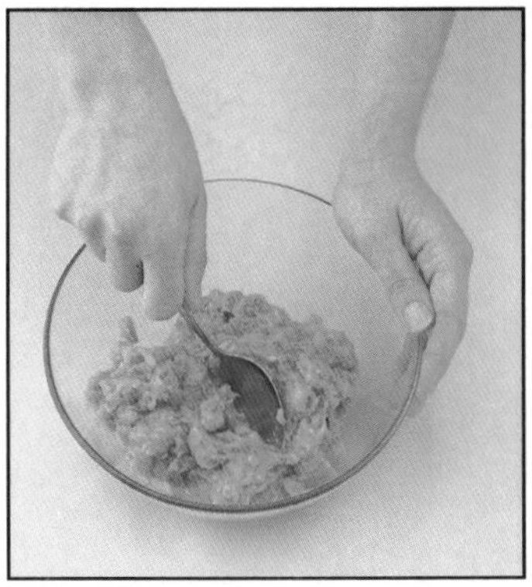

Mix minced chicken, miso, 1 tablespoon soy sauce, sugar and a little salt and grind to a smooth paste using the back of a tablespoon.

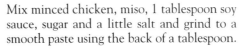

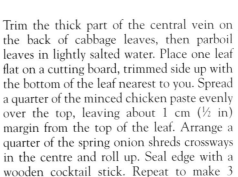

Trim the thick part of the central vein on the back of cabbage leaves, then parboil leaves in lightly salted water. Place one leaf flat on a cutting board, trimmed side up with the bottom of the leaf nearest to you. Spread a quarter of the minced chicken paste evenly over the top, leaving about 1 cm (½ in) margin from the top of the leaf. Arrange a quarter of the spring onion shreds crossways in the centre and roll up. Seal edge with a wooden cocktail stick. Repeat to make 3 more rolls.

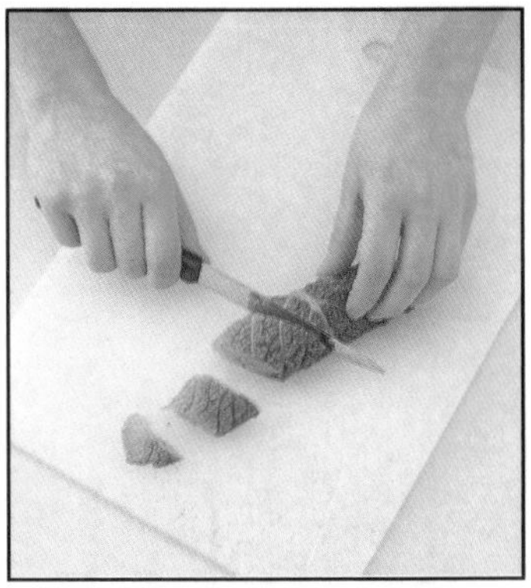

Place rolls on a large plate and sprinkle with sake. Place plate in a boiling steamer and steam rolls over high heat for 15 minutes or until chicken meat is well cooked. Drain, remove cocktail sticks and cut each roll diagonally into 4-5 pieces. Make a bed of shredded carrot on 4 individual serving plates and arrange pieces of roll on top. In a jug, mix mustard and remaining soy sauce with 2-3 tablespoons of cooking juices. Pour sauce over chicken and cabbage and serve at once.

GRILLED SKEWERED CHICKEN

8 unskinned chicken thighs, boned and cut into 2.5 cm (1 in) pieces
8 spring onions, white part only, cut into 2.5 cm (1 in) lengths
24 okra, trimmed
lemon wedges, sansho peppers and chilli powder, to garnish
TARE SAUCE:
3 tablespoons sake
70 ml (2½ fl oz/⅓ cup) soy sauce
1 tablespoon each mirin and sugar

Mix ingredients for tare sauce in a saucepan and bring to the boil. Remove from heat and set aside.

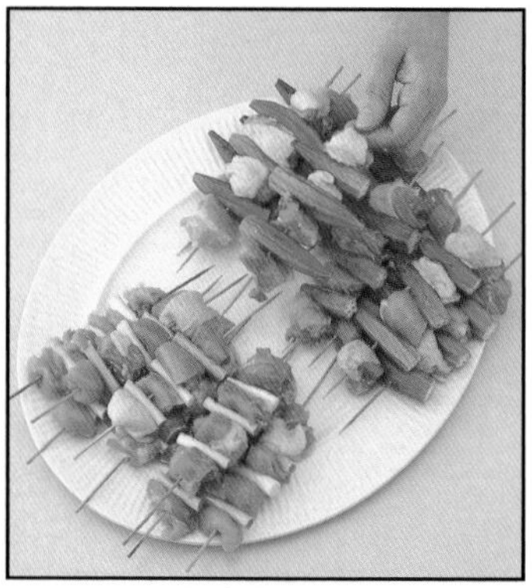

If barbecuing, prepare barbecue. Thread 4 pieces of chicken and 3 okra alternately on to a 20 cm (8 in) bamboo or stainless steel skewer. Repeat with another 7 skewers. Thread another 8 with 4 pieces of chicken and 3 pieces of spring onion. Thread any remaining ingredients on to extra skewers. Cook on barbecue, keeping skewer handles well away from fire and turning them frequently. Brush with tare sauce 2-3 times during cooking, until chicken is well cooked and golden brown.

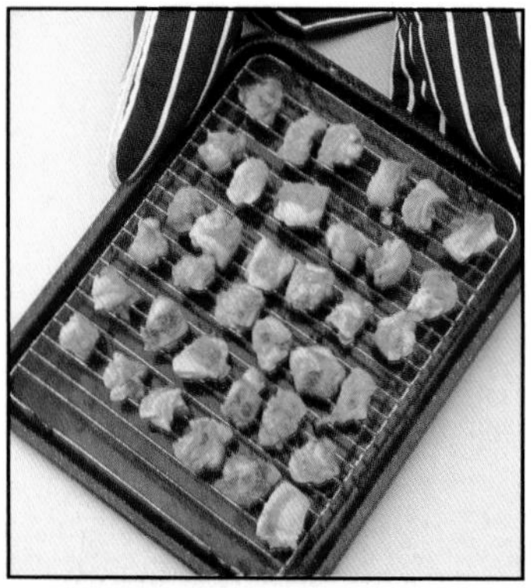

If grilling, preheat grill. On a well-oiled wire rack, spread chicken pieces well apart and cook under grill until both sides are golden brown. Dip pieces in tare sauce, put back on rack; grill for another 30 seconds on each side. Set aside. Lightly grill spring onions and okra without dipping in sauce. Thread 4 chicken pieces alternately with 3 spring onions on 8 skewers and with okra on another 8. Serve on a platter, garnished with lemon, sansho peppers and chilli powder.

Serves 4-8 as a starter.

CHAR-GRILLED YUAN CHICKEN

4 whole chicken legs, boned
8 large spring onions, white part only
lime or lemon wedges, to garnish
MARINADE:
70 ml (2½ fl oz/⅓ cup) sake or white wine
70 ml (2½ fl oz/⅓ cup) mirin or 1 tablespoon sugar
70 ml (2½ fl oz/⅓ cup) soy sauce
zest 1 lemon, in large pieces not chopped or shredded

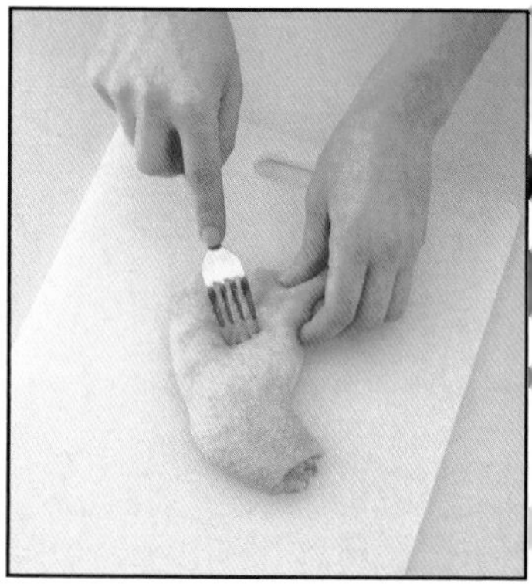

Place chicken legs on a cutting board skin-side up. Using a fork, pierce skin in a few places. Cut spring onions crossways into 4 cm (1½ in) lengths.

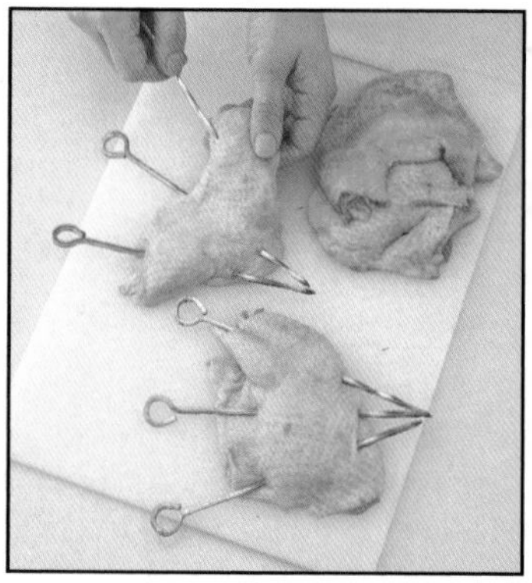

In a dish, mix sake or wine, mirin or sugar, soy sauce and lemon zest, add chicken and spring onions and leave to marinate for 30 minutes. If barbecuing, prepare barbecue. Thread 3-4 stainless steel skewers through each chicken leg parallel with skin in a fan shape. Char-grill skin-side down, over high heat for 6-7 minutes until golden brown, then turn and cook other side for 3-4 minutes. Thread spring onions, 6-8 pieces to a skewer, and char-grill. Remove skewers and serve 1 chicken leg and a quarter of the spring onions on each of 4 individual places.

If grilling, preheat grill. Lay chicken legs, unskewered, flat on a wire rack, with skin-side facing heat first and grill for about 10 minutes until golden brown. Turn and grill other side for 5-10 minutes until well cooked. Grill spring onions until both sides are golden brown. Cut chicken legs into bite-sized pieces and arrange chicken and spring onions on 4 individual plates. Serve hot, garnished with lime or lemon wedges.

Serves 4.

FRIED FISH-STUFFED CHICKEN

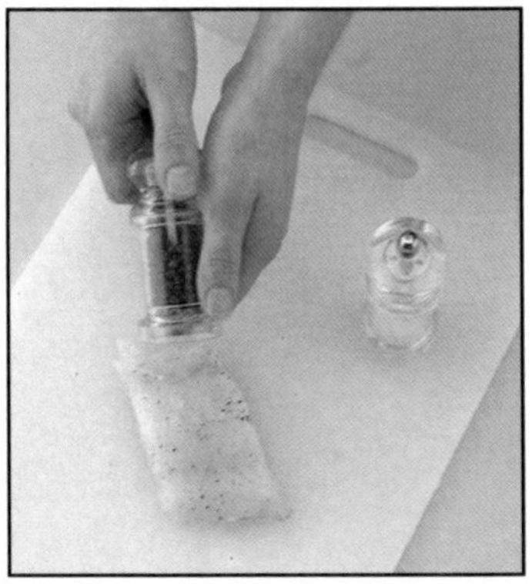

150-200 g (5-7 oz) cod fillet, skinned
salt and freshly ground black pepper
4 boneless, skinless chicken breasts
plain flour for coating
1 egg, beaten
dried bread crumbs for coating
vegetable oil for deep-frying
shredded lettuce, to serve
DIPPING SAUCE:
6 tablespoons mayonnaise
1½ tablespoons soy sauce

To make sauce, mix together mayonnaise and soy sauce. Set aside. Sprinkle cod fillet with a pinch of salt and pepper.

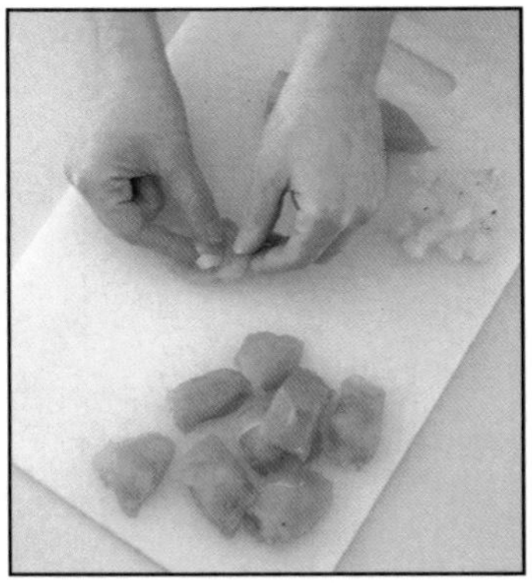

Separate one chicken fillet along its natural divide into 2 pieces and cut larger one crossways into 4 pieces and smaller one into 2 pieces. Slice 2 thickest pieces horizontally in half to make 8 pieces of even thickness, about 0.5 cm (¼ in). Repeat this with remaining 3 fillets. Make a deep slit horizontally in centre of each piece to make chicken envelopes and stuff with small pieces of seasoned cod. The chicken should completely encase the fish.

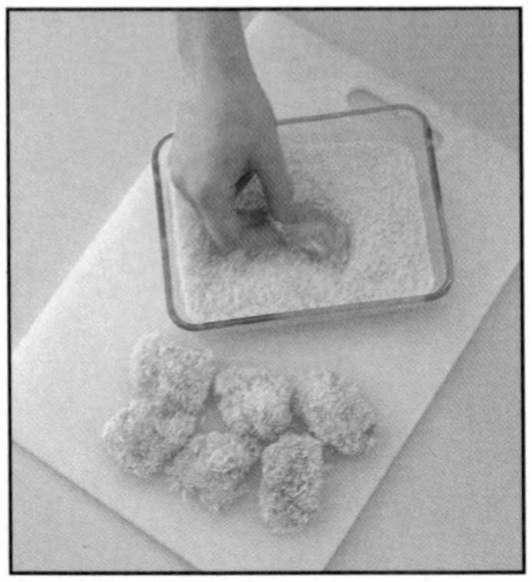

Dust stuffed chicken with plain flour, dip into beaten egg, then roll in bread crumbs and press gently to seal chicken envelope with bread crumbs. Heat oil in a wok or deep-frying pan to 170C (340F) and deep-fry chicken pieces, a few at a time, for 5-6 minutes until golden brown, turning frequently. Drain on a wire rack or absorbent kitchen paper. Make a bed of shredded lettuce on 4 individual plates. Arrange chicken on top. Serve at once with sauce.

Serves 4.

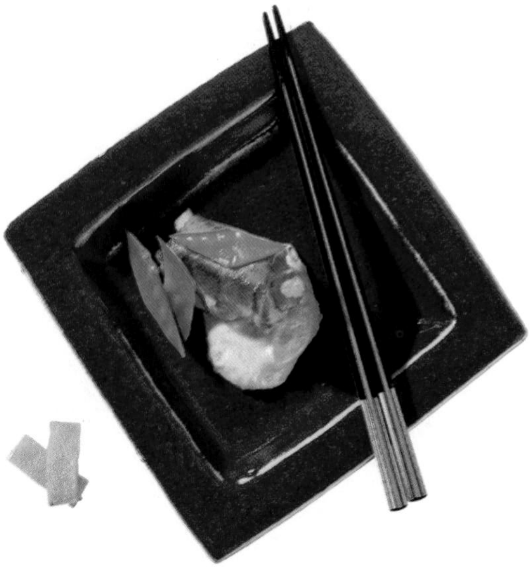

COD ROE-STUFFED CHICKEN

4 chicken thighs, boned and skinned
150 g (5 oz) smoked cod roe
vegetable oil and butter for frying
sake or white wine
parboiled mangetout, to garnish
COD ROE MAYONNAISE:
4 tablespoons mayonnaise
1 tablespoon smoked cod roe, inside only
1 tablespoon mustard

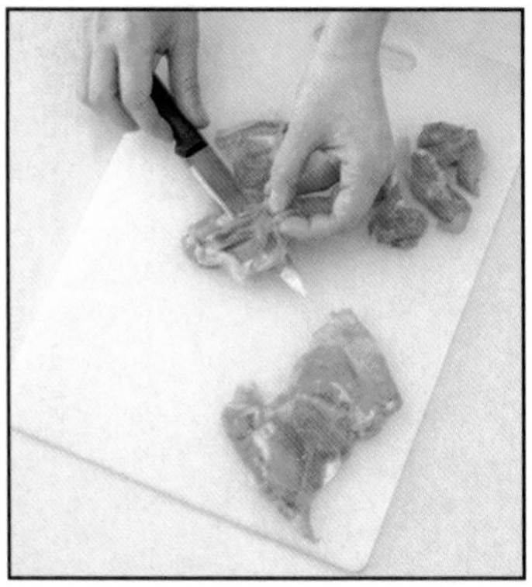

Remove any fat from chicken thighs and place on a cutting board, skinned side down. Open up inner side by making several slits lengthways and even out thickness.

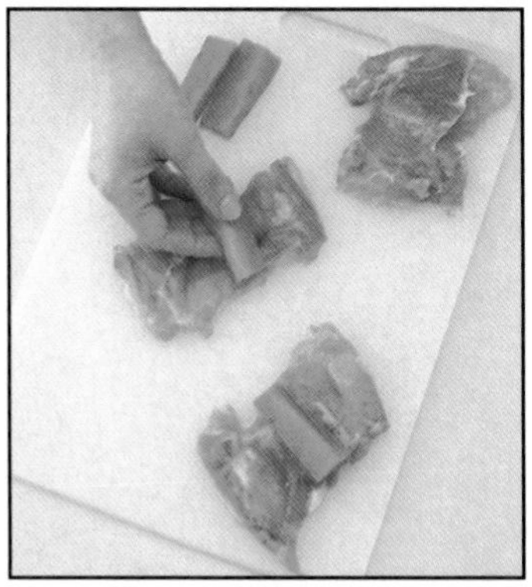

Cut cod roe lengthways into 5 strips and reserve one for making the sauce. Put a strip of cod roe on top of each chicken thigh, placing it lengthways in the centre. Roll in to the original thigh shape and seal end with a wooden cocktail stick. Heat a frying pan, add a little vegetable oil and a knob of butter and fry stuffed chicken thighs over high heat until both sides are golden brown. Drain on absorbent kitchen paper.

Transfer chicken to a large deep plate, or a shallow dish, and sprinkle generously with sake or white wine. Place chicken in a boiling steamer and steam vigorously for 10-15 minutes until well cooked. Mix mayonnaise, remaining cod roe and mustard and place a quarter in the centre of each of 4 individual plates. Remove chicken from steamer and drain. Remove cocktail sticks and place chicken on mayonnaise. Garnish with mangetout and serve.

Serves 4-6 as a starter.

CHICKEN WITH ONION SAUCE

8 chicken thighs, boned
sake, soy sauce and sesame oil
1 egg, beaten
250 g (9 oz) broccoli, separated into florets
cornflour for coating
vegetable oil for deep-frying
red pepper, shredded, to garnish
SPRING ONION SAUCE:
1-2 spring onions, finely chopped
2 tablespoons each soy sauce and sake or white wine
2 tablespoons mirin or 2 teaspoons sugar
2 teaspoons sesame oil

Cut chicken, with skin on, into bite-sized pieces and put in a large mixing bowl.

Sprinkle generously with sake, soy sauce and sesame oil and leave to marinate for about 15 minutes. Fold in beaten egg and leave for another 15 minutes. Meanwhile, make spring onion sauce by mixing together in a bowl spring onions, soy sauce, sake (or white wine), mirin (or sugar) and sesame oil. Cook broccoli in lightly salted boiling water for 3 minutes. Drain and keep warm. Roll chicken pieces in cornflour and shake off excess.

Heat vegetable oil in a wok or deep-frying pan to 170C (340F) and fry chicken pieces, several at a time, until well cooked and light golden, turning frequently. (Do not add too much chicken at a time – the pan should not be more than two-thirds full at any time.) Drain well on a wire rack or absorbent kitchen paper and arrange in the centre of a serving platter along with broccoli. Pour sauce over the top, garnish with shredded red pepper and serve at once.

Serves 4.

CHICKEN WITH WASABI SAUCE

4 boneless, skinless chicken breasts
1 tablespoon sake
watercress sprigs and lemon slices, to garnish
WASABI SAUCE:
2 teaspoons wasabi paste or powder
3 tablespoons soy sauce
juice ½ lemon
1 tablespoon sake or white wine
1 teaspoon chopped fresh chives

Inserting the knife blade diagonally, slice fillets crossways into pieces 1 cm (½ in) thick. Sprinkle with sake. To make wasabi sauce, mix wasabi paste, soy sauce, lemon juice, sake or white wine and chopped chives. (If using wasabi powder, mix with an equal quantity of water to make a paste, then combine with other sauce ingredients.)

Cook chicken slices, a few at a time, in boiling water for 2 minutes (do not overcook), then plunge into ice cold water. Drain slices and serve on individual plates, garnished with watercress and lemon slices and accompanied by small individual bowls of wasabi sauce.

Serves 4 as a starter.

MEAT

BEEF

PORK

LAMB

BEEF-STUFFED CABBAGE

2 onions
5 tablespoons vegetable oil
3 cloves garlic, crushed
2 fresh green chillies, seeded and chopped
7.5 cm (3 in) piece fresh root ginger, grated
450 g (1 lb) lean minced beef
¼ teaspoon turmeric
2 teaspoons Garam Masala (see page 224)
1 Savoy cabbage
400 g (14 oz) can chopped tomatoes
2 tablespoons lemon juice
salt and pepper
lemon or lime slices, to garnish

Chop 1 onion and slice the other.

Heat 2 tablespoons oil in a heavy-based pan, add chopped onion and cook over a medium heat, stirring, for about 8 minutes, until soft and golden brown. Add garlic, chillies and one-third of the ginger and cook for 1 minute, then remove with a slotted spoon and set aside.

Add beef to pan and cook, stirring, until browned and well broken up. Stir in turmeric and garam masala and cook for 1 minute, then add onion mixture.

Cook, covered, for 20-30 minutes, stirring occasionally, until cooking liquid is absorbed. Leave to cool. Remove core from cabbage with a sharp knife. Cook whole cabbage in boiling salted water for 8 minutes, then drain and rinse in cold water. Leave until cool enough to handle, then carefully peel off 12-16 outside leaves, keeping them whole. Finely shred remaining cabbage.

To make sauce, heat remaining oil in a heavy-based pan, add sliced onion and cook, stirring frequently, for 5 minutes or until soft but not brown. Add shredded cabbage, tomatoes, remaining ginger, lemon juice and 150 ml (5 fl oz/⅔ cup) water. Season with salt and pepper. Bring to the boil, then simmer uncovered, for 5 minutes.

Preheat oven to 190C (375F/Gas 5). Put about 2 tablespoons mince mixture on each cabbage leaf, fold sides in and roll up neatly. Pour a little sauce into the base of an ovenproof casserole, add cabbage rolls and pour over remaining sauce. Cover and cook for 40-50 minutes, until cabbage is tender. Serve hot, garnished with lemon or lime slices.

Serves 4.

MADRAS MEAT CURRY

700 g (1½ lb) braising steak
2 tablespoons vegetable oil
1 large onion, finely sliced
4 cloves
4 green cardamom pods, bruised
3 fresh green chillies, seeded and finely chopped
2 dried red chillies, seeded and crushed
2.5 cm (1 in) piece fresh root ginger, grated
2 cloves garlic, crushed
2 teaspoons ground coriander
2 teaspoons turmeric
50 ml (2 fl oz/¼ cup) tamarind water (see page 11)
salt
lettuce leaves, to garnish

Cut beef into 2.5 cm (1 in) cubes. Heat oil in a large heavy-based pan, add beef and fry until browned all over. Remove with a slotted spoon and set aside. Add onion, cloves and cardamom pods to pan and fry for about 8 minutes, stirring until onion is soft and golden brown. Stir in chillies, ginger, garlic, coriander and turmeric and fry for 2 minutes. Return beef to pan, add 50 ml (2 fl oz/¼ cup) water and simmer, covered, for 1 hour.

Stir in tamarind water and season with salt, re-cover and simmer, covered, for 15-30 minutes, until beef is tender. Serve garnished with lettuce leaves.

Serves 4.

BEEF KEBABS

700 g (1½ lb) lean minced beef
1 onion, finely chopped
5 cm (2 in) piece fresh root ginger, grated
3 cloves garlic, crushed
1 teaspoon chilli powder
1 tablespoon Garam Masala (see page 224)
1 tablespoon chopped coriander leaves
1 tablespoon ground almonds
1 egg, beaten
25 g (1 oz/¼ cup) chick-pea flour
6 tablespoons natural yogurt
2 teaspoons vegetable oil
raw onion rings and thin lemon wedges, to garnish

In a large bowl, mix together beef, onion, ginger, garlic, chilli powder, garam masala, coriander, ground almonds, egg and flour. Cover beef mixture and leave in a cool place for up to 4 hours to allow flavours to blend. Shape into 16-20 long ovals and thread on to 4 long skewers. Mix together yogurt and oil and brush over kebabs.

Heat grill. Cook kebabs for 20-25 minutes, until well browned and no longer pink in centres. Baste kebabs with more yogurt and oil mixture and turn occasionally during cooking. Serve hot, garnished with onion rings and lemon wedges.

Serves 4.

Note: The meatball mixture can be made up to 12 hours in advance and stored in the refrigerator.

GINGER BEEF WITH PINEAPPLE

450 g (1 lb) lean beef rump or sirloin steak
salt and freshly ground black pepper
1 tablespoon sweet sherry
2.5 cm (1 in) piece fresh root ginger, peeled and finely chopped
1 clove garlic, finely chopped
1 teaspoon cornflour
225 g (8 oz) fresh pineapple
1 tablespoon sunflower oil
2 red peppers, thinly sliced
4 spring onions, chopped
2 tablespoons light soy sauce
1 piece stem ginger in syrup, drained and thinly sliced

Trim any visible fat from beef and cut into 0.5 cm (¼ in) strips. Place in a bowl and season with salt and pepper. Add sherry, chopped ginger, garlic and cornflour and mix well. Cover and chill for 30 minutes. Meanwhile, peel and core pineapple and cut into 2.5 cm (1 in) cubes.

Heat oil in a wok, add beef mixture and stir-fry for 1-2 minutes or until beef is browned all over. Add peppers and stir-fry for another minute. Add spring onions, pineapple and soy sauce and simmer for 2-3 minutes to heat through. Sprinkle with stem ginger and serve on a bed of noodles.

Serves 4.

STEAKS WITH CHILLI SAUCE

4 lean beef fillet steaks, each weighing about 25 g (4 oz)
1 teaspoon dark soy sauce
1 clove garlic, finely chopped
1 teaspoon sesame oil
2 tablespoons chopped fresh chives, to garnish
CHILLI SAUCE:
1 teaspoon sunflower oil
1 fresh green chilli, seeded and finely chopped
1 shallot, finely chopped
1 teaspoon chilli sauce
2 tablespoons red rice vinegar
55 ml (2 fl oz/¼ cup) dry sherry
1 teaspoon brown sugar

Trim any fat from steaks. Tenderize lightly with a meat tenderizer or rolling pin. Preheat grill. Place steaks on grill rack. Mix together soy sauce, garlic and sesame oil and brush over steaks. Grill for 3-4 minutes on each side, brushing with soy sauce mixture to prevent drying out.

Meanwhile, make sauce. Heat oil in a wok and stir-fry chilli and shallot over a low heat for 1 minute. Add chilli sauce, red rice vinegar, dry sherry and brown sugar and simmer for 2-3 minutes. Drain cooked steaks on absorbent kitchen paper. Sprinkle with chives and serve with sauce and a salad.

Serves 4.

MANGO BEEF WITH CASHEWS

450 g (1 lb) lean beef rump or sirloin steak
1 clove garlic, finely chopped
1 tablespoon light soy sauce
1 tablespoon rice wine
1 teaspoon cornflour
salt and freshly ground pepper
2 ripe mangoes
1 tablespoon sunflower oil
2 tablespoons chopped coriander leaves
3 tablespoons unsalted cashew nuts, coarsely crushed

Trim any fat from beef and cut into 0.5 cm (¼ in) strips.

Place beef strips in a bowl and mix with garlic, soy sauce, rice wine, cornflour, salt and pepper. Cover and chill for 30 minutes. Peel mangoes and slice flesh off large flat pit in the centre of each mango. Cut flesh into thick, even slices, reserving a few small strips garnish.

Heat oil in a wok and stir-fry beef mixture for 3-4 minutes until beef is browned all over. Stir in sliced mango and cook over a low heat for 2-3 minutes to heat through. Sprinkle with chopped coriander and crushed cashews, garnish with reserved mango and serve on a bed of rice.

Serves 4.

ROAST HOISIN BEEF

450-700 g (1-1½ lb) lean beef topside
freshly ground pepper
2 cloves garlic, finely chopped
1 cm (½ in) piece fresh root ginger, peeled and finely chopped
2 teaspoons sesame oil
55 ml (2 fl oz/¼ cup) hoisin sauce
450 ml (16 fl oz/2 cups) Chinese Beef Stock (see page 16)
4 carrots
1 daikon
1 large green pepper
1 large yellow pepper
4 spring onions, shredded
spring onion rings, to garnish

Preheat oven to 180C (350F/Gas 4). Trim any fat from beef and place in non-stick roasting pan. Season with pepper. Mix together garlic, ginger, sesame oil and hoisin sauce and spread over beef. Pour half the stock into the pan and roast for 1 hour, basting occasionally to prevent drying out.

Meanwhile, peel carrots and daikon. Halve carrots and slice lengthways. Slice daikon crossways. Quarter peppers. Arrange vegetables around beef, pour in remaining stock and cook for 45-60 minutes or until tender. Drain beef and vegetables. Slice beef and serve with vegetables, topped with shredded spring onions and garnished with spring onion rings.

Serves 4.

BEEF WITH WATER CHESTNUTS

450 g (1 lb) lean beef rump or sirloin steak
1 tablespoon dark soy sauce
1 tablespoon dry sherry
1 teaspoon chilli sauce
2 teaspoons brown sugar
2 teaspoons cornflour
225 g (8 oz) broccoli
115 g (4 oz) can water chestnuts, drained
1 tablespoon sunflower oil
salt and freshly ground pepper
strips fresh red chilli, to garnish

Trim any fat from beef and cut into 2 cm (¾ in) pieces.

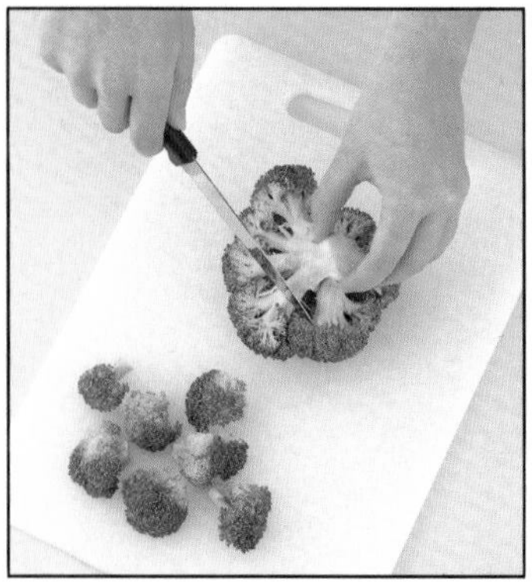

Place beef in a bowl, and mix with soy sauce, sherry, chilli sauce, sugar and cornflour. Cover and chill for 30 minutes. Meanwhile, divide broccoli into small florets. Bring a small saucepan of water to the boil and cook broccoli for 3 minutes. Drain and rinse in cold water. Halve water chestnuts.

Heat oil in a wok. Add beef mixture and stir-fry for 2-3 minutes. Add broccoli and water chestnuts, season with salt and pepper and stir-fry for 3 minutes. Garnish with red chilli strips and serve with noodles.

Serves 4.

SZECHUAN BEEF

450 g (1 lb) lean beef fillet
1 tablespoon sunflower oil
1 clove garlic, finely chopped
1cm (½ in) piece fresh root ginger, peeled and finely chopped
4 spring onions, finely chopped
1 tablespoon hoisin sauce
1 teaspoon Szechuan peppercorns, toasted and ground
115 g (4 oz) preserved vegetables
1 teaspoon sugar
shredded spring onions, to garnish

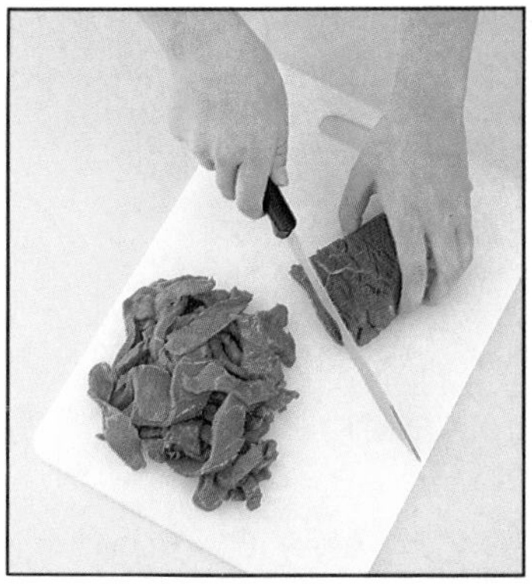

Trim any fat and silver skin from beef. Cut beef into very thin slices.

Heat oil in a wok and stir-fry beef, garlic, ginger and spring onions 1 minute or until beef is browned.

Add hoisin sauce, Szechuan peppercorns, preserved vegetables and sugar and stir-fry for 3-4 minutes or until beef is just cooked through. Garnish with shredded spring onions and serve with rice.

Serves 4.

BLACK-BEAN BEEF & RICE

1 tablespoon sunflower oil
2 shallots, chopped
2 cloves garlic, finely chopped
1 whole cinnamon stick, broken
2 star anise
225 g (8 oz) lean beef chuck, trimmed and cut into 2cm (3/4 in) cubes
3 tablespoons fermented black beans
225 g (8 oz/1 1/4 cups) long-grain white rice, rinsed
800 ml (1 1/2 pints/3 1/2 cups) Chinese Beef Stock (see page 16)
salt and freshly ground pepper
2 tablespoons chopped fresh chives, to garnish

Heat oil in a wok and stir-fry shallots, garlic, cinnamon stick, star anise, beef, black beans and rice for 2-3 minutes or until beef is browned and rice is opaque.

Pour in stock and bring to the boil. Reduce heat and simmer for 25 minutes or until liquid is absorbed and beef is tender. Discard cinnamon stick and star anise. Garnish with chives and serve with a salad.

Serves 4.

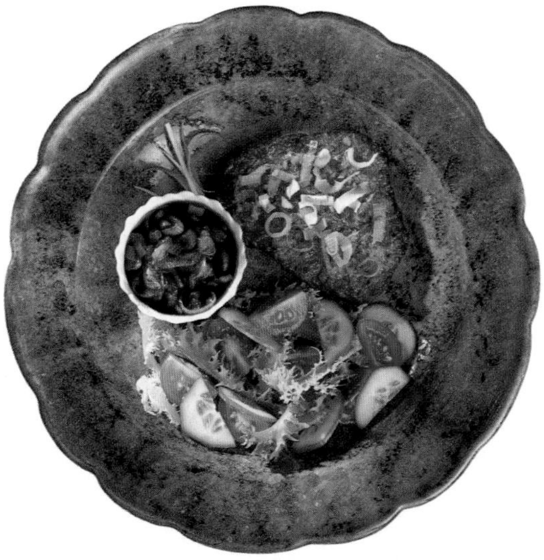

STEAKS WITH SHERRY DIP

4 lean beef fillets, each weighing about 115 g (4 oz)
freshly ground pepper
1 tablespoon dry sherry
2.5 cm (1 in) piece fresh root ginger, peeled and finely chopped
1 teaspoon sesame oil
4 spring onions, finely chopped, and spring onion strips, to garnish

DIP:
2 teaspoons sunflower oil
4 spring onions, finely chopped
1 cm (1/2 in) piece fresh root ginger, peeled and finely chopped
55 ml (2 fl oz/1/4 cup) dry sherry
2 tablespoons dark soy sauce

Trim any fat and silver skin from steaks and lightly tenderize with a meat tenderizer. Season both sides with pepper. Mix together sherry, ginger and sesame oil. Preheat grill. Place steaks on grill rack and brush with sherry mixture. Grill for 3-4 minutes on each side, basting to prevent drying out. Drain on absorbent kitchen paper.

Meanwhile, make dip. Heat oil in a wok and stir-fry spring onions and ginger for 2 minutes or until soft. Drain well on absorbent kitchen paper and place in a bowl. Mix in sherry and soy sauce. Garnish steaks with spring onion and serve with dip and a salad.

Serves 4.

BEEF WITH OYSTER SAUCE

25 g (1 oz) dried Chinese mushrooms, soaked in hot water for 20 minutes
225 g (8 oz) oyster mushrooms
1 tablespoon light soy sauce
1 tablespoon dry sherry
freshly ground pepper
2 tablespoons oyster sauce
450 g (1 lb) lean beef rump or sirloin steak, trimmed of fat and cut into 0.5cm (¼ in) strips
1 tablespoon sunflower oil
2 tablespoons chopped fresh chives, to garnish

Drain soaked mushrooms, squeezing out excess water. Discard stems and slice caps. Slice oyster mushrooms.

Mix together soy sauce, sherry, pepper and oyster sauce and set aside. Heat oil in a wok and stir-fry beef and mushrooms for 2-3 minutes or until beef is browned.

Stir soy sauce mixture into beef and stir-fry for 2-3 minutes or until beef is tender. Garnish with chives and serve on a bed of noodles with freshly cooked vegetables.

Serves 4.

GARLIC BEEF CASSEROLE

450 g (1 lb) lean beef chuck, trimmed and cut into 2 cm (¾ in) cubes
1 tablespoon groundnut (peanut) oil
2 shallots, chopped
4 cloves garlic, thinly sliced
2 large carrots, sliced
175 g (6 oz) baby sweetcorn, halved lengthways
225 g (8 oz) button mushrooms
300 ml (10 fl oz/1¼ cups) Chinese Beef Stock (see page 16)
2 tablespoons dark soy sauce
1 tablespoon rice wine
2 teaspoons five-spice powder
2 tablespoons hoisin sauce
1 teaspoon chilli sauce

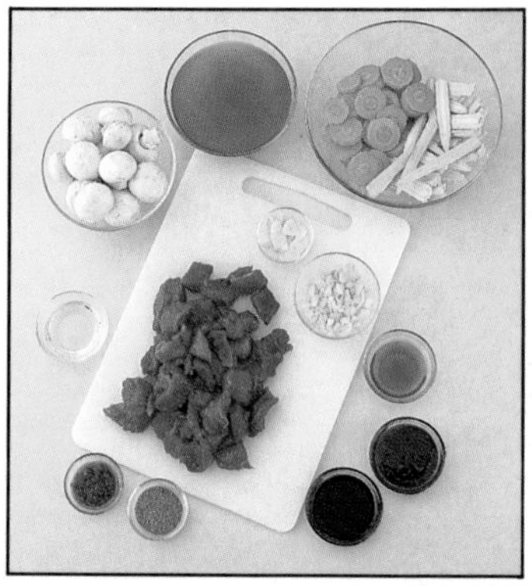

Heat oil in a wok and stir-fry beef, shallots, garlic, carrots, baby sweetcorn and mushrooms for 5 minutes. Add stock, soy sauce, rice wine, five-spice powder, hoisin sauce and chilli sauce and bring to the boil. Reduce to a simmer, cover and simmer for 1 hour.

Remove from heat and blot surface with absorbent kitchen paper to absorb surface fat. Increase the heat and boil for 10 minutes to reduce and thicken sauce. Serve with rice.

Serves 4.

BEEF IN CHILLI SAUCE

8 dried red chillies, cored, seeded and chopped
2 small onions, chopped
5 cm (2 in) piece fresh root ginger, chopped
700 g (1½ lb) lean beef, cut into bite-sized pieces
1 tablespoon ground coriander
1 tablespoon ground cumin
1 tablespoon tomato ketchup
2 teaspoons turmeric
2 teaspoons paprika
2 tablespoons vegetable oil
2 cloves garlic, crushed
2.5 cm (1 in) stick cinnamon
seeds from 3 cardamom pods, crushed
sugar
salt
1 onion, sliced into thick rings

Put chillies in a small blender. Add 4 tablespoons hot water and leave until slightly softened. Add half of the small onions and half of the ginger to the blender and mix to a paste. Put beef in a large bowl. Add spice paste from blender, coriander, cumin, tomato ketchup, turmeric and paprika. Stir together. Cover and leave for at least 1 hour to marinate.

In a wok, heat oil over medium-high heat. Add remaining onion and ginger and garlic. Fry, stirring, for 3 minutes until lightly browned. Stir in cinnamon stick and cardamom and stir-fry for 1 minute. Add meat and marinade and stir-fry for 5 minutes. Add 350 ml (12 fl oz/1½ cups) water and sugar and salt to taste. Cover pan. Simmer very gently for 1¼ hours or until beef is tender. Stir occasionally. Add onion rings and cook for 3-5 minutes or until soft.

Serves 4-6.

DRY BEEF WITH COCONUT

4 tablespoons vegetable oil
6 shallots, finely chopped
3 cloves garlic, finely chopped
1 fresh red chilli, cored, seeded and finely chopped
700 g (1½ lb) lean beef, thinly sliced and cut into 1 cm (½ in) strips
1 tablespoon light brown sugar
1½ teaspoons ground cumin
1 teaspoon ground coriander
squeeze lime juice
salt
½ fresh coconut, grated, or 225 g (8 oz/2⅔ cups) desiccated coconut

In a wok or sauté pan, heat 1 tablespoon oil over medium heat. Add shallots, garlic and chilli and fry for about 5 minutes, stirring occasionally, until softened but not browned. Add beef, sugar, cumin, coriander, lime juice, salt to taste and 150 ml (5 fl oz/⅔ cup) water. Cover pan tightly and simmer gently for 30 minutes, stirring occasionally.

Uncover pan, stir in coconut until all liquid has been absorbed. Stir in remaining oil and continue stirring until coconut begins to brown.

Serves 6.

SINGAPORE STEAMBOAT

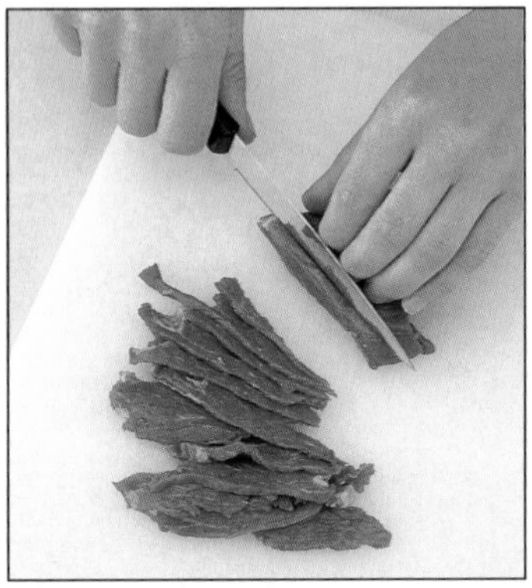

175 g (6 oz) beef fillet, well chilled
175 g (6 oz) pork fillet (tenderloin), well chilled
175 g (6 oz) lamb fillet, well chilled
175 g (6 oz) boneless, skinless chicken breasts, well chilled
350 g (12 oz) rice vermicelli
115 g (4 oz) each mangetout, French beans, baby sweetcorn, oyster mushrooms, shiitake mushrooms, asparagus spears, cut into bite-sized pieces

Thinly slice beef, pork, lamb and chicken. Cover with cling film, and set aside. Cook noodles, drain, refresh under running cold water, drain again, cover and set aside.

PRAWN BALLS
350 g (12 oz) raw, peeled prawns
1½-2½ teaspoons cornflour
2 small spring onions, finely chopped
1 small egg white, lightly beaten

Put prawns and 1½ teaspoons cornflour into blender and mix until smooth. Mix in spring onion. Stir in egg white and more cornflour if necessary to bind mixture, which should be firm enough to handle. With wet hands, roll mixture into walnut-size balls. Refrigerate until required.

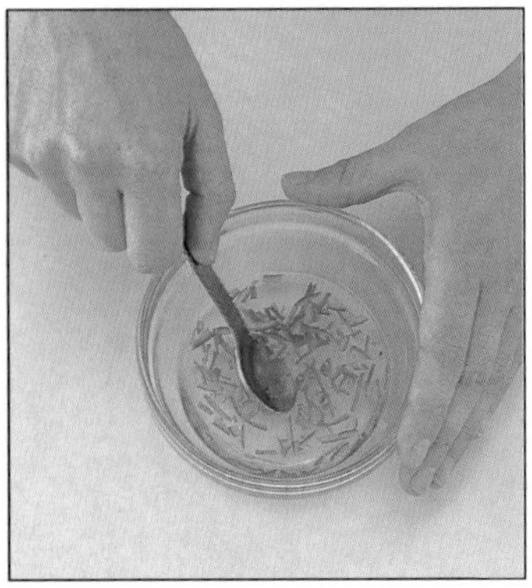

CHILLI VINEGAR
3 tablespoons rice vinegar
2 teaspoons sugar
½-1 fresh red chilli, cored seeded and finely sliced
1½ tablespoons water

DIPPING SAUCE
2 tablespoons tomato purée
1 teaspoons soy sauce
1 teaspoon toasted sesame oil
1 fresh red chilli, cored, seeded and finely chopped
2 tablespoons water

In 2 bowls, mix together all ingredients for chilli vinegar and dipping sauce.

COCONUT SAUCE
2 teaspoons groundnut (peanut) oil
1 small onion, finely chopped
5 cm (2 in) stalk lemon grass, bruised and thinly sliced
¾ teaspoon crushed coriander seeds
85 g (3 oz) piece creamed coconut
about 3 tablespoons stock

In a frying pan or saucepan, heat oil. Add onion, lemon grass and coriander seeds and fry until onion has softened. Stir in coconut cream until melted. Add enough stock to make a dipping sauce.

STOCK
1 litre (1¾ pints/4 cups) chicken or vegetable stock
1½ tablespoons chopped coriander
5 cm (2 in) thick end lemon grass stalk, thinly sliced
2 spring onions, thinly sliced

Place all stock ingredients in a saucepan and bring to the boil, then pour into a warm fondue pot or heavy flameproof casserole set over a burner. Diners serve themselves by dipping meat, prawn balls and vegetables into stock to cook, then transferring them to plates to eat with sauces and chilli vinegar.

When all meat, fish and vegetables have been eaten, either warm noodles in hotpot, or dunk them in a bowl or saucepan of boiling water, then drain and divide them among bowls. Ladle remaining stock, which will have become concentrated, into bowls.

Serves 6.

Note: Use fondue forks, chopsticks, Chinese wire mesh baskets or long wooden skewers to serve.

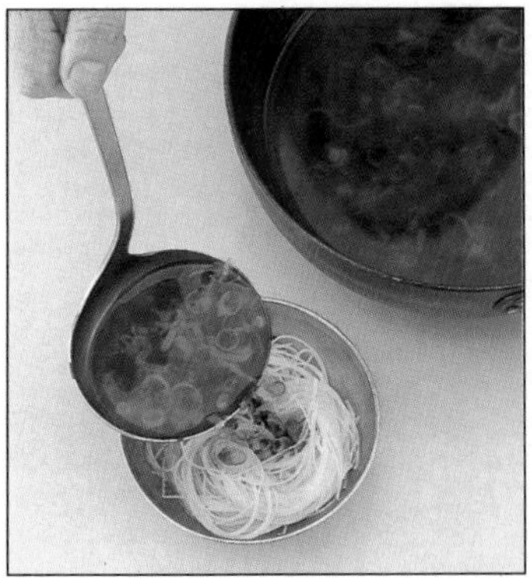

STIR-FRIED BEEF STEAK

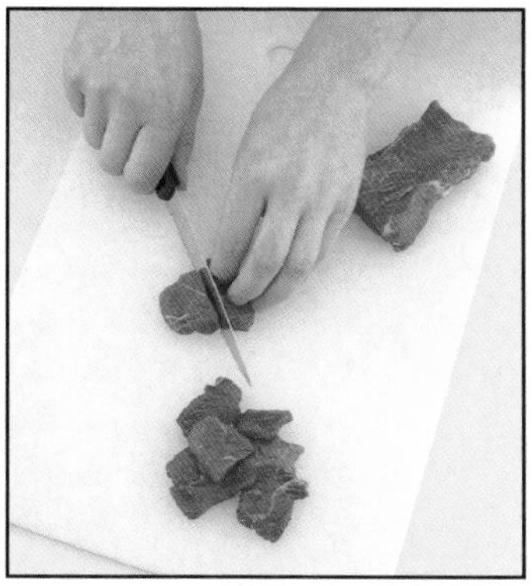

225 g (8 oz) beef steak, cut into small, thin slices, about 2.5 cm (1 in) square
¼ teaspoon freshly ground black pepper
1 teaspoon sugar
1 tablespoon fish sauce
2 tablespoons vegetable oil
1 clove garlic, chopped
1 small onion, sliced
1 green pepper, cored and cut into cubes
115 g (4 oz) sliced bamboo shoots, drained
1 firm tomato, cut into 8 wedges
2 spring onions, cut into short lengths
2 tablespoons soy or oyster sauce
2 teaspoons cornflour

Mix beef with black pepper, sugar and fish sauce and leave to marinate for 15-20 minutes. Heat oil in a wok or frying pan and stir-fry garlic and onion for about 1 minute. Add beef and stir-fry for 1 minute.

Add green pepper, bamboo shoots, tomato and spring onions. Continue stir-frying for 2-3 minutes, then blend in soy or oyster sauce. Mix cornflour with 1 tablespoon water and stir into mixture. Cook, stirring, until thickened. Serve with rice noodles.

Serves 4.

SPICY BEEF STEW

1 tablespoon vegetable oil
2 cloves garlic, chopped
1 onion, chopped
1 stalk lemon grass, chopped
450 g (1 lb) stewing beef, cut into bite-sized cubes
550 ml (20 fl oz/2½ cups) stock or water
5-6 tablespoons soy or fish sauce
1 teaspoon chilli sauce
2 teaspoons five-spice powder
1 tablespoon sugar
2-3 spring onions, chopped
freshly ground black pepper
coriander sprigs, to garnish

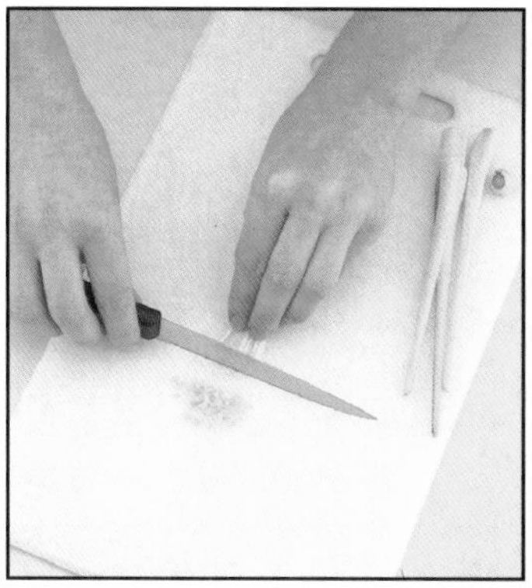

Heat oil in a clay or flameproof casserole and stir-fry garlic, onion, and lemon grass for about 1 minute. Add beef and stir-fry for 2-3 minutes, or until colour of meat changes. Add stock or water, bring to the boil, then add soy or fish sauce, chilli sauce, five-spice powder and sugar. Blend well, then reduce heat, cover and simmer gently for 45-50 minutes.

Add spring onions, season with pepper and cook for a further 5 minutes. Garnish with coriander sprigs and serve straight from the pot.

Serves 4.

Variation: Substitute curry powder for five-spice powder to make beef curry.

BEEF & SEAFOOD HOT POT

225 g (8 oz) beef fillet, very thinly sliced
115 g (4 oz) firm white fish fillet, thinly sliced
115 g (4 oz) prepared squid
6 raw peeled prawns, cut in half lengthways
1 tomato, thinly sliced
1 onion, thinly sliced
freshly ground black pepper
1 tablespoon sesame oil
2 teaspoons vegetable oil
1 clove garlic, chopped
2 shallots, chopped
1 tablespoon tomato purée
1 tablespoon sugar
1 teaspoon salt
2 tablespoons rice vinegar
675 ml (24 fl oz/3 cups) stock or water

Arrange beef, fish, squid and prawns on a platter in separate sections. Place tomato and onion slices in the centre and sprinkle pepper and sesame oil all over them. Set aside while you prepare the broth.

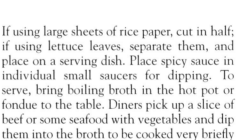

Heat vegetable oil in a saucepan and stir-fry garlic and shallots for about 30 seconds, then add tomato purée, sugar, salt and rice vinegar. Blend well, then add stock or water, bring to the boil and transfer to a Chinese hot pot or fondue.

ACCOMPANIMENTS:
55 g (2 oz) bean thread vermicelli, soaked then cut into short lengths
6-8 Chinese dried mushrooms, soaked and each cut in half or quartered
2 cakes tofu, cut into small cubes
115 g (4 oz) bok choy, cut into small pieces
dried rice paper or lettuce leaves
fresh mint and coriander leaves
Spicy Fish Sauce (see page 233)

Arrange vermicelli, mushrooms, tofu cubes and bok choy on a serving platter in separate sections.

If using large sheets of rice paper, cut in half; if using lettuce leaves, separate them, and place on a serving dish. Place spicy sauce in individual small saucers for dipping. To serve, bring boiling broth in the hot pot or fondue to the table. Diners pick up a slice of beef or some seafood with vegetables and dip them into the broth to be cooked very briefly – usually for no longer than 1 minute.

Meanwhile, they dip a piece of rice paper in hot water to soften it, then quickly remove food from broth and place in the centre of the rice paper or a lettuce leaf. They can then add a few mint and coriander leaves, then fold over to make a neat parcel, dipping parcel in Spicy Fish Sauce before eating it.

Serves 4-6.

BEEF TATAKI

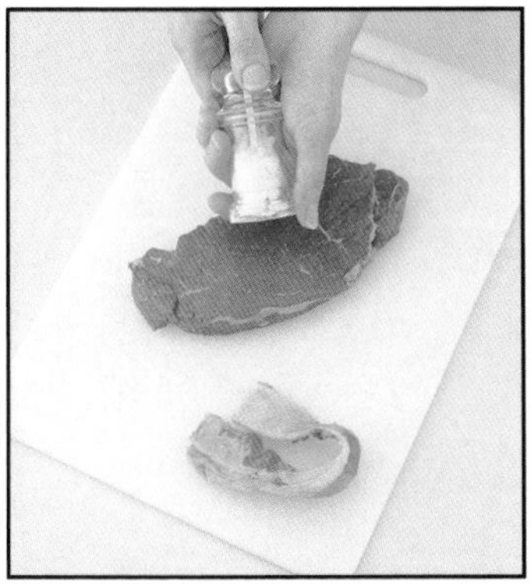

450 g (1 lb) lean sirloin steak
salt and vegetable oil for brushing
2 spring onions, finely chopped
2.5 cm (1 in) piece fresh root ginger, peeled and grated
1 tablespoon wasabi paste
½ cucumber
lime slices and watercress, to garnish
DAIKON DIP:
7.5 cm (3 in) daikon, peeled and grated
3 tablespoons soy sauce
juice ½ lime

Preheat grill. Trim fat from meat, sprinkle with a pinch of salt and brush with oil.

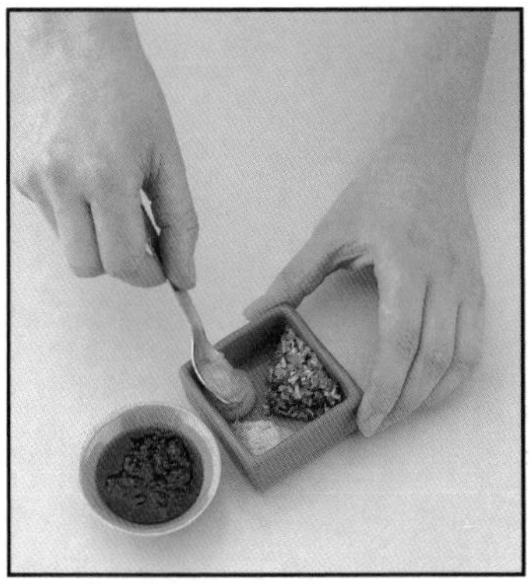

Quickly brown meat under a high grill for 2-3 minutes on each side. Remove from heat and immediately plunge into ice cold water to stop further cooking. Traditionally the meat should be golden brown outside but rare inside. Drain, pat dry and set aside while preparing daikon dip. Mix grated daikon, soy sauce and lime juice in a serving bowl. Arrange chopped spring onions, grated ginger and wasabi in separate heaps on a small plate. Cut cucumber in half lengthways, then slice crossways into paper-thin 'half-moons'.

Slice meat very thinly against the grain. Arrange each piece folded on a slice of cucumber, slightly overlapping in a circle on a large serving platter. Garnish with lime slices and watercress. Serve with bowl of daikon dip, accompanied by plate of condiments. Each diner has a small plate for mixing their own dip sauce.

Serves 4-6.

SIMMERED BEEF & POTATOES

300 g (10 oz) piece lean beef
5 medium potatoes, peeled
2 Spanish onions
2 tablespoons vegetable oil
5 tablespoons sugar
6 tablespoons soy sauce
dashi (see page 29), or water
parboiled mangetout, to garnish

Put beef in the freezer for about 1 hour to part-harden, then slice very thinly against the grain into bite-sized pieces.

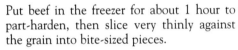

Quarter each potato and boil until tender but still slightly hard in the centre. Drain and set aside. Cut onions into thin half-moon slices. In a frying pan or a shallow saucepan, heat a little vegetable oil and stir-fry beef slices over medium heat. When beef begins to change colour, add potatoes and continue to stir. Add sugar and soy sauce to the pan and lightly fold in. Pour in enough dashi or water to just cover ingredients and bring to the boil. Skim the surface to remove any fat and lower the heat.

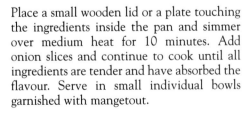

Place a small wooden lid or a plate touching the ingredients inside the pan and simmer over medium heat for 10 minutes. Add onion slices and continue to cook until all ingredients are tender and have absorbed the flavour. Serve in small individual bowls garnished with mangetout.

Serves 4.

MIXED GRIDDLE

300 g (10 oz) beef sirloin or topside or 2 boneless, skinless chicken breasts
1 squid, cleaned (optional)
4-8 scallops or raw king prawns, peeled
4-8 fresh shiitake or button mushrooms, stalks removed
1 red or green pepper, seeded
250 g (9 oz) bean sprouts, trimmed
1 lemon, cut into wedges
2-3 spring onions, finely chopped
vegetable oil for frying
DIPPING SAUCE:
15 cm (6 in) daikon, peeled
1 fresh or dried chilli
soy sauce

Prepare wafer-thin beef slices following the method used for Sukiyaki, opposite. Skin squid by holding 2 flaps together and peeling down; cut in half lengthways. Put fillets on a cutting board skinned-side up and make fine cross slits on them with a sharp knife. Cut fillets and flaps into 2.5 cm (1 in) square pieces. Separate tentacles, if large. Arrange meat and fish on separate platters. If mushrooms are large, cut them in half. Slice pepper into thin strips. Arrange all vegetables on a platter.

Make 'autumn maple leaf' relish following the method on page 145, or, alternatively, grate daikon, finely chop fresh chilli and simply mix together. Arrange daikon relish, lemon wedges and spring onion in a serving bowl or on a small plate. Place a hotplate in the centre of the dining table set with small individual bowls. Serve meat, fish and vegetable platters and condiments: diners mix their own sauce, adding soy sauce to taste, and fry their portion for themselves.

Serves 4-6.

SUKIYAKI (PAN-COOKED BEEF)

450 g (1 lb) beef sirloin or topside
2 leeks, white part only
8 fresh or dried shiitake or button mushrooms, stalks removed if fresh
sugar
250 g (9 oz) (1 cake) tofu
115 g (4 oz) watercress, trimmed
5 cm (2 in) square beef fat
70 ml (2½ fl oz/⅓ cup) sake or white wine
55 ml (2 fl oz/¼ cup) soy sauce

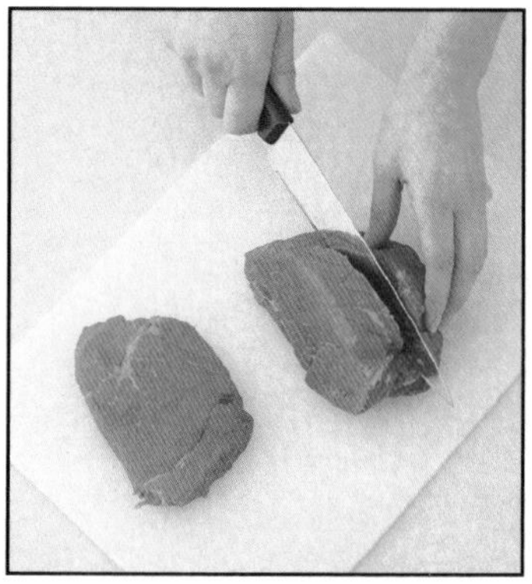

Trim any fat from beef and cut beef into 7.5 × 4 cm (3 × 1½ in) flat pieces .

Place beef pieces in separate freezer bags and freeze for 1-2 hours. Remove from freezer and leave until half thawed. Cut beef into wafer-thin slices and arrange in a circular fan on a large platter. Slice leeks diagonally. If shiitake mushrooms are large, cut in half. If using dried shiitake, soak in warm water with a pinch of sugar for 45 minutes, then remove stalks. Cut tofu into 16 cubes. Arrange all vegetables and tofu on a large platter.

Place a cast-iron pan on a portable gas ring or electric hotplate on the table together with platters of raw ingredients, jugs of water, soy sauce and sake and a sugar pot. Melt beef fat in the pan and move around to oil the entire base. Cook a few slices of beef first and sprinkle with about 2 tablespoons sugar. Pour in sake and soy sauce, and add water to taste. Diners serve themselves into individual small bowls.

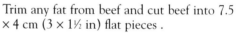

Serves 4.

SHABUSHABU (BEEF HOT POT)

450 g (1 lb) beef sirloin or topside
2 leeks, white part only
8 fresh or dried shiitake or 12 button mushrooms, stalks removed
250 g (9 oz) (1 cake) firm tofu
4-6 Chinese leaves
300 g (10 oz) spinach, trimmed
10 cm (4 in) piece dried konbu (kelp)
300 g (10 oz) udon noodles, cooked (optional)
finely chopped spring onions, to garnish

CITRUS DIP:
½ daikon, peeled
1 dried or fresh red chilli
2 spring onions, finely chopped
juice ½ lemon and ½ lime
115 ml (4 fl oz/½ cup) soy sauce

SESAME DIP:
4 tablespoons sesame paste or smooth peanut butter
115 ml (4 fl oz/½ cup) dashi (see page 29)
3 tablespoons soy sauce
1 tablespoon mirin or sweet sherry
1 tablespoon sugar
2 tablespoons sake or white wine
2 teaspoons chilli oil or chilli powder (optional)

Trim any fat from beef and cut into 7.5 × 4 cm (3 × 1½ in) flat pieces. Place in separate freezer bags and freeze for 1-2 hours.

Remove from the freezer and leave until half thawed, then cut beef into wafer-thin slices and arrange in a circular fan on a large platter. Slice leeks diagonally. If shiitake mushrooms are large cut in half. If using dried shiitake, soak in warm water with a pinch of sugar for 45 minutes, then remove stalks before use. Cut tofu into 16 cubes. Cut Chinese leaves and spinach into bite-sized pieces. Arrange vegetables and tofu on a large platter.

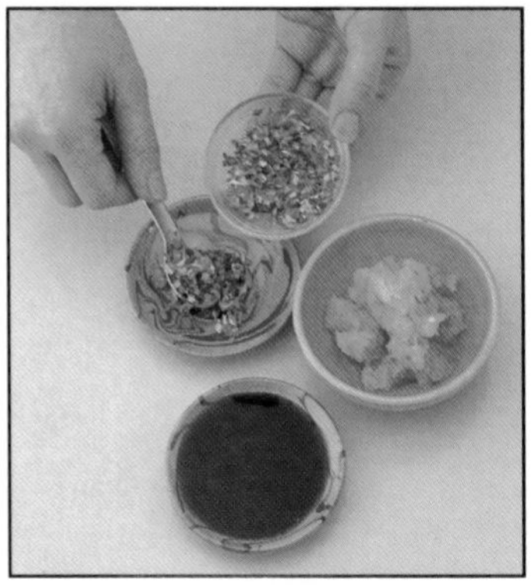

To prepare citrus dip, first make 'autumn maple leaf' relish by poking a chopstick into daikon to make a few holes lenghways. Push in red chilli strips and grate to make rust-coloured daikon. (Alternatively, grate daikon very finely, chop chilli, then mix together.) Put relish, chopped spring onion, a mixture of lemon and lime juices and soy sauce in separate small bowls. To make sesame dip, mix all ingredients together and stir until sesame paste (or peanut butter) is of a smooth runny consistency. Divide between 4-6 individual dipping bowls.

Put konbu in a large pot (ideally a clay pot, an enamelled cast-iron casserole or a copper-based Mongolian hot-pot) and fill two thirds full with water. Bring to the boil and remove konbu. Put in some of the leek, Chinese leaves, shiitake mushrooms, spinach and tofu and when it begins to come back to the boil, transfer the pot to a portable gas ring or electric hotplate on the dining table. Diners make their own citrus dip in individual dipping bowls by mixing 1-2 teaspoons each of relish, spring onion and citrus juice with some soy sauce.

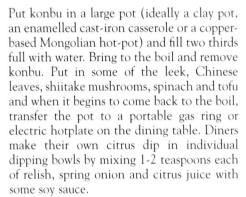

Diners serve themselves by cooking meat in the pot, adding more vegetables, and eating them dipped in either of the sauces. When ingredients are finished, skim and season the soup with soy sauce and a little salt and sugar. If using noodles, warm them in the soup, seasoned with a little soy sauce to taste, so that diners can end the meal with plain noodles garnished with chopped spring onion.

Serves 4-6.

PORK IN SPINACH SAUCE

700 g (1½ lb) fresh spinach, well rinsed
salt
700 g (1½ lb) lean boneless pork
3 tablespoons vegetable oil
2 onions, finely sliced
4 cloves garlic, crushed
2.5 cm (1 in) piece fresh root ginger, grated
3 tablespoons Garam Masala (see page 224)
½ teaspoon turmeric
1 bay leaf
2 tomatoes, skinned and chopped
2 fresh chillies, seeded and chopped
150 ml (5 fl oz/⅔ cup) natural yogurt
tomato slices and bay leaves, to garnish

Trim stems from spinach and cook leaves in boiling salted water for 2-3 minutes, until tender. Drain thoroughly and rinse under cold running water. Put in a blender or food processor fitted with a metal blade and process to a smooth purée. Set aside. Preheat oven to 160C (325F/Gas 3). Cut pork into 2.5 cm (1 in) cubes. Heat oil in a large frying pan and fry pork until browned all over. Transfer to a casserole using a slotted spoon.

Add onions to pan and cook, stirring, for 10-15 minutes, until a rich brown. Add garlic, ginger, garam masala, turmeric, bay leaf, tomatoes and chillies. Cook, stirring, for 2-3 minutes, until tomatoes have softened. Add yogurt and 150 ml (5 fl oz/⅔ cup) water and stir. Pour over pork, cover and cook for 1¼-1½ hours, until pork is cooked through. Remove bay leaf, stir in spinach and salt, re-cover and cook for a further 10 minutes. Garnish and serve.

Serves 4.

HOT SPICY RIBS

900 g-1.25 kg (2-2½ lb) meaty pork spare ribs
3 tablespoons Hot Spice Mix (see page 224)
1 teaspoon turmeric
5 cm (2 in) piece fresh root ginger, grated
1 small onion, finely chopped
1 tablespoon white wine vinegar
1 tablespoon tomato purée
spring onions and tomatoes, to garnish

Cut ribs into single rib pieces and chop into 7.5 cm (3 in) lengths.

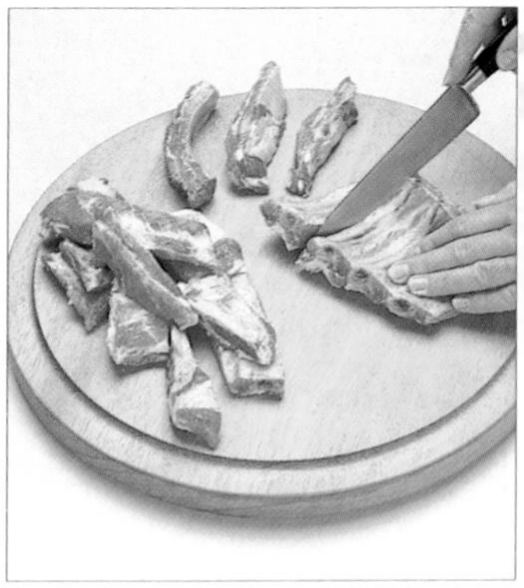

Place ribs in a large saucepan, cover with cold water and bring to the boil, then simmer for 15 minutes; drain. Put hot spice mix, turmeric, ginger, onion, vinegar and tomato purée in a blender or food processor fitted with a metal blade. Add 70 ml (2½ fl oz/⅓ cup) water and process until smooth.

Place ribs in a non-metallic dish, pour over spice mixture and stir to coat well. Cover loosely and leave in a cool place for 2-3 hours. Transfer ribs to a grill pan. Heat grill. Cook ribs for about 15 minutes, turning occasionally and basting with any remaining marinade, until well browned and very tender. Serve hot, garnished with spring onions and tomatoes.

Serves 4.

HAM & PRAWN BEAN SPROUTS

350 g (12 oz) bean sprouts
1 tablespoon sunflower oil
115 g (4 oz) lean ham, trimmed and diced
115 g (4 oz) cooked, peeled large prawns, thawed and dried if frozen
115 g (4 oz) spring onions, finely chopped
1 green pepper, chopped
2 tablespoons light soy sauce
salt and freshly ground pepper
2 tablespoons chopped fresh chives, to garnish

Cook bean sprouts in boiling water for a few seconds or until soft. Drain and rinse in cold water. Dry on absorbent kitchen paper.

Heat oil in a wok and stir-fry ham, prawns, spring onions and pepper 2 or 3 minutes or until lightly golden.

Add soy sauce, bean sprouts, salt and pepper and stir-fry 2 minutes to heat through. Garnish with chopped chives and serve with rice.

Serves 4.

HOT SWEET PORK

350 g (12 oz) lean pork fillet
1 tablespoon light soy sauce
1 tablespoon rice wine
freshly ground pepper
1 tablespoon cornflour
1 tablespoon sunflower oil
2 fresh red chillies, seeded and chopped
1 clove garlic, finely chopped
1 red pepper, diced
225 g (8 oz) courgettes, diced
115 g (4 oz) can bamboo shoots, drained
2 tablespoons red rice vinegar
2 tablespoons brown sugar
large pinch salt
1 tablespoon sesame seeds
strips fresh red chilli, to garnish

Trim any fat and silver skin from pork fillet. Cut into 1 cm (½ in) strips. Place in a bowl and mix with soy sauce, rice wine, pepper and cornflour. Cover and chill for 30 minutes.

Heat oil in a wok and stir-fry pork mixture for 1-2 minutes until pork is browned. Add chillies, garlic, red pepper, courgettes, bamboo shoots, rice vinegar, sugar and salt and stir-fry for 4-5 minutes until vegetables are just cooked through. Sprinkle with sesame seeds, garnish with chilli strips and serve with noodles.

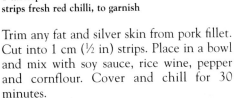

Serves 4.

GRILLED CITRUS PORK CHOPS

4 lean pork chops, each weighing about 115 g (4 oz)
grated zest and juice 1 lime, 1 small lemon and 1 small orange
1 teaspoon sesame oil
2 tablespoons dry sherry
2 tablespoons light soy sauce
1 tablespoon sugar
large pinch ground white pepper
1 teaspoon cornflour mixed with 2 teaspoons water
lime, lemon and orange slices and strips zest, to garnish

Trim fat from chops and score in a crisscross pattern. Place in a shallow dish, sprinkle with citrus zests and top with juices.

Cover and chill for 30 minutes. Drain chops well, reserving juices. Preheat grill. Place chops on grill rack and brush lightly with sesame oil. Grill for 3-4 minutes on each side or until cooked through. Drain on absorbent kitchen paper and keep warm. Place reserved juices in a small saucepan with sherry, soy sauce, sugar, pepper and cornflour mixture. Bring to the boil, stirring until thickened.

Slice pork chops and arrange on serving plates with lime, lemon and orange slices. Top with sauce and garnish with strips of citrus zest to serve.

Serves 4.

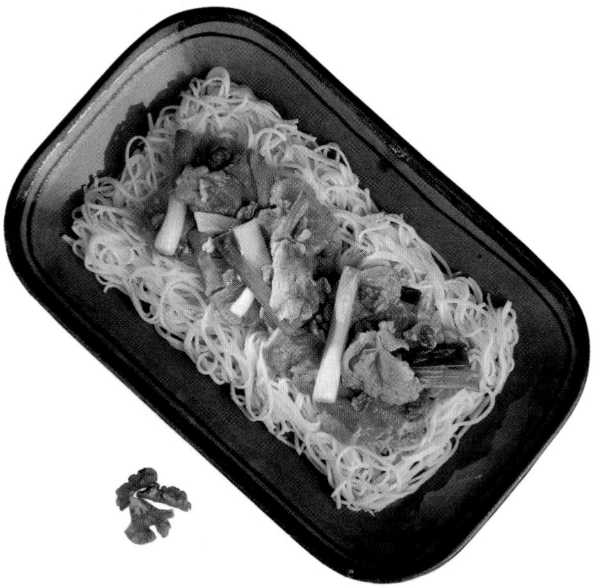

PORK WITH WALNUTS

450 g (1 lb) lean pork fillet
1 tablespoon rice wine
1 tablespoon light soy sauce
1 teaspoon cornflour
1 bunch spring onions
2 teaspoons sunflower oil
1 teaspoon sugar
salt and freshly ground pepper
25 g (1 oz) walnut pieces

Trim any fat and silver skin from pork and cut fillet into 0.5 cm (¼ in) strips. Place in a bowl and mix in rice wine, soy sauce and cornflour. Cover and chill for 30 minutes.

Trim spring onions, discarding any damaged outer leaves. Cut spring onions into 5 cm (2 in) pieces.

Heat oil in a wok and stir-fry pork mixture for 2-3 minutes or until browned. Add spring onions, sugar, salt and pepper and stir-fry for 3 minutes. Sprinkle with walnut pieces and serve with noodles.

Serves 4.

DRY PORK CURRY

350 g (12 oz) lean boneless pork, trimmed and cut into 2 cm (¾ in) cubes
1 tablespoon light brown sugar
350 g (12 oz) potatoes
225 g (8 oz) carrots
225 g (8 oz) shallots
1 tablespoon sunflower oil
2.5 cm (1 in) piece fresh root ginger, peeled and finely chopped
2 tablespoons Madras curry paste
150 ml (5 fl oz/⅔ cup) coconut milk
300 ml (10 fl oz/1¼ cups) Chinese Chicken Stock (see page 16)
salt and freshly ground pepper
2 tablespoons chopped coriander leaves

In a bowl, mix together pork and brown sugar and set aside. Cut potatoes and carrots into 2 cm (¾ in) chunks. Peel and halve shallots.

Heat oil in a wok and stir-fry pork, ginger, potatoes, carrots and shallots for 2-3 minutes or until lightly browned. Blend curry paste with coconut milk, stock, salt and pepper. Stir into pork mixture and bring to the boil. Reduce heat and simmer for 40 minutes. Sprinkle with coriander and serve on a bed of rice.

Serves 4.

ROAST PORK WITH HONEY

450 g (1 lb) piece lean pork fillet
4 tablespoons chopped coriander leaves
1 teaspoon Szechuan peppercorns, toasted and ground
1 tablespoon honey
2 teaspoons brown sugar
1 tablespoon dark soy sauce
2.5 cm (1 in) piece fresh root ginger, peeled and finely chopped
1 clove garlic, finely chopped

Preheat oven to 190C (375F/Gas 5). Trim any fat and silver skin from pork and place fillet on a rack in a roasting pan. Pour in enough water to cover bottom of pan.

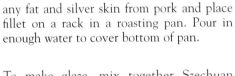

To make glaze, mix together Szechuan peppercorns, honey, brown sugar, soy sauce, ginger and garlic and brush generously over pork. Roast for 1 hour or until cooked through, brushing occasionally with glaze and adding more water to pan if it dries out.

Remove cooked pork from rack and sprinkle with chopped coriander until coated all over. Slice and serve with rice and vegetables.

Serves 4.

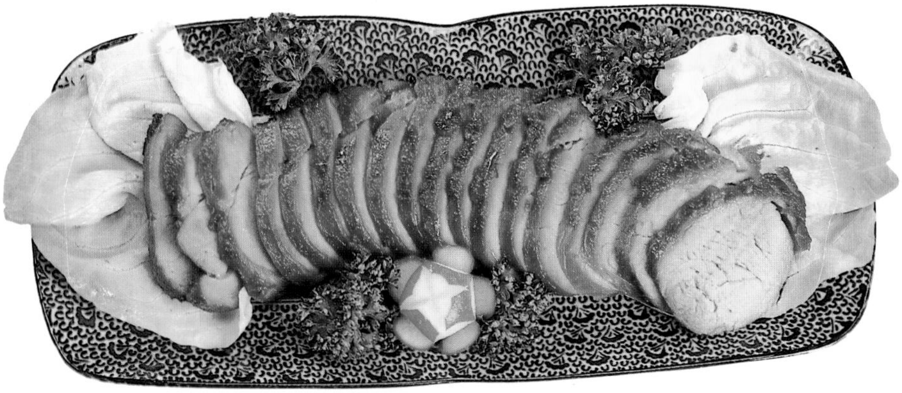

CHAI SUI ROAST PORK

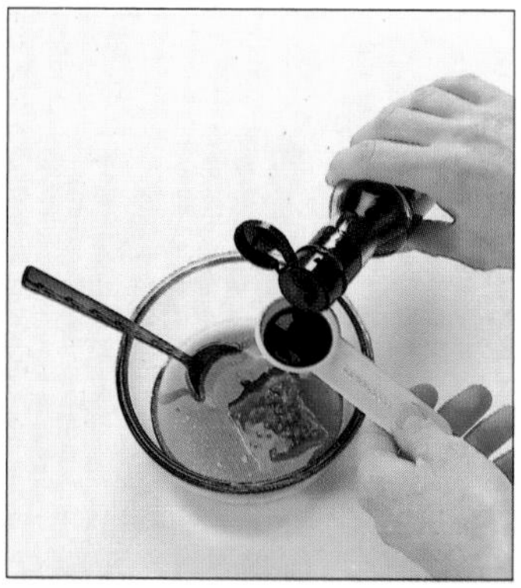

2 tablespoons rice wine or dry sherry
3 tablespoons brown sugar
3 tablespoons groundnut (peanut) oil
1 tablespoon yellow bean paste
2 tablespoons dark soy sauce
2 tablespoons red fermented tofu
450 g (1 lb) pork fillet

In a bowl, mix together rice wine or dry sherry, brown sugar, groundnut oil, yellow bean paste, soy sauce and fermented tofu.

Spoon sauce over pork and leave to marinate at room temperature for 1 hour. Meanwhile, pre-heat oven to 200C (400F/Gas 6).

Put pork fillet on a rack in a roasting tin and roast for 15-20 minutes until juices run clear and outside is richly coloured.

Serves 4.

PORK WITH CASHEW NUTS

1 teaspoon rice wine or dry sherry
1 teaspoon sea salt
1 teaspoon sugar
1 tablespoon cornflour
450 g (1 lb) pork tenderloin, cubed
550 ml (20 fl oz/2½ cups) groundnut (peanut) oil
115 g (4 oz/¾ cup) cashew nuts
3 cloves garlic, finely chopped
2 spring onions, coarsely chopped
4 dried winter mushrooms, soaked in hot water for 25 minutes, drained
½ red pepper and ½ green pepper, seeded and diced
1 teaspoon light soy sauce
¼ teaspoon ground white pepper
70 ml (2½ fl oz/⅓ cup) Chinese Chicken Stock (see page 16)

In a bowl, mix together rice wine or dry sherry, ½ teaspoon of sea salt, sugar and 2 teaspoons of cornflour. Stir in pork to coat evenly. Leave for 30 minutes. In a wok, heat oil until very hot, add pork and deep-fry for 3-4 minutes until cooked through. Using a slotted spoon, lift out pork and drain on absorbent kitchen paper. Place cashew nuts in a small wire basket, lower into oil and deep-fry for a few seconds until lightly coloured. Drain on absorbent kitchen paper.

SWEET AND SOUR PORK

2 teaspoons rice wine or dry sherry
1 large egg, beaten
½ teaspoon sea salt
450 g (1 lb) belly pork, cubed
115 g (4 oz/1 cup) cornflour
550 ml (20 fl oz/2½ cups) groundnut (peanut) oil
3 spring onions, thinly sliced
85 g (3 oz) can bamboo shoots, drained, thinly sliced
1 green pepper, seeded and thinly sliced
2 cloves garlic, finely chopped
1 teaspoon sesame oil
SAUCE:
2 tablespoons brown sugar
1 tablespoon vegetable oil
3 tablespoons malt vinegar
1 teaspoon cornflour

In a bowl, mix together rice wine or dry sherry, egg and salt. Stir in pork to coat evenly. Remove pork and roll in cornflour to coat evenly. In a wok, heat groundnut oil until smoking and deep-fry pork for about 5 minutes until crisp and well cooked. Using a slotted spoon, lift pork from oil and drain on absorbent kitchen paper. Pour oil from wok, leaving just 2 tablespoonsful. Add spring onions, bamboo shoots, green pepper and garlic and stir-fry for 3 minutes. Stir in pork and mix thoroughly.

To make sauce, in a saucepan, stir together brown sugar, vegetable oil, malt vinegar and cornflour and place over a moderate heat for 4 minutes, stirring continuously until hot and well blended. Pour over pork and briefly heat together. Sprinkle with sesame oil and serve.

Serves 4.

SZECHUAN PORK

3 tablespoons vegetable oil
175 g (6 oz) Szechuan preserved cabbage, soaked for 1 hour, drained and shredded
450 g (1 lb) pork tenderloin, very thinly sliced
3 spring onions, finely chopped
3 slices fresh root ginger, peeled and finely chopped
1 fresh red chilli, seeded and very finely sliced
1 red pepper, seeded and cut into strips
1 tablespoon light soy sauce
2 tablespoons rice wine or dry sherry
½ teaspoon brown sugar

In a wok, heat oil, add cabbage and pork and stir-fry for 2 minutes until pork changes colour. Stir in spring onions, ginger, chilli and pepper.

In a small bowl, mix together soy sauce, rice wine or dry sherry and brown sugar. Stir into wok and cook for 2 minutes.

Serves 4.

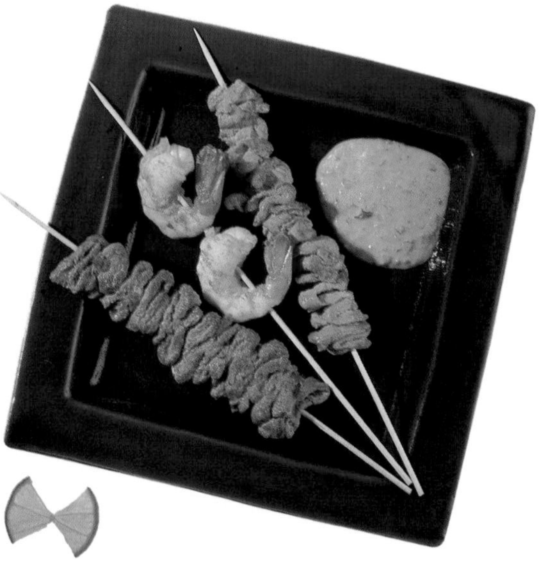

MIXED SATAY

350 g (12 oz) pork fillet, chilled, thinly sliced
350 g (12 oz) steak, chilled, thinly sliced
½ lime
2 teaspoons ground coriander
2 teaspoons ground cumin
1 teaspoon ground turmeric
1 tablespoon light brown sugar
4 tablespoons coconut milk
12 large raw prawns, peeled, tails left on, deveined
oil for brushing
Satay Sauce (see page 227)

Lay each pork slice between sheets of cling film and beat with a rolling pin until fairly thin. Cut slices into 2.5 cm (1 in) wide strips.

Cut steak into strips about the same size as pork. Put meats into a non-reactive bowl and squeeze lime juice over. In a small bowl, mix together coriander, cumin, turmeric, sugar and coconut milk to make a fairly dry paste. Add prawns to dish with meat and spoon coconut mixture over to coat thoroughly. Cover and marinate for 1 hour, or overnight in a refrigerator.

Heat barbecue or grill. Soak bamboo skewers in water for 20-30 minutes. Thread pork strips, steak strips and prawns onto separate skewers. Brush with oil and cook at a very high heat for 10 minutes, turning frequently. Prawns should have turned opaque with bright pink tails, pork should be cooked through and beef still be pink in the centre. Meanwhile, heat satay sauce. Serve sauce with skewers.

Serves 6.

PORK WITH TAMARIND

4 dried red chillies, cored and seeded
1 large onion, chopped
4 candlenuts or cashew nuts
2 tablespoons vegetable oil
700 g (1½ lb) pork shoulder, cut into large bite-sized pieces
2 tablespoons tamarind paste (see page 11)
2 tablespoons dark soy sauce
1 tablespoon yellow bean sauce
1 tablespoon light brown sugar
sliced fresh chillies, to garnish (optional)

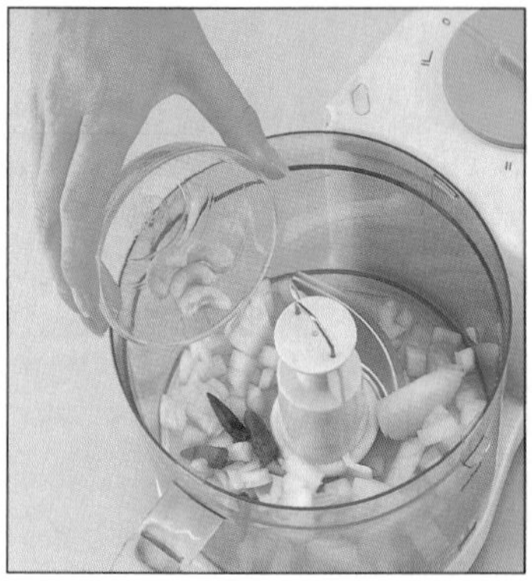

Put chillies in a blender. Add 4 tablespoons hot water and leave until slightly softened. Add onion and nuts; mix to a smooth paste.

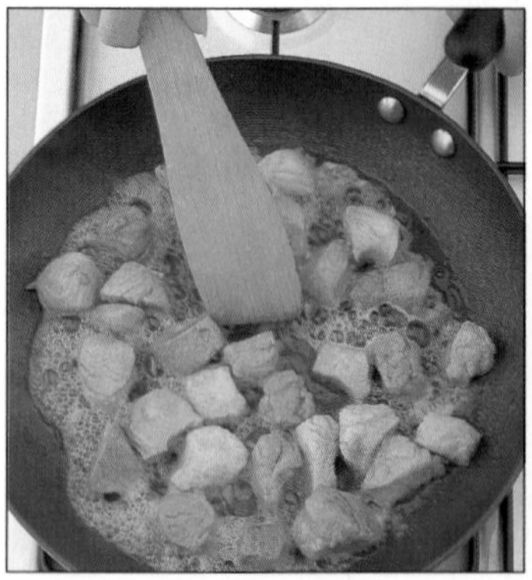

In a sauté pan, preferably non-stick, heat oil over medium-high heat. Add meat in batches and fry until an even light brown. Using a slotted spoon transfer to absorbent kitchen paper to drain.

Add chilli paste to pan and fry for about 5 minutes. Stir in pork, tamarind paste, soy sauce, yellow bean sauce, sugar and 350 ml (12 fl oz/1½ cups) water. Bring to a simmer, cover pan then cook gently for 30-40 minutes, stirring occasionally, until pork is very tender. Serve garnished with sliced fresh chillies, if wished.

Serves 4.

PORK WITH WATER CHESTNUTS

1½ tablespoons vegetable oil
4 cloves garlic, chopped
2 fresh red chillies, seeded and finely chopped
350 g (12 oz) lean pork, cubed
10 canned water chestnuts, chopped
1 teaspoon fish sauce
freshly ground black pepper
3 tablespoons chopped coriander leaves
6 spring onions, chopped
3-4 spring onion brushes (see page 14), to garnish

In a wok, heat oil, add garlic and chillies and cook, stirring occasionally, until garlic becomes golden.

Stir in pork and stir-fry for about 2 minutes until almost cooked through. Add water chestnuts, heat for 2 minutes, then stir in fish sauce, 4 tablespoons water and add plenty of black pepper. Stir in coriander and spring onions. Serve garnished with spring onion brushes.

Serves 3-4.

BARBECUED SPARE RIBS

2 tablespoons chopped coriander stalks
3 cloves garlic, chopped
1 teaspoon black peppercorns, cracked
1 teaspoon grated kaffir lime zest
1 tablespoon Green Curry Paste (see page 230)
2 teaspoons fish sauce
1½ teaspoons crushed palm sugar
175 ml (6 fl oz/¾ cup) coconut milk
900 g (2 lb) pork spare ribs, trimmed
spring onion brushes (see page 14), to garnish

Using a pestle and mortar or small blender, pound or mix together coriander, garlic, peppercorns, lime zest, curry paste, fish sauce and sugar. Stir in coconut milk. Place spare ribs in a shallow dish and pour over spiced coconut mixture. Cover and leave in a cool place for 3 hours, basting occasionally.

Preheat a barbecue or moderate grill. Cook ribs for about 5 minutes a side, until cooked through and brown, basting occasionally with coconut mixture. Garnish with spring onion brushes.

Serves 4-6.

Note: The ribs can also be cooked on a rack in a roasting tin in an oven preheated to 200C (400F/Gas 6) for 45-60 minutes, basting occasionally.

STIR-FRIED PORK & BEANS

2 tablespoons vegetable oil
6 cloves garlic, chopped
350 g (12 oz) lean pork, finely chopped
350 g (12 oz) long beans or slim green beans
12 water chestnuts
115 g (4 oz) cooked peeled prawns
1 tablespoon fish sauce
½ teaspoon crushed palm sugar
freshly ground black pepper

In a wok, heat oil, add garlic and fry, stirring occasionally, until golden.

Add pork and beans and stir-fry for 2 minutes, then add water chestnuts. Stir for 1 minute.

Add prawns, fish sauce, sugar, plenty of black pepper and about 3 tablespoons water. Simmer for a minute or two, then transfer to a warmed serving plate.

Serves 4.

THAI PORK CURRY

115 ml (4 fl oz/½ cup) coconut cream (see page 8)
1 onion, chopped
1 cloves garlic, finely crushed
2 tablespoons Fragrant Curry Paste (see page 231)
2 teaspoons fish sauce
½ teaspoon crushed palm sugar
350 g (12 oz) lean pork, diced
3 kaffir lime leaves, shredded
25 Thai holy basil leaves
1 long fresh red chilli, seeded and cut into strips, and Thai holy basil sprig, to garnish

In a wok, heat 85 ml (3 fl oz/⅓ cup) coconut cream until oil begins to separate. Stir in onion and garlic and cook, stirring occasionally, until lightly browned. Stir in curry paste and continue to stir for about 2 minutes. Stir in fish sauce and sugar, then pork to coat. Cook for 3-4 minutes.

Add lime and basil leaves and cook for 1 more minute. If necessary, add a little water, but final dish should be dry. Serve garnished with a trail of remaining coconut cream, chilli strips and basil sprig.

Serves 3.

PORK WITH SPRING ONIONS

550 ml (20 fl oz/2½ cups) coconut milk
450 g (1 lb) lean pork, cut into 2.5 cm (1 in) cubes
1 tablespoon fish sauce
½ teaspoon crushed palm sugar
100 g (3½ oz/⅔ cup) skinned peanuts
3 fresh red chillies, seeded and chopped
3 cm (1¼ in) piece galangal, chopped
4 cloves garlic
1 stalk lemon grass
4 tablespoons coconut cream (see page 8)
8 spring onions, chopped
900 g (2 lb) young spinach leaves
warmed coconut cream (see page 8), and dry-roasted peanuts, to serve

In a wok, heat coconut milk until just simmering; adjust heat so liquid barely moves. Add pork and cook for about 25 minutes until very tender. Meanwhile, using a small blender or food processor, mix fish sauce, sugar, peanuts, chillies, galangal, garlic and lemon grass to a paste. In another wok, or a frying pan, heat coconut cream until oil separates. Add spring onions and peanut paste, and cook, stirring frequently, for 2-3 minutes.

Stir in milk from pork and boil until lightly thickened. Pour over pork, stir and cook for 5 minutes more. Rinse spinach leaves, then pack into a saucepan with just the water left on them. Gently cook for about 3 minutes until just beginning to wilt. Arrange on a warmed serving plate. Spoon pork and sauce onto centre. Trickle over coconut cream and scatter over dry-roasted peanuts.

Serves 4-6.

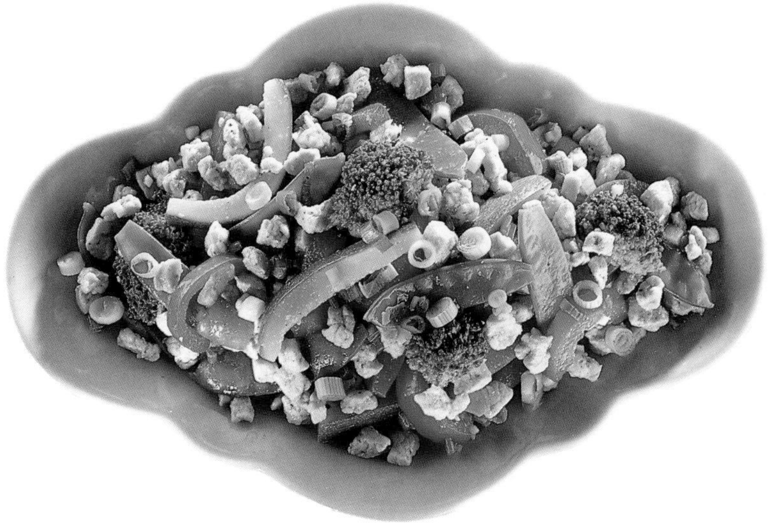

MIXED VEGETABLES & PORK

225 g (8 oz) lean pork, finely chopped
freshly ground black pepper
2 tablespoons vegetable oil
3 cloves garlic, finely chopped
450 g (1 lb) prepared mixed vegetables, such as mangetout, broccoli florets, red pepper and courgettes
1 tablespoon fish sauce
½ teaspoon crushed palm sugar
3 spring onions, finely chopped

In a bowl, mix together pork and plenty of black pepper. Set aside for 30 minutes.

In a wok or frying pan, heat oil, add garlic and cook, stirring occasionally, for 2-3 minutes, then stir in pork. Stir briefly until pork changes colour.

Stir in mixed vegetables, then fish sauce, sugar and 115 ml (4 fl oz/½ cup) water. Stir for 3-4 minutes until mangetout are bright green and vegetables still crisp. Stir in spring onions. Heat through and serve.

Serves 4.

SPICY PORK HOT POT

1 tablespoon vegetable oil
2 cloves garlic, chopped
2 shallots, chopped
450 g (1 lb) lean pork, cut into bite-sized pieces
3 tablespoons sugar
3 tablespoons fish sauce
1 teaspoon five-spice powder
about 250 ml (9 fl oz/1 cup) stock or water
salt and freshly ground black pepper
2-3 spring onions, cut into short sections, to garnish
mangetout and peppers, to serve (optional)

Heat oil in a clay pot or flameproof casserole and stir-fry garlic and shallots for about 1 minute until fragrant.

Add pork pieces and stir-fry them for about 2 minutes, or until pork turns almost white in colour.

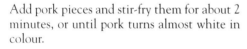

Add sugar, fish sauce and five-spice powder, stir for 1 minute, then add stock or water. Bring to the boil, reduce heat, cover and simmer for 15-20 minutes. Adjust seasoning, garnish with spring onions and serve, with mangetout and peppers, if wished.

Serves 4.

Variation: Chicken, lamb, veal or beef can all be cooked in the same way; increase the cooking time by 10-15 minutes for lamb and veal, 20-25 minutes for beef.

SPICY PORK & LEMON GRASS

1 clove garlic, chopped
2 shallots, chopped
3 tablespoons chopped lemon grass
1 tablespoon sugar
1 tablespoon fish sauce
salt and freshly ground black pepper
350 g (12 oz) pork fillet, cut into small, thin slices
2-3 tablespoons vegetable oil
2-3 sticks celery, thinly sliced
115 g (4 oz) straw mushrooms, halved lengthways
4 small red chillies, seeded and shredded
2 spring onions, shredded
1 tablespoon soy sauce
about 55 ml (2 fl oz/¼ cup) stock or water
2 teaspoons cornflour
coriander sprigs, to garnish

Using a pestle and mortar, pound garlic, shallots and lemon grass to a paste. Transfer to a mixing bowl and add sugar, fish sauce, salt and pepper. Blend well, then add pork slices, turning to coat them with mixture, and leave to marinate for 25-30 minutes.

Heat oil in a wok or frying pan and stir-fry pork slices for 2 minutes. Add celery, straw mushrooms, chillies, spring onions and soy sauce and stir-fry for 2-3 minutes. Use stock to rinse out marinade bowl and add to pork. Bring to the boil. Mix cornflour with 1 tablespoon water and add to sauce to thicken it. Garnish with coriander sprigs and serve at once, with a mixture of rice and wild rice.

Serves 4.

PORK WITH VEGETABLES

225 g (8 oz) pork fillet, thinly shredded
salt and freshly ground black pepper
3 tablespoons vegetable oil
2 shallots, finely chopped
1 teaspoon chopped fresh root ginger
225 g (8 oz) bean sprouts
1 small red pepper, cored and thinly sliced
2-3 spring onions, shredded
2 tablespoons soy sauce
coriander sprigs, to garnish

In a bowl, season pork with salt and pepper and leave for 10-15 minutes.

Heat oil in a wok or frying pan and stir-fry shallots and ginger for about 1 minute. Add pork and stir-fry for 2-3 minutes, until shreds are separated and pork turns almost white in colour.

Add beans sprouts, red pepper, spring onions and soy sauce and stir-fry for a further 2-3 minutes. Garnish with coriander sprigs and serve at once.

Serves 4.

STIR-FRIED PORK

1 teaspoon minced garlic
2 shallots, finely chopped
½ teaspoon chopped fresh root ginger
1 teaspoon sugar
1 tablespoon fish sauce
salt and freshly ground black pepper
450 g (1 lb) pork fillet, cut into small slices or cubes
2-3 tablespoons vegetable oil
115 g (4 oz) sliced bamboo shoots, drained
2 small red chillies, seeded and chopped
2 spring onions, chopped
2 tablespoons oyster sauce
about 55 ml (2 fl oz/¼ cup) stock or water
2 teaspoons cornflour
½ teaspoon sesame oil
coriander sprigs and cucumber slices, to serve

In a bowl, mix garlic, shallots, ginger, sugar, fish sauce and salt and pepper. Add pork and leave to marinate for 25-30 minutes.

Heat oil in a wok or frying pan and stir-fry pork pieces for 2 minutes, then add bamboo shoots, chillies, spring onions and oyster sauce and stir-fry for 4-5 minutes. Rinse out marinade bowl with stock or water and add to pork mixture. Bring to the boil. Mix cornflour with 1 tablespoon water and stir into sauce. Cook, stirring, until thickened. Add sesame oil, garnish with coriander sprigs and serve with halved cucumber slices.

Serves 4.

FRIED PORK CUTLETS

4 pork loin cutlets or boneless chops
salt and freshly ground black pepper
plain flour for coating
2 eggs, beaten
dried bread crumbs for coating
vegetable oil for deep-frying
shredded cabbage and lemon wedges, to garnish
TONKATSU SAUCE:
4 tablespoons tomato ketchup
1 tablespoon soy sauce
2 teaspoons Worcestershire sauce
2 teaspoons mustard plus extra for serving

Make a few slits in the fat of the cutlets or chops to prevent them curling when cooked.

Sprinkle both sides of pork cutlets with salt and pepper and dredge with flour, shaking off any excess. Dip in beaten egg, then coat in bread crumbs. Heat oil in a wok or a deep-frying pan to 180C (350F). Gently slide in pork cutlets, 1 or 2 at a time, and deep-fry for 5-7 minutes until golden brown, turning once or twice. Drain on absorbent kitchen paper. In between each batch, clean oil with a mesh ladle. Meanwhile, mix together tomato ketchup, soy sauce, Worcestershire sauce and mustard in a small serving bowl.

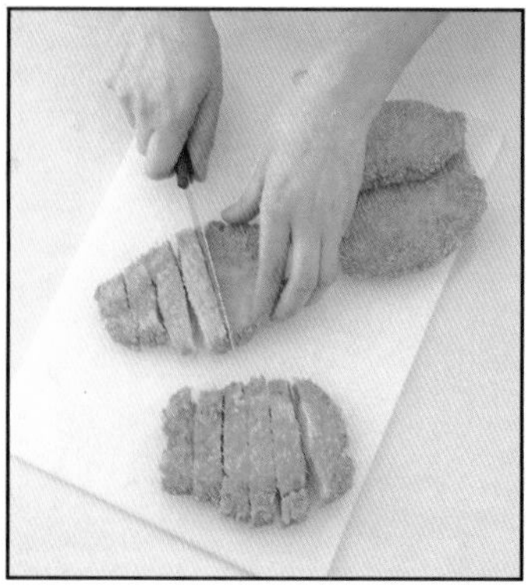

When all cutlets have been cooked, place them on a cutting board and cut each one crossways into 2.5 cm (1 in) lengths. Arrange on 4 individual plates and garnish with very finely shredded raw cabbage and lemon wedges. Serve with sauce and extra mustard, if wished.

Serves 4.

Note: This dish is called Tonkatsu in Japanese.

GINGER PORK

450 g (1 lb) pork fillets or boneless chops
5 cm (2 in) piece fresh root ginger, peeled and grated
4 tablespoons soy sauce
boiled rice and lightly cooked mangetout, to serve

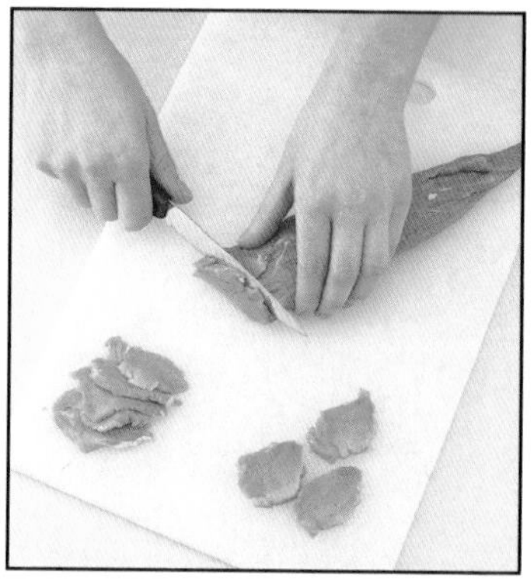

Inserting the blade of a knife diagonally, slice pork fillets crossways into very thin, 2.5 cm (1 in) diameter discs. If using chops, discard fat and cut roughly 5 x 2.5 cm (2 x 1 in) thin pieces.

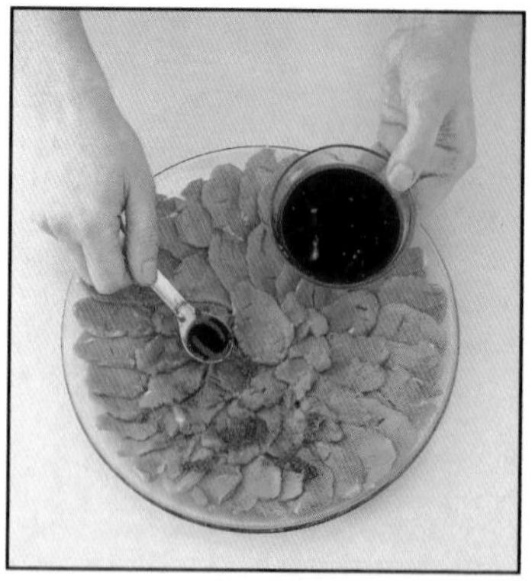

Place pork slices on a large plate, spreading as widely apart as possible, and sprinkle all over with grated ginger, together with its juice, and soy sauce. Leave to marinate for 15 minutes.

Heat a frying pan, add 2-3 tablespoons vegetable oil and fry pork slices for 2-3 minutes on each side until they are well cooked and both sides are golden brown. Arrange a quarter of the cooked pork slices on a bed of boiled rice, garnish with mangetout and serve at once.

Serves 4.

GRILLED PORK WITH MISO

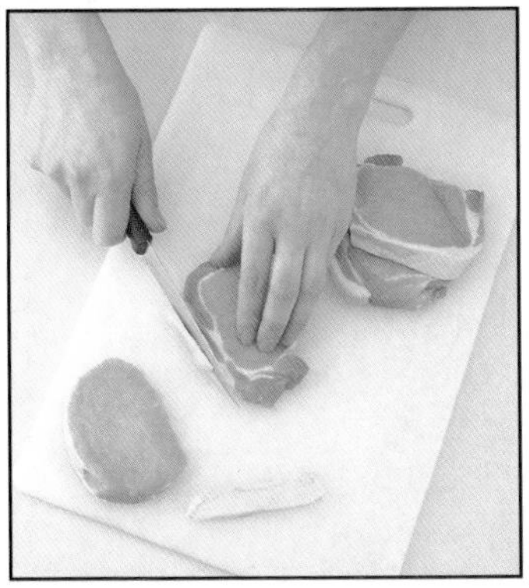

4 pork loin steaks
lemon wedges, to garnish
MISO SAUCE:
3 tablespoons red miso
3 spring onions, finely chopped
2 teaspoons sake
2 teaspoons fresh root ginger juice

Remove any fat from pork. If pork is more than 1.5 cm (⅔ in) thick, slice in half horizontally.

Preheat grill. Heat a well-oiled wire rack under hot grill and place pork steaks on it. Gently grill pork for 3-4 minutes on each side or until both sides are golden brown and well cooked.

Meanwhile, in a bowl, make miso sauce by mixing red miso, spring onions, sake and ginger juice. Lower the heat and remove the rack from the grill. Spoon miso sauce evenly on to the centre of the pork steaks and put back under medium hot grill for 1 minute until miso sauce is fairly dry. Transfer steaks to 4 individual plates, garnish with lemon wedges and serve.

Serves 4.

PORK WITH CITRUS SOY SAUCE

450 g (1 lb) pork loin or gammon
3 spring onions, cut in half
5 cm (2 in) piece fresh root ginger, peeled and cut into 3-4 pieces
CITRUS SOY SAUCE:
juice ½ lemon
1 tablespoon lime juice
1 tablespoon rice vinegar
2 tablespoons soy sauce
½ tablespoon mirin
2 spring onions, finely chopped
2.5 cm (1 in) fresh root ginger, peeled, finely chopped

Put pork, spring onions, ginger and a pinch of salt in a large pot and cover with water.

Bring to the boil, cover pot and simmer gently for 2 hours. Drain meat, put it in a bowl of ice cold water and refrigerate until chilled. Remove pork from water, pat dry and then slice it crossways against the grain as thinly as possible. Arrange slices, fanning them out around the edge of a large serving platter.

To make citrus soy sauce, mix together lemon and lime juice, rice vinegar, soy sauce, mirin, spring onions and ginger. and stir well. Transfer it to a serving bowl or a ramekin and place in the centre of the pork circle. Serve cold.

Serves 4.

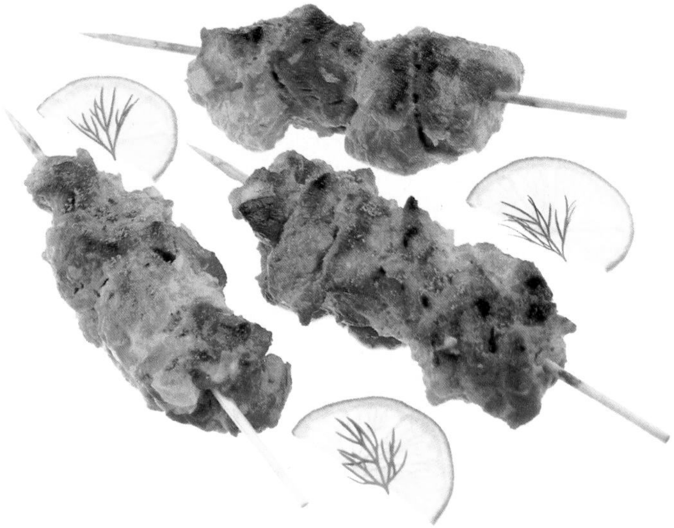

LAMB TIKKA

900 g (2 lb) boneless leg of lamb, trimmed of fat and cut into 4 cm (1½ in) cubes
1 teaspoon ground cumin
¼ teaspoon turmeric
salt
6 tablespoons natural yogurt
½ small onion, finely chopped
5 cm (2 in) piece fresh root ginger, grated
2 cloves garlic, crushed
few drops red food colouring, optional
1 teaspoon Garam Masala (see page 224)

Put lamb in a bowl and add cumin, turmeric, salt, yogurt, onion, ginger and garlic.

Mix together well, then, if you wish, add enough colouring to give mixture a red tinge. Cover and leave in refrigerator for 4-6 hours to marinate. Drain lamb from marinade and thread cubes on to 8 short skewers, pressing cubes closely together.

Heat grill. Cook kebabs for 15-20 minutes, basting kebabs with any remaining marinade and turning occasionally during cooking, until well browned and done to taste. Sprinkle with garam masala and serve at once.

Serves 4.

Note: These kebabs can be cooked on a barbecue using metal skewers. Cooking time depends on heat of barbecue.

KASHMIR MEATBALL CURRY

700 g (1½ lb) minced lamb
25 g (1 oz/¼ cup) chick-pea flour
3 tablespoons Garam Masala (see page 224)
¼ teaspoon cayenne pepper
6 tablespoons natural yogurt
salt
2 tablespoons vegetable oil
7.5 cm (3 in) cinnamon stick
6 green cardamom pods, bruised
2 fresh bay leaves
6 whole cloves
5 cm (2 in) piece fresh root ginger, grated
2 tablespoons chopped coriander leaves, to garnish

Put lamb, chick-pea flour, garam masala, cayenne and 3 tablespoons of yogurt in a bowl. Season with salt and mix together well. Shape into 16 long ovals. Heat oil in a shallow heavy-based pan, add cinnamon, cardamom pods, bay leaves and cloves. Stir-fry for a few seconds, then add meatballs and fry until lightly browned on all sides. Add ginger and fry for a few seconds more. Stir remaining 3 tablespoons of yogurt into 225 ml (8 fl oz/1 cup) cold water and pour over meatballs.

Cover pan and bring to the boil. Reduce heat and simmer for about 30 minutes, stirring gently 2 or 3 times, until meatballs are cooked and almost all the sauce has been absorbed. Sprinkle with coriander and serve at once.

Serves 4.

Note: If meatballs release a lot of fat during initial frying, drain it off before adding yogurt liquid.

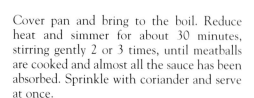

LAMB KORMA

700 g (1½ lb) boneless leg of lamb
55 ml (2 fl oz/¼ cup) vegetable oil
1 large onion, finely chopped
1 quantity Cashew Nut Masala (see page 224)
2 tablespoons Garam Masala (see page 224)
3 dried red chillies, seeded and crushed
2.5 cm (1 in) piece fresh root ginger, grated
1 tablespoon chopped coriander leaves
225 ml (8 fl oz/1 cup) single cream
salt
2 teaspoons lemon juice
coriander leaves and lemon wedges, to garnish

Wipe lamb, trim off excess fat and cut into 5 cm (2 in) cubes.

Heat oil in a heavy-based pan, add lamb and fry until browned all over. Add onion and cook for about 5 minutes, stirring frequently, until soft. Stir in masala, chillies and ginger and cook for 2 minutes more.

Add chopped coriander, cream and 70 ml (2½ fl oz/⅓ cup) water and season with salt. Bring to the boil and simmer, covered, for about 1 hour or until lamb is tender. Stir in lemon juice and serve hot, garnished with coriander and lemon wedges.

Serves 4.

RED LAMB & ALMOND CURRY

700 g (1½ lb) boneless leg of lamb
55 ml (2 fl oz/¼ cup) vegetable oil
6 green cardamom pods, bruised
1 teaspoon turmeric
1 teaspoon chilli powder
1 teaspoon ground cumin
1 tablespoon paprika
1 teaspoon ground coriander
1 small piece rattan jog (type of bark which stains food red), optional
1 quantity Almond Masala (see page 224)
150 ml (5 fl oz/⅔ cup) natural yogurt
400 g (14 oz) can chopped tomatoes
1 large onion, finely chopped

Trim excess fat from lamb and cut lamb into 4 cm (1½ in) cubes. Heat oil in a heavy-based pan, add cardamom pods, turmeric, chilli powder, cumin, paprika, coriander, rattan jog, if using, and almond masala. Fry, stirring, for 2-3 minutes, then stir in yogurt and tomatoes and bring to the boil. Add onion and cook for 3-4 minutes. Add lamb cubes, stir well and cover.

Bring to the boil again, then reduce heat and cook for 40-50 minutes, stirring occasionally, until lamb is tender and liquid makes a thick sauce.

Serves 4.

Note: On special occasions, this dish can be garnished with real silver leaf, available from Indian shops. Just before serving, place a sheet, silver side down, on top and peel off backing paper.

LAMB WITH ONIONS

700 g (1½ lb) shoulder of lamb, boned
1 teaspoon turmeric
1 teaspoon ground cumin
1 teaspoon ground coriander
2.5 cm (1 in) piece fresh root ginger, grated
2 cloves garlic, crushed
45 ml (1½ fl oz/3 tablespoons) vegetable oil
1 tablespoon caster sugar
4 large onions, sliced into thin rings
450 g (1 lb) potatoes, cut into large chunks
salt and cayenne pepper
1 teaspoon Garam Masala (see page 224)
rosemary sprig, to garnish

Wipe lamb, trim and cut into cubes.

Put lamb in a glass or china bowl. Mix together turmeric, cumin, coriander, ginger and garlic and add to lamb. Stir well, then cover loosely and leave in a cool place for 2-3 hours. Heat oil in heavy-based pan until smoking. Stir in sugar, then add onions and cook over a medium to high heat for 10 minutes, stirring frequently, until a rich brown. Remove onions with a slotted spoon and set aside.

Add lamb to pan and fry until browned all over. Add potatoes and fry, stirring for 2 minutes. Return onions to pan, add 225 ml (8 fl oz/1 cup) water and season with salt and pepper. Bring to the boil and simmer, covered, for 1¼ hours, or until lamb is tender, stirring occasionally. Stir in garam masala and serve, garnished with rosemary sprigs.

Serves 4.

LEG OF LAMB & PISTACHIOS

1.5-1.8 kg (3½-4 lb) leg of lamb, boned, rolled and tied
2 cloves garlic, crushed
2.5 cm (1 in) piece fresh root ginger, grated
1 teaspoon ground cumin
2 teaspoons Murghal Masala (see page 224)
salt and cayenne pepper
115 g (4 oz/¾ cup) shelled pistachio nuts
2 tablespoons lemon juice
2 tablespoons soft brown sugar
115 ml (4 fl oz/½ cup) natural yogurt
2 pinches saffron threads
2 tablespoons boiling water
1 tablespoon cornflour
2 tablespoons shelled pistachio nuts, sliced, to garnish

Prick lamb all over with the point of a knife and place in a large glass bowl. Put garlic, ginger, cumin, masala, salt and cayenne pepper to taste, pistachio nuts, lemon juice, sugar and yogurt in a blender or food processor fitted with a metal blade and process until smooth. Pour over lamb and leave to marinate for 24 hours, turning lamb occasionally. Preheat oven to 180C (350F/Gas 4). Transfer lamb to a flameproof casserole, add 150 ml (5 fl oz/⅔ cup) water and bring to the boil.

Cover tightly and cook in the oven for 1½ hours. Reduce heat to 140C (275F/Gas 1) and cook for a further 30 minutes. Turn off oven and leave for 30 minutes. Soak saffron in water for 20 minutes, then blend in cornflour. Remove lamb and keep warm. Skim excess fat from sauce, add saffron mixture and boil, stirring, until thick. Slice lamb, pour a little sauce over and garnish with nuts. Serve remaining sauce separately.

Serves 6-8.

LAMB IN GARLIC SAUCE

450 g (1 lb) lamb tenderloin, very thinly sliced
3 tablespoons dark soy sauce
5 tablespoons groundnut (peanut) oil
2 tablespoons rice wine or dry sherry
½ teaspoon ground Szechuan pepper
½ teaspoon sea salt
2 cloves garlic, chopped
8 spring onions, chopped
1 tablespoon rice vinegar
2 tablespoons sesame oil

In a shallow dish, combine lamb with 1 tablespoon soy sauce, 2 tablespoons oil, rice wine or dry sherry, pepper and salt.

Leave meat to marinate for 30 minutes. In a wok, heat remaining 3 tablespoons groundnut oil until smoking, then add garlic and lamb. Stir-fry for 2 minutes until lamb just changes colour; remove from wok. Pour oil from wok, leaving just 1 tablespoonful. Add spring onions and stir-fry for 2 minutes. Add remaining 2 tablespoons soy sauce and rice vinegar.

Continue stir-frying for another minute then add lamb slices and sesame oil. Stir-fry for 1 minute making sure lamb and sauce are thoroughly combined.

Serves 4.

LAMB WITH SPRING ONIONS

1 egg white
55 g (2 oz/½ cup) cornflour
1 teaspoon sea salt
1 tablespoon rice wine or dry sherry
450 g (1 lb) lamb fillet, cut into strips
300 ml (10 fl oz/1¼ cups) vegetable oil
10 spring onions, chopped
1 cm (½ in) piece fresh root ginger, peeled and finely chopped
2 cloves garlic, finely chopped
1 teaspoon brown sugar
2 teaspoons dark soy sauce
¼ teaspoon ground white pepper
1 teaspoon sesame oil to serve

In a bowl, mix together egg white, cornflour, ½ teaspoon salt, and rice wine or dry sherry. Stir in lamb strips to coat thoroughly. In a wok, heat oil until smoking, add lamb in small batches, keeping strips separate, and stir-fry for 2 minutes.

Using a slotted spoon remove lamb from wok, drain on absorbent kitchen paper and keep warm. Pour oil from wok, leaving just 1 tablespoonful. Stir in spring onions, ginger, garlic, remaining ½ teaspoon salt, sugar, soy sauce and pepper. Add lamb and heat through thoroughly. Serve sprinkled with sesame oil.

Serves 4.

RED-COOKED LAMB FILLET

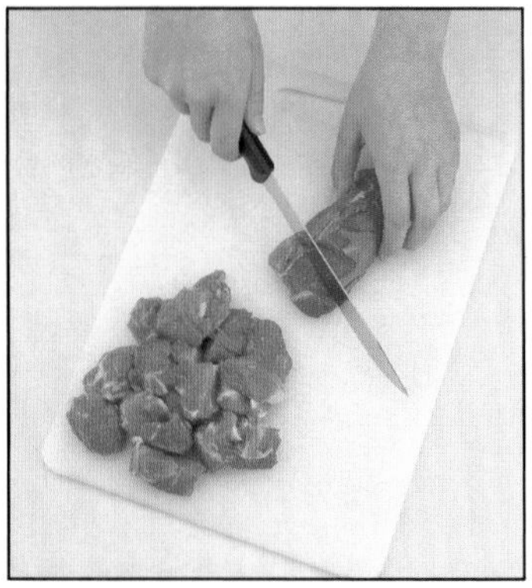

450 g (1 lb) lean lamb fillet
3 tablespoons dry sherry
1 cm (½ in) piece fresh root ginger, peeled and chopped
2 cloves garlic, thinly sliced
1 teaspoon five-spice powder
3 tablespoons dark soy sauce
300 ml (10 fl oz/1¼ cups) Chinese Vegetable Stock (see page 17)
2 teaspoons sugar
2 teaspoons cornflour mixed with 4 teaspoons water
salt and freshly ground pepper
shredded spring onions, to garnish

Trim any excess fat and silver skin from lamb and cut lamb into 2 cm (¾ in) cubes.

Cook lamb in a saucepan of boiling water for 3 minutes. Drain well. Heat a wok and add lamb, sherry, ginger, garlic, five-spice powder and soy sauce. Bring to the boil, reduce heat and simmer for 2 minutes, stirring. Pour in stock, return to boil, then simmer for 25 minutes.

Add sugar, cornflour mixture, salt and pepper and stir until thickened. Simmer for 5 minutes. Garnish with shredded spring onions and serve on a bed of rice.

Serves 4.

STIR-FRIED MEATBALLS

1 aubergine, weighing about 450 g (1 lb)
55 ml (2 fl oz/¼ cup) salt
1 tablespoon sunflower oil
2 tablespoons rice wine
115 g (4 oz) can bamboo shoots, drained and cut into strips
4 spring onions, finely chopped, to garnish
MEATBALLS:
350 g (12 oz) lean minced lamb
4 spring onions, finely chopped
2 cloves garlic, finely chopped
2 tablespoons chopped fresh chives
salt and ground white pepper
1 teaspoon ground cinnamon
2 teaspoons cornflour
1 egg white

Cut aubergine into 0.5 cm (¼ in) slices and layer in a bowl, sprinkling generously with salt. Set aside for 30 minutes. Meanwhile, make meatballs, by mixing together minced lamb, spring onions, garlic, chives, salt and pepper, cinnamon, cornflour and egg white. Divide mixture into 24 portions and roll into balls, flouring hands with extra cornflour. Set aside. Transfer aubergine to a colander and rinse well under cold running water, pressing gently to remove all salt. Drain well and pat dry with absorbent kitchen paper.

Heat oil and rice wine in a wok and stir-fry aubergine for 2-3 minutes or until softened. Add meatballs and carefully stir-fry for 5 minutes. Add bamboo shoots and stir-fry for 2 minutes. Remove meatballs and vegetables with a slotted spoon. Garnish with chopped spring onions and serve with a salad.

Serves 4.

YELLOW BEAN LAMB

115 g (4 oz) rice vermicelli
350 g (12 oz) lean boneless lamb
1 tablespoon groundnut (peanut) oil
1 clove garlic, finely chopped
2 spring onions, finely chopped
115 g (4 oz) mangetout, sliced
2 tablespoons yellow bean sauce
freshly ground pepper
2 tablespoons chopped fresh chives, to garnish

Bring a saucepan of water to the boil. Remove from heat and add noodles. Leave to soak for 2-3 minutes or until soft, then drain well and set aside.

Trim any far from lamb and cut into 1 cm (½ in) strips. Heat oil in a wok and stir-fry lamb, garlic, spring onions and mangetout for 2-3 minutes or until lamb is browned.

Stir in yellow bean sauce and noodles, season with pepper and stir-fry for 3 minutes. Garnish with chopped chives and serve with a mixed salad.

Serves 4.

STIR-FRIED SESAME LAMB

350 g (12 oz) lean lamb fillet
1 tablespoon sunflower oil
115 g (4 oz) shallots, sliced
1 red pepper, sliced
1 green pepper, sliced
1 clove garlic, finely chopped
1 tablespoon light soy sauce
1 teaspoon white rice vinegar
1 teaspoon sugar
freshly ground black pepper
2 tablespoons sesame seeds

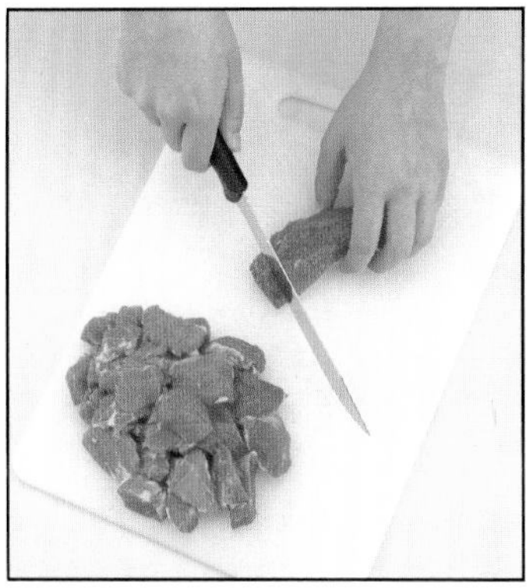

Trim any fat and silver skin from lamb fillet. Cut fillet into 0.5 cm (¼ in) cubes.

Heat oil in a wok and stir-fry lamb for 1-2 minutes or until browned. Remove with a slotted spoon and set aside. Stir-fry shallots, peppers and garlic for 2 minutes or until just softened.

Return lamb to wok with soy sauce, rice vinegar, sugar and black pepper. Stir-fry for 2 minutes. Sprinkle with sesame seeds and serve with rice and vegetables.

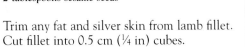

Serves 4.

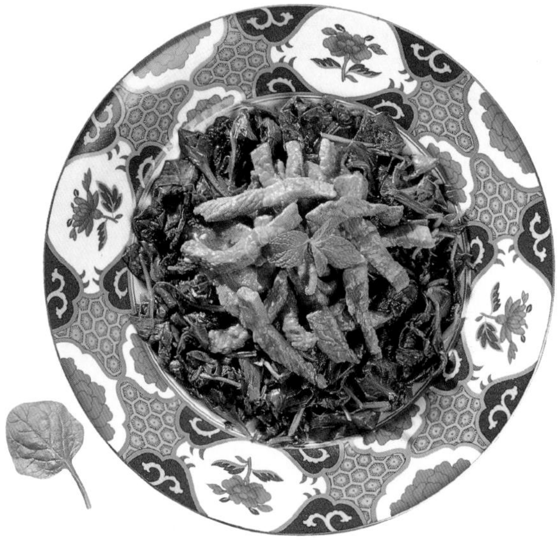

LAMB WITH SPICY HOT SAUCE

300g (10 oz) lamb steak, thinly sliced
salt and freshly ground black pepper
1 teaspoon minced garlic
1 teaspoon chopped fresh root ginger
1 tablespoon fish sauce
3 tablespoons vegetable oil
225 g (8 oz) spinach or any green vegetable
1 tablespoon oyster sauce
2-3 tablespoons Vietnamese Hot Sauce (see page 234)
about 2-3 tablespoons stock or water
½ teaspoon sesame oil
fresh mint and/or coriander sprigs, to garnish

Marinate lamb slices with salt, pepper, garlic, ginger and fish sauce for 2-3 hours.

Heat about half of the oil in a wok or pan and stir-fry spinach or other green vegetable for about 2 minutes. Blend in oyster sauce, then place on a warmed serving dish.

Wipe clean the wok or pan and add remaining oil. When hot, add lamb slices and Vietnamese Hot Sauce and stir-fry for 2 minutes. Rinse out remaining marinade with stock or water and add to lamb. Bring to the boil and cook for 2-3 minutes, stirring all the time. Add sesame oil, then spoon lamb over spinach or green vegetable. Garnish with mint and/or coriander sprigs and serve at once.

Serves 4.

MALAYSIAN LAMB CURRY

2 onions, chopped
3 cloves garlic, crushed
4 fresh red chillies, cored, seeded and chopped
1 stalk lemon grass, chopped
1½ tablespoons chopped fresh root ginger
2 teaspoons ground coriander
1 teaspoon ground cumin
800 ml (1½ pints/3½ cups) coconut milk
1 kg (2¼ lb) lean mature lamb or mutton shoulder, cut into 5 cm (2 in) cubes
juice 1 lime
1½ teaspoons light brown sugar
salt

Put onions, garlic, chillies, lemon grass, ginger, coriander and cumin in a blender. Add about 150 ml (5 fl oz/⅔ cup) of the coconut milk and mix together well. Pour into a large saucepan. Stir in 300 ml (10 fl oz/1¼ cups) coconut milk and 700 ml (25 fl oz/3 cups + 2 tablespoons) water and bring to a simmer. Add lamb and lime juice. Simmer gently, uncovered, stirring occasionally, for about 2 hours until meat is tender and liquid has evaporated.

Add a little boiling water if liquid evaporates too quickly. Stir in remaining coconut milk and sugar. Add salt to taste and simmer for about 5 minutes. Serve with boiled rice.

Serves 4-6.

VEGETABLES

MIXED VEGETABLE CURRY

3 tablespoons vegetable oil
1 onion, sliced
1 teaspoon ground cumin
1 teaspoon chilli powder
2 teaspoons ground coriander
1 teaspoon turmeric
225 g (8 oz) potatoes, diced
175 g (6 oz) cauliflower florets
115 g (4 oz) green beans, sliced
175 g (6 oz) carrots, diced
4 tomatoes, skinned and chopped
300 ml (10 fl oz/1¼ cups) hot vegetable stock
onion rings, to garnish

Heat oil in a large saucepan, add onion and fry for 5 minutes, until softened. Stir in cumin, chilli powder, coriander and turmeric and cook for 2 minutes, stirring occasionally. Add potatoes, cauliflower, green beans and carrots, tossing them in spices until coated.

Add tomatoes and stock and cover. Bring to the boil, then reduce heat and simmer for 10-12 minutes or until vegetables are just tender. Serve hot, garnished with onion rings.

Serves 4.

Variation: Use any mixture of vegetables to make a total of 700 g (1½ lb) – turnips, swedes, courgettes, aubergines, parsnips and leeks are all suitable for this curry.

CARROTS WITH FRESH DILL

450 g (1 lb) carrots
1 tablespoon vegetable oil
25 g (1 oz/2 tablespoons) butter or ghee
¾ teaspoon cumin seeds
pinch ground asafoetida
1 cm (½ in) piece fresh root ginger, finely chopped
2 fresh green chillies, seeded and finely sliced
1 teaspoon ground coriander
¼ teaspoon turmeric
4 tablespoons chopped fresh dill
salt
dill sprigs, to garnish

Cut carrots into 0.3 × 2.5 cm (⅛ × 1 in) sticks and set aside.

Heat oil and butter or ghee in a heavy-based pan and fry cumin seeds for about 30 seconds, until they begin to pop. Add asafoetida, ginger, chillies, coriander and turmeric and fry for 2 minutes. Stir in carrots and 6 tablespoons water.

Cook over a medium heat, covered, for 5 minutes or until carrots are just tender. Uncover, add chopped dill, season with salt and cook over a high heat for about 2 minutes to evaporate any excess liquid. Serve hot, garnished with dill sprigs.

Serves 4.

Note: This recipe is also delicious chilled and served as a salad.

TAMIL NADU VEGETABLES

115 g (4 oz/2/3 cup) red split lentils
1/2 teaspoon turmeric
1 small aubergine
55 ml (2 fl oz/1/4 cup) vegetable oil
25 g (1 oz/1/3 cup) desiccated coconut
1 teaspoon cumin seeds
1/2 teaspoon mustard seeds
2 dried red chillies, crushed
1 red pepper, seeded and sliced
115 g (4 oz) courgettes, thickly sliced
85 g (3 oz) green beans, cut into 2 cm (3/4 in) pieces
150 ml (5 fl oz/2/3 cup) vegetable stock
salt
red pepper strips, to garnish

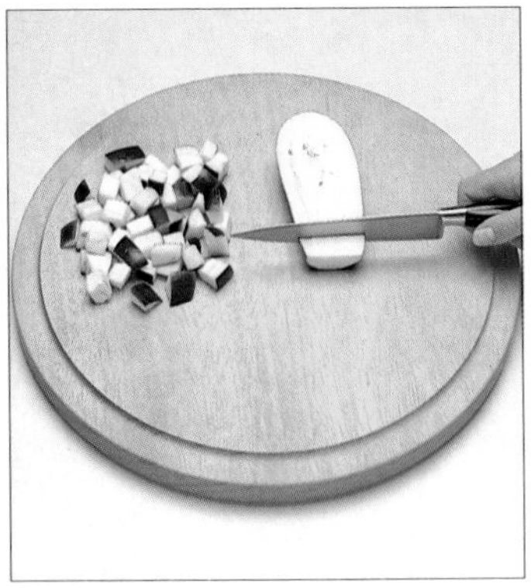

Wash lentils and put into a large saucepan with turmeric and 550 ml (20 fl oz/2 1/2 cups) water. Bring to the boil, then reduce heat and simmer, covered, for 15-20 minutes, until lentils are soft. Meanwhile, cut aubergine into 1 cm (1/2 in) dice. Heat oil in a large shallow pan, add coconut, cumin, mustard seeds and chillies.

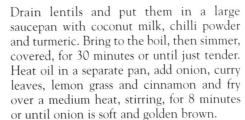

Fry for 1 minute, then add aubergine, red pepper, courgettes, green beans, stock and salt. Bring to the boil, then simmer, covered, for 10-15 minutes, until vegetables are just tender. Stir in lentils and any cooking liquid and cook for a further 5 minutes. Serve hot, garnished with red pepper strips.

Serves 4.

SPICED BROWN LENTILS

225 g (8 oz/1 1/4 cups) whole brown lentils
300 ml (10 fl oz/1 1/4 cups) coconut milk (see page 224)
1/4 teaspoon chilli powder
1/2 teaspoon turmeric
2 tablespoons vegetable oil
1 onion, finely chopped
4 curry leaves
1/2 stalk lemon grass
7.5 cm (3 in) cinnamon stick
sprigs lemon thyme, to garnish

Wash lentils, put in a bowl, cover with cold water and leave to soak for 6 hours or overnight.

Drain lentils and put them in a large saucepan with coconut milk, chilli powder and turmeric. Bring to the boil, then simmer, covered, for 30 minutes or until just tender. Heat oil in a separate pan, add onion, curry leaves, lemon grass and cinnamon and fry over a medium heat, stirring, for 8 minutes or until onion is soft and golden brown.

Stir into lentil mixture and simmer for a further 10 minutes or until liquid has evaporated and lentils are soft but not broken up. Remove whole spices and serve hot, garnished with thyme sprigs.

Serves 4.

Note: Substitute a few sprigs of lemon thyme if lemon grass is unavailable.

MUSHROOM CURRY

450 g (1 lb) button mushrooms
2 fresh green chillies, seeded
2 teaspoons ground coriander
1 teaspoon ground cumin
½ teaspoon chilli powder
2 cloves garlic, crushed
1 onion, cut into wedges
150 ml (5 fl oz/⅔ cup) coconut milk (see page 224)
salt
25 g (1 oz/2 tablespoons) butter or ghee
bay leaves, to garnish

Wipe mushrooms and trim stalks, then set aside.

Put chillies, ground coriander, cumin, chilli powder, garlic, onion, coconut milk and salt to taste in a blender or food processor fitted with a metal blade and blend until smooth.

Melt butter in a saucepan, add mushrooms and fry for 3-4 minutes, until golden brown. Pour over spicy coconut milk and simmer, uncovered, for 10 minutes or until mushrooms are tender. Serve hot, garnished with bay leaves.

Serves 4.

PEPPERS WITH CAULIFLOWER

55 ml (2 fl oz/¼ cup) vegetable oil
1 large onion, sliced
2 cloves garlic, crushed
2 green chillies, seeded and chopped
1 cauliflower, divided into small florets
½ teaspoon turmeric
1 teaspoon Garam Masala (see page 224)
1 green pepper
1 red pepper
1 orange or yellow pepper
salt and pepper
1 tablespoon chopped coriander leaves, to garnish

Heat oil in a large saucepan, add onion and fry over a medium heat for 8 minutes or until soft and golden brown. Stir in garlic, chillies and cauliflower and fry for 5 minutes, stirring continuously. Stir in turmeric and garam masala and fry for 1 minute.

Reduce heat, add 55 ml (2 fl oz/¼ cup) water and cook, covered, for 10-15 minutes, until cauliflower is almost tender. Cut peppers in half lengthways, remove stalks and seeds, then slice peppers finely. Add to pan and cook for a further 3-5 minutes, until softened. Season with salt and pepper. Serve hot, garnished with chopped coriander.

Serves 4.

SPICY OKRA

350 g (12 oz) okra
2 tablespoons vegetable oil
2.5 cm (1 in) piece fresh root ginger, grated
1 teaspoon turmeric
½ teaspoon chilli powder
1 teaspoon chick-pea flour
salt
300 ml (10 fl oz/1¼ cups) natural yogurt
2 tablespoons chopped coriander leaves, to garnish

Wash okra and pat dry with absorbent kitchen paper, then cut into thick slices.

Heat oil in a saucepan, add okra and fry, stirring continuously, for 4 minutes. Stir in ginger, turmeric, chilli powder and chick-pea flour. Season with salt and fry for 1 minute more.

Stir in 3 tablespoons water, then cover and cook gently for 10 minutes or until okra is tender. Stir in yogurt and reheat gently. Serve hot, sprinkled with coriander.

Serves 4.

Note: Choose okra pods that are about 10 cm (4 in) long – larger pods are tough and stringy to eat.

DRY POTATO CURRY

450 g (1 lb) waxy potatoes
salt
2 tablespoons vegetable oil
1 teaspoon mustard seeds
1 onion, finely sliced
2 cloves garlic, crushed
2.5 cm (1 in) piece fresh root ginger, grated
1 fresh green chilli, seeded and chopped
1 teaspoon turmeric
½ teaspoon cayenne pepper
1 teaspoon ground cumin
green pepper strips, to garnish (optional)

Cut potatoes into 2 cm (¾ in) chunks.

Cook potatoes in boiling salted water for 6-8 minutes, until just tender, then drain and set aside. Heat oil in a large saucepan, add mustard seeds and fry for 30 seconds or until they begin to pop. Add onion and fry for 5 minutes, until soft but not brown. Stir in garlic and ginger and fry for 1 minute more.

Add potatoes, chilli, turmeric, cayenne and cumin and stir well. Cook, covered, for 3-5 minutes, stirring occasionally, until potatoes are very tender and coated with spices. Serve hot, garnished with green pepper strips.

Serves 4.

VEGETARIAN EIGHT TREASURE

2 tablespoons vegetable oil
4 spring onions, sliced
1 cloves garlic, finely chopped
55 g (2 oz) green pepper, seeded and diced
55 g (2 oz) red pepper, seeded and diced
2 fresh hot green chillies, seeded and sliced
115 g (4 oz) canned water chestnuts, diced
2 cakes spiced tofu
6 dried black winter mushrooms, soaked in hot water for 25 minutes, drained
115 g (4 oz) cucumber, diced
2 tablespoons black bean paste
1 teaspoon red bean paste
1 teaspoon rice wine or dry sherry
1 teaspoon dark soy sauce
1 teaspoon brown sugar
¼ teaspoon ground white pepper
115 g (4 oz) deep-fried gluten balls (see Note), if wished
1 teaspoon sesame oil, to serve

In a wok, heat vegetable oil, add spring onions and garlic, and stir-fry for 3-4 minutes until just beginning to colour. Add pepper, chillies and water chestnuts; stir-fry for 1 minute.

Stir in mushrooms, cucumber, black and red bean pastes, rice wine, soy sauce, brown sugar, white pepper, deep-fried gluten balls (if using) and 2 tablespoons water and cook for 3 minutes. Sprinkle with sesame oil and serve.

Serves 4.

Note: Deep-fried gluten balls are available in packets in Chinese food shops, and speciality delicatessens.

VEGETARIAN NEW YEAR

550 ml (20 fl oz/2½ cups) vegetable oil
4 cakes tofu, cut into bite-sized pieces
6 pieces white ji stick (see Note), if wished
55 g (2 oz) dried cloud mushrooms, soaked in hot water for 20 minutes, drained
55 g (2 oz) dried black winter mushrooms, soaked in hot water for 25 minutes, drained
85 g (3 oz) can bamboo shoots, drained and sliced
85 g (3 oz) can water chestnuts, drained and sliced
55 g (2 oz) golden needles (see Note), soaked in warm water for 10 minutes, drained
55 g (2 oz/⅓ cup) shelled ginko nuts, or almonds, skinned
1 cake red tofu
1 teaspoon brown sugar
1 tablespoon dark soy sauce

In a wok, heat vegetable oil until smoking, add tofu and ji sticks (if using) and fry for 3-4 minutes until golden and puffy. Remove and drain on absorbent kitchen paper. Pour oil from wok leaving just 4 tablespoonsful. Add mushrooms, bamboo shoots, water chestnuts and golden needles and stir-fry for 5 minutes. Add nuts, stir-fry for 1 minute, then stir in a few tablespoons water to prevent vegetables drying out. Reduce heat and simmer for 4 minutes. Add ji sticks.

In a bowl mix together red tofu, sugar and soy sauce, then stir into wok. Cover and simmer for 10 minutes; if mixture begins to dry out, add a little more water. Stir in deep-fried tofu to heat through.

Serves 4.

Note: Ji sticks are strips of tofu. Golden needles are dried lilies (they may also be called 'tiger lilies'), and add a subtle flavour.

SESAME GARLIC VEGETABLES

225 g (8 oz) broccoli
1 large green pepper
2 small courgettes
225 g (8 oz) asparagus
2 cloves garlic, thinly sliced
2 teaspoons sesame oil
1 tablespoon sesame seeds
soy sauce, for dipping

Cut broccoli into small florets. Cut pepper into 8. Slice courgettes into 2.5 cm (1 in) pieces and halve. Trim away tough ends from asparagus and slice into 5 cm (2 in) pieces. Place vegetables in a colander and rinse well.

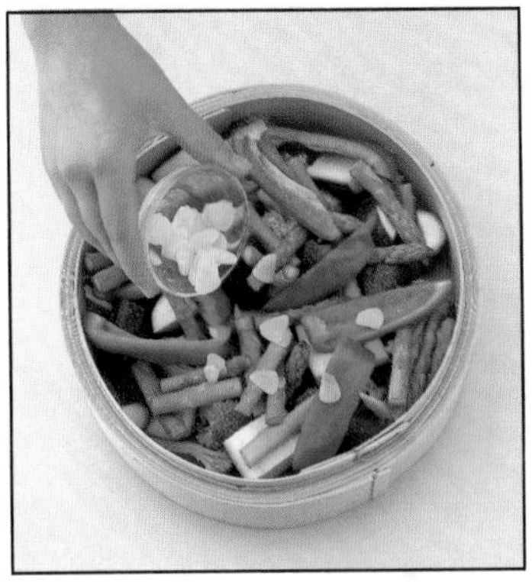

Bring a wok or large saucepan of water to the boil. Arrange vegetables on a layer of non-stick baking parchment in a steamer and place over water. Sprinkle with garlic and sesame oil. Cover and steam for 10 minutes.

Remove vegetables from steamer and place on warmed serving plates. Sprinkle with sesame seeds and serve with soy sauce, for dipping.

Serves 4.

Note: This makes an ideal accompaniment to Five-Spice Salmon Steaks (see page 73).

RED-ROAST VEGETABLES

450 g (1 lb) sweet potatoes, cut into 5 x 1 cm (2 x ½ in) pieces
350 g (12 oz) turnips, cut into 2.5 cm (1 in) pieces
3 large carrots, cut into 2.5 cm (1 in) pieces
1 tablespoon sunflower oil
2 fresh red chillies, seeded and chopped
1 clove garlic, finely chopped
1 cm (½ in) piece fresh root ginger, peeled and chopped
2 tablespoons hoisin sauce
55 ml (2 fl oz/¼ cup) dark soy sauce
85 ml (3 fl oz/⅓ cup) Chinese Vegetable Stock (see page 17)
strips fresh root ginger, to garnish

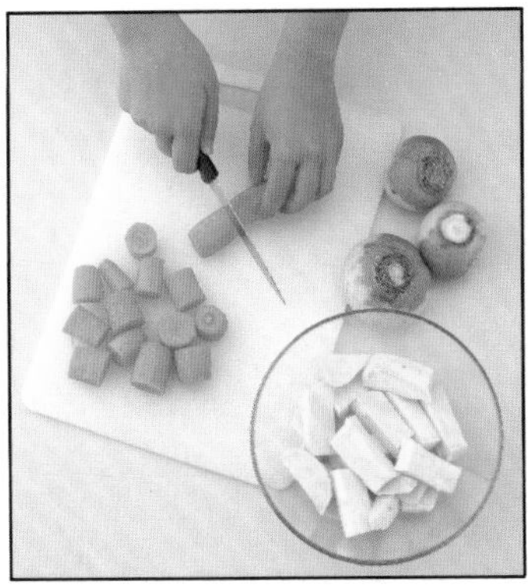

Preheat oven to 200C (400F/Gas 6). Bring a large saucepan of water to the boil, add prepared vegetables and cook for 5 minutes. Drain well. Place drained vegetables in a non-stick roasting pan.

In a small bowl, mix together oil, chillies, garlic, ginger, hoisin sauce, soy sauce and stock and spoon over vegetables. Stir thoroughly to coat vegetables and roast for 30 minutes, basting occasionally, until tender. Garnish with strips of ginger and serve.

Serves 4.

Note: This makes an ideal accompaniment to roast meats such as Roast Pork with Honey (see page 149).

SPICY STIR-FRIED CABBAGE

450 g (1 lb) bok choy
½ head Chinese leaves
1 tablespoon groundnut (peanut) oil
2 cloves garlic, finely chopped
1 tablespoon light soy sauce
1 teaspoon five-spice powder
1 teaspoon chilli sauce
salt and freshly ground pepper
sliced fresh red chilli, to garnish

Discard outer leaves of bok choy and Chinese leaves. Break bok choy leaves from stem, rinse and dry on absorbent kitchen paper. Discard coarse stem at base of leaves then shred finely.

Bring a large saucepan of water to the boil and cook bok choy for a few seconds until just wilted. Drain well then rinse in cold water. Drain thoroughly and pat dry with absorbent kitchen paper. Remove core from Chinese leaves and shred finely.

Heat oil in a wok and stir-fry bok choy and garlic for 2 minutes. Add Chinese leaves, soy sauce, five-spice powder, chilli sauce and salt and pepper and stir-fry for 2 minutes. Garnish with sliced red chilli and serve immediately.

Serves 4.

Note: This makes an ideal accompaniment to Beef with Oyster Sauce (see page 138).

GARLIC AUBERGINE

450 g (1 lb) aubergine
4 tablespoons salt
1 tablespoon sunflower oil
2 cloves garlic, thinly sliced
3 tablespoons dark soy sauce
70 ml (2½ fl oz/⅓ cup) rice wine
1 tablespoon yellow bean sauce
freshly ground pepper
4 spring onions, finely chopped
shredded and sliced spring onions, to garnish

Halve aubergine lengthways. Halve again and cut into 1 cm (½ in) thick pieces.

Layer aubergine in a bowl with salt and leave for 30 minutes. Rinse well and dry on absorbent kitchen paper. Heat oil in a wok and stir-fry aubergine and garlic for 2-3 minutes or until lightly browned.

Add soy sauce, rice wine, yellow bean sauce and pepper. Bring to the boil, reduce heat and simmer for 5 minutes or until softened. Stir in chopped spring onions, garnish with shredded and sliced spring onions and serve.

Serves 4.

Note: This makes an ideal accompaniment to Stir-fried Sesame Lamb (see page 165).

CHILLI ROAST PEPPERS

1 large red pepper
1 large orange pepper
1 large green pepper
1 large yellow pepper
1 tablespoon dark soy sauce
1 teaspoon chilli sauce
1 tablespoon sunflower oil
freshly ground pepper
2 tablespoons chopped fresh chives

Halve peppers lengthways, remove core and seeds, then halve again. Place in a roasting pan.

Preheat over to 190C (375F/Gas 5). In a small bowl, mix together soy sauce, chilli sauce, oil and ground pepper and spoon over peppers, turning to make sure they are well coated. Roast for 30 minutes, or until softened, basting occasionally.

Transfer roast peppers to warmed serving plates, sprinkle with chives and serve.

Serves 4.

Note: This makes an ideal accompaniment to Ginger Chicken Patties (see page 102).

PAN-COOKED VEGETABLES

25 g (1 oz) dried Chinese mushrooms, soaked in hot water for 20 minutes
1 tablespoon groundnut (peanut) oil
1 whole cinnamon stick, broken
115 g (4 oz) shallots, quartered
225 g (8 oz) baby sweetcorn
115 g (4 oz) small broccoli florets
2 tablespoons dark soy sauce
55 ml (2 fl oz/¼ cup) dry sherry
1 tablespoon brown sugar
115 g (4 oz) mangetout
115 g (4 oz) can water chestnuts, rinsed
115 g (4 oz) can bamboo shoots, drained and sliced
salt and freshly ground pepper

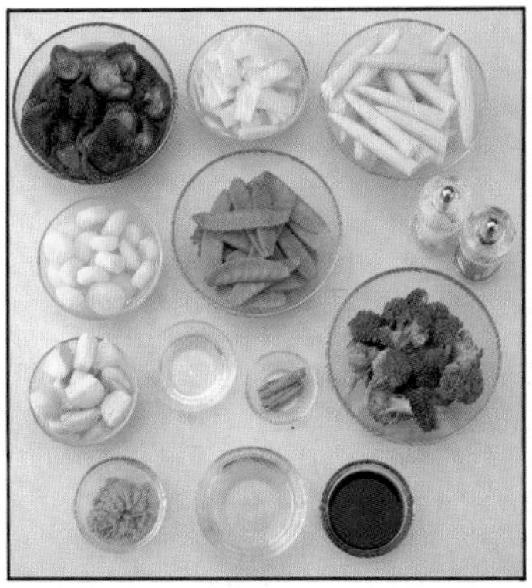

Drain mushrooms and squeeze out any excess water. Discard stems and thinly slice caps. Heat oil in a wok and stir-fry mushrooms, cinnamon, shallots, baby sweetcorn and broccoli for 2-3 minutes until lightly browned.

Add soy sauce, sherry and sugar and bring to the boil. Reduce heat and simmer for 5 minutes. Add mangetout, water chestnuts, bamboo shoots and salt and pepper, mix well and cook for 3 minutes. Discard cinnamon and serve with noodles.

Serves 4.

STIR-FRIED SUGAR SNAP PEAS

225 g (8 oz) sugar snap peas
1½ tablespoons vegetable oil
6 cloves garlic with skins on, lightly bruised
115 g (4 oz) raw peeled medium prawns
2 tablespoons light soy sauce
1½ tablespoons oyster sauce
1 teaspoon rice wine
115 ml (4 fl oz/½ cup) fish stock or water mixed with 1 teaspoon cornflour
freshly ground black pepper (optional)

Add sugar snap peas to a pan of boiling water. Boil for 5 seconds then drain thoroughly.

Heat oil in a wok or large frying pan over high heat. Add garlic and stir-fry for a few seconds. Add prawns and stir-fry until they turn pink. Add sugar snap peas, soy sauce, oyster sauce and rice wine. Stir-fry for 30 seconds.

Stir in cornflour mixture and bring to the boil, stirring. Add black pepper, if wished, and serve.

Serves 4.

VEGETABLE STIR-FRY

2 tablespoons groundnut (peanut) oil
2 fresh red chillies, cored, seeded and finely chopped
2.5 cm (1 in) piece fresh root ginger, grated
2 cloves garlic, crushed
115 g (4 oz) carrots, cut into matchsticks
115 g (4 oz) French beans
115 g (4 oz) broccoli florets
115 g (4 oz) baby sweetcorn, halved
1 red pepper, cut into fine strips
1 small bok choy, coarsely chopped
4 spring onions, including some green, sliced
1 tablespoon hot curry paste
300 ml (10 fl oz/1¼ cups) coconut milk
2 tablespoons Satay Sauce (see page 227)
2 tablespoon soy sauce
1 teaspoon light brown sugar
4 tablespoons chopped coriander leaves
whole roasted peanut, to garnish

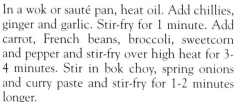

In a wok or sauté pan, heat oil. Add chillies, ginger and garlic. Stir-fry for 1 minute. Add carrot, French beans, broccoli, sweetcorn and pepper and stir-fry over high heat for 3-4 minutes. Stir in bok choy, spring onions and curry paste and stir-fry for 1-2 minutes longer.

Stir in coconut milk, satay sauce, soy sauce and sugar. Bring to the boil then simmer for 1-2 minutes until vegetables are just tender. Add coriander, then serve garnished with peanuts.

Serves 4-6.

OKRA IN SPICE SAUCE

2 tablespoons dried shrimp
3 fresh red chillies, cored, seeded and chopped
4 cloves garlic, chopped
1½ teaspoons shrimp paste
3 shallots, chopped
3 tablespoons vegetable oil
225 g (8 oz) fresh okra, trimmed
1 tablespoon lime juice
freshly ground black pepper

Soak dried shrimp in hot water for 10 minutes. Drain and put in a blender. Add chillies, garlic, shrimp paste and shallots. Mix to a paste, adding water if necessary.

In a wok or frying pan, heat oil over medium-high heat. Add okra and stir-fry for about 5 minutes. Remove with a slotted spoon and set aside.

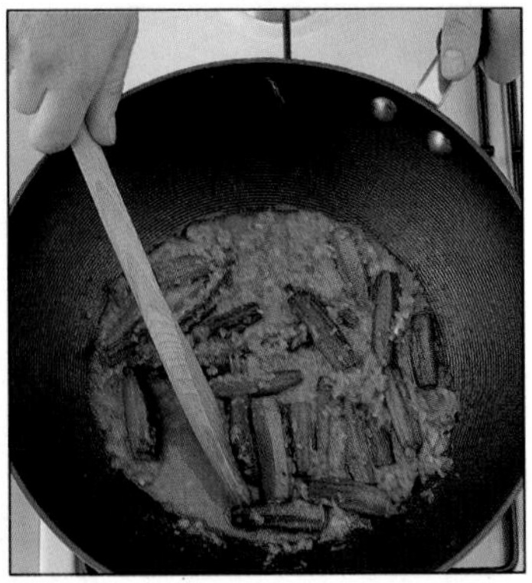

Add spice paste to pan and stir-fry for 1 minute. Lower heat and return okra to pan with lime juice, 4 tablespoons water and plenty of black pepper. Bring to a simmer then cook gently, stirring occasionally, for 5 minutes or until okra is tender.

Serves 3-4 as a side dish.

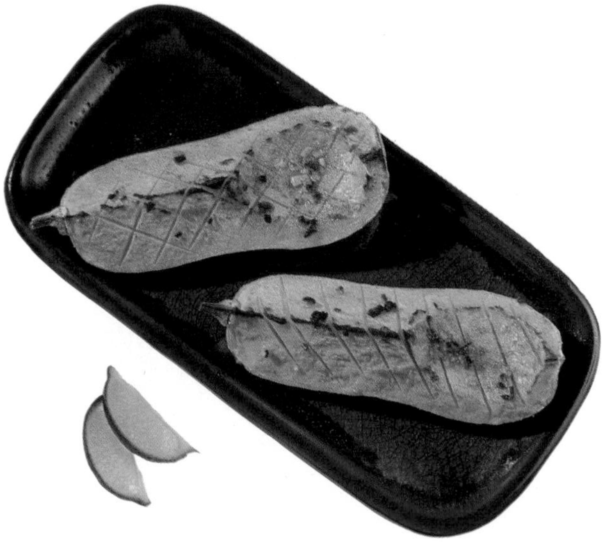

SPICED GRILLED SQUASH

2 small butternut squash, quartered and seeded
2 cloves garlic, finely chopped
2 teaspoons ground cumin
2-3 tablespoons vegetable oil
½ lime
salt and freshly ground black pepper

Using a small, sharp knife make shallow criss-cross cuts in flesh of each squash quarter.

In a bowl, mix together garlic, cumin, oil, a good squeeze of lime juice and salt and pepper to taste. Brush over flesh side of each piece of squash, working it well into cuts.

Preheat barbecue or grill. Cook squash quarters for 10-15 minutes, until lightly browned and flesh is tender. Brush occasionally with any remaining cumin mixture.

Serves 4 as a side dish.

COCONUT MILK & VEGETABLES

1½ teaspoons tamarind
2 tablespoons groundnut (peanut) oil
2 small onions, chopped
2 cloves garlic, chopped
2 fresh red chillies, cored, seeded and chopped
¼ teaspoon ground turmeric
175 g (6 oz) French beans, cut in 5 cm (2 in) lengths
300 ml (10 fl oz/1¼ cups) coconut milk
225 g (8 oz) Chinese leaves, shredded
2 tomatoes, peeled, seeded and chopped
salt

Soak tamarind in 1½ tablespoons hot water. Strain through a fine sieve, extracting as much liquid as possible. Reserve liquid.

In a wok or sauté pan, heat oil over medium heat. Add onion, garlic and chillies and cook for about 4 minutes until softened but not coloured. Stir in turmeric.

Add beans and 175 ml (6 fl oz/¾ cup) coconut milk to pan. Bring to the boil and simmer for 5 minutes. Add Chinese leaves and cook for a further 4 minutes until vegetables are just tender. Stir in tamarind liquid, tomatoes and remaining coconut milk. Heat, stirring, for 1-2 minutes. Season with salt to taste.

Serves 4 as a side dish.

SPINACH WITH SESAME

1½ tablespoons oyster sauce
450 g (1 lb) young spinach leaves
1½ tablespoons vegetable oil
2 cloves garlic, thinly sliced
1 teaspoon sesame oil
toasted sesame seeds, to garnish

Mix oyster sauce with 1 tablespoon boiling water. Set aside. Bring a large saucepan of water to the boil. Quickly add spinach and return to the boil for 30 seconds. Drain very well.

Transfer spinach to a warm serving dish. Trickle oyster sauce mixture over spinach. Keep warm.

Meanwhile, in a wok or small frying pan heat oil. Add garlic and fry until just turning golden. Scatter over spinach and trickle a little sesame oil over. Scatter sesame seeds on top and serve.

Serves 4 as a side dish.

VEGETARIAN STIR-FRY

8 dried Chinese black mushrooms
225 g (8 oz) firm tofu, rinsed
1 tablespoon cornflour
3 tablespoons groundnut (peanut) oil
3 cloves garlic, finely chopped
1 fresh red chilli, cored, seeded and chopped
225 g (8 oz) long beans or French beans, cut into 5 cm (2 in) lengths
2 carrots, thinly sliced diagonally
½ cauliflower, divided into florets
175 g (6 oz) mangetout
3 tablespoons soy sauce
2 teaspoons dark sesame oil
2 teaspoons light brown sugar

Soak mushrooms in 115 ml (4 fl oz/½ cup) warm water for 30 minutes. Drain through muslin; reserve liquid. Slice mushroom caps and discard stalks. Pat tofu dry. Cut tofu into 2.5 cm (1 in) cubes. Put cornflour on a plate and dip tofu into to coat evenly; press cornflour in firmly. In a wok or frying pan, heat oil; add tofu and fry for 6-8 minutes until browned on all sides. Using a slotted spoon transfer to absorbent kitchen paper to drain.

Add garlic, chilli, beans, carrots and cauliflower to pan and stir-fry for 1 minute. Add mangetout and stir-fry for 1 minute longer. Add black mushrooms and reserved mushroom liquid. Stir-fry for about 5 minutes until vegetables are tender. Stir soy sauce, sesame oil and sugar into vegetables. Add fried tofu and toss gently until hot and coated with liquid.

Serves 4.

GREEN BEANS IN SPICED SAUCE

2 cloves garlic, chopped
1 stalk lemon grass, chopped
6 shallots, chopped
3 tablespoons vegetable oil
2 strips lime zest
2 fresh red chillies, cored, seeded and finely chopped
2 spring onions, thickly sliced diagonally
700 g (1½ lb) green beans, cut into 4 cm (1½ in) lengths
225 ml (8 fl oz/1 cup) coconut milk
salt

Put garlic, lemon grass and shallots in a blender. Add 2 tablespoons water and mix to a paste.

In a large frying pan, heat oil over medium-high heat. Add spice paste from blender and fry, stirring, for 5 minutes until paste is lightly browned. Add lime zest, chillies and spring onions. Stir for a further minute then add beans and coconut milk.

Pour in 225 ml (8 fl oz/1 cup) water. Bring to the boil. Lower heat, cover and simmer gently for about 20 minutes until beans are tender. Add salt to taste.

Serves 4-6 as a side dish.

STUFFED AUBERGINES

2 aubergines, each weighing about 225 g (8 oz)
2 cloves garlic, finely chopped
2 stalks lemon grass, chopped
2 tablespoons vegetable oil
1 small onion, finely chopped
175 g (6 oz) boneless, skinless chicken breast, finely chopped
2 teaspoons fish sauce
25 Thai holy basil leaves
freshly ground black pepper
Thai holy basil leaves, to garnish

Preheat grill. Place aubergines under grill and cook, turning as necessary, for about 20 minutes until evenly charred.

Meanwhile, using a pestle and mortar, pound together garlic and lemon grass; set aside. Heat oil in a wok, add onion and cook, stirring occasionally, until lightly browned. Stir in garlic mixture, cook for 1-2 minutes, then add chicken. Stir-fry for 2 minutes. Stir in fish sauce, basil leaves and plenty of black pepper.

Using a sharp knife, slice each charred aubergine in half lengthways. Using a teaspoon, carefully scoop aubergine flesh into a bowl; keep skins warm. Using kitchen scissors, chop flesh. Add to wok and stir ingredients together for about 1 minute. Place aubergine skins on a large warmed plate and divide chicken mixture between them. Garnish with basil leaves.

Serves 4.

STIR-FRIED MANGETOUT

2 tablespoons vegetable oil
3 cloves garlic, finely chopped
115 g (4 oz) lean pork, very finely chopped
450 g (1 lb) mangetout
½ teaspoon crushed palm sugar
1 tablespoon fish sauce
55 g (2 oz) cooked peeled prawns, chopped
freshly ground black pepper

In a wok, heat oil over a medium heat, add garlic and fry until lightly coloured. Add pork and stir-fry for 2-3 minutes.

Add mangetout and stir-fry for about 3 minutes until cooked but still crisp.

Stir in sugar, fish sauce, prawns and black pepper. Heat briefly and serve.

Serves 4-6.

VEGETABLES WITH SAUCE

1 aubergine, weighing about 225 g (8 oz)
115 g (4 oz) long beans or green beans
85 g (3 oz) cauliflower florets
450 ml (16 fl oz/2 cups) coconut milk
2 red shallots, chopped
2 cloves garlic, chopped
4 coriander roots, chopped
2 dried red chillies, seeded and chopped
1 stalk lemon grass, chopped
3 cm (1¼ in) piece galangal, chopped
grated zest 1 kaffir lime
4 tablespoons coconut cream (see page 8)
1½ tablespoons ground roasted peanuts
3 tablespoons tamarind water (see page 11)
1 tablespoon fish sauce
2 teaspoons crushed palm sugar

Cut aubergine into 4 cm (1½ in) cubes; cut beans into 5 cm (2 in) lengths. Put aubergine, beans and cauliflower into a saucepan, add coconut milk and bring to the boil. Cover and simmer for 10 minutes until vegetables are tender. Remove from heat, uncover and set aside. Using a pestle and mortar or small blender, pound or mix together shallots, garlic, coriander roots, chillies, lemon grass, galangal and lime zest.

Mix in 4 tablespoons liquid from vegetables. Place in a small, heavy frying pan, stir in coconut cream and heat, stirring, until oil is released and paste is thick. Stir into vegetables with peanuts, tamarind water, fish sauce and sugar. Heat through gently for about 1 minute.

Serves 6.

SPICED CABBAGE

14 black peppercorns
2 tablespoons coconut cream (see page 8)
2 shallots, chopped
115 g (4 oz) lean pork, very finely chopped
about 450 g (1 lb) white cabbage, finely sliced
300 ml (10 fl oz/1¼ cups) coconut milk
1 tablespoon fish sauce
1 fresh red chilli, seeded and very finely chopped

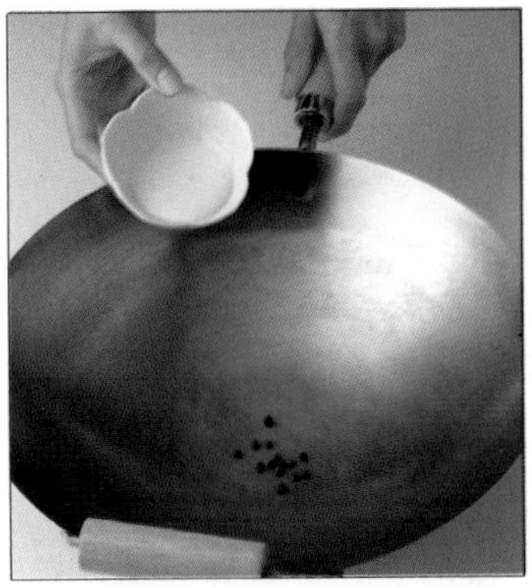

In a wok, heat peppercorns for about 3 minutes until aroma changes. Stir in coconut cream, heat for 2-3 minutes, then stir in shallots.

Stir-fry for a further 2-3 minutes, then stir in pork and cabbage. Cook, stirring occasionally, for 3 minutes, then add coconut milk and bring just to the boil. Cover and simmer for 5 minutes.

Uncover and cook for about 10 minutes until cabbage is tender but retains some bite. Stir in fish sauce. Serve sprinkled with finely chopped chilli.

Serves 4-5.

TOSSED GREENS

2 tablespoons groundnut (peanut) oil
225 g (8 oz) boneless, skinless chicken breast, very finely chopped
6 cloves garlic, finely chopped
700 g (1½ lb) spinach leaves, torn into large pieces if necessary
1½ tablespoons fish sauce
freshly ground black pepper
1½ tablespoons dry-fried unsalted peanuts, chopped
fresh seeded chilli, seeded and thinly sliced, to garnish

In a wok, heat oil, add chicken and stir-fry for 2-3 minutes. Using a slotted spoon, transfer to absorbent kitchen paper; set aside.

Add garlic to wok and fry until just coloured. Using a slotted spoon, transfer half to absorbent kitchen paper; set aside. Increase heat beneath wok so oil is lightly smoking. Quickly add all spinach, stir briefly to coat with oil and garlic.

Scatter chicken over, sprinkle with fish sauce and pepper. Reduce heat, cover wok and simmer for 2-3 minutes. Scatter over peanuts and reserved garlic and garnish with sliced chilli. Serve immediately.

Serves 4.

MUSHROOMS & BEAN SPROUTS

2 tablespoons vegetable oil
2 fresh red chillies, seeded and thinly sliced
2 cloves garlic, chopped
225 g (8 oz) shiitake mushrooms, sliced
115 g (4 oz) bean sprouts
115 g (4 oz) cooked peeled prawns
2 tablespoons lime juice
2 red shallots, sliced into rings
1 tablespoon fish sauce
½ teaspoon crushed palm sugar
1 tablespoon ground browned rice (see page 10)
6 coriander sprigs, stalks and leaves finely chopped
10 Thai mint leaves, shredded
Thai mint leaves, to garnish

In a wok, heat oil, add chillies and garlic and cook, stirring occasionally, for 2-3 minutes. Add mushrooms and stir-fry for 2-3 minutes.

Add bean sprouts and prawns, stir-fry for 1 minute, then stir in lime juice, shallots, fish sauce and sugar. When hot, remove from heat and stir in rice, coriander and mint. Serve garnished with mint leaves.

Serves 4.

FRIED FRENCH BEANS

2 tablespoons vegetable oil
1 clove garlic, chopped
1 small onion, sliced
450 g (1 lb) french beans, topped, tailed, and halved
about 2 tablespoons stock or water
2-3 small red chillies, seeded and shredded
2 firm tomatoes, cut into wedges
salt and freshly ground black pepper
½ teaspoon sugar
chopped coriander leaves, to garnish (optional)

Heat oil in a wok or frying pan and stir-fry garlic and onion for about 1 minute.

Add French beans and stir-fry for 2-3 minutes, adding a little stock or water if beans seem to be too dry.

Add chillies and tomatoes, and stir-fry for a further 1 minute, then add salt, pepper and sugar and blend well. Serve beans hot or cold, garnished with chopped coriander, if wished.

Serves 4.

COURGETTES WITH GINGER

2 tablespoons vegetable oil
small piece fresh root ginger, peeled and sliced
1 teaspoon minced garlic
450 g (1 lb) courgettes, peeled and cut into small wedges
1 small carrot, sliced
2-3 tablespoons stock or water
55 g (2 oz) straw mushrooms, halved lengthways
1 tomato, sliced
2 spring onions, cut into short lengths
salt and freshly ground pepper
½ teaspoon sugar
1 tablespoon fish sauce

Heat oil in a wok or frying pan and stir-fry ginger and garlic for about 30 seconds until fragrant. Add courgettes and carrot and stir-fry for about 2 minutes, then add stock or water to create steam, and continue stirring for another 1-2 minutes.

Add straw mushrooms, tomato and spring onions with salt, pepper and sugar. Blend well and cook for a further 1-2 minutes. Sprinkle with fish sauce and serve at once.

Serves 4.

Variation: Other fresh delicate vegetables, such as asparagus, mangetout, green peppers or cucumber, can also be cooked in this way.

AUBERGINES IN SPICY SAUCE

450 g (1 lb) aubergines, cut into small strips, rather like potato chips
2-3 tablespoons vegetable oil
1 clove garlic, chopped
2 shallots, finely chopped
salt and freshly ground black pepper
½ teaspoon sugar
2-3 small hot red chillies, seeded and chopped
2 tomatoes, cut into wedges
1 tablespoon soy sauce
1 teaspoon chilli sauce
1 tablespoon rice vinegar
about 115 ml (4 fl oz/½ cup) vegetarian stock
2 teaspoons cornflour
½ teaspoon sesame oil
coriander sprigs, to garnish

Stir-fry aubergines in a dry wok or frying pan for 3-4 minutes until soft and a small amount of natural juice has appeared. Remove and set aside. Heat oil and stir-fry garlic and shallots for about 30 seconds. Add aubergines, salt, pepper, sugar and chillies and stir-fry for 2-3 minutes.

Add tomatoes, soy sauce, chilli sauce, rice vinegar and stock, blend well and bring to the boil. Reduce heat and simmer for 3-4 minutes. Mix cornflour with 1 tablespoon water and stir into sauce to thicken it. Blend in sesame oil, garnish and serve at once.

Serves 4.

Variation: For non-vegetarians, fish sauce or shrimp paste can be used instead of soy sauce. Chicken stock can be used instead of vegetarian stock.

SPICY TOFU

vegetable oil for deep-frying
2 cakes tofu, cut into small cubes
1 clove garlic, chopped
2 shallots, chopped
2-3 small red chillies, seeded and chopped
2 leeks, sliced
about 15 g (½ oz) black fungus, soaked and cut into small pieces
salt and freshly ground black pepper
½ teaspoon sugar
1 tablespoon rice vinegar
1 tablespoon crushed black bean sauce
about 55 ml (2 fl oz/¼ cup) stock or water
2 teaspoons cornflour
½ teaspoon sesame oil
chopped spring onions, to garnish

Heat oil in a wok or deep-fat fryer and deep-fry tofu cubes until browned on all sides. Remove and drain. Pour off excess oil, leaving about 1 tablespoon in the wok. Add garlic, shallots, and chillies and stir-fry for about 30 seconds, then add leeks and stir-fry for 2-3 minutes.

Add tofu, black fungus and salt and pepper. Stir-fry for 1 minute, then blend in sugar, vinegar, black bean sauce and stock or water. Bring to the boil and simmer for 1-2 minutes. Mix cornflour with 1 tablespoon water and stir into mixture with sesame oil. Serve garnished with chopped spring onions.

Serves 4.

Note: For a non-vegetarian dish, add about 175 g (6 oz) chopped beef with leeks in step 2, and increase seasonings by half.

STIR-FRIED VEGETABLES

2 tablespoons vegetable oil
1 clove garlic, chopped
1 teaspoon chopped fresh root ginger
1 carrot, sliced
115 g (4 oz) baby sweetcorn, halved
1-2 young leeks, sliced
1-2 bok choy, cut into small pieces
115 g (4 oz) mangetout
115 g (4 oz) bean sprouts
salt and freshly ground black pepper
1 tablespoon soy sauce
2 teaspoons cornflour
½ teaspoon sesame oil (optional)

Heat oil in a wok or frying pan and stir-fry garlic and ginger for about 30 seconds. Add carrot, baby sweetcorn, leeks, bok choy and mangetout and stir-fry for about 2 minutes.

Add bean sprouts and continue stir-frying for 1 minute. Add salt, pepper and soy sauce and stir-fry for a further 2 minutes. Mix cornflour with 1 tablespoon water and stir into gravy to thicken it. Finally blend in sesame oil, if using, then serve vegetables hot or cold.

Serves 4-6.

Variation: Fish or oyster sauce can be used instead of soy sauce for non-vegetarians.

VEGETABLES IN SPICY SAUCE

2-3 tablespoons vegetable oil
1 cake tofu, cut into small cubes
½ teaspoon minced garlic
2 shallots, sliced
1 tablespoon curry powder
2 tablespoons soy sauce
1 tablespoon chopped lemon grass
1 tablespoon chopped fresh root ginger
1 teaspoon chilli sauce (optional)
250 ml (9 fl oz/1 cup) coconut milk
1 tablespoon sugar
2 small carrots, sliced
1 onion, sliced
115-175 g (4-6 oz) cauliflower florets
225 g (8oz) green beans, trimmed and cut in half
2 firm tomatoes, cut into wedges

Heat oil in a wok or large frying pan and fry tofu until browned on all sides. Remove and drain. Stir-fry garlic and shallots in the same oil for about 1 minute, then add curry powder, soy sauce, lemon grass, ginger and chilli sauce, if using, and continue cooking for a further minute. Add coconut milk, sugar and ½ teaspoon salt and bring to the boil.

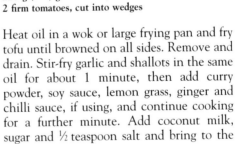

Add carrots, onion, cauliflower, beans and tofu and stir-fry for 3-4 minutes, then add tomatoes. Blend well and cook for a further 2 minutes. Serve at once.

Serves 4-6.

Variation: For non-vegetarians, either fish sauce or oyster sauce can be used instead of soy sauce for this dish.

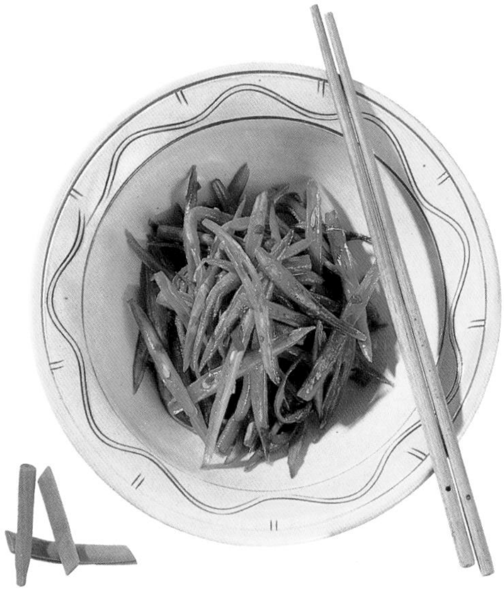

FRENCH BEANS KINPIRA

225 g (8 oz) french beans, trimmed, or 3 carrots or parsnips, peeled
1 dried or fresh red chilli
2 tablespoons vegetable oil
2 tablespoons sake
2 tablespoons soy sauce
1 tablespoon sugar

Cut french beans diagonally into thin strips. If using carrots or parsnips, cut them into 5 cm (2 in) pieces, slicing lengthways and then cut into strips.

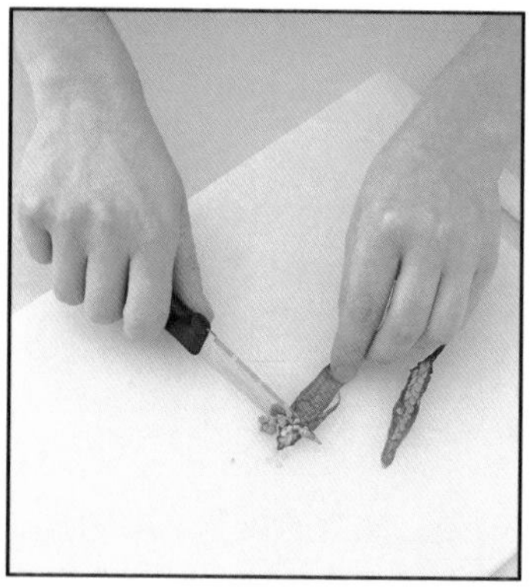

If using dried chilli, soak it in warm water for 10-15 minutes until outer skin is soft. To seed fresh or dried chilli, cut it lengthways and scrape out seeds with the back of the knife blade. Chop chilli very finely.

Heat a wok or a large frying pan, add oil and tilt the pan to spread it over the base. Stir in chilli and French bean, or carrot or parsnip, strips and stir-fry over high heat for about 3 minutes until vegetable strips begin to soften. Lower heat and sprinkle with sake, soy sauce and sugar. Stir-fry over moderate heat until liquid is almost completely absorbed. Serve hot or at room temperature in one deep serving dish or in small, deep individual dishes.

Serves 4.

GRILLED AUBERGINE

4 aubergines, stems removed
vegetable oil for frying
GINGER SAUCE:
70 ml (2½ fl oz/⅓ cup) dashi (see page 29)
2 tablespoons soy sauce
2 tablespoons mirin or 2 teaspoons sugar
2 tablespoons sake
4-5 cm (1½-2 in) piece fresh root ginger, peeled
8 fresh mint leaves
SESAME SAUCE:
3 tablespoons white sesame seeds
3 tablespoons dashi
1½ tablespoons soy sauce
½ tablespoon sugar
salt

To make ginger sauce, put dashi, soy sauce, mirin or sugar and sake in a saucepan and boil for 1 minute. Remove from heat and set aside. Grate ginger with a Japanese daikon grater or a cheese grater. Finely shred mint leaves. To make sesame sauce, toast sesame seeds in a small dry saucepan, then grind them to a paste in a suribachi (Japanese grinding bowl) or a mortar. Mix in dashi and soy sauce. Season with sugar and a pinch salt. Slice aubergines lengthways into quarters and fry, in batches, in a little oil over high heat for 1-2 minutes on each side.

Place 2 slices on each of 8 small plates. Arrange grated ginger and mint slices on top of 4 of the plates and add ginger sauce. Pour sesame sauce over aubergine slices on the other 4 plates. Serve one of each type to each person.

Serves 4.

Note: This dish is also excellent cooked on a barbecue.

SALADS

SWEET & SOUR FISH SALAD

225 g (8 oz) trout fillets
225 g (8 oz) cod fillets
300 ml (10 fl oz/1¼ cups) Chinese Vegetable Stock (see page 17)
2 tablespoons dry sherry
2 shallots, sliced
2 pineapple slices, chopped
1 small red pepper, diced
1 bunch watercress
pineapple pieces and watercress leaves, to garnish
DRESSING:
2 teaspoons sunflower oil
1 tablespoon red rice vinegar
pinch chilli powder
1 teaspoon honey
salt and freshly ground black pepper

Rinse and pat dry trout and cod fillets and place in a wok. Add stock and sherry. Bring to the boil and simmer for 7-8 minutes or until fish just begins to flake. Leave to cool in cooking liquor. Drain, remove skin and flake flesh into a bowl.

Carefully mix flaked fish with shallots, pineapple and pepper. Arrange watercress on 4 serving plates and top with fish mixture. Mix together oil, vinegar, chilli powder, honey, salt and pepper and pour over salad. Garnish with pineapple pieces and watercress leaves and serve.

Serves 4.

SZECHUAN PRAWN SALAD

1 teaspoon chilli oil
1 teaspoon Szechuan peppercorns, toasted and ground
pinch salt
1 tablespoon white rice vinegar
1 teaspoon sugar
350 g (12 oz) cooked, peeled large prawns, thawed and dried, if frozen
½ large cucumber
1 tablespoon sesame seeds
½ head Chinese leaves, shredded
fresh red chilli strips and lemon wedges, to garnish

In a large bowl, mix together chilli oil, peppercorns, salt, vinegar and sugar.

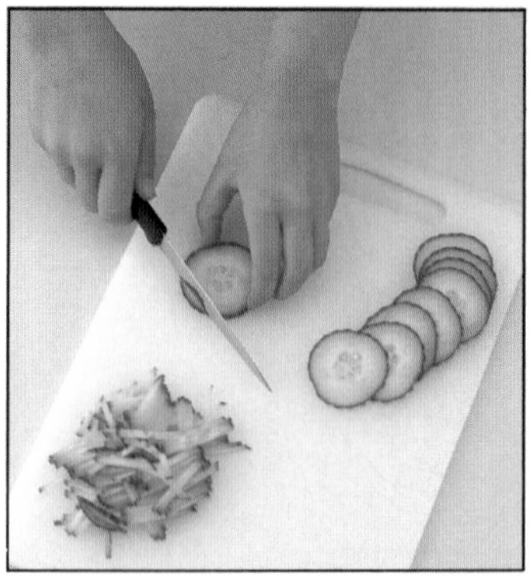

Add prawns and mix well. Cover and chill for 30 minutes. Thinly slice cucumber and slice each piece into thin strips. Pat dry with absorbent kitchen paper and mix into prawns with sesame seeds.

Arrange Chinese leaves on 4 serving plates and top with prawn mixture. Garnish with chilli strips and lemon wedges and serve immediately.

Serves 4.

CORIANDER CHICKEN

2 teaspoons sunflower oil
1 clove garlic, finely chopped
1 shallot, finely chopped
350 g (12 oz) lean cooked skinless chicken, diced
1 teaspoon ground coriander
2 teaspoons dark soy sauce
freshly ground pepper
2 tablespoons chopped coriander leaves
115 g (4 oz) bean sprouts
1 large carrot, grated
25 g (1 oz) coriander leaves
2 nectarines, sliced
2 bananas, halved, sliced and tossed in
juice 1 small lemon

Heat oil in a wok and stir-fry garlic and shallot for 1 minute. Add chicken, coriander, soy sauce and pepper and stir-fry for 2-3 minutes or until chicken is lightly browned. Remove from heat and stir in chopped coriander.

Mix together bean sprouts, grated carrot and coriander leaves. Place on serving plates and top with warm chicken mixture. Arrange nectarine and banana slices around edge of each salad and serve immediately.

Serves 4.

EIGHT-TREASURE SALAD

350 g (12 oz) lean cooked skinless turkey
1 red, 1 green and 1 yellow pepper
115 g (4 oz) mangetout
55 g (2 oz) oyster mushrooms
1 bunch spring onions
55 g (2 oz/⅓ cup) salted cashew nuts, crushed, to garnish
DRESSING:
2 teaspoons sesame oil
1 tablespoon white rice vinegar
1 teaspoon honey
freshly ground pepper

Cut turkey into 0.5 cm (¼ in) slices and arrange in the centre of 4 serving plates.

Halve and seed peppers. Cut into thin slices and arrange around turkey. Diagonally slice mangetout. Shred oyster mushrooms and spring onions. Arrange on serving plates.

Mix together sesame oil, vinegar, honey and pepper. Pour dressing over each salad, garnish with cashew nuts and serve.

Serves 4.

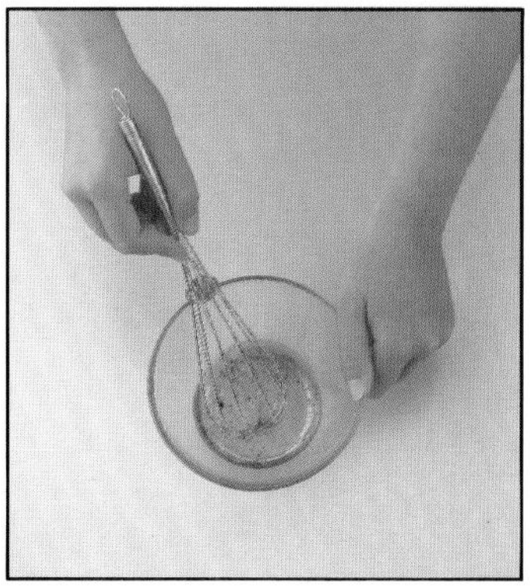

BEEF & ORANGE SALAD

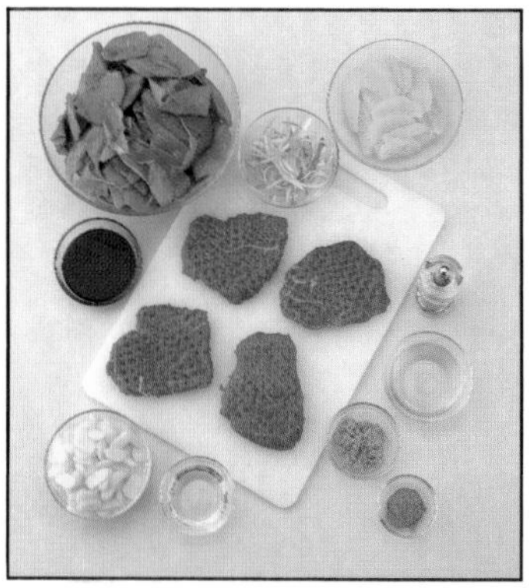

1 tablespoon groundnut (peanut) oil
4 lean beef steaks, each weighing about 115 g (4 oz), trimmed
3 tablespoons dark soy sauce
3 tablespoons dry sherry
1 teaspoon ground cinnamon
1 tablespoon brown sugar
freshly ground pepper
175 g (6 oz) fresh young spinach leaves
115 g (4 oz) can water chestnuts, rinsed and sliced
115 g (4 oz) spring onions, shredded
2 oranges, peeled and segmented
strips orange zest, to garnish

Heat oil in a wok and fry beef steaks for 2 minutes on each side. Drain on absorbent kitchen paper and wipe out wok. Mix together soy sauce, dry sherry, cinnamon, brown sugar and pepper. Return steaks to wok, add water chestnuts and soy sauce mixture. Bring to the boil, reduce heat and simmer for 5-6 minutes, turning steaks halfway through.

Arrange spinach leaves on serving plates and top each with a steak, water chestnuts and sauce. Sprinkle with spring onions and top with orange segments. Garnish with strips of orange zest and serve immediately.

Serves 4.

HOISIN BEEF SALAD

350 g (12 oz) lean roast beef, thinly sliced
½ head Chinese leaves
2 large carrots
225 g (8 oz) daikon
4 tablespoons chopped fresh chives
carrot and daikon flowers (see page 14), to garnish
DRESSING:
2 tablespoons hoisin sauce
1 teaspoon brown sugar
1 tablespoon red rice vinegar
1 teaspoon sesame oil

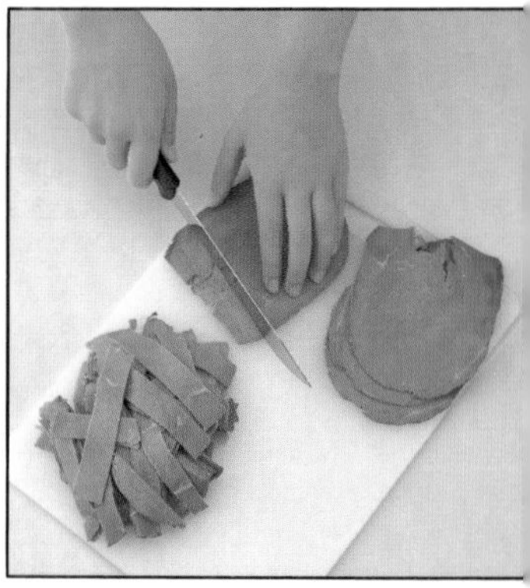

Trim any fat from beef slices and cut into 1 cm (½ in) strips.

Discard damaged outer layer of Chinese leaves and cut out centre core. Shred leaves finely and arrange on 4 serving plates. Peel and grate carrot and daikon and arrange on top of Chinese leaves.

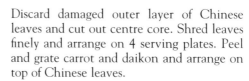

Arrange beef strips in the centre and sprinkle each plate with chives. In a small bowl, mix together hoisin sauce, sugar, vinegar and oil and drizzle over beef. Garnish with carrot and daikon flowers and serve.

Serves 4.

SUMMER NOODLE SALAD

175 g (6 oz) dried egg noodles
1 teaspoon sesame oil
2 tablespoons crunchy peanut butter
2 tablespoons light soy sauce
2 teaspoons sugar
pinch chilli powder
450 g (1 lb) tomatoes, thinly sliced
1 bunch spring onions, finely chopped
115 g (4 oz) bean sprouts
1 large carrot, grated
8 pitted dates, finely chopped

Cook noodles in boiling water for 4-5 minutes or until tender but firm to the bite. Drain well, rinse in cold water and set aside.

Mix together sesame oil, peanut butter, soy sauce, sugar and chilli powder. Drain noodles well, place in a large bowl and mix in peanut sauce. Arrange tomato slices on a serving plate.

Using chopsticks or 2 forks, toss spring onions, bean sprouts, grated carrot and dates into noodles and mix well. Pile on top of sliced tomato and serve.

Serves 4.

STIR-FRIED TOFU SALAD

350 g (12 oz) tofu, drained and rinsed
2 tablespoons dark soy sauce
2 tablespoons rice wine
115 g (4 oz) mangetout
115 g (4 oz) baby sweetcorn
2 small red peppers, quartered
2 tablespoons ground almonds
2 cloves garlic, finely chopped
2 tablespoons cornflour
salt and freshly ground pepper
1 tablespoon sunflower oil
2 tablespoons chopped fresh chives, to garnish

Cut tofu into 1 cm (½ in) cubes, spoon over soy sauce and wine; cover and chill for 1 hour.

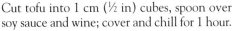

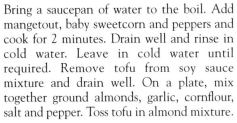

Bring a saucepan of water to the boil. Add mangetout, baby sweetcorn and peppers and cook for 2 minutes. Drain well and rinse in cold water. Leave in cold water until required. Remove tofu from soy sauce mixture and drain well. On a plate, mix together ground almonds, garlic, cornflour, salt and pepper. Toss tofu in almond mixture.

Heat oil in a wok and stir-fry tofu for 4-5 minutes or until golden. Drain well on absorbent kitchen paper. Drain vegetables and arrange on serving plates. Top with tofu, garnish with chives and serve.

Serves 4.

MIXED VEGETABLE SALAD

3 large carrots, cut into thin 7.5 cm (3 in) long sticks
10 long beans, or 85 g (3 oz) French beans, cut into 5 cm (2 in) pieces
½ small cauliflower, divided into florets
1 cucumber, peeled, halved, seeded and cut into matchsticks
225 g (8 oz) green cabbage, cored and shredded
2 cloves garlic, crushed
6 candlenuts or cashew nuts, chopped
2 fresh red chillies, cored, seeded and chopped
6 shallots, chopped
1½ teaspoons ground turmeric
4 tablespoons vegetable oil
100 g (3½ oz) light brown sugar
115 ml (4 fl oz/½ cup) rice vinegar
45 g (1½ oz/¼ cup) roasted unsalted peanuts

Bring a large saucepan of water to the boil. Add carrots, beans and cauliflower. Simmer for 2-3 minutes until tender but still crisp. Add cucumber and cabbage and simmer 1 minute longer. Drain, rinse under cold running water and drain thoroughly. Put garlic, nuts, chillies, shallots and turmeric in a blender. Mix to a paste.

Heat oil in a wok or frying pan over medium heat. Add spice paste and cook, stirring, for 3-5 minutes until slightly thickened and spices are fragrant. Add sugar, vinegar and salt to taste. Bring to the boil. Add vegetables to pan. Stir and toss to coat thoroughly. Transfer to a bowl. Cover tightly and leave at room temperature for about 1 hour. To serve, mound vegetables in a serving dish and sprinkle peanuts on top.

Serves 8-10.

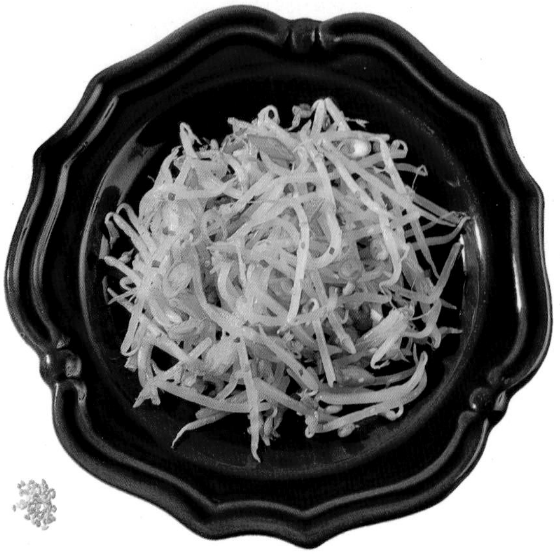

BEAN SPROUT SALAD

salt
575 (1¼ lb) bean sprouts
1 tablespoon sesame seeds
1 fresh red chilli, cored, seeded and chopped
2 cloves garlic, finely chopped
2 tablespoons sesame oil
4 spring onions including green, very thinly sliced

Bring a large saucepan of salted water to the boil. Add bean sprouts all at once. Cover the pan and quickly return to the boil. Uncover the pan and boil for 30 seconds.

Tip bean sprouts into a colander and rinse under running cold water. Press bean sprouts gently to squeeze out surplus water. Transfer bean sprouts to a bowl. Heat a small heavy frying pan. Add sesame seeds and dry-fry, stirring, until fragrant and lightly browned. Add to bean sprouts.

Add chilli, garlic, sesame oil and spring onions to bowl with bean sprouts. Toss to mix ingredients thoroughly.

Serves 4 as a side dish.

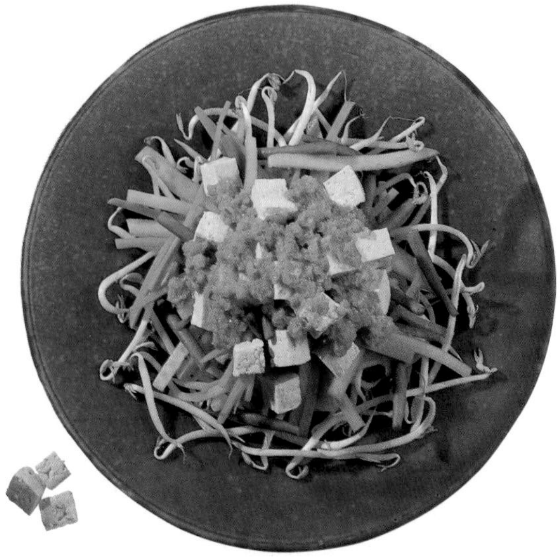

TOFU & PEANUT SALAD

225 g (8 oz) firm tofu
3 large carrots, cut into 7.5 cm (3 in) long sticks
10 long beans, or 85 g (3 oz) French beans, cut into 5 cm (2 in) pieces
1 cucumber, peeled, seeded and cut into matchsticks
225 g (8oz) bean sprouts
PEANUT DRESSING:
2 cloves garlic, crushed
6 shallots, chopped
2 fresh red chillies, cored, seeded and chopped
85 g (3 oz/½ cup) roasted unsalted peanuts
3 tablespoons groundnut (peanut) oil
2 tablespoons light brown sugar
4 tablespoons rice vinegar
1 tablespoon soy sauce
juice 1 lime

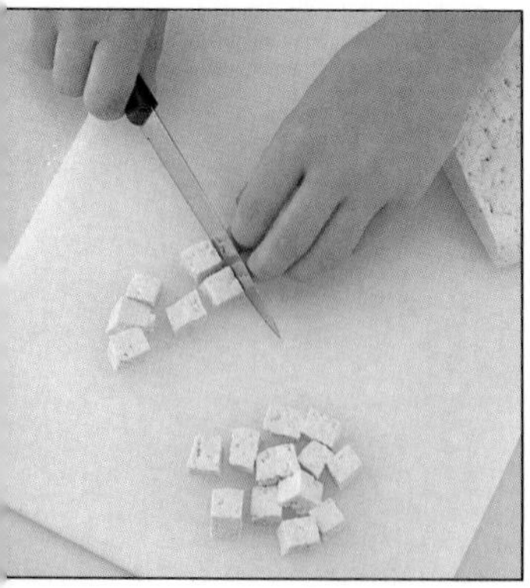

Half-fill a saucepan with water. Bring to the boil. Add tofu and simmer, turning once, for 10 minutes. Drain, cool on absorbent kitchen paper then cut into 1 cm (½ in) cubes. Bring a large saucepan of water to the boil. Add carrots and beans. Simmer for 2 minutes until tender but still crisp. Add cucumber and simmer 1 minute more. Drain, rinse under cold running water and drain thoroughly. To make dressing, put garlic, shallots, chillies and nuts in a blender. Mix to a paste.

Heat oil in a wok or frying pan over medium heat. Add spice paste and cook, stirring, for 3-5 minutes until slightly thickened and fragrant. Add sugar, vinegar, soy sauce, lime juice and 4 tablespoons water. Bring to the boil. Remove pan from heat. Arrange bean sprouts on a serving plate. Top with other vegetables and tofu. Spoon some dressing over. Cover and chill for 1 hour. Serve remaining dressing separately.

Serves 4.

CUCUMBER & PINEAPPLE SALAD

150 g (5 oz) peeled pineapple
175 g (6 oz) cucumber, peeled
2 shallots, thinly sliced
½-1 thin fresh red chilli, cored, seeded and thinly sliced
15-20 mint leaves, torn into small pieces
2 tablespoons lime juice
1¼ teaspoons light brown sugar
salt

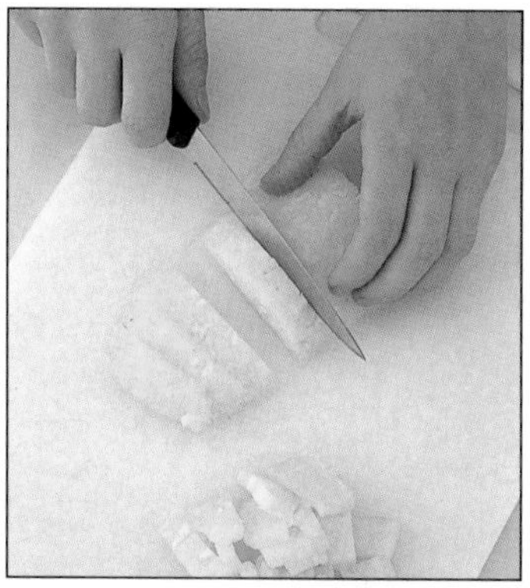

Cut pineapple and cucumber into about 5 cm (2 in) long strips. Put into a non-reactive bowl.

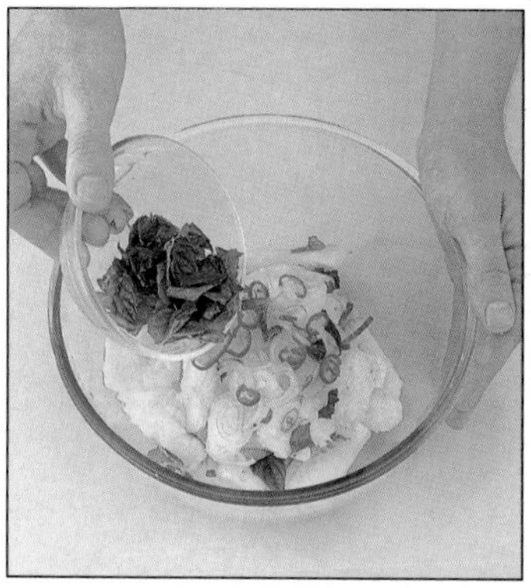

Add shallots, chilli, mint leaves, lime juice and sugar to bowl. Stir together.

Season salad with salt to taste. Adjust levels of chilli, mint, lime juice and sugar to taste if necessary.

Serves 4-6.

SQUID SALAD

450 g (1 lb) small or medium squid
2 tablespoons vegetable oil
½ small red pepper, seeded and halved lengthways
1 tablespoon fish sauce
3 tablespoons lime juice
1 teaspoon crushed palm sugar
2 cloves garlic, very finely crushed
1 stalk lemon grass, very finely chopped
1 fresh red chilli, seeded and thinly sliced
10 Thai mint leaves, cut into strips
2 tablespoons chopped coriander leaves
2 spring onions, chopped
1 cucumber, peeled if wished, thinly sliced
coriander sprigs, to garnish

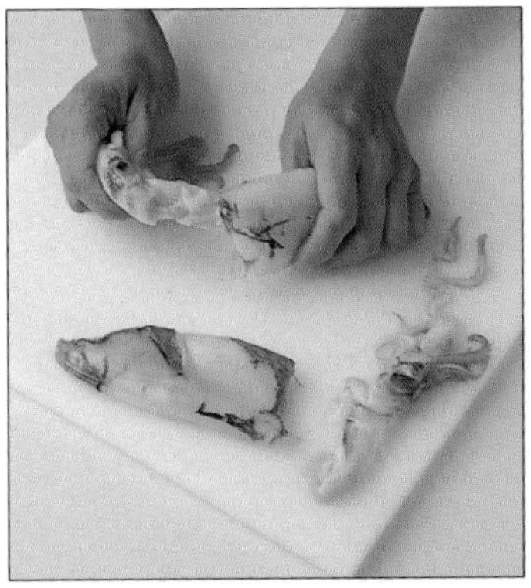

Clean squid. Holding head just below eyes, gently pull away from body pouch. Discard soft innards that come away with it. Carefully remove ink sac; retain if desired. Pull quill-shaped pen free from pouch and discard. Slip your fingers under skin on body pouch and slip it off.

Cut off edible fins on either side of pouch. Cut off tentacles just below eyes; discard head. Squeeze out beak-like mouth from in between tentacles and discard. Rinse tentacles, pouch and fins thoroughly. Dry well, then slice into rings.

Heat oil in a wok, add squid and fry gently, stirring occasionally, for about 10-15 minutes until tender. Using a slotted spoon, transfer to absorbent kitchen paper to drain.

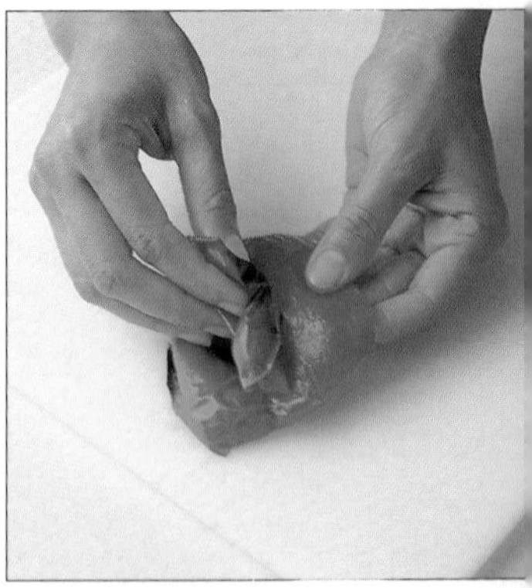

Meanwhile, preheat grill, then grill red pepper, turning frequently, for 8-10 minutes until evenly charred. Leave until cool enough to handle, then remove skin. Seed and roughly chop.

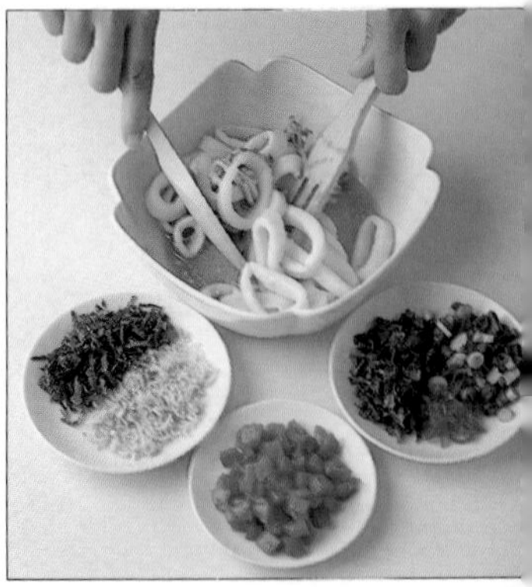

In a bowl, mix together fish sauce, lime juice, sugar and garlic. Add squid and mix together, then toss with lemon grass, chilli, red pepper, mint, coriander and spring onions. Arrange cucumber slices on a plate. Place squid salad on cucumber and garnish with coriander sprigs.

Serves 3-4.

Variation: Instead of cucumber, serve with small celery leaves.

CHICKEN & WATERCRESS SALAD

2 cloves garlic, finely chopped
3 cm (1¼ in) piece galangal, finely chopped
1 tablespoon fish sauce
3 tablespoons lime juice
1 teaspoon crushed palm sugar
2 tablespoons groundnut (peanut) oil
225 g (8 oz) boneless, skinless chicken breast, finely chopped
about 25 dried shrimp
1 bunch watercress, weighing about 115 g (4 oz), coarse stalks removed
3 tablespoons chopped dry-roasted peanuts
2 fresh red chillies, seeded and cut into fine strips

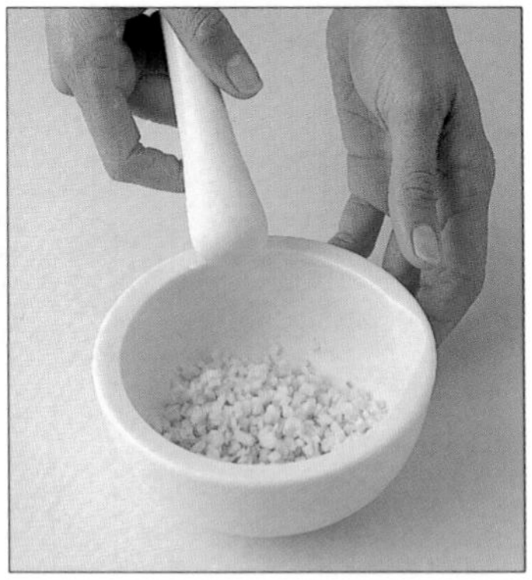

Using a pestle and mortar, pound together garlic and galangal. Mix in fish sauce, lime juice and sugar; set aside. In a wok, heat oil, add chicken and stir-fry for about 3 minutes until cooked through. Using a slotted spoon, transfer to absorbent kitchen paper to drain. Put into a serving bowl and set aside.

Chop half of the dried shrimp and add to bowl. Mix in watercress, peanuts and half of chillies. Pour over garlic mixture and toss to mix. Sprinkle with remaining chillies and shrimp.

Serves 3-4.

PRAWN SALAD WITH MINT

16-20 raw large prawns, peeled and deveined
juice 2 limes
2 teaspoons vegetable oil
2 teaspoons crushed palm sugar
2 tablespoons tamarind water (see page 11)
1 tablespoon fish sauce
2 teaspoons Red Curry Paste (see page 230)
2 stalks lemon grass, very finely chopped
4 tablespoons coconut cream (see page 8)
10 Thai mint leaves, shredded
5 kaffir lime leaves, shredded
1 small crisp lettuce, divided into leaves
1 small cucumber, thinly sliced
Thai mint leaves, to garnish

Put prawns in a bowl, pour over lime juice and leave for 30 minutes. Remove prawns, allow excess liquid to drain into bowl; reserve liquid. Heat oil in a wok, add prawns and stir-fry for 2-3 minutes until just cooked – marinating in lime juice partially 'cooks' them.

Meanwhile, stir sugar, tamarind water, fish sauce, curry paste, lemon grass, coconut cream, mint and lime leaves into reserved lime liquid. Stir in cooked prawns. Set aside until cold. Make a bed of lettuce on a serving plate, place on a layer of cucumber slices. Spoon prawns and dressing on top. Garnish with mint leaves.

Serves 3-4.

THAI BEEF SALAD

- 350 g (12 oz) lean beef, very finely chopped
- 1 tablespoon fish sauce
- 2 tablespoons lime juice
- 2 teaspoons crushed palm sugar
- 1½ tablespoons long-grain white rice, browned and coarsely ground (see page 10)
- 2 fresh green chillies, seeded and finely chopped
- 2 cloves garlic, finely chopped
- 8 Thai mint leaves
- 4 kaffir lime leaves, torn
- 8 Thai holy basil leaves
- lettuce leaves, to serve
- chopped spring onions and a chilli flower (see page 14), to garnish

Heat a wok, add beef and dry-fry for about 2 minutes until tender. Transfer to a bowl. In a small bowl, mix together fish sauce, lime juice and sugar. Pour over warm beef, add rice and toss together. Cover and leave until cold.

Add chillies, garlic, mint, lime and basil leaves to bowl and toss ingredients together. Line a plate with lettuce leaves and spoon beef mixture into centre. Scatter over spring onions and garnish with a chilli flower.

Serves 3-4.

PORK & BAMBOO SHOOT SALAD

- 3 tablespoons vegetable oil
- 3 cloves garlic, chopped
- 1 small onion, thinly sliced
- 225 g (8 oz) lean pork, very finely chopped
- 1 egg, beaten
- 225 g (8 oz) can bamboo shoots, drained and cut into strips
- 1 tablespoon fish sauce
- 1 teaspoon crushed palm sugar
- 3 tablespoons lime juice
- freshly ground black pepper
- lettuce leaves, to serve

In a wok, heat 2 tablespoons oil, add garlic and onion and cook, stirring occasionally, until lightly browned. Using a slotted spoon, transfer to absorbent kitchen paper to drain; set aside. Add pork to wok and stir-fry for about 3 minutes until cooked through. Using a slotted spoon, transfer to absorbent kitchen paper; set aside. Using absorbent kitchen paper, wipe out wok.

Heat remaining oil, pour in egg to make a thin layer and cook for 1-2 minutes until just set. Turn egg over and cook for 1 minute more. Remove egg from wok and roll up. Cut across into strips. In a bowl, toss together pork, bamboo shoots and egg. In a small bowl, stir together fish sauce, sugar, lime juice and pepper. Pour over pork mixture and toss. Serve on lettuce leaves and sprinkle with garlic and onion.

Serves 3-4.

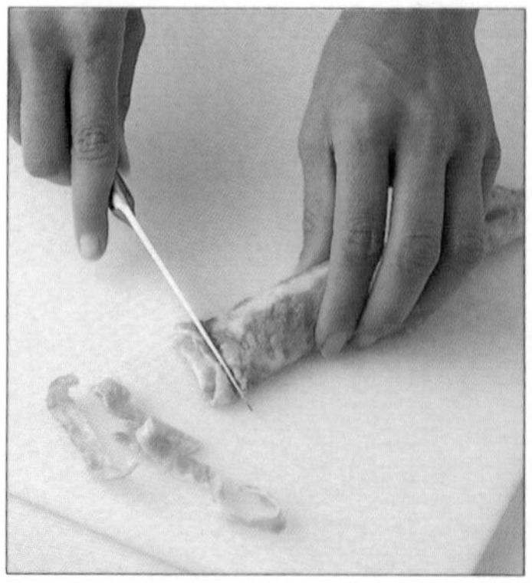

BEAN SALAD

2 tablespoons lime juice
2 tablespoons fish sauce
½ teaspoon crushed palm sugar
1½ tablespoons Nam Prik (see page 232)
2 tablespoons ground roasted peanuts
2 tablespoons vegetable oil
3 cloves garlic, chopped
3 shallots, thinly sliced
¼ dried red chilli, seeded and finely chopped
2 tablespoons coconut cream (see page 8)
225 g (8 oz) French beans, very thinly sliced

In a small bowl, mix together lime juice, fish sauce, sugar, nam prik, peanuts and 2 tablespoons water; set aside. In a small saucepan, heat oil, add garlic and shallots and cook, stirring occasionally, until beginning to brown. Stir in chilli and cook until garlic and shallots are browned. Using a slotted spoon, transfer to absorbent kitchen paper; set aside.

In a small saucepan over a low heat, warm coconut cream, stirring occasionally. Bring a saucepan of water to the boil, add beans, return to the boil and cook for about 30 seconds. Drain and refresh under cold running water. Drain well. Transfer to a serving bowl and toss with shallot mixture and contents of small bowl. Spoon over warm coconut cream.

Serves 3-4.

HOT BAMBOO SHOOT SALAD

1 tablespoon fish sauce
2 tablespoons tamarind water (see page 11)
½ teaspoon crushed palm sugar
1 clove garlic, chopped
1 small fresh red chilli, seeded and finely chopped
175 g (6 oz) bamboo shoots, cut into fine strips
1 tablespoon coarsely ground browned rice (see page 10)
2 spring onions, including some green part, sliced
coriander leaves, to garnish

In a saucepan, heat fish sauce, tamarind water, sugar, garlic, chilli and 2 tablespoons water to the boil. Stir in bamboo shoots and heat for 1-2 minutes.

Stir in rice, then turn into a warmed dish, scatter over spring onion and garnish with coriander leaves.

Serves 2-3.

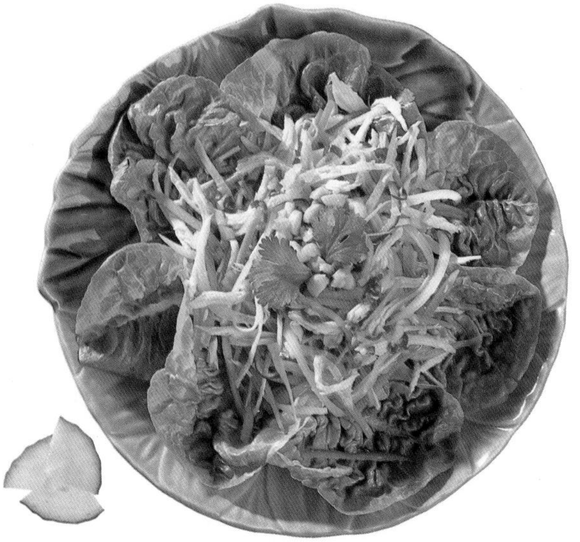

SPICY CHICKEN SALAD

225-300 g (8-10 oz) cooked chicken meat, shredded
½ cucumber, thinly shredded
1 carrot and 1 small onion, thinly shredded
salt and freshly ground black pepper
few lettuce leaves
2 small red chillies, seeded and shredded
1 tablespoon roasted peanuts, crushed
coriander sprigs, to garnish
DRESSING:
1 clove garlic, chopped
1 teaspoon chopped fresh root ginger
1-2 small red or green chillies, chopped
1 tablespoon sugar
2 tablespoons fish sauce
2 tablespoons lime juice
1 tablespoon sesame oil

In a bowl, mix together chicken, cucumber, carrot and onion and season with salt and pepper. Arrange a bed of lettuce leaves on a serving dish or plate and spoon chicken mixture on top.

To make dressing, using a pestle and mortar, pound garlic, ginger, chillies and sugar to a fine paste. Blend paste with fish sauce, lime juice and sesame oil. Pour dressing all over salad just before serving, and garnish with chillies, peanuts and coriander sprigs.

Serves 4-6.

Note: Do not toss and mix salad with dressing until ready to serve.

VIETNAMESE SALAD

4-6 soft lettuce leaves
½ cucumber, cut into thin strips lengthways
1-2 carrots, peeled and cut into thin strips
1 small onion, thinly shredded
2 firm tomatoes, cut into wedges
2-3 small red chillies, seeded and chopped
fresh mint leaves
coriander leaves
Spicy Fish Sauce or Vegetarian Dipping Sauce (see page 233), to serve

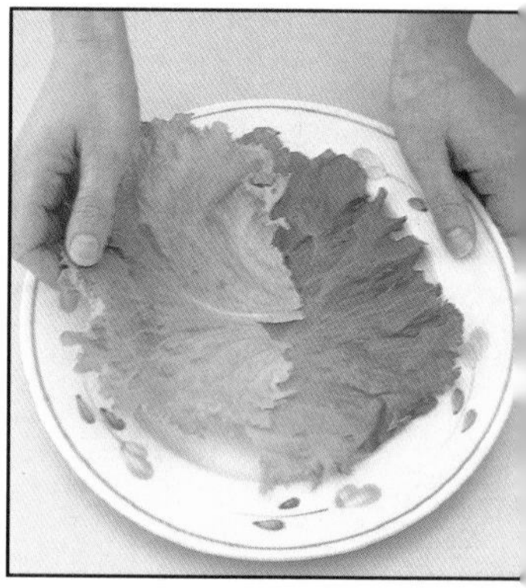

Line a serving platter with lettuce leaves.

Arrange separate sections of cucumber and carrot strips, shredded onion and tomato wedges on bed of lettuce leaves.

Arrange separate mounds of chopped red chillies, mint and coriander leaves on top of vegetables. Serve with either Spicy Fish Sauce or Vegetarian Dipping Sauce poured over the salad at the table.

Serves 4.

Note: At Vietnamese meals this vegetable platter is served either as a starter or as a side dish, and vegetables can be varied according to seasonal availability.

CHINESE LEAVES & KIMCHEE

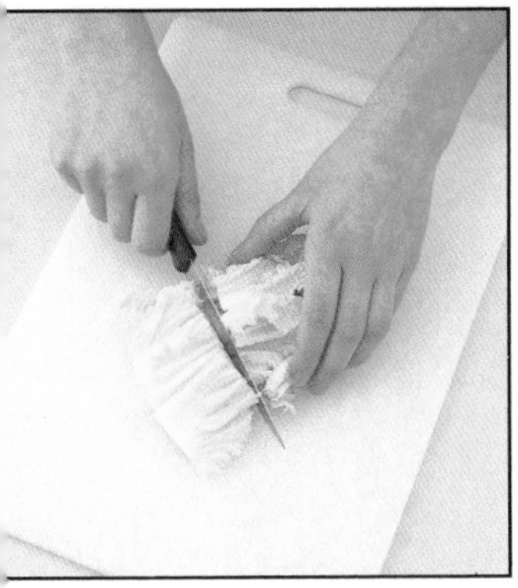

20 Chinese leaves
1-2 fresh red or green chillies, seeded
2 teaspoons salt
2 tablespoons kimchee dressing (Korean chilli and garlic dressing)
finely shredded lemon zest, to garnish

Wash and trim Chinese leaves. Cut in half lengthways, then crossways into 5 cm (2 in) pieces. Chop chilli into fine half-rings.

Put a quarter of Chinese leaves in a freezer bag and sprinkle with one quarter of the salt and chilli. Add another quarter of the leaves on top and sprinkle with another quarter of the salt and chilli. Repeat this 2 more times with remaining ingredients and shake the bag to spread salt and chilli pieces evenly throughout leaves. Tie the bag almost air-tight and leave in the refrigerator for at least 1-2 days, preferably 1 week.

Keeping leaves in the bag, squeeze out the water, then turn out cabbage into a mixing bowl. Add kimchee dressing, mix well and arrange on a serving dish. Garnish with shredded lemon and serve.

Serves 4-8.

Note: Kimchee dressing is available in jars at oriental shops.

TRICOLOUR SALAD

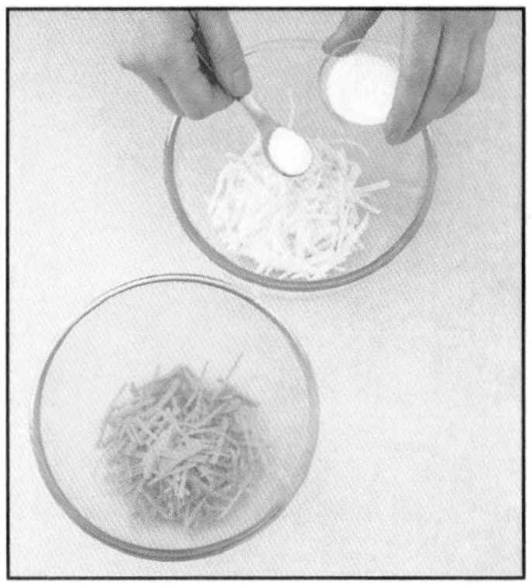

1 carrot
8 cm (3½ in) piece large daikon, peeled
150 g (5oz) mangetout, trimmed
DRESSING:
1 tablespoon soy sauce
3 tablespoons vegetable oil
2 tablespoons rice vinegar
⅓ teaspoon salt
freshly ground black pepper

Chop carrot and daikon separately into 4 cm (1½ in) shreds. Put them in 2 large mixing bowls and sprinkle each with a pinch salt. Leave for 15 minutes.

Cook mangetout in salted boiling water for 1-2 minutes until tender but still crisp. Drain and immediately rinse under cold running water. Slice each mangetout slightly diagonally into 3 pieces. Arrange different vegetable shreds on a serving dish, each occupying one third of the dish.

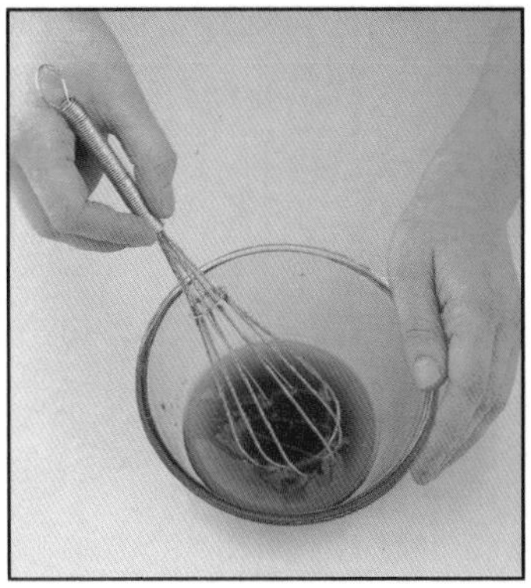

In a bowl, mix soy sauce, oil and vinegar. Add salt and a pinch of pepper. Blend vigorously with a whisk and pour into a serving bowl or a gravy boat. Vegetables and dressing are served separately and mixed together at table before eating.

Serves 4.

NAMASU SALAD

15 cm (6 in) piece daikon, peeled
1-2 carrots
1 teaspoon salt
70 ml (2½ fl oz/⅓ cup) rice vinegar
3 tablespoons sugar
finely shredded lime zest, to garnish

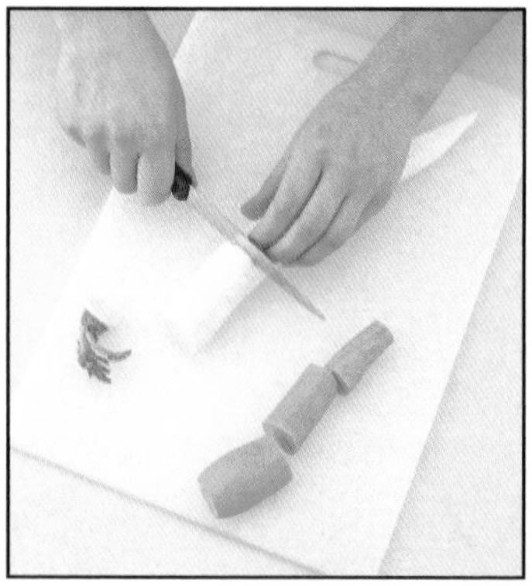

Cut daikon and carrots into three 5 cm (2 in) pieces and slice each piece very thinly lengthways and then shred into thin matchsticks.

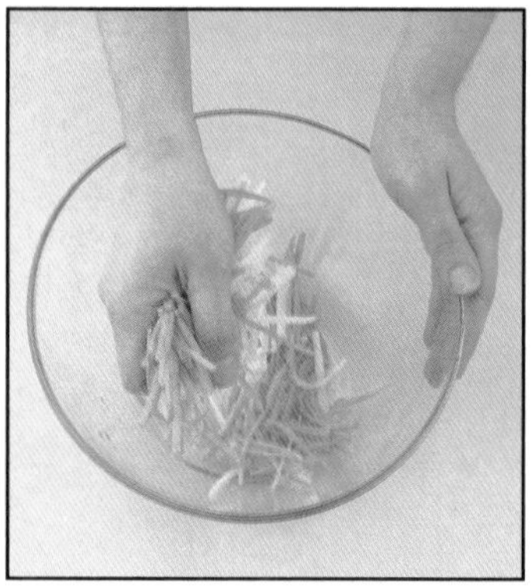

Place daikon and carrot matchsticks in a mixing bowl and sprinkle with salt. Using your hand, gently squash them, then leave for 15-20 minutes. Lightly squeeze out water between your hands (do not press too hard) and put in another mixing bowl.

Mix rice vinegar and sugar and stir well until sugar has dissolved. Pour mixture into daikon and carrot shreds and gently fold in to mix 2 colours evenly. Heap it on a serving dish and garnish with finely shredded lime zest.

Serves 4.

Note: The Japanese regard the combination of red and white as celebration colours, so this dish is considered essential for a New Year's Day brunch table.

SQUID & CUCUMBER SALAD

500 g (1 lb 2 oz) squid, cleaned (see page 194)
½ cucumber
salt
DRESSING:
1 teaspoon mustard
2 tablespoons soy sauce
1 teaspoon sake
1 teaspoon sesame oil

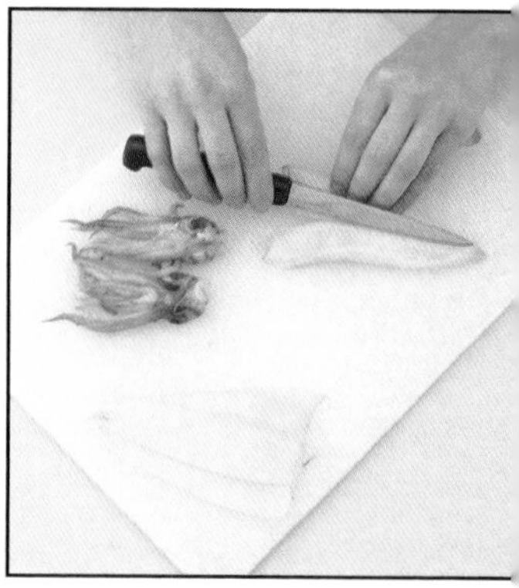

Peel the outer skin off the squid, then cut squid in half lenghways. Wash inside well and parboil, with the tentacles, for 1 minute. Drain and immediately rinse under cold running water to stop further cooking.

Cut the body parts in half lengthways and then crossways into 0.5 cm (¼ in) strips. Separate the tentacles and chop each into 4-5 cm (1½-2 in) pieces. Put the squid in a large mixing bowl.

Halve the cucumber lengthways. Using a tablespoon, scoop out the seeds. Slice the cucumber into thick half-moons and sprinkle with a pinch of salt. Lightly squash with a hand to squeeze out the water, then add to squid in the bowl. In a small cup, mix mustard, soy sauce, sake and sesame oil and pour into the squid and cucumber mixture. Toss the squid and cucumber in the dressing and serve in small individual dishes.

Serves 4 as a starter.

RICE

SWEET SAFFRON RICE

225 g (8 oz/1¼ cups) basmati rice
1 teaspoon saffron threads
3 tablespoons boiling water
3 tablespoons vegetable oil
6 cloves
6 green cardamom pods, bruised
7.5 cm (3 in) cinnamon stick
85 g (3 oz/½ cup) raisins
3 tablespoons sugar
salt
parsley sprigs, to garnish

Place rice in a sieve and wash under cold running water until water runs clear.

Put rice in a bowl with 550 ml (20 fl oz/2½ cups) water and soak for 30 minutes. Put saffron in a small bowl, add boiling water and leave to soak for 5 minutes. Heat oil in a heavy-based saucepan, add cloves, cardamom pods and cinnamon and fry for 1 minute. Drain rice and reserve soaking water. Add rice to the pan and fry for 2-3 minutes, until opaque and light golden.

Stir in reserved water, saffron and its soaking water, raisins and sugar and season with salt. Bring to the boil, then lower the heat and simmer, covered, for 12-15 minutes, stirring once or twice, until liquid is absorbed and rice is very tender. Serve hot, garnished with parsley.

Serves 4.

Note: The whole spices in the rice are not meant to be eaten.

FRAGRANT FRIED RICE

175 g (6 oz/1 cup) basmati rice
3 tablespoons vegetable oil
8 cloves
4 black cardamom pods, bruised
1 bay leaf
7.5 cm (3 in) cinnamon stick
1 teaspoon black peppercorns
1 teaspoon cumin seeds
1 teaspoon coriander seeds
1 onion, sliced into rings
1 small cauliflower, divided into small florets
salt
onion rings and bay leaves, to garnish

Place rice in a sieve and wash under cold running water until water runs clear. Put in a bowl with 550 ml (20 fl oz/2½ cups) water and soak for 30 minutes. Heat oil in a heavy-based saucepan, add cloves, cardamom pods, bay leaf, cinnamon, peppercorns and cumin and coriander seeds and fry for 1 minute. Add onion and cook for 5 minutes, until softened. Drain rice and reserve soaking water.

Add rice to the pan and fry for 2-3 minutes, until opaque and light golden. Stir in reserved water and cauliflower and season with salt. Bring to the boil, lower heat and simmer, covered, for 12-15 minutes, stirring once or twice, until liquid is absorbed and rice and cauliflower are tender. Serve hot, garnished with onion rings and bay leaves.

Serves 4.

Note: Do not eat the whole spices.

EGG FRIED RICE

150 g (5 oz/¾ cup) long-grain white rice
3 eggs, beaten
2 tablespoons vegetable oil
1 clove garlic, chopped
3 spring onions, finely chopped
115 g (4 oz) peas, cooked, or frozen and thawed
1 tablespoon light soy sauce
1 teaspoon sea salt

Cook rice in boiling water for 15 minutes until tender but still firm. Drain and rinse with boiling water. In a small saucepan, cook eggs over moderately low heat, stirring until lightly scrambled. Remove and keep warm.

In a wok, heat oil, add garlic, spring onions and peas and stir-fry for 1 minute. Stir in rice to mix thoroughly.

Add soy sauce, eggs and salt. Stir to break up egg and mix thoroughly.

Serves 4.

YANGCHOW FRIED RICE

150 g (5 oz/¾ cup) long-grain white rice
3 tablespoons groundnut (peanut) oil
2 medium onions, finely sliced
3 slices fresh root ginger, peeled and finely chopped
115 g (4 oz) pork tenderloin, minced
1 tablespoon light soy sauce
1 teaspoon brown sugar
½ teaspoon sea salt
2 eggs, beaten
3 dried black winter mushrooms, soaked in hot water for 25 minutes, drained and squeezed
2 large tomatoes, peeled, seeded and chopped
55 g (2 oz) peas, cooked, or frozen and thawed

Cook rice in plenty of boiling water for 15 minutes until tender but still firm to the bite. Drain and rinse with boiling water. In a wok, heat oil, add onion and ginger and stir-fry for 2 minutes. Stir in pork, continue stirring for 3 minutes until crisp, then add soy sauce and sugar. Stir-fry for 1 minute, then stir in rice.

Remove to a warmed dish and keep warm. Pour eggs into wok, season with salt and pepper, then cook stirring for 2-3 minutes until just beginning to set. Stir in mushrooms, tomatoes and peas. Cook for 2-3 minutes, then stir in rice mixture.

Serves 4.

GREEN RICE

225 g (8 oz/1¼ cups) long-grain white rice, rinsed
800 ml (1½ pints/3½ cups) Chinese Vegetable Stock (see page 17)
225 g (8 oz) small broccoli florets
225 g (8 oz) fresh spinach, tough ribs removed
1 tablespoon groundnut (peanut) oil
2 cloves garlic, finely chopped
1 fresh green chilli, seeded and chopped
1 bunch spring onions, finely chopped
225 g (8 oz) frozen green peas
2 tablespoons light soy sauce
salt and freshly ground black pepper
4 tablespoons chopped fresh chives
fresh chives, to garnish

Place rice and stock in a large saucepan, bring to the boil, reduce heat and simmer for 25 minutes or until rice is cooked and liquid has been absorbed. Cook broccoli in a saucepan of boiling water for 2 minutes. Drain and set aside. Blanch spinach in a saucepan of boiling water for a few seconds or until just wilted. Drain well, shred and set aside.

Heat oil in a wok and stir-fry garlic, chilli, spring onions and broccoli for 1 minute. Add cooked rice, spinach, frozen peas and soy sauce. Season with salt and pepper and simmer for 5 minutes. Stir in chopped chives. Garnish with chives to serve.

Serves 4.

CORIANDER TURKEY RICE

1 tablespoon sunflower oil
2 shallots, chopped
2 cloves garlic, finely chopped
25 g (1 oz) prosciutto, trimmed and cut into strips
225 g (8 oz/1¼ cups) long-grain white rice, rinsed
1 teaspoon ground coriander
salt and freshly ground black pepper
1 litre (1¾ pints/4 cups) Chinese Chicken Stock (see page 16)
115 g (4 oz) asparagus, cut into 2.5 cm (1 in) pieces, blanched
225 g (8 oz) frozen green peas
225 g (8 oz) cooked turkey, skinned and diced
4 tablespoons chopped coriander leaves

Heat oil in a wok and stir-fry shallots, garlic, ham, rice and ground coriander for 2 minutes. Season with salt and pepper.

Pour in stock and bring to the boil. Reduce heat and simmer for 20 minutes. Gently stir in asparagus, peas, turkey and coriander and cook over low heat for 5 minutes or until heated through, stirring to prevent sticking. Serve immediately.

Serves 4.

SPICED RICE

5 cm (2 in) cinnamon stick
1 tablespoon coriander seeds, lightly crushed
seeds from 1 green cardamom pod, lightly crushed
2 whole star anise
1 small onion, chopped
2 cloves garlic, chopped
2 cm (¾ in) piece fresh root ginger, chopped
1 tablespoon vegetable oil
225 g (8 oz/1¼ cups) long-grain white rice, rinsed
1 teaspoon dark soy sauce
1 tablespoon candlenuts nuts or cashew nuts
2 tablespoons raisins

Put cinnamon, coriander, cardamom seeds and star anise in a saucepan.

Add 800 ml (1½ pints/3½ cups) water and simmer uncovered until reduced to 450 ml (16 fl oz/2 cups). Set aside to cool, then strain. Put onion, garlic and ginger in a blender and mix to a paste, adding a little of spiced water if necessary. In a saucepan, heat oil over medium-high heat. Add paste and fry for 3-4 minutes, stirring occasionally.

Stir in rice. Add strained spiced water and soy sauce and bring to the boil. Stir, cover and simmer until rice is tender and liquid has been absorbed. Add nuts and raisins and fluff up rice with chopsticks or a fork.

Serves 4 as a side dish.

MALAYSIAN FRIED RICE

225 g (8 oz/1¼ cups) long-grain white rice, rinsed
3 tablespoons vegetable oil
2 eggs, beaten
1 onion, chopped
2 fresh red chillies, cored, seeded and chopped
2 cloves garlic, crushed
1 teaspoon shrimp paste
175 g (6 oz) boneless, skinless chicken breast, cut into thin strips
115 g (4 oz) raw, large prawns, peeled and deveined
2 tablespoons dark soy sauce
1 tablespoon light brown sugar
2 spring onions, including some green, sliced diagonally

Bring rice to the boil in 500 ml (18 fl oz/2¼ cups) water. Stir, cover pan and simmer over low heat for 12 minutes until rice is tender and water is absorbed. Without lifting lid, remove pan from heat and leave for 15 minutes. Uncover and stir. Spread on an oiled tray and leave for 30-60 minutes. Heat 1 tablespoon oil in a wok. Add eggs to make an omelette. When cool, roll up and slice. Mix onion, chillies, garlic and shrimp paste to a paste in a blender. Heat remaining oil in wok over medium-high heat. Add paste and cook for 30 seconds.

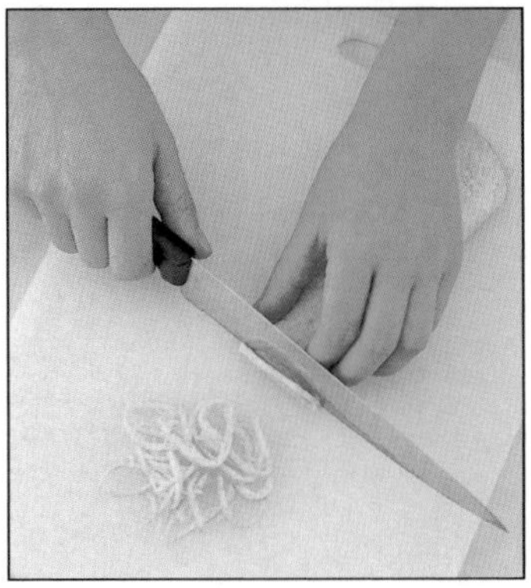

Increase heat to high. Add chicken and stir-fry for 2-3 minutes until opaque. Add prawns and stir-fry for 1-1½ minutes until just pink. Transfer chicken and prawns to absorbent kitchen paper. Lower heat to medium; add rice and stir for 1-2 minutes. Cover and cook for 3 minutes, stirring twice. Add soy sauce, sugar and spring onions. Stir-fry for 1 minute. Return chicken and prawns to wok. Add egg strips and cook over high heat for 2-3 minutes.

Serves 4.

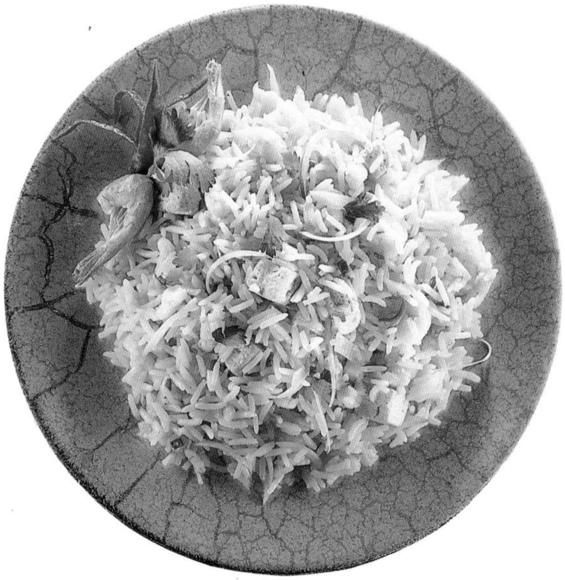

RICE, PRAWNS & TOFU

175 g (6 oz/1 cup) long-grain white rice
3 tablespoons vegetable oil
3 cloves garlic, chopped
1 small onion, chopped
115 g (4 oz) tofu, drained and cut into about 1cm (½ in) cubes
2 small fresh red chillies, seeded and finely chopped
1 tablespoon fish sauce
175 g (6 oz) peeled prawns
1 shallot, thinly sliced
chilli flower (see page 14), prawns in their shells and coriander leaves, to garnish

Rinse rice several times in cold running water. Put into a heavy saucepan with 300 ml (10 fl oz/1¼ cups water), cover and bring quickly to boil. Uncover and stir vigorously until water has evaporated. Reduce heat to very low, cover pan, and steam for 20 minutes until rice is tender, lightly and fluffy. In a wok, heat oil, add garlic and onion and cook, stirring occasionally, for 3-4 minutes until lightly browned. Add tofu and fry for about 3 minutes until browned. Add chillies and stir-fry briefly. Stir in fish sauce and rice for 2-3 minutes, then stir in prawns.

Add shallot, stir quickly to mix, then transfer to a warmed serving plate. Garnish with chilli flower and prawns in their shells and scatter coriander leaves over rice mixture.

Serves 4.

SPICY FRIED RICE

175 g (6 oz/1 cup) long-grain white rice
2 tablespoons vegetable oil
1 large onion, finely chopped
3 cloves garlic, chopped
2 fresh green chillies, seeded and finely chopped
2 tablespoons Red Curry Paste (see page 230)
55 g (2 oz) lean pork, very finely chopped
3 eggs, beaten
1 tablespoon fish sauce
55 g (2 oz) cooked peeled prawns
finely sliced red chilli, shredded coriander leaves and spring onion brushes (see page 14), to garnish

Cook rice following method on page 206. In a wok, heat oil, add onion, garlic and chillies and cook, stirring occasionally, until onion has softened. Stir in curry paste and continue to stir for 3-4 minutes. Add pork and stir-fry for 2-3 minutes. Stir in rice to coat with ingredients, then push to sides of wok.

Pour eggs into centre of wok. When just beginning to set, mix evenly into the rice, adding fish sauce at the same time. Stir in prawns, then transfer to a shallow, warmed serving dish. Garnish with chilli, coriander and spring onion brushes.

Serves 4.

THAI FRIED RICE

175 g (6 oz/1 cup) long-grain white rice
115 g (4 oz) long beans, or French beans, cut into 2.5 (1 in) lengths
3 tablespoons vegetable oil
2 onions, finely chopped
3 cloves garlic, crushed
85 g (3 oz) lean pork, very finely chopped
85 g (3 oz) boneless, skinless chicken breast, very finely chopped
2 eggs, beaten
2 tablespoons Nam Prik (see page 232)
1 tablespoon fish sauce
85 g (3 oz) cooked peeled prawns
coriander leaves, sliced spring onions and lime wedges, to garnish

Cook rice following method on page 206. Add beans to a saucepan of boiling water and cook for 2 minutes. Drain and refresh under cold running water. Drain well. In a wok, heat oil, add onions and garlic and cook, stirring occasionally, until softened. Stir in pork and chicken and stir-fry for 1 minute. Push to side of wok.

Pour eggs into centre of wok, leave until just beginning to set, then stir in pork mixture followed by nam prik, fish sauce and rice. Stir for 1-2 minutes, then add beans and prawns. Serve garnished with coriander leaves, spring onions and lime wedges.

Serves 4.

CHICKEN & MUSHROOM RICE

175 g (6 oz/1 cup) long-grain white rice
2 tablespoons vegetable oil
1 small onion, finely chopped
2 cloves garlic, finely chopped
2 fresh red chillies, seeded and cut into slivers
225 g (8 oz) boneless, skinless chicken breast, finely chopped
85 g (3 oz) bamboo shoots, chopped or cut into matchstick strips
8 pieces dried Chinese black mushrooms, soaked for 30 minutes, drained and chopped
2 tablespoons dried shrimp
1 tablespoon fish sauce
about 25 Thai holy basil leaves
Thai holy basil sprig, to garnish

Cook rice following method on page 206. In a wok, heat oil, add onion and garlic and cook, stirring occasionally, until golden. Add chillies and chicken and stir-fry for 2 minutes.

Stir in bamboo shoots, mushrooms, dried shrimp and fish sauce. Continue to stir for 2 minutes, then stir in rice and basil. Serve garnished with basil sprig.

Serves 4.

STEAMED CHICKEN & RICE

salt and freshly ground black pepper
1 teaspoon each sugar and sesame oil
1 tablespoon fish sauce
2 teaspoons chopped garlic
300 g (10 oz) chicken thigh meat, boned and skinned, cut into bite-sized pieces
3 tablespoons vegetable oil
4 shallots, finely chopped
450 g (1 lb/2½ cups) long-grain white rice
550 ml (20 fl oz/2½ cups) chicken stock
8 dried Chinese mushrooms, soaked and cut into small pieces
115 g (4 oz) canned straw mushrooms, drained
1 tablespoon each soy sauce and oyster sauce
2 spring onions, chopped
coriander sprigs, to garnish

In a bowl, mix salt, pepper, sugar, sesame oil, fish sauce and half the garlic. Add chicken and leave to marinate for 25-30 minutes. Heat about 2 tablespoons vegetable oil in a clay pot or flameproof casserole and stir-fry remaining garlic and half of the chopped shallots for about 1 minute. Add rice and stir-fry for about 5 minutes, then add stock. Stir and bring to the boil, then reduce the heat to very low, cover and cook gently for 8-10 minutes.

Heat remaining oil in a wok or saucepan and stir-fry remaining shallots until opaque. Add chicken pieces and stir-fry for 2-3 minutes. Add mushrooms and soy sauce and continue stirring for about 5 minutes. Uncover rice and fluff up with a fork. Spoon chicken and mushroom mixture on top of rice, add oyster sauce and spring onions, cover and cook for a further 5 minutes. Garnish with coriander sprigs and serve at once.

Serves 4-6.

SEAFOOD FRIED RICE

225 g (8 oz/1¼ cups) long-grain white rice
3 tablespoons vegetable oil
1 clove garlic, chopped
2 shallots, chopped
115 g (4 oz) small cooked peeled prawns
115 g (4 oz) crab meat, flaked
salt and freshly ground black pepper
2-3 eggs, beaten
2 tablespoons fish or soy sauce
chopped spring onions, to garnish

The day before, cook rice following method on page 206, then refrigerate it, so that it is cold and dry when required.

Heat about 1 tablespoon oil in a wok or frying pan and stir-fry garlic and shallots for about 30 seconds, then add prawns and crab meat with salt and pepper. Stir-fry for 2-3 minutes, remove from pan and set aside.

Heat remaining oil in the pan and lightly scramble beaten eggs. When just beginning to set hard, add rice and stir-fry mixture for 2-3 minutes. Add prawns and crab meat with fish or soy sauce and blend well. Garnish with chopped spring onions and serve at once.

Serves 4.

RICE BALLS

400 g (14 oz/2 cups) Japanese rice
salt
160 g (5½ oz) salmon steak
55 g (2 oz) smoked cod roe, skinned
2 teaspoons sake
red chilli powder (optional)
2 tablespoons black or white sesame seeds
1-2 sheets nori (wafer-thin dried seaweed), optional

Boil rice following the method given opposite. Heavily salt salmon and leave for at least 30 minutes. Preheat grill.

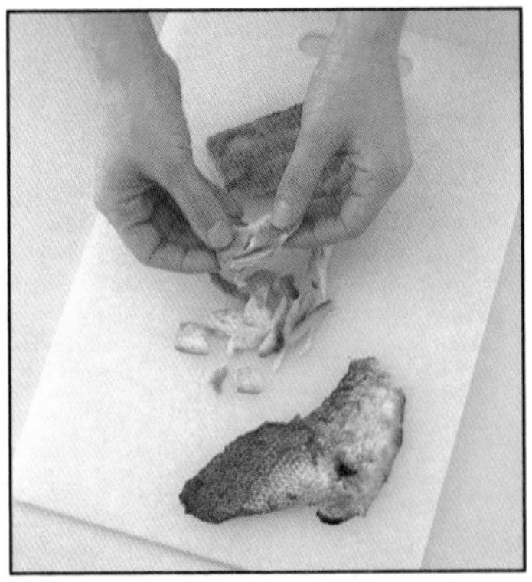

Wipe off salt from salmon with absorbent kitchen paper and grill salmon under high heat until both sides are lightly burnt. Remove skin and break flesh into rough flakes. Put cod roe in a small bowl, sprinkle with sake and make into a paste. Add a pinch of chilli powder, if wished. Put sesame seeds in a small saucepan and quickly toss over high heat. Place a sheet of nori over low heat and swiftly turn over a few times to bring out the flavour. Using kitchen scissors, cut it into 8 pieces. Repeat if using a second sheet.

Put 2 tablespoons rice into each of 4 wet teacups. Make a hole in centre of each, put 1 teaspoonful salmon into each one and press to cover with rice. Wet hands and rub with salt. Turn out rice on to your hand and squeeze, shaping it into a round. Sprinkle with sesame seeds and partly wrap with nori. Make 4 more with cod roe inside but with no sesame seeds. Mix rest of the rice with remaining ingredients to make 4 or 5 rice balls.

Makes about 12.

BOILING RICE & SUMESHI

400 g (14 oz/2 cups) Japanese rice
VINEGARY SUMESHI:
70 ml (2½ fl oz/⅓ cup) rice vinegar
1 tablespoon sugar
1 teaspoon salt

Wash the rice thoroughly, changing the water several times until it becomes clear.

Put the rice in a deep 15-18 cm (5-6 in) saucepan, with 25 per cent more cold water than rice. To do this, first cover rice with water, then add another 1 cup of water – the water level should be about 2 cm (¾ in) above rice. Leave for 1 hour. Place the pan, covered, over high heat for 5 minutes or until you hear a sizzling noise. Reduce heat and simmer gently for 10 minutes. To make sumeshi, put vinegar, sugar and salt in a jug and mix until sugar and salt have dissolved.

Transfer rice to a large bowl and gradually fold in vinegar mixture, using a wooden spatula. Do not stir. Cool rice to room temperature using a fan; this will make it shiny. It is now ready to make sushis.

Serves 4.

Variation: To make sweet sumeshi, add 1 tablespoon mirin to rice cooking water. Mix 55 ml (2 oz/¼ cup) rice vinegar, 1½ tablespoons sugar and ½ tablespoon salt. Fold into the cooked rice, as above.

BABY CLAM RICE

575 g (1¼ lb/3 cups) Japanese rice
2 tablespoons sake or white wine
2 tablespoons soy sauce
1 teaspoon sugar
250 g (9 oz) canned baby clams, drained
⅔ teaspoon salt
2 spring onions, finely shredded

Put rice in a deep enamelled cast-iron casserole and wash well, changing water several times until water becomes clear. Leave to soak in just enough water to cover rice for 1 hour.

Meanwhile, in a saucepan mix sake, soy sauce and sugar over high heat and quickly toss in clams. Skim surface and remove from heat. Pour juice from pan into a measuring jug and keep clams warm in the pan.

Drain rice. Add enough water to jug to make pan juices up to 250 ml (9 fl oz/1 cup) and dissolve salt in it. Pour mixture over rice, cover and place on high heat. bring to the boil and cook for 7-8 minutes until it sizzles, then lower heat and simmer for 10 minutes. Place clams and spring onions on top. Cover and cook over high heat for 2 seconds. Remove from heat and leave to stand for 10-15 minutes. Gently mix clams and spring onions into rice. Serve in rice bowls.

Serves 4-6.

TEMPURA RICE BOWL

575 g (1¼ lb/3 cups) Japanese rice
12 raw king prawns
12 okra, trimmed
1 egg
115 g (4 oz/1 cup) plain flour
vegetable oil for deep-frying
TARE SAUCE:
2 tablespoons sugar
3 tablespoons soy sauce
115 ml (4 fl oz/½ cup) dashi (see page 29)

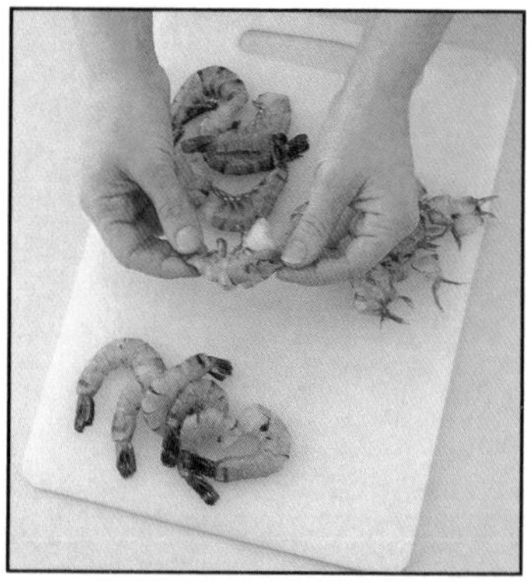

Boil rice (see page 209) and keep warm. Peel prawns, retaining tail, and devein. Make a slit along the belly to prevent curling.

To make tare sauce, dissolve sugar with soy sauce and dashi in a saucepan over medium heat and set aside. Beat egg in a measuring jug and add enough water to make up to 250 ml (9 fl oz/1 cup). Add flour to jug and gently fold in a few times: do not stir as the batter should be lumpy. Heat oil in a wok or deep-frying pan to 170C (340F). Plunge prawns and okra, one or two at a time, into batter and deep-fry until light golden. Drain on absorbent kitchen paper.

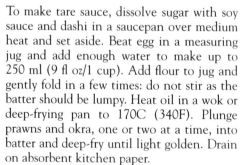

Divide rice between 4 large individual bowls. Pour about 1 tablespoon of tare sauce over each portion. Arrange 3 prawns and 3 okra on top of each portion of rice and pour remaining tare sauce over the top. Serve hot.

Serves 4.

Note: Cold left-over tempura (see page 92), can be used for this dish. Gently reheat tempura in tare sauce before placing it on top of boiled rice.

NOODLES

NOODLES WITH CHOP SUEY

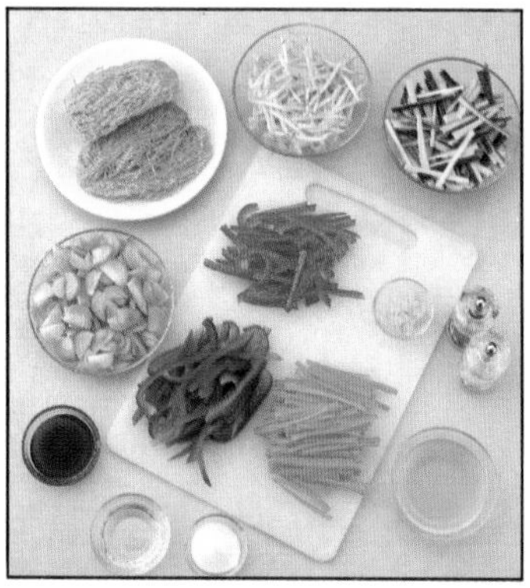

1 tablespoon groundnut (peanut) oil
2 cloves garlic, finely chopped
1 green pepper, thinly sliced
1 red pepper, thinly sliced
225 g (8 oz) shallots, chopped
2 small courgettes, cut into matchstick strips
2 large carrots, cut into matchstick strips
115 g (4 oz) bean sprouts
2 teaspoons sugar
2 tablespoons light soy sauce
55 ml (2 fl oz/¼ cup) Chinese Vegetable Stock (see page 17)
salt and freshly ground pepper
225 g (8 oz) dried egg noodles

Heat oil in a wok and stir-fry garlic, green and red peppers, shallots, courgettes and carrots for 2-3 minutes or until just softened. Add bean sprouts, sugar, soy sauce, stock and salt and pepper. Bring to the boil, reduce heat and simmer for 6-7 minutes.

Meanwhile, bring a large saucepan of water to the boil, add noodles and cook for 5 minutes or until just tender. Drain well and transfer to warmed serving plates. Top with vegetable mixture and serve.

Serves 4.

PRAWN NOODLES

225 g (8 oz) rice vermicelli
25 g (1 oz) dried Chinese mushrooms, soaked in hot water for 20 minutes
2 teaspoons chilli oil
4 spring onions, shredded
225 g (8 oz) cooked, peeled large prawns, thawed and dried, if frozen
225 g (8 oz) frozen green peas
1 tablespoon oyster sauce
grated zest 1 lemon
1 egg, lightly beaten

Bring a large saucepan of water to the boil. Turn off heat and add noodles. Loosen with 2 forks and let soak 3 minutes.

Drain noodles well and rinse in cold water. Drain mushrooms and squeeze out excess water. Discard stems and slice caps. Heat half chilli oil in a wok and stir-fry mushrooms, spring onions, prawns and peas for 2 minutes. Add oyster sauce, lemon zest and noodles and stir-fry for 2 minutes. Keep warm.

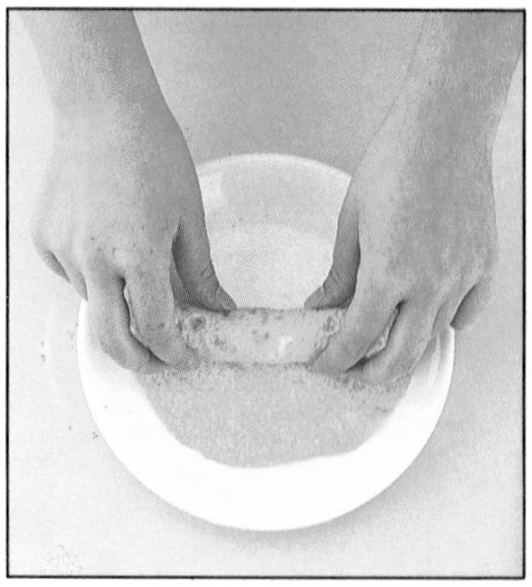

Heat remaining oil in a small non-stick skillet and cook egg for 1-2 minutes on each side or until set. Slide on to a plate, roll up and cut into thin slices. Garnish noodles with egg and serve immediately.

Serves 4.

FRIED RICE NOODLES

225 g (8 oz) dried rice noodles, 1 cm (½ in) wide
2 tablespoons vegetable oil
3 small onions, sliced into thin rings
2 cloves garlic, finely chopped
3 fresh red chillies, seeded, cored and finely chopped
3 Chinese pork sausages, total weight about 175 g (6 oz), thinly sliced diagonally
225 g (8 oz) raw tiger prawns, peeled and deveined
2 eggs, beaten
115 g (4 oz) bean sprouts
3 tablespoons light soy sauce
4 tablespoons chicken stock
2 spring onions, including some green, cut diagonally into 0.5 cm (¼ in) pieces

In a bowl, soak rice vermicelli in hot water for 30 minutes or until softened. Drain well. In a wok or sauté pan, heat oil over medium-high heat. Add onions and stir-fry for 3-4 minutes or until starting to brown. Add garlic, chillies and Chinese sausage and stir-fry for about 30 seconds until fragrant. Add prawns and stir-fry for 1-1½ minutes until they just turn pink.

Increase heat to high. Quickly stir in eggs, then add bean sprouts, rice sticks, soy sauce and stock. Stir for about 1 minute. Serve sprinkled with spring onions.

Serves 4.

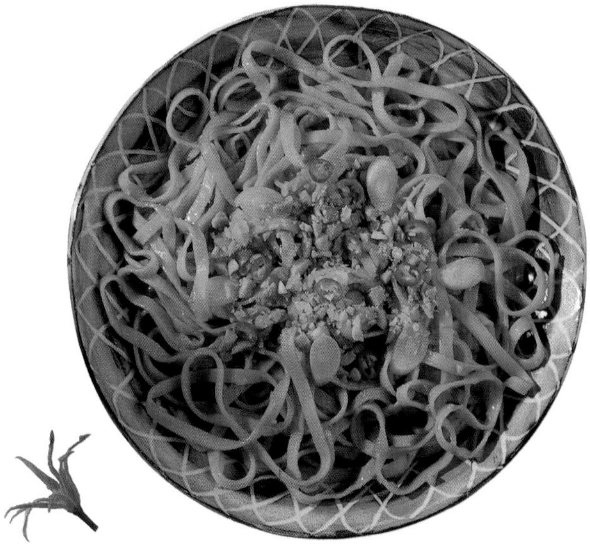

NOODLES WITH PEANUT SAUCE

225 g (8 oz) fresh thin egg noodles
2 tablespoons sesame oil
4 tablespoons unsalted roast peanuts
1 clove garlic, crushed
1 tablespoon light soy sauce
2 teaspoons Chinese black vinegar
1 teaspoon light brown sugar
1 tablespoon groundnut (peanut) oil
few drops hot chilli oil
white part spring onion, thinly sliced, to garnish
fresh red chilli, very thinly sliced, to garnish

Bring a large saucepan of water to the boil. Add noodles, return to boil, stir, then cover pan and boil until just tender.

Drain well and tip into a serving bowl. Toss with 1 tablespoon sesame oil. Set aside. In a blender or a spice grinder, or using a pestle and mortar, crush 1 tablespoon peanuts. Set aside. Put remaining peanuts and sesame oil, garlic, soy sauce, vinegar, sugar and groundnut oil in a blender. Add 55 ml (2 fl oz/ ¼ cup) water. Mix to a smooth paste. Add chilli oil to taste.

To serve, pour peanut sauce over noodles. Toss to mix. Sprinkle crushed peanuts on top, and garnish with spring onion and chilli slices.

Serves 3-4 as a side dish.

NOODLES WITH BEAN SPROUTS

225 g (8 oz) fresh thin egg noodles
2 tablespoons sesame oil
1 clove garlic, finely crushed
3 tablespoons light soy sauce
1 tablespoon rice vinegar
½ teaspoon light brown sugar
½ fresh red chilli, cored, seeded and finely chopped
115 g (4 oz) bean sprouts
4 crisp inner Cos lettuce leaves, shredded

Bring a large saucepan of water to the boil. Add noodles, return to boil, stir, then cover and boil according to packet instructions, until just tender.

Drain well and tip into a warm serving bowl. Toss with 1 tablespoon sesame oil. Set aside. Put remaining sesame oil, garlic, soy sauce, vinegar, sugar and chilli in a blender. Mix together.

Scatter bean sprouts and lettuce shreds over noodles. Stir sesame oil dressing and pour over noodles and vegetables. Transfer to serving dish, toss and serve.

Serves 3-4 as a side dish.

CHICKEN & PRAWN NOODLES

225 g (8 oz) chicken breast fillet, very thinly sliced
225 g (8 oz) raw prawns, peeled and deveined
5 tablespoons groundnut (peanut) oil
1 tablespoon sesame oil
1 teaspoon ground coriander
pinch Chinese five-spice powder
115 g (4 oz) dried thin egg noodles
55 g (2 oz) mangetout
55 g (2 oz) French beans, halved
2 cloves garlic, finely crushed
1½ teaspoons grated fresh root ginger
2 fresh red chillies, cored, seeded and finely chopped
1 tablespoon dark soy sauce
1 tablespoon lime juice
2 tablespoons chopped coriander leaves
toasted candlenuts or cashew nuts

Put chicken and prawns into a non-reactive bowl. Stir together 1 tablespoon groundnut (peanut) oil, 1 teaspoon sesame oil, ground coriander and five-spice powder. Pour over chicken and prawns. Stir until evenly coated. Cook noodles according to packet instructions. Meanwhile, in a wok or sauté pan, heat 2 tablespoons groundnut oil. Add chicken and prawns and stir-fry for 2 minutes. Using a slotted spoon, transfer to absorbent kitchen paper to drain. Add mangetout and French beans to pan and stir-fry for 1 minute.

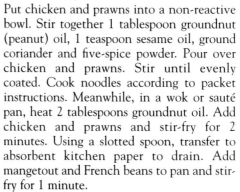

Transfer chicken and prawns to serving bowl. Keep warm. In a small pan, heat remaining groundnut oil and sesame oil. Add garlic, ginger and chillies and fry gently for 4-5 minutes until softened but not coloured. Whisk in soy sauce, lime juice and 2 tablespoons water. Bring to the boil then remove from heat. Drain noodles and quickly toss with chicken and garlic mixtures. Serve warm or cold sprinkled with chopped coriander and toasted nuts.

Serves 4.

NOODLES WITH FISH

3 tablespoons tamarind
225 g (8 oz) rice vermicelli
350 g (12 oz) mixed white fish and snapper, salmon or trout fillets
4 fresh red chillies, cored, seeded and finely chopped
1 stalk lemon grass, crushed and thinly sliced
8 spring onions, thinly sliced
1½ teaspoons shrimp paste, roasted (see page 11)
175 g (6 oz) peeled raw medium prawns
225 g (8 oz) dried medium egg noodles
1 tablespoon light brown sugar
¼ teaspoon ground turmeric
6 shallots, very thinly sliced
leaves from small bunch mixed basil and mint

Soak tamarind in 3 tablespoons boiling water for 3 hours. Strain through muslin and set aside. Soak rice sticks in boiling water until softened. Put fish, chillies, lemon grass, spring onions and shrimp paste in a saucepan. Add 1.75 litres (3 pints/7½ cups) water. Bring to the boil. Add prawns and poach until fish just flakes and prawns turn pink. Remove fish and prawns and keep warm.

Bring fish stock to the boil then simmer for 5 minutes. Add egg noodles. Stir, then boil, uncovered, until just tender. Cut fish into bite-sized pieces. Drain both types of noodle. Add sugar and turmeric to stock, and return to a simmer. Divide noodles between 6 warm bowls. Top with fish, prawns and shallots. Strain over enough stock to moisten well. Add mint and basil leaves. Serve tamarind juice separately, or sprinkle over noodles before serving.

Serves 6.

NOODLES WITH TOFU

175 g (6 oz) dried thin egg noodles
2 tablespoons vegetable oil
6 shallots, finely chopped
3 cloves garlic, finely crushed
2 fresh red chillies, cored, seeded and chopped
5 eggs
225 g (8 oz) firm tofu, cut into thin strips
2 tablespoons soy sauce
55 ml (2 fl oz/¼ cup) rice vinegar
1½ tablespoons light brown sugar
salt
grated zest ½ lime
2 spring onions, white and green parts, thinly sliced
3 tablespoons chopped coriander leaves
115 g (4 oz) bean sprouts

Cook noodles according to packet instructions. Meanwhile, in a wok or sauté pan over medium heat, heat oil. Add shallots, garlic and chillies and stir-fry until shallots are lightly browned.

Break all eggs into the pan. Stir for 1 minute, breaking up yolks. Add tofu, soy sauce, vinegar, sugar and salt to taste. Toss ingredients together until eggs are set. Drain noodles. Toss with egg and tofu mixture, lime zest, spring onions and coriander. Scatter bean sprouts on top.

Serves 4.

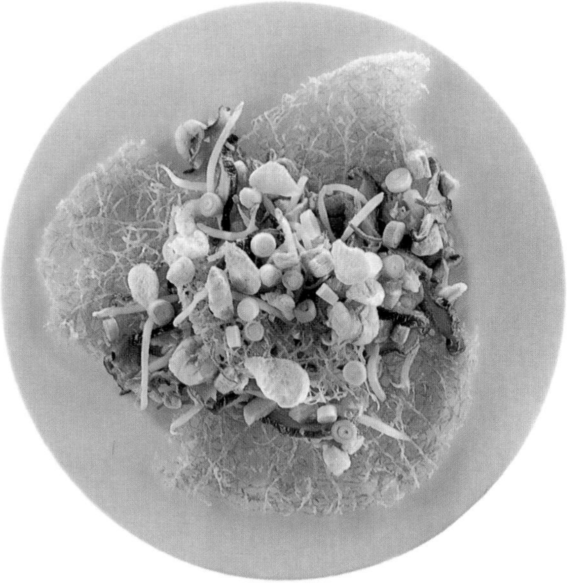

CRISPY NOODLES

175 g (6 oz) rice vermicelli
6 pieces dried Chinese black mushrooms
115 g (4 oz) lean pork
115 g (4 oz) boneless, skinless chicken breast
vegetable oil for deep-frying
2 eggs
4 cloves garlic, finely chopped
3 shallots, thinly sliced
1 fresh red chilli, seeded and sliced
1 fresh green chilli, seeded and sliced
6 tablespoons lime juice
1 tablespoon fish sauce
1 tablespoon crushed palm sugar
45 g (1½ oz) cooked peeled prawns
115 g (4 oz) bean sprouts
3 spring onions, thickly sliced

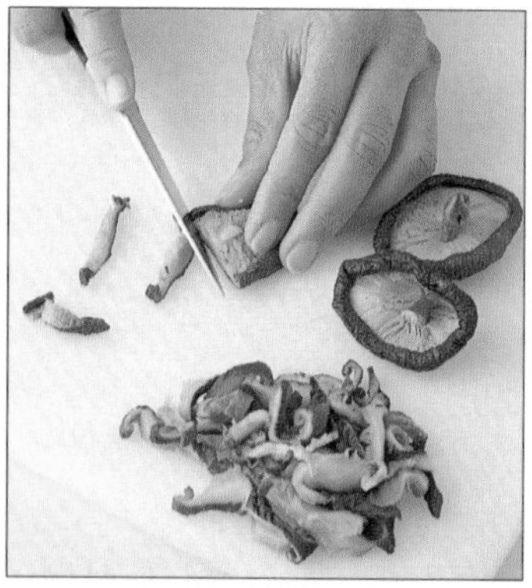

Soak vermicelli in water for 20 minutes, then drain and set aside. Soak mushrooms in water for 20 minutes, then drain, chop and set aside. Cut pork and chicken into 2.5 cm (1 in) strips or small dice. Set aside.

For garnish, heat 2 tablespoons oil in a wok. In a small bowl, beat eggs with 2 tablespoons water, then drip small amounts in batches in tear shapes on to wok. Cook for 1½-2 minutes until set. Remove using a fish slice or thin spatula. Set aside.

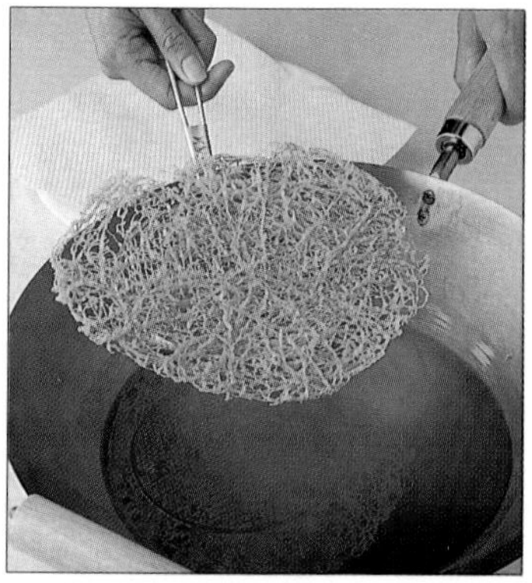

Add more oil to wok until there is sufficient for deep-frying. Heat to 190C (375F). Add vermicelli in batches and fry until puffed, light golden and crisp. Transfer to absorbent kitchen paper. Set aside.

Pour off oil leaving 3 tablespoons. Add garlic and shallots and cook, stirring occasionally, until lightly browned. Add pork, stir-fry for 1 minute, then mix in chicken and stir for 2 minutes. Stir in chillies, mushrooms, lime juice, fish sauce and sugar.

Bubble until liquid becomes very lightly syrupy. Add prawns, bean sprouts and noodles, tossing to coat with sauce without breaking up noodles. Serve with spring onions scattered over and garnished with egg 'tears'.

Serves 4.

THAI FRIED NOODLES

3 tablespoons vegetable oil
4 cloves garlic, crushed
1 tablespoon fish sauce
3-4 tablespoons lime juice
1 teaspoon crushed palm sugar
2 eggs, beaten
350 g (12 oz) rice vermicelli, soaked in water for 20 minutes, drained
115 g (4 oz) cooked peeled prawns
115 g (4 oz) bean sprouts
4 spring onions, sliced
2 tablespoons ground dried shrimp, finely chopped, roasted peanuts, coriander leaves and lime slices, to garnish

In a wok, heat oil, add garlic and cook, stirring occasionally, until golden. Stir in fish sauce, lime juice and sugar until sugar has dissolved. Quickly stir in eggs and cook for a few seconds. Stir in vermicelli to coat with garlic and egg, then add shrimp, 85 g (3 oz) bean sprouts and half of the chopped spring onions.

When noodles are tender, transfer contents of wok to a warmed serving dish. Garnish with remaining bean sprouts and spring onions, dried shrimp, peanuts, coriander leaves and lime slices.

Serves 4.

NOODLES & THAI HERB SAUCE

70 ml (2½ fl oz/⅓ cup) vegetable oil
2 tablespoons raw shelled peanuts
1 small fresh green chilli, seeded and sliced
2 cm (¾ in) piece galangal, chopped
2 large cloves garlic, chopped
leaves from bunch Thai holy basil (about 90)
leaves from small bunch Thai mint (about 30)
leaves from small bunch coriander (about 45)
2 tablespoons lime juice
1 teaspoon fish sauce
350-450 g (12-16 oz) dried egg noodles, soaked for 5-10 minutes

Over a high heat, heat oil in a wok, add peanuts and cook, stirring, for about 2 minutes until browned. Using a slotted spoon, transfer nuts to absorbent kitchen paper to drain; reserve oil.

Using a small blender, roughly grind nuts. Add chilli, galangal and garlic. Mix briefly. Add basil, mint, coriander, lime juice, fish sauce and reserved oil. Drain noodles, shake loose, then cook in a pan of boiling salted water for 2 minutes until soft. Drain well, turn into a warmed dish and toss with sauce.

Serves 4.

CRAB & AUBERGINE NOODLES

225 g (8 oz) brown and white crab meat
175 g (6 oz) dried egg thread noodles
3 tablespoons vegetable oil
1 aubergine, weighing about 225 g (8 oz), cut into 5 × 0.5 cm (2 × ¼ in) strips
2 cloves garlic, very finely chopped
1 cm (½ in) slice galangal, finely chopped
1 fresh green chilli, seeded and finely chopped
6 spring onions, sliced
1 tablespoon fish sauce
2 teaspoons lime juice
1½ tablespoons chopped coriander leaves

In a bowl, thoroughly mash brown crab meat and roughly mash white crab meat. Set aside.

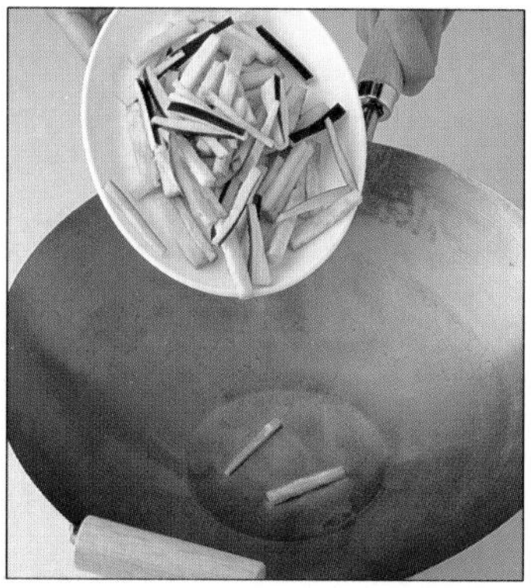

Add noodles to a saucepan of boiling salted water and cook for about 4 minutes until just tender. Drain well. Meanwhile, in a wok, heat 2 tablespoons oil, add aubergine and stir-fry for about 5 minutes until evenly and well coloured. Using a slotted spoon, transfer to absorbent kitchen paper; set aside.

Add remaining oil to wok, heat, then one by one stir in garlic, galangal, chilli and, finally, spring onions. Add noodles, toss together for 1 minute, then toss in crab meats and aubergine. Sprinkle over fish sauce, lime juice and coriander, and toss to mix.

Serves 3.

NOODLES WITH BROCCOLI

450 g (1 lb) wet rice noodles
225 g (8 oz) broccoli
2 tablespoons vegetable oil
3 cloves garlic, finely chopped
225 g (8 oz) lean pork, finely chopped
4 tablespoons roasted peanuts, chopped
2 teaspoons fish sauce
½ teaspoon crushed palm sugar
1 fresh red chilli, seeded and cut into thin slivers, to garnish

Remove wrapping from noodles and immediately cut into 1 cm (½ in) strips; set aside. Cut broccoli diagonally into pieces 5 cm (2 in) wide and cook in a saucepan of boiling salted water for 2 minutes. Drain, refresh under cold running water and drain well; set aside.

In a wok, heat oil, add garlic and fry, stirring occasionally, until golden. Using a slotted spoon, transfer to absorbent kitchen paper; set aside. Add pork to wok and stir-fry for 2 minutes. Add noodles, stir quickly, then add broccoli and peanuts and stir-fry for 2 minutes. Stir in fish sauce, sugar and 3 tablespoons water. Stir briefly and serve garnished with reserved garlic and chilli slivers.

Serves 4.

VEGETARIAN FRIED NOODLES

2 tablespoons vegetable oil
1 clove garlic, chopped
1 onion, sliced
2-3 small red chillies, seeded and shredded
1 carrot, thinly shredded
225 g (8 oz) bean sprouts
salt and freshly ground black pepper
225 g (8 oz) rice vermicelli, soaked in hot water for 5 minutes, drained and cut into short lengths
2 tablespoons soy sauce
shredded spring onions, to garnish

Heat oil in a wok or frying pan and stir-fry garlic and onion for 1 minute until opaque.

Add chillies and carrot shreds, continue stirring for 2 minutes, then add bean sprouts with salt and pepper. Blend well and stir-fry for 2 more minutes.

Add rice vermicelli with soy sauce, mix and toss, then cook for 2-3 minutes. Garnish with shredded spring onions and serve at once.

Serves 4.

Note: Serve this dish with chilli sauce or Spicy Fish Sauce (see page 233), if wished.

SPICY COLD NOODLES

225 g (8 oz) rice vermicelli
3 tablespoons vegetable oil
2 eggs, beaten
1 clove garlic, finely chopped
2 shallots, chopped
115 g (4 oz) pork, shredded
115 g (4 oz) peeled raw prawns
1 tablespoon dried shrimp, soaked
1-2 tablespoons preserved vegetables, chopped
55 g (2 oz) bean sprouts
2 small red chillies, seeded and chopped
salt and freshly ground black pepper
2 tablespoons fish sauce
3 tablespoons crushed peanuts
2-3 spring onions, shredded
coriander sprigs, to garnish

Cook vermicelli in boiling water for 5 minutes; drain, rinse and set aside. Heat about 1 tablespoon oil in a wok or pan and scramble eggs until just set, then break up into small pieces and remove. Heat remaining oil and stir-fry garlic and shallots for about 30 seconds. Add pork and prawns and continue stir-frying for 1-2 minutes. Add dried shrimp, preserved vegetables, bean sprouts, scrambled eggs, chillies, salt, pepper and fish sauce. Blend well to make a dressing and stir-fry for 2-3 minutes. Set aside.

Place vermicelli on a large serving dish or plate, add spicy dressing with a mound of crushed peanuts and spring onions on top. Serve garnished with coriander.

Serves 4.

Note: Serve with chilli sauce and/or Spicy Fish Sauce (see page 233), if wished.

BEEF & RICE NOODLE SOUP

1.35 kg (3 lb) oxtail, cut into pieces
2 stalks lemon grass, chopped
1 large piece fresh root ginger, peeled
1 onion, sliced
5-6 whole star anise
6 cloves
1 cinnamon stick (optional)
1 tablespoon sugar
1 teaspoon salt
2 tablespoons fish sauce
450 g (1 lb) flat rice noodles, soaked in hot water for 10 minutes, then drained
225-300 g (8-10 oz) sirloin beef steak, cut into small paper-thin slices

Trim off as much excess fat from oxtail as possible. Place pieces in a large pot, add lemon grass, ginger, onion, star anise, cloves and cinnamon stick, if using. Add 2 litres (3½ pints/9 cups) water and bring to the boil. Reduce heat and simmer oxtail for at least 2½ hours, skimming the surface occasionally to remove scum.

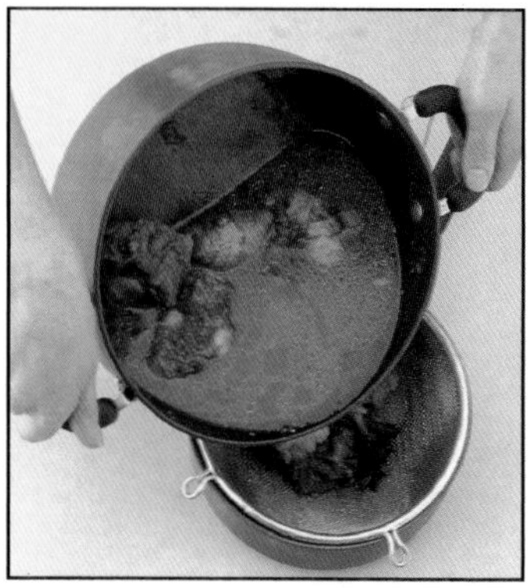

Strain stock and discard oxtail and flavouring ingredients (the meat from the bones can be used for another dish). Add sugar, salt, and fish sauce to clear stock, bring back to the boil and simmer for 2-3 minutes. (At this stage, stock can be cooled and refrigerated for 1-2 days, if wished. Fat can be removed from surface and stock reheated ready for use.)

SOUP ACCOMPANIMENTS
115 g (4 oz) bean sprouts
½ cucumber, thinly shredded
4-5 lettuce leaves, shredded
1 onion, thinly sliced
4 small red chillies, seeded and chopped
2 limes, cut into wedges
fresh mint, basil and coriander leaves
chilli sauce

Arrange accompaniments on a serving platter. Place a portion of rice noodles in each of 4-6 large individual serving bowls.

Bring beef broth to a rolling boil. Place a few slices of beef steak on top of noodles and pour in boiling broth to fill the bowls about three-quarters full. Bring them to the table.

Each person takes a small amount of bean sprouts, cucumber, lettuce, onion, chillies and herbs and places them on top of the noodles, with a squeeze of lime and more seasonings as desired.

Serves 4-6.

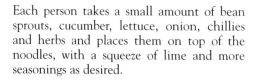

Note: This is almost a meal on its own, and traditionally may be eaten as breakfast, lunch or as a snack at any time of day.

SOY SAUCE RAMEN WITH PORK

500 g (1 lb 2 oz) egg noodles
85 ml (3 fl oz/⅓ cup) soy sauce
3 tablespoons sake
250 g (9 oz) pork, shredded
85 g (3 oz) fine green beans, trimmed and halved
200 g (7 oz) bean sprouts, trimmed
vegetable oil for frying
salt and freshly ground pepper
BROTH:
2.5 cm (1 in) piece fresh root ginger, peeled
2 cloves garlic
2 spring onions
1.35 litres (2¼ pints/6 cups) chicken stock
2 teaspoons salt

To make broth, roughly chop root ginger, garlic and spring onions and add to chicken stock. Bring to the boil over medium heat and simmer, half-covered, for 30 minutes. Meanwhile, cook noodles in plenty of boiling water, following packet instructions. Wash away starch and drain. Sprinkle 1 tablespoon sake and 2 tablespoons soy sauce over pork and set aside. Parboil beans, then drain. Stir-fry bean sprouts in a little oil over high heat for 1 minute. Add beans and stir-fry for 1-2 minutes. Season with salt and pepper and remove to a plate.

Add pork to pan and stir-fry for 5-6 minutes until well cooked. Strain broth into another pan, discarding ginger, garlic and spring onions. Season with remaining soy sauce and sake, salt and pepper. Bring to the boil, add noodles and cook over medium heat for 1 minute. Divide noodles between 4 individual noodle bowls, keeping broth at a gentle simmer. Divide cooked ingredients between bowls. Pour broth over them and serve garnished with chilli oil, if wished.

Serves 4.

POT-COOKED UDON

4 fresh or dried shiitake or any mushrooms, stalks removed, plus sugar and soy sauce if using dried shiitake
900 g (2 lb) fresh cooked udon noodles or 400 g (14 oz) dried uncooked udon noodles
4 eggs
4 raw king prawns, peeled and deveined.
4 fish balls or cakes (optional)
55 g (2 oz) cress or watercress
BROTH:
1.35 litres (2¼ pints/6 cups) second dashi (see page 29), or water and 2 teaspoons dashi-no-moto
1½ teaspoons salt
4 tablespoons soy sauce
1 tablespoon sugar
2 tablespoons mirin

Make a cross slit on top of fresh shiitake caps. If using dried ones, soak in warm water with a pinch sugar for about 1 hour, then cook in mixture of 115 ml (4 fl oz/½ cup) soaking water and 2 tablespoons each of sugar and soy sauce. Meanwhile, if using dried udon noodles cook them in plenty of boiling water until tender, following packet instructions. Wash away starch from noodles under running water and drain. To make broth, in a saucepan over medium heat, put second dashi, salt, soy sauce, sugar and mirin. Keep at a gentle simmer.

Lightly poach eggs. Place noodles in an earthenware pot or cast-iron casserole and add mushrooms, prawns, fish balls or cakes (if using) and cress or watercress. Place poached eggs on top. Ladle in enough broth to just cover ingredients, then bring to the boil, covered, over medium heat and simmer for another 4-5 minutes until all ingredients are hot and cooked. Serve at once in noodle bowls.

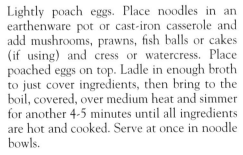

Serves 4.

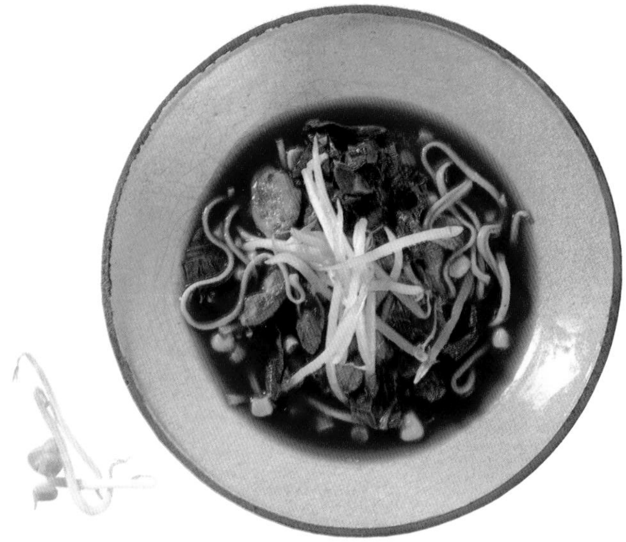

MISO RAMEN WITH CHICKEN

2 boneless, skinless chicken breasts
2.5 cm (1 in) piece fresh root ginger, peeled, grated
3-4 tablespoons soy sauce
500 g (1 lb 2 oz) egg noodles
200 g (7 oz) bean sprouts, trimmed
vegetable oil for frying
salt and freshly ground black pepper
8 tablespoons cooked sweetcorn kernels
150 g (5 oz) spinach, trimmed
BROTH:
1.35 litres (2¼ pints/6 cups) chicken stock
2.5 cm (1 in) piece fresh root ginger, peeled, sliced
2 cloves garlic
2 spring onions, cut into 3 pieces
8 tablespoons miso (white, if available)
2 tablespoons each soy sauce and sake

To make broth, put stock in a saucepan with sliced ginger, garlic and spring onions. Bring to the boil and simmer over medium heat for 30 minutes. Slice chicken into 0.5 cm (¼ in) thick, bite-sized pieces. Spread pieces on a large plate, pour over grated ginger and 3-4 tablespoons soy sauce and leave to marinate for 10 minutes. Cook noodles following packet instructions and wash off any starch. Stir-fry bean sprouts in a little oil for 1-2 minutes, season with salt and pepper and remove to a plate. Drain chicken and fry in a little oil until all sides are golden brown.

Blanch sweetcorn in boiling water for 1 minute; drain. Cook spinach in lightly salted water for 1-2 minutes, drain, squeeze out water and cut into 2.5cm (1 in) pieces. Strain broth into a large pan, discarding ginger, garlic and onions; bring to the boil. Add 2 tablespoons soy sauce and sake and miso diluted with a little broth. Add noodles, bring to the boil and simmer for 2 minutes. Remove noodles to individual bowls, put rest of ingredients on top and pour over hot broth.

Serves 4.

SOBA WITH DIPPING SAUCE

450 g (1 lb) dried soba (buckwheat) noodles
1 sheet nori (wafer-thin dried seaweed)
3-4 teaspoons wasabi paste or powder
2 spring onions, finely chopped
DIPPING SAUCE:
450 ml (16 fl oz/2 cups) second dashi (see page 29), or water and 1 teaspoon dashi-no-moto (freeze-dried dashi powder)
115 ml (4 fl oz/½ cup) soy sauce
4 tablespoons mirin
1 teaspoon sugar

Cook noodles in plenty of boiling water, following packet instructions. Wash away starch under running water and drain.

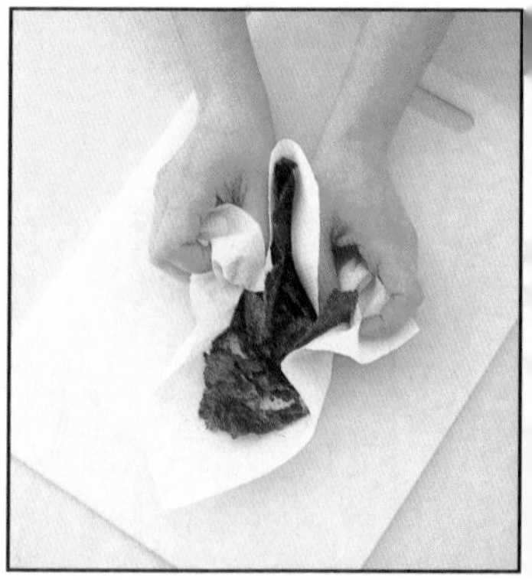

Lightly toast both sides of nori sheet over low heat and crush into pieces in absorbent kitchen paper or cut into 2.5 cm (1 in) long shreds with kitchen scissors. If using wasabi powder, make a paste by mixing it with the same amount of water. To make dipping sauce, mix together second dashi, soy sauce, mirin and sugar in a saucepan and simmer over medium heat until sugar has dissolved. Half fill 4 small individual bowls or tea cups with sauce and put remaining sauce in a jug.

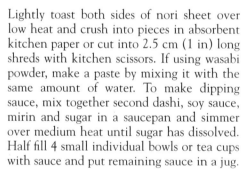

Refresh noodles under cold running water for a second and arrange a quarter on each of 4 individual bamboo mats placed on large plates, or directly on to plates. Sprinkle nori on top. Serve with small plates of chopped spring onion and wasabi paste and sauce. Diners dip some noodles into their own sauce mixed with condiments.

Serves 4.

DIPS, SAUCES, CURRY PASTES & PICKLES

SPICE MIXES & COCONUT MILK

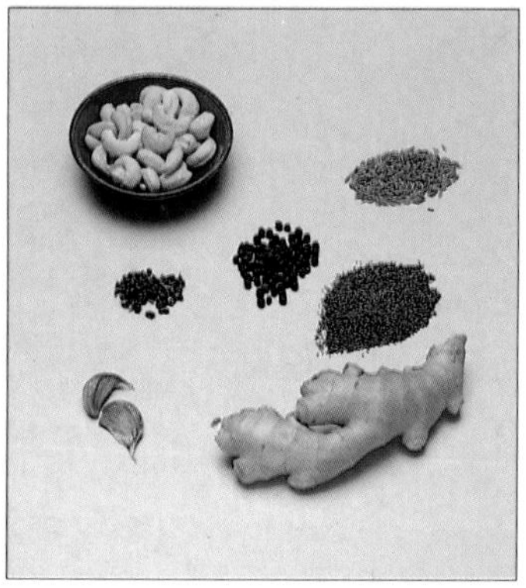

NUT MASALA
2 tablespoons vegetable oil
1 teaspoon cumin seeds
1 teaspoon cardamom seeds
1 tablespoon poppy seeds
1 teaspoon black peppercorns
2 cloves garlic, crushed
2.5 cm (1 in) piece fresh root ginger, grated
55 g (2 oz/⅓ cup) blanched almonds or unsalted cashew nuts, chopped
70 ml (2½ fl oz/⅓ cup) boiling water

Heat oil in a heavy-based frying pan, add cumin, cardamom and poppy seeds and black peppercorns and fry over a medium heat for 5-10 minutes, until golden brown, stirring constantly. Add garlic and ginger and cook for 2 minutes more, then leave to cool. Put spice mixture in a blender or food processor fitted with a metal blade. Add almonds or cashew nuts and water and grind to a smooth paste. Cover tightly and store in a cool place for up to 1 week.

MURGHAL MASALA
seeds from 55 g (2 oz) green cardamom pods
two 7.5 cm (3 in) cinnamon sticks, crushed
1 tablespoon whole cloves
1 tablespoon black peppercorns
1 teaspoon grated nutmeg

Grind spices to a fine powder using a coffee grinder or pestle and mortar. Store in a small, airtight jar for up to 2 months.

GARAM MASALA
4 teaspoons cardamom seeds
two 7.5 cm (3 in) cinnamon sticks, crushed
2 teaspoons whole cloves
4 teaspoons black peppercorns
3 tablespoons cumin seeds
3 tablespoons coriander seeds

Put spices in a heavy-based frying pan and fry over medium heat for 5-10 minutes, until browned, stirring. Cool, then grind to a fine powder. Store for up to 2 months.

HOT SPICE MIX
4 tablespoons cumin seeds
8 dried red chillies
1 tablespoon black peppercorns
1 tablespoon cardamom seeds
7.5 cm (3 in) cinnamon stick, crushed
4 teaspoons black mustard seeds
1 tablespoon fenugreek seeds

Prepare as for Garam Masala (above). Store in an airtight jar for up to 2 months.

COCONUT MILK
100 g (3½ oz/1 cup) desiccated, fresh or creamed coconut
450 ml (16 fl oz/2 cups) hot water

Put coconut and water in a blender or food processor fitted with a metal blade; process for 1 minute. Strain through a nylon sieve, squeezing out liquid, then discard coconut. (There is no need to sieve creamed coconut.)

Makes about 450 ml (16 fl oz/2 cups).

FRESH MANGO CHUTNEY

2 mangoes
1 red chilli, seeded and finely sliced
3 tablespoons cashew nuts, chopped
25 g (1 oz/2½ tablespoons) raisins
2 tablespoons chopped fresh mint
pinch asafoetida
½ teaspoon ground cumin
¼ teaspoon cayenne pepper
½ teaspoon ground coriander
mint sprigs, to garnish

Peel and stone mangoes, then very thinly slice flesh.

Put mango slices in a bowl with chilli, cashew nuts, raisins and mint and stir gently. In a small bowl, mix asafoetida, cumin, cayenne and coriander together, then sprinkle over mango mixture.

Stir gently to coat mango mixture in spices, then cover and chill for 2 hours. Serve chilled, garnished with mint sprigs.

Makes about 225 g (8 oz).

LIME PICKLE

12 limes
55 g (2 oz/¼ cup) coarse sea salt
1 tablespoon fenugreek seeds
1 tablespoon mustard seeds
2 tablespoons chilli powder
1 tablespoon ground turmeric
225 ml (8 fl oz/1 cup) vegetable oil, such as sunflower or peanut
coriander sprigs, to garnish

Cut each lime lengthways into 8 thin wedges. Place in a large sterilised bowl, sprinkle with salt and set aside.

Put fenugreek and mustard seeds in a frying pan and dry roast over a medium heat for 1-2 minutes, until they begin to pop. Put them in a mortar and grind them to a fine powder with a pestle.

Add chilli powder and turmeric and mix well. Sprinkle spice mixture over limes and stir. Pour over oil and cover with a dry cloth. Leave in a sunny place for 10-12 days, until softened. Pack into sterilised jars, then seal and store in a cool, dark place. It can be kept for 1-2 weeks. Serve at room temperature, garnished with coriander.

Makes about 1.5 kg (3½ lb).

Variation: To make Lemon Pickle, substitute 8 lemons for limes.

CUCUMBER RAITA

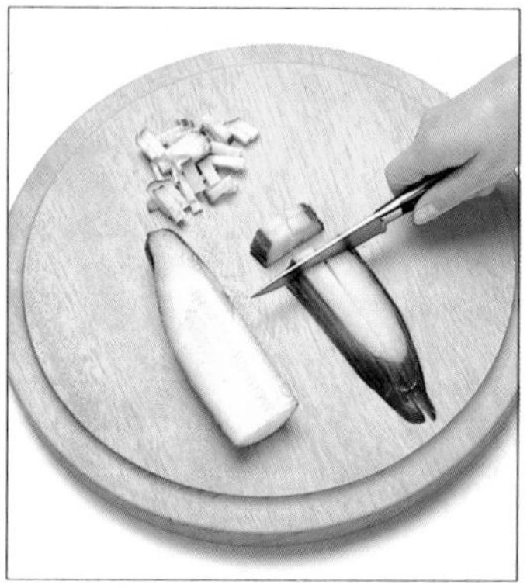

1/3 cucumber
225ml (8 fl oz/1 cup) natural yogurt
1 tablespoon chopped coriander leaves
1 tablespoon chopped fresh mint
1 green chilli, seeded and finely chopped
salt
1 teaspoon cumin seeds
1 teaspoon mustard seeds
coriander or mint leaves, to garnish

Cut cucumber into 0.3 cm × 1 cm (1/8 × 1/2 in) sticks and place in a bowl.

Add yogurt, coriander, mint and chilli and stir gently to mix. Season with salt. Chill for 30 minutes.

Meanwhile, put cumin and mustard seeds in a frying pan and dry roast over a medium heat for 1-2 minutes, until they begin to pop. Leave to cool, then sprinkle over yogurt mixture. Serve chilled, garnished with coriander or mint leaves.

Makes about 350 ml (12 fl oz/1 1/2 cups).

CARROT & PISTACHIO RAITA

25 g (1 oz/1/4 cup) coarsely chopped pistachio nuts
55 g (2 oz/1/3 cup) raisins
85 ml (3 fl oz/1/3 cup) boiling water
4 carrots, coarsely grated
175 ml (6 fl oz/3/4 cup) natural yogurt
1 tablespoon chopped fresh mint
1/2 teaspoon chilli powder
1/2 teaspoon cardamom seeds, crushed
1/2 teaspoon ground cumin

Put pistachio nuts and raisins in a small bowl and pour over boiling water. Leave to soak for 30 minutes, then drain and pat dry with absorbent kitchen paper.

Put carrots, yogurt, chopped mint, chilli powder, cardamom seeds and cumin in a bowl, season with salt and stir to mix.

Chill for 30 minutes. Stir all but 2 tablespoons pistachio nuts and raisins into yogurt, then sprinkle remainder on top. Serve raita chilled.

Makes about 350 ml (12 fl oz/1 1/2 cups).

Variation: Substitute chopped blanched almonds for pistachio nuts.

MALAYSIAN SAUCES

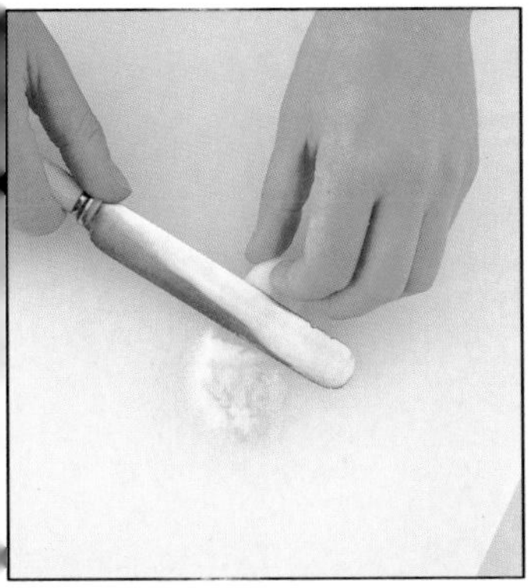

DIPPING SAUCE:
1 clove garlic, crushed
4 tablespoons light soy sauce
2½ tablespoons lime juice
1 tablespoon very finely sliced spring onion
1 teaspoon light brown sugar
1-2 drops chilli sauce

Mash garlic with a very small pinch of salt. In a small dish, put garlic, soy sauce, lime juice, spring onion and sugar. Add chilli sauce to taste. Stir before serving.

Serves 4.

SPICY SAUCE:
4 dried red chillies, cored, seeded and chopped
6 tablespoons groundnut (peanut) oil
4 shallots, finely chopped
8 cloves garlic, finely chopped
150 g (5 oz) ripe tomato, coarsely chopped
1 teaspoon ground coriander seeds
1 teaspoon ground cumin seeds
1 teaspoon light brown sugar

In a bowl, soak chillies in 3 tablespoons hot water for 15 minutes. Drain and reserve. Heat oil in a frying pan over medium-low heat. Add shallots and fry until softened.

Add garlic, tomato, coriander seeds, cumin seeds and sugar to pan. Bring to the boil then simmer for 3-4 minutes. Pour into a fine sieve placed over a bowl. Press through as much of the contents of sieve as possible. Cover and keep in a cool place until required.

Serves 6.

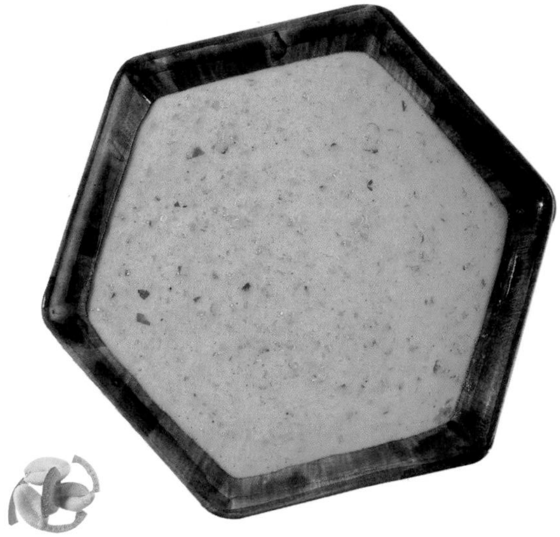

SATAY SAUCE

85 g (3 oz/½ cup) roasted peanuts
1 fresh red chilli, cored, seeded and chopped
1 clove garlic, chopped
4 tablespoons red curry paste
375 ml (13 fl oz/1⅔ cups) coconut milk
squeeze lime juice
2 tablespoons light brown sugar

Put peanuts, chilli and garlic in a blender. Mix together, then add curry paste, 2 tablespoons of coconut milk and a squeeze of lime juice. Mix to blend evenly.

Pour mixture into a saucepan. Stir in remaining coconut milk and sugar. Bring to the boil, stirring, then boil for 2 minutes.

Lower heat and simmer for 10 minutes, stirring occasionally. Add a little water if sauce becomes too thick.

Serves 6.

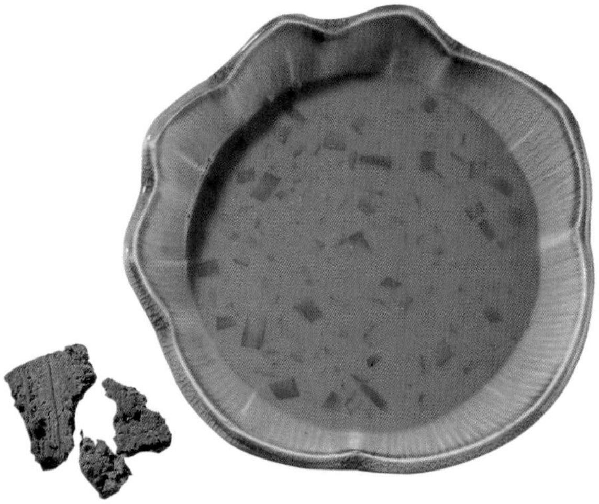

SHRIMP PASTE RELISH

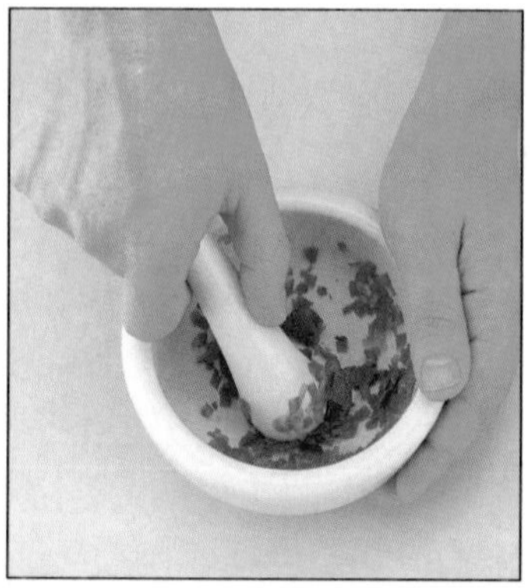

8 fresh red chillies, cored, seeded and chopped
1 tablespoon shrimp paste, roasted (see page 11)
2½ tablespoons lime juice

In a mortar or small bowl, pound chillies with a pestle or end of a rolling pin. Add shrimp paste and pound thoroughly.

Gradually add lime juice, using pestle or end of rolling pin to work lime juice into pounded chillies.

Serve relish in a non-reactive bowl, or store in a covered glass jar.

Serves 4-6.

COCONUT SAMBAL

55 g (2 oz) dried shrimp
175 g (6 oz/2 cups) desiccated coconut
2 fresh red chillies, cored, seeded and chopped
1 small onion, chopped
2 cloves garlic, crushed
1 stalk lemon grass, chopped
3 tablespoons vegetable oil

In a mortar or small bowl, pound shrimp with a pestle or end of a rolling pin, until fairly fine. Add coconut and work in lightly.

Put chillies, onion, garlic and lemon grass in a blender. Mix to a paste.

Heat oil in a wok or small frying pan over medium heat. Add spice paste and fry, stirring, for about 3 minutes until very fragrant. Add coconut mixture and fry until coconut is crisp and golden. Transfer to a small serving bowl and leave until cold. Store in a covered glass jar in the refrigerator.

Serves 6.

FRESH MINT SAMBAL

55 g (2 oz) mint leaves
1 cm (½ in) piece fresh root ginger, coarsely chopped
1 small onion, coarsely chopped
4 tablespoons lime juice
salt

Put mint, ginger, onion and lime juice in a blender. Mix to a paste. Season with salt to taste.

Transfer sambal to a serving small bowl. Serve sambal with curries or Curry Puffs (see page 40).

Makes about 225 ml (8 fl oz/1 cup).

QUICK MIXED PICKLE

2 fresh red chillies, cored, seeded and chopped
7 shallots, 5 chopped, 2 left whole
6 cloves garlic, 3 chopped, 3 left whole
4 cm (1½ in) piece fresh root ginger, grated
175 g (6 oz) cauliflower florets
4 small carrots, cut into fine sticks
175 g (6 oz) unpeeled cucumber, cut into fine sticks
3 tablespoons vegetable oil
1 tablespoon curry powder
½ teaspoon black mustard seeds
½ teaspoon ground turmeric
2 teaspoons light brown sugar
4 tablespoons rice vinegar
salt
1 tablespoon sesame oil
1 tablespoon toasted sesame seeds

Put chillies, chopped shallots and chopped garlic and three-quarters of the ginger in a blender. Add 1 tablespoon water and mix to a paste. Bring a large saucepan of water to the boil. Add cauliflower and carrots. Quickly return to the boil. After 30 seconds add cucumber and boil for about 3 seconds. Tip into a colander and rinse under running cold water.

Heat oil in a large saucepan. Add spice paste and fry for 1 minute. Add whole shallots and whole garlic and remaining ginger. Stir-fry for 30 seconds. Reduce heat to medium low. Stir in curry powder, mustard seeds, turmeric and sugar. Add vinegar, blanched vegetables and 1½ teaspoons salt. Bring to the boil. Remove from heat and stir in sesame oil and sesame seeds. Cool, then ladle into a warm jar and cover with a non-reactive lid. Refrigerate when cold.

Makes 1 litre (1¾ pints/4 cups).

GREEN CURRY PASTE

2 teaspoons coriander seeds
1 teaspoon cumin seeds
1 teaspoon black peppercorns
8 fresh green chillies, seeded and chopped
3 shallots, chopped
4 cloves garlic, crushed
3 coriander roots, chopped
2.5 cm (1 in) piece galangal, chopped
2 stalks lemon grass, chopped
2 kaffir lime leaves, chopped
2 teaspoons shrimp paste
2 tablespoons chopped coriander leaves

Heat a wok, add coriander and cumin seeds and heat until aroma rises.

Using a pestle and mortar or small blender, crush coriander and cumin seeds with peppercorns.

Add chillies, shallots, garlic, coriander roots, galangal, lemon grass, lime leaves, shrimp paste and chopped coriander and pound or mix to a smooth paste. Store in an airtight jar in the refrigerator for up to 4 weeks.

Makes about 8 tablespoons.

Note: Yield and heat of this paste will vary according to size and heat of chillies.

RED CURRY PASTE

1 tablespoon coriander seeds
1 teaspoon cumin seeds
1 teaspoon black peppercorns
4 cloves garlic, chopped
3 coriander roots, chopped
8 dried red chillies, seeded and chopped
2 stalks lemon grass, chopped
grated zest ½ kaffir lime
3 cm (1¼ in) piece galangal, chopped
2 teaspoons shrimp paste

Heat a wok, add coriander and cumin seeds and heat until aroma rises. Using a pestle and mortar or small blender, crush coriander and cumin seeds with peppercorns.

Add garlic, coriander roots, chillies, lemon grass, lime zest, galangal and shrimp paste and pound or mix to a smooth paste. Store in an airtight jar in the refrigerator for up to 4 weeks.

Makes about 4 tablespoons.

Note: Yield and heat of this paste will vary according to size and heat of chillies.

FRAGRANT CURRY PASTE

2 cloves garlic, chopped
1 shallot, chopped
4 dried red chillies, seeded and chopped
1 thick stalk lemon grass, chopped
3 coriander roots, chopped
finely grated zest 2 kaffir limes
1 kaffir lime leaf, torn
4 black peppercorns, cracked
½ teaspoon shrimp paste

Using a pestle and mortar or small blender, pound or mix together garlic, shallot, chillies, lemon grass and coriander roots.

Add lime zest, lime leaf, peppercorns and shrimp paste and pound or mix to a smooth paste. Store in an airtight jar in the refrigerator for up to 4 weeks.

Makes about 4 tablespoons.

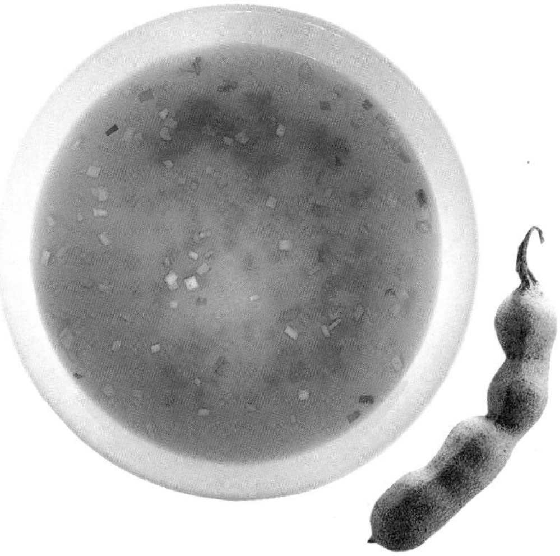

THAI DIPPING SAUCE 1

8 tablespoons tamarind water (see page 11)
½-¾ tablespoon crushed palm sugar
1-2 drops fish sauce
½ teaspoon very finely chopped spring onion
½ teaspoon very finely chopped garlic
½ teaspoon finely chopped fresh red chilli

In a small saucepan, gently heat tamarind water and sugar until sugar has dissolved.

Remove pan from heat and add fish sauce. Stir in spring onion, garlic and chilli. Pour into a small serving bowl and leave to cool.

Serves 4.

THAI DIPPING SAUCE 2

6 tablespoons lime juice
1½-2 teaspoons crushed palm sugar
½ teaspoon fish sauce
½ teaspoon very finely chopped red shallot
½ teaspoon very finely chopped fresh green chilli
½ teaspoon finely chopped fresh red chilli

In a small bowl, stir together lime juice and sugar until sugar has dissolved. Adjust amount of sugar, if wished.

Stir in fish sauce, shallot and chillies. Pour into a small serving bowl. Serve with deep-fried fish, fish fritters, won tons or spring rolls.

Serves 4.

NAM PRIK

1 tablespoon fish sauce
about 22 whole dried shrimp, chopped
3 cloves garlic, chopped
4 dried red chillies with seeds, chopped
2 tablespoons lime juice
1 fresh red or green chilli, seeded and chopped
about 1 tablespoon pea aubergines, chopped (optional)

Using a pestle and mortar or small blender, pound or mix fish sauce, shrimp, garlic, dried chillies and lime juice to a paste.

Stir in fresh red or green chilli and pea aubergines, if using. Transfer paste to a small bowl.

Serve with a selection of raw vegetables. Store in a covered jar in the refrigerator for several weeks.

Serves 6-8.

SPICY FISH SAUCE

2 cloves garlic
2 small red or green chillies, seeded and chopped
1 tablespoon sugar
2 tablespoons lime juice
2 tablespoons fish sauce

Using a pestle and mortar, pound garlic and chillies until finely ground. If you do not have a pestle and mortar, just finely mince garlic and chillies.

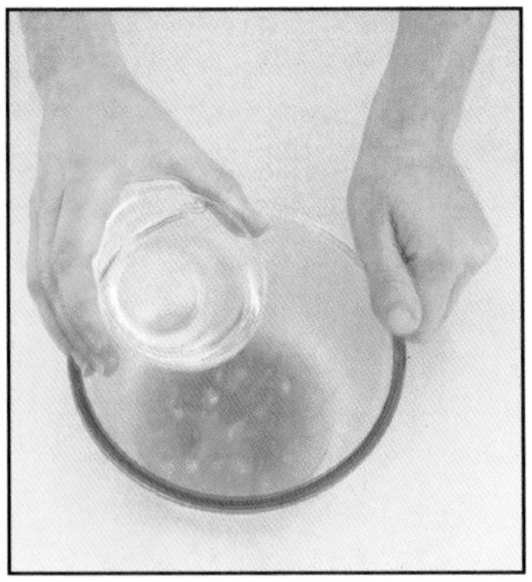

Place mixture in a bowl and add sugar, lime juice, fish sauce and 2-3 tablespoons water. Blend well. Serve in small dipping saucers.

Serves 4.

Note: This sauce is known as nuoc cham. You can make a large quantity of the base for later use by boiling lime juice, fish sauce and water with sugar in a pan. It will keep for months in a tightly sealed jar or bottle in the refrigerator. Add freshly minced garlic and chillies for serving.

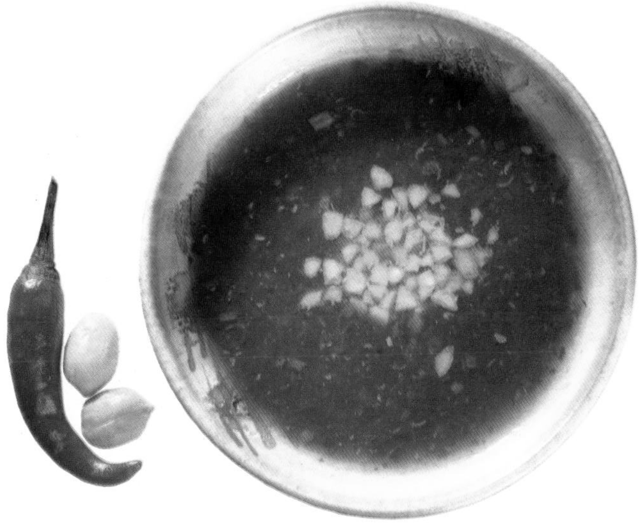

VEGETARIAN DIPPING SAUCE

1 tablespoon sugar
2 tablespoons chilli sauce
2-3 tablespoons water
1 small red or green chilli, seeded and chopped
1 tablespoon roasted peanuts, coarsely chopped

In a small bowl, mix sugar with chilli sauce and water.

Add chopped chilli and transfer sauce to 4 individual saucers to serve. Sprinkle chopped peanuts over the top as a garnish.

Serves 4.

Note: This sauce is known as nuoc leo. The liquid base can be made in advance; add freshly chopped chilli and peanuts just before serving.

SWEET & SOUR SAUCE

2 tablespoons vegetable oil
1 clove garlic, chopped
2 shallots or ½ onion, chopped
1 teaspoon chilli sauce
2 tablespoons tomato ketchup
2 tablespoons soy sauce
i tablespoon fish sauce
2 tablespoons sugar
2 tablespoons red rice vinegar
about 115 ml (4 fl oz/½ cup) chicken stock
2 tablespoons cornflour

Heat oil in a medium saucepan and gently stir-fry garlic and shallots or onion until golden but not brown.

Add chilli sauce, tomato ketchup, soy and fish sauces, sugar and vinegar. Stir to blend well, then add stock and bring to the boil, stirring continuously.

Taste sauce to check sweet and sour balance and adjust seasoning if necessary. Mix cornflour with 2-3 tablespoons water and add to sauce, stirring until smooth, then remove from heat and serve.

Makes about 450 ml (16 fl oz/2 cups).

Note: This sauce is traditionally used for fried or grilled dishes, or it can be used as a dip at table.

VIETNAMESE HOT SAUCE

1 clove garlic, chopped
2 small red or green chillies, seeded and chopped
1 teaspoon finely chopped fresh root ginger
1 tablespoon chilli sauce
2 stalks lemon grass, peeled and chopped
2 tablespoons vegetable oil
2 tablespoons soy sauce
1 tablespoon fish sauce
2 tablespoons sugar
2 tablespoons lime juice with pulp
4-6 tablespoons chicken stock or water
2 tablespoons chopped coriander leaves
1 tablespoon cornflour

Using a pestle and mortar, pound garlic, chillies, ginger, chilli sauce and lemon grass to a paste. Heat oil in a medium saucepan and gently stir-fry paste with soy sauce, fish sauce, sugar, lime juice and stock or water, then bring to the boil.

Blend in chopped coriander. Mix cornflour with 2 tablespoons water and stir paste into sauce to thicken it. Remove from heat and serve.

Makes about 350 ml (12 fl oz/1½ cups).

Note: This highly spiced sauce goes well with all sorts of meat or fish dishes – it can form the base for curry sauce, or it can be served as a dip.

DESSERTS

FRITTERS & FRAGRANT SYRUP

450 g (1 lb/2 cups) caster sugar
5 green cardamom pods, bruised
1 teaspoon rose water
pinch saffron threads
115 g (4 oz/1 cup) plain flour
1 tablespoon baking powder
175 g (6 oz/2½ cups) low-fat milk powder
15 g (½ oz/1 tablespoon) butter, melted
150 ml (5 fl oz/⅔ cup) natural yogurt
about 115 ml (4 fl oz/½ cup) milk
55 g (2 oz/⅓ cup) raisins
vegetable oil for frying
rose petals, to decorate (optional)

Put sugar and 450 ml (16 fl oz/2 cups) water in a heavy-based pan and heat gently, stirring occasionally, until sugar dissolves. Bring to the boil, then boil for about 5 minutes or until thickened and syrupy. Stir in cardamom pods, rose water and saffron threads and keep warm. Meanwhile, sift flour and baking powder together into a mixing bowl and stir in milk powder. Mix in butter and yogurt and enough milk to make a soft dough.

With floured hands, divide dough into 24 pieces. Make a depression in centre of each and press in 2 or 3 raisins. Cover raisins with dough and roll into balls. Half-fill a deep-fat pan or fryer with oil and heat to 190C (375F). Fry 4 or 5 balls at a time, for 3-5 minutes, until a deep golden brown. Drain on absorbent kitchen paper, then add to syrup. Serve hot, decorated with rose petals, if wished.

Serves 4-6.

CARDAMOM & NUT ICE CREAM

2 litres (3½ pints/8 cups) milk
12 green cardamom pods, bruised
85 g (3 oz/⅓ cup) caster sugar
45 g (1½ oz/⅓ cup) chopped blanched almonds, toasted
45 g (1½ oz/⅓ cup) chopped pistachio nuts
mint sprigs, to decorate

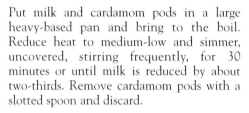

Put milk and cardamom pods in a large heavy-based pan and bring to the boil. Reduce heat to medium-low and simmer, uncovered, stirring frequently, for 30 minutes or until milk is reduced by about two-thirds. Remove cardamom pods with a slotted spoon and discard.

Stir in sugar, almonds and half the pistachio nuts and simmer for 5 minutes more. Leave to cool. Pour reduced milk into a plastic container, cover and freeze for 2-3 hours, until frozen around edge. Spoon into a food processor fitted with a metal blade and process, or whisk with an electric hand whisk, until smooth and light. Return to container, cover and freeze for 1 hour. Meanwhile, put 6 individual 175 ml (6 fl oz/¾ cup) moulds into freezer to chill.

Spoon semi-frozen mixture into moulds, pressing down firmly. Cover and freeze for 2-3 hours, until solid. To serve, dip moulds in hot water for a few seconds and turn out onto plates. Serve at once, sprinkled with remaining pistachio nuts and decorated with mint sprigs.

Serves 6.

SAFFRON YOGURT

550 ml (20 fl oz/2½ cups) natural yogurt
pinch saffron threads
2 tablespoons boiling water
seeds from 6 cardamom pods
3 tablespoons caster sugar
lemon zest and cardamom seeds, to decorate

Pour yogurt into a nylon sieve lined with muslin and leave in refrigerator overnight to drain.

Put saffron and water in a small bowl and leave to soak for 30 minutes. Tip drained yogurt into a bowl and stir in saffron and its soaking liquid.

Put cardamom seeds in a mortar and crush lightly with a pestle. Stir into yogurt with sugar. Serve chilled, decorated with lemon zest and cardamom seeds.

Serves 4-6.

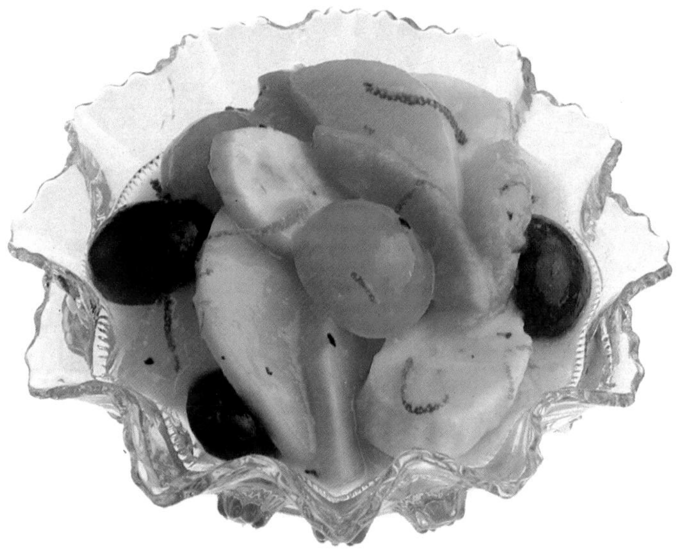

INDIAN FRUIT SALAD

2 mangoes
2 bananas
2 oranges
55 g (2 oz) black grapes
55 g (2 oz) green grapes
1 papaya
grated zest and juice 1 lime
55 g (2 oz/¼ cup) caster sugar
freshly ground black pepper
natural yogurt, to serve

Peel and stone mangoes and cut flesh into thin slices, reserving any scraps. Peel and diagonally slice bananas.

Peel and segment oranges, working over a bowl to catch juices. Halve and pip both black and green grapes. Peel and halve papaya, scoop out seeds and cut flesh into slices, reserving any scraps. Put fruit in a serving bowl and stir to combine.

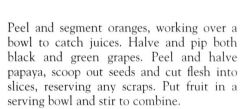

Put orange juice, lime juice, sugar and scraps of mango and papaya in a blender or food processor fitted with a metal blade and process until smooth. Add lime zest and pepper. Pour over fruit and chill for at least 1 hour before serving with yogurt.

Serves 4-6.

Variation: Use other fruits, such as melon, guava or pineapple, if preferred.

GOLDEN SEMOLINA PUDDING

115 g (4 oz/½ cup) caster sugar
45 g (1½ oz/3 tablespoons) butter or ghee
115 g (4 oz/¾ cup) semolina
seeds from 3 cardamom pods
25 g (1 oz/2½ tablespoons) raisins
55 g (2 oz/⅓ cup) flaked almonds, toasted
natural yogurt, to serve (optional)

Put sugar in a heavy-based saucepan with 150 ml (5 fl oz/⅔ cup) water. Cook over a low heat, stirring occasionally, until sugar has dissolved. Bring to the boil and boil for 1 minute, then remove from heat and set aside.

Melt butter or ghee in a large heavy-based frying pan, add semolina and cook for 8-10 minutes over a medium heat, stirring constantly, until semolina turns golden brown.

Remove from heat and leave to cool slightly, then stir in sugar syrup and cardamom seeds. Cook over a low heat for 3-5 minutes, stirring frequently, until thick. Stir in half the raisins and almonds. Serve warm, decorated with remaining raisins and almonds, and with natural yogurt, if wished.

Serves 4-6.

COCONUT LAYER CAKE

55 g (2 oz/½ cup) plain flour
400 ml (14 fl oz/1¾ cups) coconut milk (see page 224)
6 egg yolks, beaten
115 g (4 oz/½ cup) caster sugar
seeds from 4 green cardamom pods, crushed
pinch freshly grated nutmeg
115 g (4 oz/½ cup) butter, melted
natural yogurt and slices banana, to serve

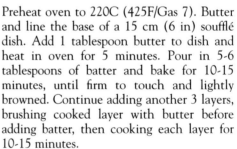

Put flour in a mixing bowl, whisk in coconut milk, egg yolks, sugar, cardamom seeds and nutmeg, then leave batter to stand for 30 minutes.

Preheat oven to 220C (425F/Gas 7). Butter and line the base of a 15 cm (6 in) soufflé dish. Add 1 tablespoon butter to dish and heat in oven for 5 minutes. Pour in 5-6 tablespoons of batter and bake for 10-15 minutes, until firm to touch and lightly browned. Continue adding another 3 layers, brushing cooked layer with butter before adding batter, then cooking each layer for 10-15 minutes.

Put soufflé dish in a roasting tin half-filled with boiling water, then continue adding final 3 layers in same way as before. When last layer is cooked, remove dish from oven and leave to cool. Run a knife around edge of dish to loosen cake and turn out onto a serving plate. Serve warm, with yogurt and sliced bananas.

Serves 4-6.

APRICOT DESSERT

225 g (8 oz) ready-to-eat dried apricots
225 g (8 oz/1 cup) caster sugar
225 ml (8 fl oz/1 cup) whipping cream
55 g (2 oz/⅓ cup) blanched almonds, chopped and toasted

Put apricots in a saucepan with 225 ml (8 fl oz/1 cup) water and bring to the boil, then simmer, covered, for about 25 minutes or until very soft.

Meanwhile, put sugar and 450 ml (16 fl oz/2 cups) water in a heavy-based saucepan and heat gently, stirring occasionally, until sugar has dissolved. Bring to the boil and boil for 3 minutes or until syrupy. Drain apricots and purée in a blender or food processor fitted with a metal blade. Add syrup and process again.

Pour mixture into a bowl and leave to cool, then chill for at least 1 hour. Whip cream until holding soft peaks, fold half into apricot purée, leaving it slightly marbled, and spoon into serving dishes. Chill for 30 minutes, then top with remaining cream and scatter with chopped almonds.

Serves 4-6.

PISTACHIO HALVA

175 g (6 oz/1⅓ cups) shelled pistachio nuts
225 ml (8 fl oz/1 cup) boiling water
2 tablespoons milk
115 g (4 oz/½ cup) sugar
25 g (1 oz/2 tablespoons) butter or ghee
few drops vanilla essence

Put pistachio nuts in a bowl, pour over boiling water and leave to soak for 30 minutes. Grease and line the base of an 18 cm (7 in) square tin.

Drain pistachio nuts thoroughly and put in a blender or food processor fitted with a metal blade. Add milk and process until finely chopped, scraping mixture down from sides once or twice. Stir in sugar. Heat a large non-stick frying pan, add butter or ghee and melt over a low to medium heat. Add nut paste and cook for about 15 minutes, stirring constantly, until mixture is very thick.

Stir in vanilla essence, then spoon into prepared tin and spread evenly. Leave to cool completely, then cut into 20 squares using a sharp knife.

Makes about 20 squares.

Note: This halva will keep for 2-3 weeks, stored in the refrigerator.

TOASTED ALMOND TOFFEE

450 g (1 lb/2 cups) sugar
150 g (5 oz/2 cups) low-fat milk powder
few drops vanilla essence
25 g (1 oz/¼ cup) flaked almonds, toasted

Grease and line the base of an 18 cm (7 in) square tin. Put sugar in a large heavy-based saucepan with 225 ml (8 fl oz/1 cup) water and heat gently, stirring occasionally, until sugar is dissolved.

Bring to the boil, then boil over a medium-high heat until a few drops of mixture will form a soft ball in cold water. Stir in milk powder and cook for 3-4 minutes more, stirring constantly, until mixture begins to dry on spoon. Stir in vanilla.

Pour into prepared tin and spread evenly. Scatter almonds over top and press into surface. Leave to cool slightly, then cut into 25 squares with a sharp knife while still warm. Leave in tin until cold and firm.

Makes 25 squares.

CASHEW NUT FUDGE

225 g (8 oz/1½ cups) unsalted cashew nuts
350 ml (12 fl oz/1½ cups) boiling water
2 tablespoons milk
150 g (5 oz/⅔ cup) sugar
15 g (½ oz/1 tablespoon) butter or ghee
few drops vanilla essence
few sheets silver leaf (see page 161)

Put cashew nuts in a bowl, pour over boiling water and leave to soak for 1 hour. Grease and line the base of an 18 cm (7 in) square tin.

Drain cashew nuts thoroughly and put in a blender or food processor fitted with a metal blade. Add milk and process until smooth, scraping mixture down from sides once or twice. Stir in sugar. Heat a large non-stick frying pan, add butter or ghee and melt over a low to medium heat. Add nut paste and cook for about 20 minutes, stirring constantly, until mixture is very thick.

Stir in vanilla essence, then spoon into prepared tin and spread evenly. Leave to cool completely, then press silver leaf onto surface. Cut fudge into about 25 diamond shapes using a wet sharp knife.

Makes about 25 pieces.

Note: This fudge will keep for 2-3 weeks if stored in an airtight tin.

PEKING APPLES

1 egg, beaten
115 g (4 oz/1 cup) plain flour
4 crisp eating apples
SYRUP:
1 tablespoon vegetable oil
6 tablespoons brown sugar
2 tablespoons golden syrup
iced water to set

In a large bowl, stir egg and 115 ml (4 fl oz/½ cup) water into flour to make a thick batter. Peel, core and thickly slice apples. Dip each apple slice in batter to evenly coat; allow excess to drain off.

In a wok, heat oil until smoking. Add apple pieces in batches and deep-fry for 3 minutes until golden brown. Using a slotted spoon, remove to absorbent kitchen paper to drain.

To make syrup, in a small saucepan, gently heat oil, sugar and 2 tablespoons water, stirring until sugar has dissolved. Simmer for 5 minutes, stirring. Stir in golden syrup and boil for 5-10 minutes until hard and stringy. Reduce heat to very low. Dip each piece of apple into syrup to coat then place in ice cold water for a few seconds to set syrup. Remove to a serving dish. Repeat with remaining apple. Serve immediately.

Serves 4.

CHINESE FRUIT SOUP

115 ml (4 fl oz/½ cup) rice wine or dry sherry
juice and zest 2 limes
800 ml (1½ pints/3½ cups) water
225 g (8 oz/1 cup) granulated sugar
1 piece lemon grass
4 whole cloves
5 cm (2 in) stick cinnamon
1 vanilla pod, split
pinch ground nutmeg
1 teaspoon coriander seeds, lightly crushed
45 g (1½ oz) piece fresh root ginger, peeled and thinly sliced
25 g (1 oz/2½ tablespoons) raisins
450 g (1 lb) prepared sweet fruits, e.g. mango, strawberries, lychees, star fruit, kiwi fruit

In a saucepan, place rice wine or dry sherry, lime juice and zest, water, sugar, lemon grass, cloves, cinnamon, vanilla, nutmeg, coriander seeds and ginger. Heat gently, stirring until sugar dissolves, then bring to the boil. Reduce heat and simmer for 5 minutes. Leave to cool, then strain into a bowl. Add raisins then chill.

Arrange a selection of prepared fruit in 4 individual serving dishes and spoon over syrup.

Serves 4.

GREEN TEA FRUIT SALAD

4 teaspoons jasmine tea leaves
2 tablespoons dry sherry
2 tablespoons sugar
1 lime
2 kiwi fruit
225 g (8 oz) fresh lychees
¼ honeydew melon
115 g (4 oz) seedless green grapes
lime slices, to decorate

Place tea leaves in a small bowl and add 300 ml (10 fl oz/1¼ cups) boiling water. Leave to steep for 5 minutes. Strain through a sieve into a saucepan.

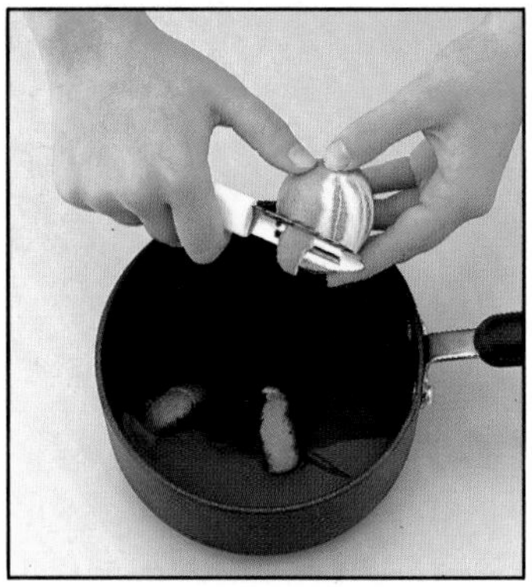

Stir in sherry and sugar. Using a vegetable peeler, pare zest from lime and add to pan. Squeeze juice from lime and add juice to pan. Bring to the boil, reduce heat and simmer for 5 minutes. Leave to cool, then discard lime zest.

Peel and thinly slice kiwi fruit. Peel, halve and stone lychees. Peel melon and slice thinly. Arrange prepared fruits and grapes in small clusters on serving plates. Spoon cooled tea syrup over fruit, decorate and serve.

Serves 4.

CARAMEL SESAME BANANAS

4 bananas
juice 1 lemon
115 g (4 oz/½ cup) sugar
2 tablespoons sesame seeds
mint sprigs and lemon slices, to decorate

Peel bananas and cut into 5 cm (2 in) pieces. Place in a bowl, add lemon juice and stir to coat.

Place sugar and 55 ml (2 fl oz/¼ cup) water in a saucepan and heat gently, stirring, until sugar dissolves. Bring to the boil and cook for 5-6 minutes or until mixture caramelizes and turns golden brown. Drain bananas well and arrange on non-stick baking parchment.

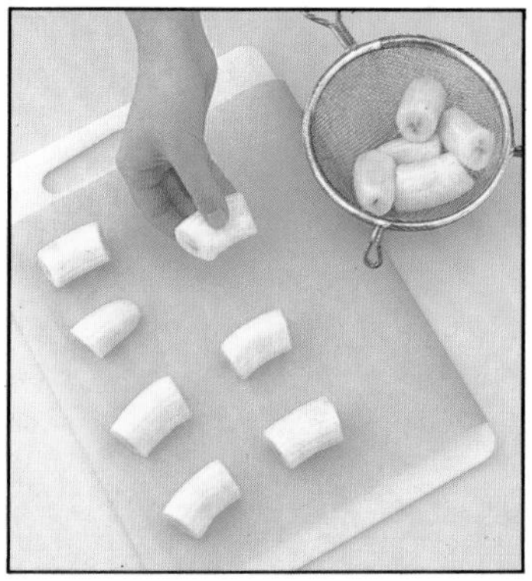

Drizzle caramel over bananas, working quickly as caramel sets within a few seconds. Sprinkle with sesame seeds. Leave to cool for 5 minutes, then carefully peel away from paper, decorate and serve.

Serves 4.

Note: Tossing banana in lemon juice prevents it from turning brown.

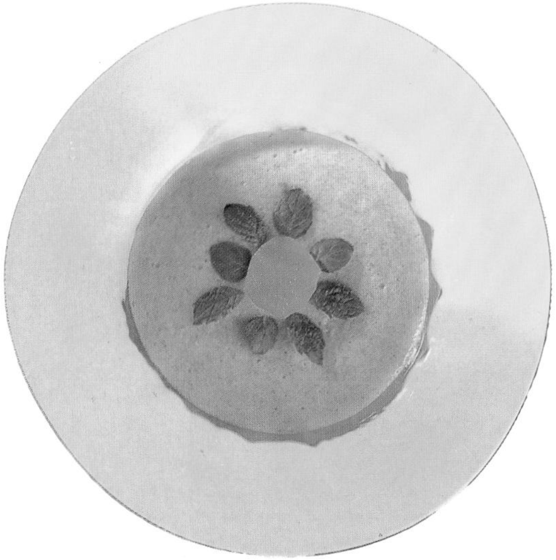

LYCHEE & GINGER MOUSSE

350 g (12 oz) fresh lychees, peeled and pitted
½ teaspoon ground ginger
3 tablespoons sweet sherry
2 pieces stem ginger in syrup, chopped
25 g (1 oz/¼ cup) ground almonds
2 teaspoons powdered gelatine dissolved in 2 tablespoons boiling water
2 egg whites
sliced stem ginger and mint leaves, to decorate

Put lychees in a food processor with ground ginger, sherry and chopped ginger. Blend until smooth. Transfer to a small bowl and stir in ground almonds and gelatine mixture.

Chill for 30-40 minutes or until beginning to set. In a large, grease-free bowl, whisk egg whites until very stiff. Using a large metal spoon, carefully fold in lychee mixture.

Divide mixture among 4 sundae glasses or dishes and chill for 1 hour or until set. Decorate with stem ginger and mint leaves and serve.

Serves 4.

FRUIT-FILLED WHITE CRÊPES

3 egg whites, lightly beaten
25 g (1 oz/¼ cup) cornflour
1 teaspoon sunflower oil
mint sprigs, to decorate
FILLING:
4 slices fresh pineapple, chopped
2 kiwi fruit, peeled and quartered
½ mango, peeled, pitted and sliced
½ papaya, peeled, seeded and chopped
2 tablespoons dry sherry
1 tablespoon brown sugar
1 whole cinnamon stick, broken
2 star anise

Place all filling ingredients in a wok and mix gently. Bring to the boil, reduce heat and simmer very gently for 10 minutes. Remove and discard cinnamon stick and star anise. Set aside. Meanwhile, make crêpes. Put egg whites and cornflour in a bowl and stir in 3 tablespoons of water, mixing well to form a smooth paste.

Brush a non-stick or well-seasoned crêpe pan with a little oil and heat. Pour in a quarter of the mixture, tilting pan to cover the bottom. Cook for 1 minute on one side only, until set. Drain on absorbent kitchen paper, layer with greaseproof paper and keep warm while making remaining 3 crêpes. Lay crêpes cooked-side up, fill with fruit and fold crêpes over filling. Decorate and serve.

Serves 4.

STUFFED RAMBUTANS

1 small banana, chopped
grated zest and juice 1 lime
16 rambutans
12 stoned dates, chopped
1 papaya, peeled, seeded and chopped
strips lime zest, to decorate

Mix banana with lime zest and juice and set aside. Slice top off rambutans, exposing tip of stone. Using a sharp, small-bladed knife, carefully slice down around stone, loosening flesh away from stone.

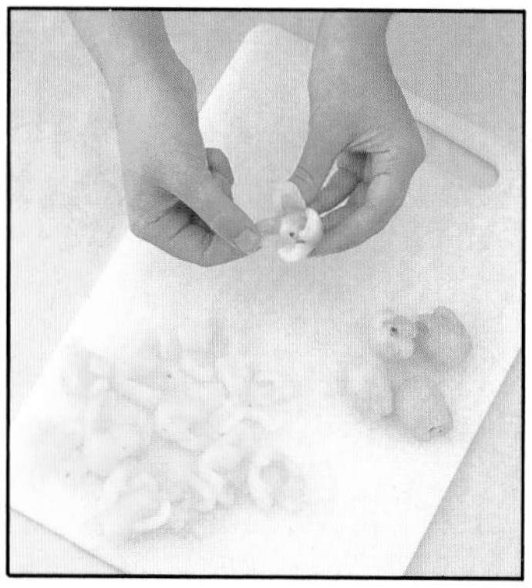

Peel away skin, and slice lengthways through flesh at quarterly intervals. Gently pull down flesh to expose stone and carefully cut away stone. The flesh should now resemble a four-petalled flower.

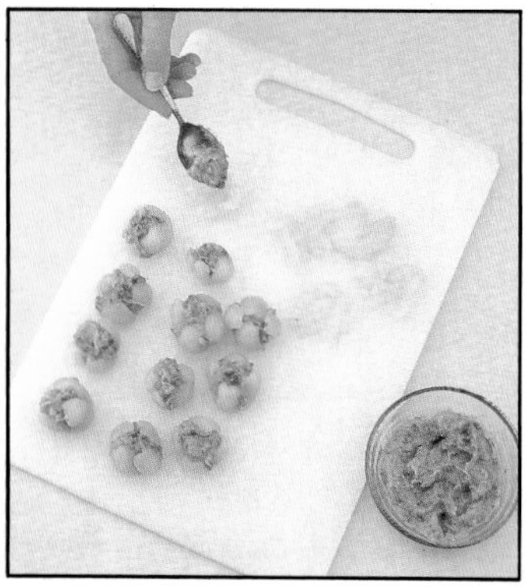

In a food processor or blender, blend banana and dates until smooth. Place a teaspoon of filling in the centre of each rambutan and bring up sides to enclose filling. Cover and chill for 30 minutes. Blend papaya in a food processor or blender until smooth, pass through a sieve and spoon onto 4 serving plates. Top with rambutans, decorate with strips of lime zest and serve.

Serves 4.

STEAMED FRUIT DUMPLINGS

1 small banana, chopped
grated zest and juice 1 small lemon
25 g (1 oz) dried mango or dried apricots, chopped
8 stoned dates, chopped
25 g (1 oz/¼ cup) ground almonds
large pinch ground cinnamon
12 round won ton skins
1 egg white, lightly beaten
2 teaspoons icing sugar
strips dried mango and date and mint sprigs, to decorate

Place banana, lemon zest and juice, mango, dates, almonds and cinnamon in a food processor and blend until smooth.

Divide fruit mixture among won ton skins, placing it in the centre of each one. Brush edges of won ton skins with egg white, fold in half to form crescent shapes and press edges together to seal.

Bring a wok or large saucepan of water to the boil. Place dumplings on a sheet of non-stick baking parchment in a steamer and place over water. Cover and steam for 10 minutes or until soft. Dust with icing sugar, decorate and serve.

Serves 4.

COCONUT CUSTARDS

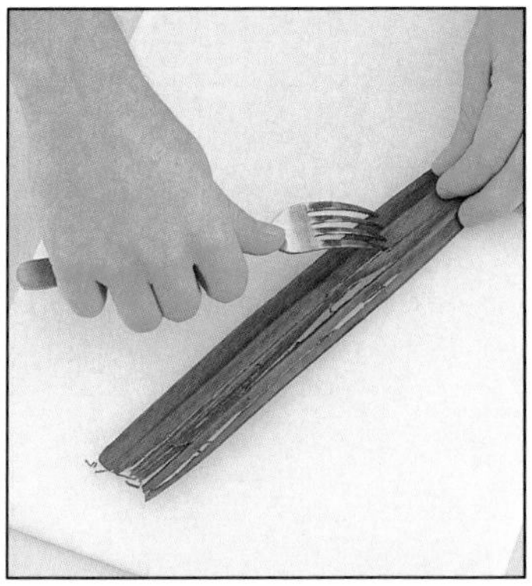

1 pandan leaf (optional)
550 ml (20 fl oz/2½ cups) coconut milk
3 whole eggs
3 egg yolks
about 85 g (3 oz/⅓ cup) caster sugar
115 ml (4 fl oz/½ cup) single cream

Run tines of a fork through pandan leaf, if using. Tie in a knot. Pour coconut milk into a non-stick saucepan, add pandan leaf and bring to just below a simmer. Remove from heat, cover and leave for 20 minutes. Discard pandan leaf.

Preheat oven to 180C (350F/Gas 4). Reheat (or heat) coconut milk to the boil. In a bowl, whisk together eggs, egg yolks and sugar until evenly blended. Slowly pour in coconut milk, whisking constantly. Stir in cream.

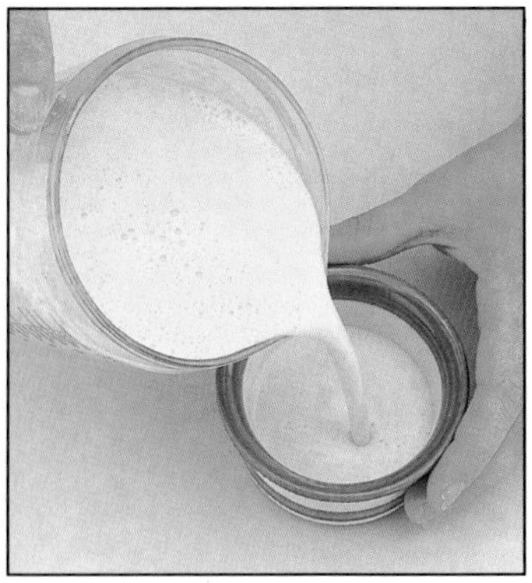

Strain into a jug and pour into 8 ramekin dishes. Set ramekins in a roasting tin and pour boiling water into tin to come halfway up sides of ramekins. Cook in the oven for 20-25 minutes until a skewer inserted in the centre comes out clean. Remove ramekins from tin and leave to cool. Chill until required.

Serves 8.

PINEAPPLE WITH COCONUT

100 g (3½ oz/½ cup) caster sugar
3.5 cm (1½ in) piece fresh root ginger, grated
100 g (3½ oz/½ cup) light brown sugar
12 thin slices fresh pineapple
3-4 tablespoons toasted coconut flakes

Put caster sugar, ginger and light brown sugar in a heavy-based saucepan. Stir in 375 ml (13 fl oz/1⅔ cups) water. Heat gently, stirring with a wooden spoon, until sugars have melted. Bring to the boil. Simmer until reduced by about one third.

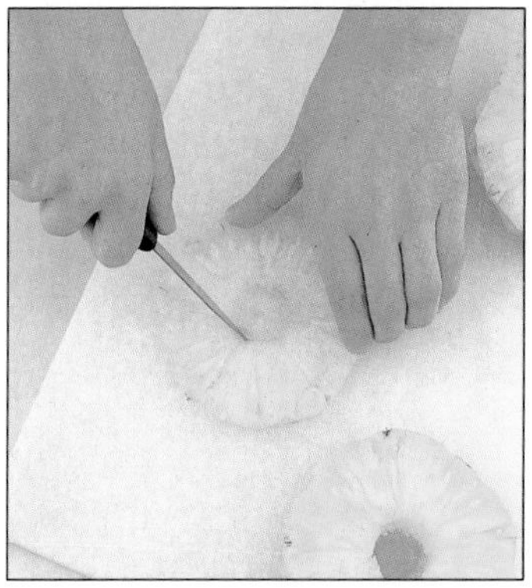

Remove cores from slices of pineapple using a small sharp knife or a small pastry cutter. Strain syrup over pineapple rings and leave to cool. Cover and chill.

To serve, lay 2 pineapple rings on each plate. Spoon some of the syrup over and scatter toasted coconut flakes on top.

Serves 6.

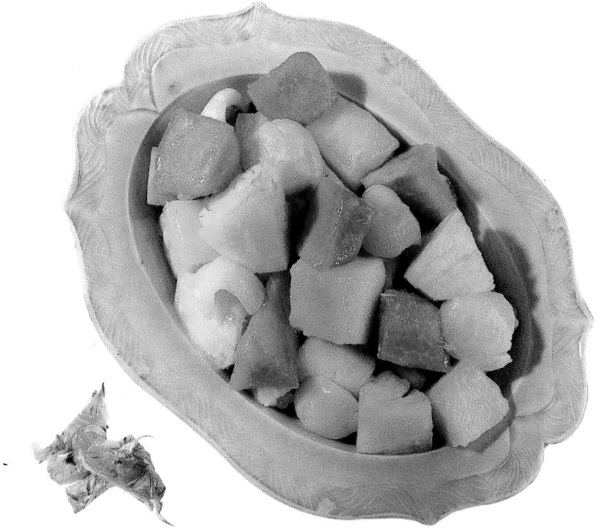

MALAYSIAN FRUIT SALAD

55 g (2 oz/⅓ cup) light brown sugar
grated zest and juice 1 lime
1 small pineapple, peeled, cored and cubed
700 g (1½ lb) lychees, peeled, halved and stoned
3 ripe mangoes, peeled, stoned and chopped
1 papaya, peeled, seeded and chopped

Put sugar, lime zest and juice and 150 ml (5 fl oz/⅔ cup) water in a saucepan. Heat gently, stirring with a wooden spoon, until sugar has dissolved.

Heat syrup to boiling point then simmer for 1 minute. Remove from heat and leave to cool.

Put pineapple, lychees, mangoes and papaya in a serving dish. Pour over cool syrup. Cover dish with cling film and put in the refrigerator to chill.

Serves 4.

SAGO PUDDING

450 ml (16 fl oz/2 cups) milk or water
175 g (6 oz) sago, rinsed
350 ml (12 fl oz/1½ cups) coconut milk
55 ml (2 fl oz/¼ cup) single cream
SYRUP:
150 g (5 oz/¾ cup) palm sugar or brown sugar
small piece fresh root ginger or lemon grass
1 pandan leaf (optional)

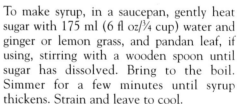

In a saucepan, bring milk or water to the boil. Add sago, stir and simmer for 10-15 minutes, stirring occasionally, until tender. Cool slightly and spoon into individual glass dishes. Cool completely then refrigerate.

To make syrup, in a saucepan, gently heat sugar with 175 ml (6 fl oz/¾ cup) water and ginger or lemon grass, and pandan leaf, if using, stirring with a wooden spoon until sugar has dissolved. Bring to the boil. Simmer for a few minutes until syrup thickens. Strain and leave to cool.

Mix together coconut milk and cream, then chill. To serve, pour creamy coconut milk around edges of sago puddings. Make a well in the centre of the puddings and pour in some of the syrup.

Serves 6.

MANGO WITH STICKY RICE

225 g (8 oz/1¼ cups) sticky rice, soaked overnight in cold water
250 ml (8 fl oz/1 cup) coconut milk
pinch salt
2-4 tablespoons sugar, to taste
2 large ripe mangoes, peeled and halved
3 tablespoons coconut cream (see page 8)
mint leaves to decorate

Drain and rinse rice thoroughly. Place in a steaming basket lined with a double thickness of muslin. Steam over simmering water for 30 minutes. Remove from heat.

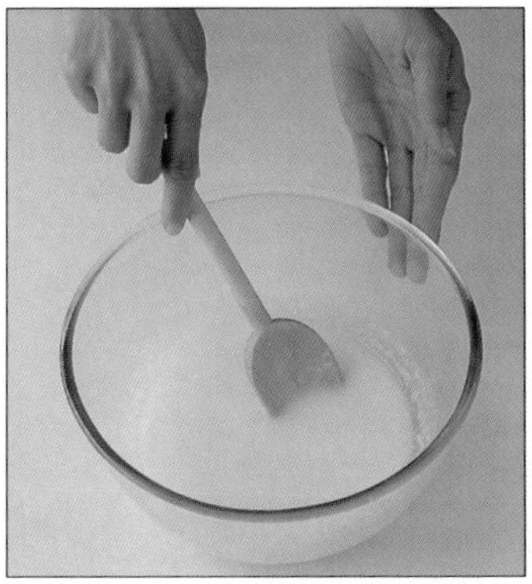

In a bowl, stir together coconut milk, salt and sugar to taste until sugar has dissolved. Stir in warm rice. Set aside for 30 minutes.

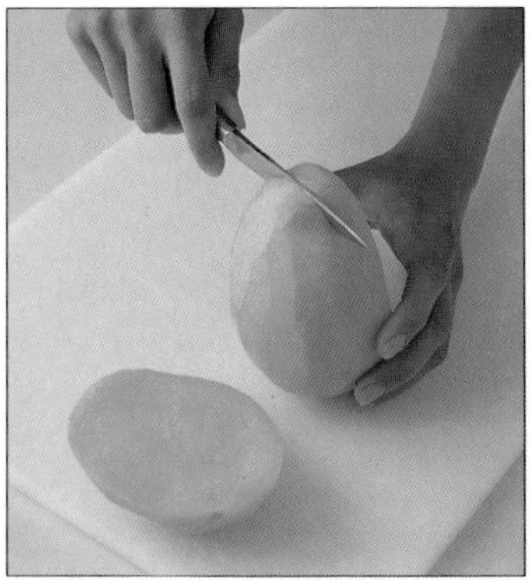

Thinly slice mangoes by cutting lengthways through flesh to the stone. Discard stones. Spoon rice into a mound in centre of serving plates and arrange mango slices around. Pour coconut cream over rice. Decorate with mint leaves.

Serves 4.

COCONUT PANCAKES

115 g (4 oz/⅔ cup) rice flour
85 g (3 oz/⅓ cup) caster sugar
pinch salt
85 g (3 oz/1 cup) desiccated coconut
2 eggs, beaten
550 ml (20 fl oz/2½ cups) coconut milk
green and red food colouring (optional)
vegetable oil for frying
mandarin segments, to serve (optional)

In a bowl, stir together rice flour, sugar, salt and coconut.

Form a well in the centre, add egg, then gradually fold in flour, slowly pouring in coconut milk at same time, to make a smooth batter. If desired, divide batter evenly between 3 bowls; stir green food colouring into one bowl to colour batter pale green; colour another batch pink and leave remaining batch plain. Heat a 15 cm (6 in) crêpe or omelette pan over a moderate heat, swirl around a little oil, then pour off excess. Stir batter well, then add 2-3 spoonfuls to pan.

Rotate to cover base, then cook over moderate heat for about 4 minutes until lightly browned underneath and quite firmly set. Carefully turn over and cook briefly on other side. Transfer to a warmed plate and keep warm while cooking remaining batter. Serve rolled up with mandarin segments, if wished.

Makes about 10 pancakes.

Note: The mixture is quite delicate and the first few pancakes may be troublesome.

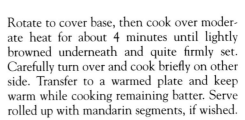

GREEN & WHITE JELLIES

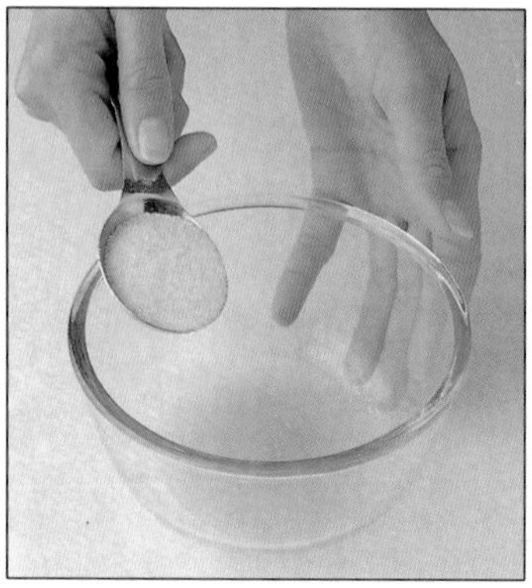

1 tablespoon powdered gelatine
200 ml (7 fl oz/scant 1 cup) coconut milk
5 tablespoons caster sugar
85 ml (3 fl oz/⅓ cup) coconut cream (see page 8)
2 pieces pandanus leaf, each 7.5 cm (3 in) long, or ¾-1 teaspoon kewra water
green food colouring

Sprinkle 1½ teaspoons gelatine over 1½ tablespoons water in a small bowl and leave to soften for 5 minutes. Stand bowl in a small saucepan of hot water and stir until dissolved. Remove from heat.

Put coconut milk and half the sugar into a medium saucepan and heat gently, stirring until sugar has dissolved. Remove from heat and stir in coconut cream.

Stir a little into dissolved gelatine, then stir back into medium pan. Divide between 4 or 6 individual moulds. Place in refrigerator to set.

Put remaining sugar in a medium saucepan with 300 ml (10 fl oz/1¼ cups) water and pandanus leaf or kewra water. Heat gently, stirring, until sugar dissolves. Bring to the boil, simmer for 2-3 minutes, cover and remove from the heat. Set aside for 15 minutes, then remove pandanus leaf, if used.

Dissolve remaining gelatine in the same way as first half. Stir in a little pandanus liquid, then stir back into medium pan. Add green food colouring to colour.

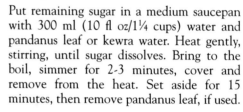

Set aside until cold but not set, then pour over set coconut mixture. Place in refrigerator to set. Dip moulds into hot water for 1-2 seconds, then turn out onto cold plates.

Serves 4-6.

Note: If pandanus leaf or kewra water are unavailable, flavour with rose water and colour pink with red food colouring to make Pink & White Jellies.

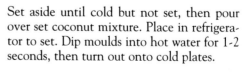

LYCHEES & COCONUT CUSTARD

3 egg yolks
3-4 tablespoons caster sugar
200 ml (7 fl oz/scant 1 cup) coconut milk
85 ml (3 fl oz/⅓ cup) coconut cream (see page 8)
about 1 tablespoon triple-distilled rose water
red food colouring
about 16 fresh lychees, peeled, halved and stoned
rose petals, to decorate

In a bowl, whisk together egg yolks and sugar.

In a medium non-stick saucepan, heat coconut milk to just below boiling point, then slowly stir into eggs yolk and sugar mixture. Return to pan and cook very gently, stirring with a wooden spoon, until custard coats the back of the spoon.

Remove from heat and stir in coconut cream, rose water to taste and sufficient red food colouring to colour pale pink. Leave until cold, stirring occasionally. Spoon a thin layer of rose-flavoured custard into 4 small serving bowls. Arrange lychees on custard. Decorate with rose petals. Serve remaining custard separately to pour over lychees.

Serves 4.

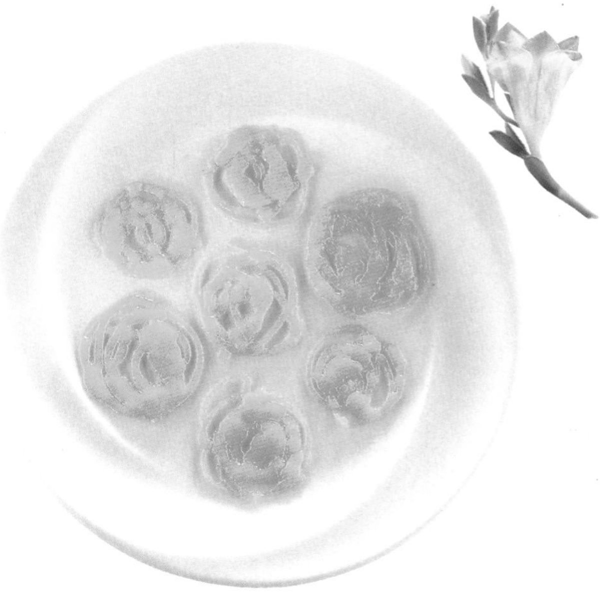

GOLDEN THREADS

6 egg yolks
1 teaspoon egg white
450 g (1 lb/2 cups) sugar
few drops jasmine essence

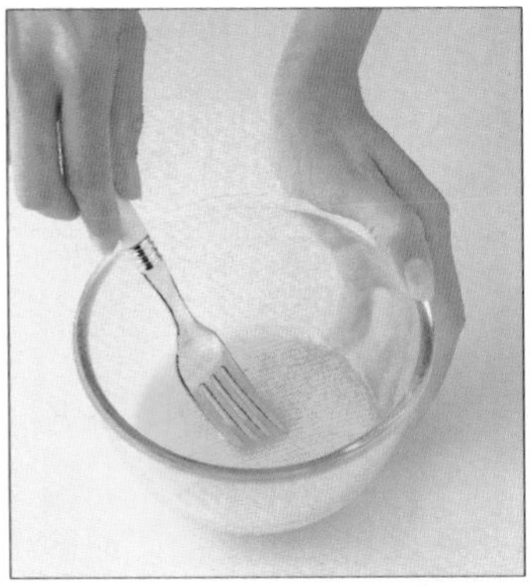

Strain egg yolks through muslin into a small bowl. Beat lightly with egg white. In a saucepan, gently heat sugar, jasmine essence and 250 ml (8 fl oz/1 cup) water, stirring until sugar dissolves, then boil until thickened slightly. Adjust heat so syrup is hot but not moving.

Spoon a small amount of egg yolk into a piping bag fitted with a very fine nozzle or a cone of nonstick baking parchment with very small hole in pointed end. Using a circular movement, carefully dribble a trail into syrup, making swirls about 4-5 cm (1½-2 in) in diameter with a small hole in centre. Make a few at a time, cooking each briefly until set.

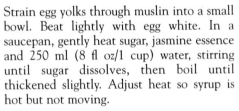

Using a skewer inserted in hole in centre of spiral, transfer each nest to a plate. Continue making similar nests with remaining egg yolks. When nests are cool, arrange on a serving plate.

Serves 4.

LYCHEE SORBET

450 g (1 lb) fresh lychees in their shells or 175 g (6 oz) canned lychees
about 115 ml (4 fl oz/½ cup) syrup (see opposite)
fresh mint sprigs, to decorate

Peel fresh lychees and stone them. Place lychees in a food processor or blender with syrup and process to a smooth purée.

Pour purée into a freezerproof container and place in the freezer for about 2 hours until almost set.

Break up iced mixture and whip until smooth. Return mixture to the freezer for 30-45 minutes to set until solid. Serve sorbet decorated with mint leaves.

Serves 4-6.

Variation: 2 teaspoons grated fresh root ginger can be added to sorbet mixture before blending, if wished.

VIETNAMESE FRUIT SALAD

115 g (4 oz/⅔ cup) rock candy or crystal sugar
about 350 ml (12 fl oz/1½ cups) boiling water
½ small watermelon or a whole honeydew melon
4-5 different fruits (fresh or canned), such as pineapple, grapes, lychees, rambutan, banana, papaya, mango or kiwi fruit
crushed ice cubes

Make a syrup by dissolving rock candy in boiling water, then leave to cool.

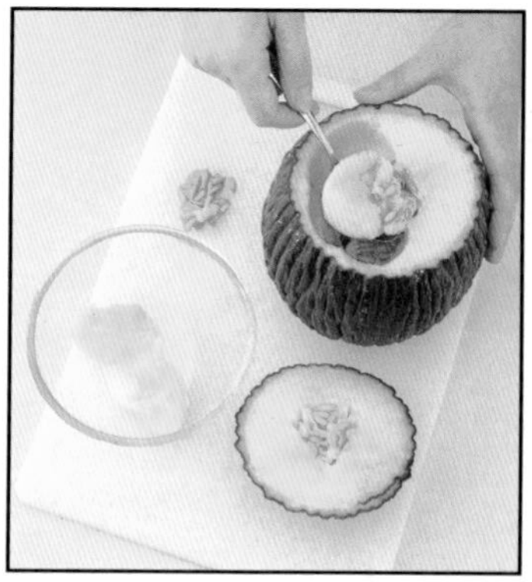

Slice about 7.5 cm (3 in) from top of melon, scoop out flesh, discarding seeds, and cut flesh into small chunks. Prepare all other fruits by cutting them into small chunks the same size as the melon chunks.

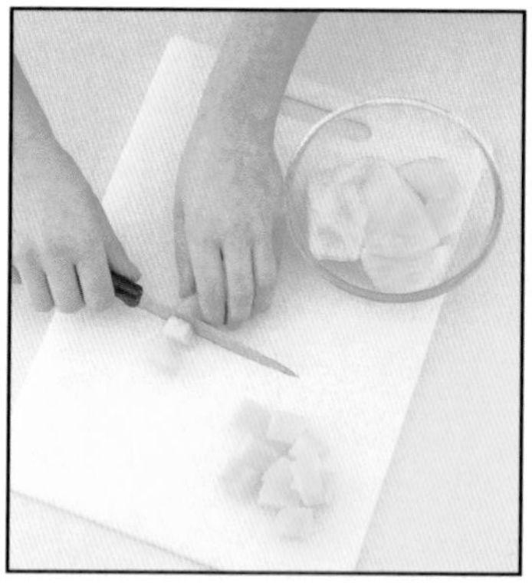

Fill melon shell with fruit and syrup. Cover with cling film and chill in the refrigerator for at least 2-3 hours. Serve on a bed of crushed ice.

Serves 4-6.

Note: If using canned fruit with syrup or natural juice, you can use this instead of making syrup for the dessert.

FRUIT SALAD WITH KANTEN

half 5 g stick dried kanten (agar-agar)
2 tablespoons sugar
1 small red apple, cut into 6 wedges and cored
salt
300 g (10 oz) can peeled tangerines or satsumas, syrup reserved
4 canned pear quarters, sliced in half
20 green grapes, cut in half and seeded
strawberries, hulled, to decorate
single cream and 115 g (4 oz) sweet azuki (red bean) paste, to serve
SYRUP:
4-5 tablespoons pouring sugar syrup
250 ml (9 fl oz/1 cup) syrup from canned tangerines or satsumas

Rinse kanten and soak in water for 30-60 minutes, then squeeze out water and tear kanten into small pieces. Put in a saucepan with 200 ml (7 fl oz/scant 1 cup) water and cook over moderate heat until kanten has dissolved. Stir in sugar and, when it has dissolved, strain. Put liquid back into the pan and continue to cook, stirring, for another 3 minutes. Pour into a wet square mould, leave to cool, then chill in the refrigerator. To make dressing, dissolve sugar syrup in tangerine or satsuma syrup and chill in the refrigerator.

Slice apple wedges into thin half-open fan-shaped pieces and plunge into salted water to prevent discoloration. Drain and pat dry. Cut hardened kanten into 1.5 cm (⅔ in) dice. Put all fruits and kanten in a large salad bowl, pour syrup dressing over them and fold in. Decorate with strawberries and serve with cream and sweet azuki (red bean) paste.

Serves 4-6.

PANCAKES & RED BEAN PASTE

3 eggs, beaten
150 g (5 oz/⅔ cup) sugar
1 tablespoon pouring sugar syrup
175 g (6 oz/1½ cups) plain flour
1 teaspoon baking powder
vegetable oil for frying
250-300 g (9-10 oz) sweet azuki (red bean) paste

In a mixing bowl, mix eggs, sugar and syrup. Using a whisk, beat until sugar has dissolved and mixture has a smooth consistency. Add flour, a little at a time, and mix well.

Dissolve baking powder in 150 ml (5 fl oz/⅔ cup) water and slowly stir into batter. Beat well. Place a small frying pan over medium heat and when hot wipe base with oil-soaked absorbent kitchen paper. Reduce heat to lowest setting and slowly ladle batter into centre of the pan. The size of the ladle determines the size of the 'gong' pancake, which should be about 13 cm (5 in) in diameter. Cook for about 3 minutes; when bubbles appear on the surface turn pancake over and cook other side for about 2 minutes. Remove to a plate.

Repeat process of oiling and baking until remaining batter is used up. As the pan gets hotter, gradually reduce the cooking time by 1 minute on each side. Spread about 2 tablespoons of sweet azuki (red bean) paste in the centre of a pancake and cover with another pancake to make a 'gong'. Alternatively, make a half gong, by folding 1 pancake with 1 tablespoonful of paste inside. Serve hot or cold, accompanied by Japanese green tea, if wished.

Makes 6-8 gongs or 12-16 half gongs.

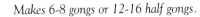